LEGAL RIGHTS OF TEACHERS AND STUDENTS

NELDA H. CAMBRON-McCABE

Miami University, Oxford, Ohio

MARTHA M. McCARTHY

Loyola Marymount University, Los Angeles

SUZANNE E. ECKES

Indiana University, Bloomington, Indiana

Boston   Columbus   Indianapolis   New York   San Francisco   Upper Saddle River   Amsterdam
Cape Town   Dubai   London   Madrid   Milan   Munich   Paris   Montreal   Toronto
Delhi   Mexico City   São Paulo   Sydney   Hong Kong   Seoul   Singapore   Taipei   Tokyo

Vice President and Editorial Director: *Jeffery W. Johnston*	**Production Manager:** *Laura Messerly*
	Senior Art Director: *Jayne Conte*
Senior Acquisitions Editor: *Meredith Fossel*	**Cover Designer:** *Karen Salzbach*
Editorial Assistant: *Krista Slavicek*	**Cover Image:** *Fotolia*
Vice President, Director of Marketing: *Margaret Waples*	**Full-Service Project Management:** *Rashmi Tickyani, Aptara®, Inc.*
Senior Marketing Manager: *Darcy Betts*	**Composition:** *Aptara®, Inc.*
Senior Managing Editor: *Pamela D. Bennett*	**Printer/Binder:** *LSC Communications*
Development Project Management: *Leslie Lahr, Aptara®, Inc.*	**Cover Printer:** *LSC Communications*
	Text Font: *10/12 Times New Roman*

Credits and acknowledgments for material borrowed from other sources and reproduced, with permission, in this textbook appear on the appropriate page within the text.

Every effort has been made to provide accurate and current Internet information in this book. However, the Internet and information posted on it are constantly changing, so it is inevitable that some of the Internet addresses listed in this textbook will change.

Library of Congress Cataloging-in-Publication Data
Cambron-McCabe, Nelda H.
   Legal rights of teachers and students / Nelda H. Cambron-McCabe, Miami University, Oxford, Ohio, Martha M. McCarthy, Loyola Marymount University, Los Angeles, Suzanne E. Eckes, Indiana University, Bloomington, Indiana.—Third edition.
      pages cm
   ISBN-13: 978-0-13-261943-1
   ISBN-10: 0-13-261943-1
   1. Teachers—Legal status, laws, etc.—United States.   2. Students—Legal status, laws, etc.—United States.   I. McCarthy, Martha M.   II. Eckes, Suzanne.   III. Title.
   KF4119.M388 2014
   344.73′078—dc23

2013009158

ISBN 10:   0-13-261943-1
ISBN 13: 978-0-13-261943-1

PREFACE

It has never been more imperative for teachers to understand the law. Since World War II, lawmakers have significantly reshaped educational policy. Most school personnel are aware of the escalating litigation and legislation, and some are familiar with the names of a few landmark U.S. Supreme Court decisions. But many educators do not understand basic legal principles that are being applied to educational questions. As a result, they are uncertain about the legality of daily decisions they must make in schools. Information provided in this book should help alleviate concerns voiced by educators who feel that the scales of justice have been tipped against them.

NEW TO THIS EDITION

Material in the third edition of *Legal Rights of Teachers and Students* is drawn from the newly revised seventh edition of *Public School Law: Teachers' and Students' Rights* (2014), also authored by three of us. The content of all chapters and figures has been updated since the second edition, and new sections have been added to capture emerging issues of legal concern. More than 300 cases have been added to the chapters, and at least 40 new or recently amended state and federal laws are addressed. Among new features of the third edition are discussions of legal concerns pertaining to:

- employee and student use of the Internet and social media;
- state legislation and First Amendment challenges pertaining to student bullying;
- educators' free expression rights following the Supreme Court's ruling in *Garcetti v. Ceballos*;
- changes in public employees' bargaining rights;
- charter schools and other alternatives to traditional public schools;
- efforts to provide government aid to private schools through tax credit programs and voucher plans; and
- affirmative action in pupil assignment plans.

For this book, we have selected topics particularly pertinent to classroom teachers. In analyzing specific school situations, we have explored the tension between government controls and individual freedoms in the school context. We discuss the implications of legal mandates and provide guidelines for educators. Throughout the chapters, we have highlighted in bold type or placed in boxes some of the most important legal concepts. Also, we have included a number of tables, figures, and scenarios to make the information presented more meaningful.

We have attempted to cover the topics thoroughly but in a nontechnical manner, avoiding the extensive use of legal terms. However, the topics are documented in footnotes that appear at the bottom of the pages if the reader wants to explore specific cases or points of law in greater detail. These notes provide additional information on selected cases and should assist the reader in understanding specific concepts. Also, a glossary of basic legal terms and a table of selected Supreme Court cases are provided at the end of the book.

NATURE OF THE LAW

A few comments about the nature of the law might assist the reader in using this book. Laws are not created in a vacuum; they reflect the social and philosophical attitudes of society. Moreover, individuals who have personal opinions and biases make laws. Although one may prefer to think that the law is always objective, personal considerations and national political trends do have an impact on the development and interpretation of legal principles.

Also, the law is not static, but rather is continually evolving as courts reinterpret constitutional and statutory provisions and as legislatures enact new laws. In the 1960s and early 1970s, courts and legislative bodies tended to focus on the expansion of personal rights through civil rights laws and constitutional interpretations favoring the individual's right to be free from unwarranted government intrusions. However, since 1975, judicial rulings in the school context have supported government authority to impose restraints on individual freedoms in the interest of the collective welfare. Although the themes of educational equity and individual rights, which dominated litigation earlier, remain important, efforts to attain educational excellence have generated a new genre of legal activity pertaining to teachers' qualifications and performance standards for students.

In this book, much of the discussion of the law focuses on court cases because the judiciary plays a vital role in interpreting constitutional and legislative provisions. Decisions are highlighted that illustrate points of law or legal trends, with particular emphasis on recent litigation. A few cases are pursued in depth to provide the reader with an understanding of the rationale behind the decisions. Reviewing the factual situations that have generated these controversies should make it easier for educators to identify potential legal problems in their own school situations.

As we completed this book, judicial decisions were being rendered and statutes being proposed that could alter the status of the law vis-à-vis teachers and students. Additionally, some questions confronting school personnel have not yet been addressed by the Supreme Court and have generated conflicting decisions among lower courts. It may be frustrating to a reader who is searching for concrete answers to learn that in some areas, the law is far from clear.

In spite of unresolved issues, certain legal principles have been established and can provide direction in many school situations. It is important for educators to become familiar with these principles and to use them to guide their decisions. Although the issues generating legal concern will change over time, knowledge of the logic underlying the law can make teachers more confident in dealing with questions that have not been clarified by courts or legislatures.

ORGANIZATION OF THE TEXT

We have attempted to arrange the chapters in logical sequence for those reading the book in its entirety or using it as a text for school law classes. An introductory chapter establishes the legal context for the subsequent examination of students' and teachers' rights, and a concluding chapter provides a summary of the major legal principles. Subheadings appear within chapters to facilitate using this book for reference if a specific issue is of immediate interest. The reader is encouraged, however, to read the entire text because some topics are addressed in several chapters from different perspectives, and many of the principles of law transcend chapter divisions. Taken together, the chapters provide an overall picture of the relationship among issues and the applicable legal principles.

The material will assist school personnel in understanding the current application of the law, but it is not intended to serve as a substitute for legal counsel. Educators confronting legal problems should always seek the advice of an attorney. Also, there is no attempt here to predict the future course of courts and legislatures. Given the dynamic nature of the law, no single text can serve to keep teachers abreast of current legal developments. If we can provide an awareness of rights and responsibilities, motivate educators to translate the basic concepts into actual practice, and generate an interest in further study of the law, our purposes in writing this book will have been achieved.

ACKNOWLEDGMENTS

A number of people contributed to the completion of this text. We are extremely grateful to the following individuals who provided valuable assistance in reviewing drafts of chapters, locating legal materials, and verifying citations: Aaron Butler, Colleen Chesnut, Ozair Shariff, and Jessica Ulm from Indiana University; Elise Scanlon from Loyola Marymount University; Mark Allen from Loyola Law School–Los Angeles; and Rosmarie Shaughnessy from Oxford, Ohio. We would also like to extend our sincere gratitude to the reviewers of this edition of our text: Deborah Elaine Bembry, Albany State University; Joseph S. Freedman, Alabama State University; Brenda R. Kallio, University of North Dakota; and T.C. Mattocks, Bridgewater State College.

This text would not have been completed without the support of our families, who offered constant encouragement as they do in all of our professional endeavors. Their contributions simply cannot be measured.

Nelda H. Cambron-McCabe
Martha M. McCarthy
Suzanne E. Eckes

BRIEF CONTENTS

CONTENTS

CHAPTER FOUR
Instructional Issues   70

CHAPTER FIVE
Student Expression, Association, and Appearance   96

CHAPTER SIX

Student Classifications   119

CHAPTER SEVEN

Rights of Students with Disabilities   144

CHAPTER EIGHT

Student Discipline   170

CHAPTER TEN

Teachers' Substantive Constitutional Rights   233

CHAPTER ELEVEN

Discrimination in Employment   257

CHAPTER TWELVE

Termination of Employment   285

CHAPTER THIRTEEN

Summary of Legal Generalizations   312

CHAPTER ONE

LEGAL FRAMEWORK OF PUBLIC EDUCATION

The authority for the establishment and control of American public education, which served approximately 55.5 million students in the 2011–2012 school year,[1] is grounded in law. State and federal constitutional and statutory provisions provide the framework within which school operational decisions are made. Policies and practices at any level of the educational enterprise must be consistent with legal mandates from higher authorities. The overlapping jurisdictions of federal and state constitutions, Congress and state legislatures, federal and state courts, and various governmental agencies (including local school boards and school-based councils) present a complex environment for educators attempting to comply with legal requirements. In an effort to untangle the various legal relationships, this chapter describes the major sources of law and how they interact to form the legal basis for public education. This overview establishes a context for subsequent chapters in which legal principles are discussed more fully as they apply to specific school situations.

STATE CONTROL OF EDUCATION

Since the U.S. Constitution does not authorize Congress to provide for education, the legal control of public education resides with the state as one of its sovereign powers.

The Tenth Amendment to the U.S. Constitution stipulates that "the powers not delegated to the United States by the Constitution, nor prohibited by it to the states, are reserved to the states respectively, or to the people." The Supreme Court repeatedly has affirmed the comprehensive authority of the states and school officials to control public schools so long as actions are consistent with fundamental federal constitutional safeguards. The state's authority over education is considered comparable to its powers to tax and to provide for the general welfare of its citizens. Although each state's educational system has unique features, many similarities are found across states.

[1]Press Release, U.S. Census Bureau, *Facts for Features, Back to School: 2011–2012* (June 27, 2011), http://www.census.gov/newsroom/releases/archives/facts_for_features_special_editions/cb11-ff15.html.

It is a widely held perception that local school boards control public education, but local boards have only those powers conferred by the state. Courts consistently have reiterated that the authority for public education is not a local one but rather is a central power residing in the state legislature. School buildings are state property, local school board members are state officials, and teachers are state employees. Public school funds, regardless where collected, are state funds.

State Legislation

All state constitutions specifically address the legislative responsibility for establishing public schools. Usually the legislature is charged with providing for a uniform, thorough and efficient, or adequate system of public education. In contrast to the federal government, which has only those powers specified in the U.S. Constitution, state legislatures retain all powers not expressly forbidden by state or federal constitutional provisions. **Thus, the state legislature has plenary, or absolute, power to make laws governing education.** State legislatures pass laws (otherwise referred to as statutes) on a variety of issues affecting public schools. For example, all fifty states require that students between specified ages (usually six to sixteen) attend a public or private school or receive equivalent instruction.

Legislatures also can authorize other school governance arrangements, such as state-funded charter schools that operate outside many regulations on the basis of a charter granted by the state, the local board of education, or other entities. In some instances, when state laws are subject to several interpretations, courts are called on to clarify legislative intent or to assess the constitution of provisions. If the judiciary misinterprets the law's purpose, the legislature can amend the law in question to clarify its meaning. However, if a law is invalidated as abridging state or federal constitutional provisions or federal civil rights laws, the legislature must abide by the judicial directives. A state's attorney general may be asked to interpret a law or to advise school boards on the legality of their actions, and such opinions are binding unless overruled by the judiciary.

State Administrative Agencies

It has been neither feasible nor desirable to include in statutes every minor detail governing public schools. Thus, state agencies play a role in providing details for state laws by adopting regulations. **The regulations are often referred to as administrative law, and they help provide guidance to the laws passed by the state legislature.** Most states have established a state board of education that typically supplies the structural details for implementing broad legislative mandates. Members of the state board of education usually are elected by the citizenry or appointed by the governor, and the board usually functions immediately below the legislature in the hierarchy of educational governance.

Accreditation is an important tool used by state boards to compel local school districts to abide by their directives. School districts often must satisfy state accreditation requirements as a condition of receiving state funds. Though accreditation models vary, it is common for states to assess student outcomes as well as establish minimum standards in areas such as curriculum, teacher qualifications, instructional materials, and facilities.

In some states, different grades of school accreditation exist, with financial incentives in place to encourage local schools to increase student achievement. **Since the mid-1980s, there has been a movement toward performance-based accreditation under which a school's performance is assessed against predicted outcomes calculated for the school in areas such as pupil achievement, absenteeism, and student retention.**

Within legislative parameters, the state board of education can issue directives governing school operations. In some states, rules pertaining to such matters as proficiency testing for students and programs for children with disabilities are embodied in state board rules rather than state law. Courts generally have upheld decisions made by state boards of education unless the boards have violated legislative or constitutional mandates. In addition to the state board, generally considered a policy-making body, all states have designated a chief state school officer (CSSO) to function in an executive capacity. The duties of the CSSO, who is often known as the superintendent of public instruction or commissioner of education and functions in an executive capacity, have been regulatory in nature. Each state also has established a state department of education, consisting of educational specialists who provide consultation to the state board, CSSO, and local school boards. State department personnel often collect data from school districts to ensure that legislative enactments and state board policies are properly implemented.

Local School Boards

Although public education in the United States is state controlled, it is for the most part locally administered. All states except Hawaii have created local school boards in addition to state education agencies and have delegated certain administrative authority over schools to these local boards. **Nationwide, there are approximately 13,592 local districts, ranging from a few students to several hundred thousand.**[2] Some states, particularly those with a large number of small school districts, have established intermediate or regional administrative units that perform regulatory or service functions for several local districts.

As with the delegation of authority to state agencies, assignment of powers to local school boards is handled differently across states. Some states with a deeply rooted tradition of local control over education give local boards a great deal of latitude in making operational decisions about schools. In states that tend toward centralized control of education (e.g., Florida), local boards must function within the framework of detailed legislative directives. **State legislatures retain the legal responsibility for education and can restrict the discretion of local boards by enacting legislation to that effect.**

The citizenry within the school district usually elects local school board members. The U.S. Supreme Court has recognized that the Equal Protection Clause requires each qualified voter to be given an opportunity to participate in the election of board members, with each vote given the same weight as far as practicable. When board members are

---

[2]Patrick Keaton, U.S. Dep't of Educ., Nat'l Ctr. for Educ. Statistics, NCES 2012-326, *Numbers and Types of Public Elementary and Secondary Local Education Agencies from the Common Core of Data: School Year 2010–11* (Nov. 2012), http://nces.ed.gov/pubs2012/2012326rev.pdf.

elected from geographical districts, such districts must be established to protect voting rights under the "one person, one vote" principle. If "at-large" elections result in a dilution of the minority vote, an abridgment of the federal Voting Rights Act may be found.[3]

A local board must act as a body; individual board members are not empowered to make policies or perform official acts on behalf of the board. School boards have some discretion in adopting operational procedures and policies, but they are legally bound to adhere to such procedures once established. **Although courts are reluctant to interfere with decisions made by boards of education and will not rule on the wisdom of such decisions, they will invalidate any board action that is arbitrary, capricious, or outside the board's legal authority (i.e., an *ultra vires* act).**

School board meetings and records must be open to the public.[4] Most states have enacted "sunshine" or open meeting laws, acknowledging that the public has a right to be fully informed regarding the actions of public agencies. Certain exceptions to open meeting requirements are usually specified in the laws. For example, in many states, school boards can meet in executive session to discuss matters that threaten public safety or pertain to pending or current litigation, personnel matters, collective bargaining, or the disposition of real property. Although discussion of these matters may take place in closed meetings, statutes usually stipulate that formal action must occur in open meetings.[5]

Local school boards hold powers specified or implied in state law and other powers considered necessary to achieve the purposes of the express powers. These delegated powers generally encompass the authority to determine the specifics of the curriculum offered within the school district, raise revenue to build and maintain schools, select personnel, and enact other policies necessary to implement the educational program pursuant to law. Courts have recognized that even without specific enabling legislation, local boards have discretionary authority to enter into contracts and make decisions necessary to operate the schools. But local school boards cannot delegate their decision-making authority to other agencies or associations.

Since the mid-1980s, the objective of decentralizing many operational decisions to the school level (i.e., site-based management) has been increasingly important. Therefore, school-based councils have become more prevalent. How a school-based council works may vary greatly from district to district. For example, whereas one school-based council may include teachers, parents, and administrators with the authority to make curricular and personnel decisions, another district's school-based council might be made up of only teachers who have very limited authority. Where school-based councils have been created and delegated authority in certain domains (e.g., curriculum, personnel), their decisions

---

[3]42 U.S.C. § 1971 (2012). Section 1973(a) states that "[n]o . . . practice or procedure shall be imposed or applied . . . in a manner which results in a denial or abridgment of the right . . . to vote on account of race . . . ." *See, e.g.*, Moore v. Itawamba Cnty., Miss., 431 F.3d 257 (5th Cir. 2005).

[4]However, a New Jersey court has indicated that handwritten notes used by the board secretary to prepare the official minutes were not public records. *See* O'Shea v. W. Milford Bd. of Educ., 918 A.2d 735 (N.J. Super. Ct. App. Div. 2007).

[5]*See, e.g.*, *In re* Kansas City Star Co., 73 F.3d 191 (8th Cir. 1996) (holding that a closed session between the desegregation monitoring committee and school board did not violate the Missouri Sunshine Act).

have the force of law.[6] Only if councils act beyond their scope of authority or impair protected rights will their decisions be invalidated by the judiciary.

Charter Schools

The charter school movement has been characterized as one of the fastest-growing education reform efforts nationally. Since 1991, forty-one states and the District of Columbia have enacted laws authorizing charter schools, usually specifying a cap on the number of charters granted to existing public or private schools or groups starting new schools. Charter schools are public schools that are not subject to some of the same rules and laws as traditional public schools. They are most often new schools, but it is also possible for a traditional public or private school to convert to charter school status. What makes charter schools different from traditional public schools is their charter, which is a performance contract that establishes each school and details the school's mission and goals. Functioning as a public school, the school receives a charter from a public agency, usually a state or local school board. The charter is typically reviewed every three to five years, as determined by state law. The entity that issues the charter is known as a sponsor or authorizer, and this entity plays a key role in the charter school system. In return for greater autonomy, charter schools are held to a higher level of accountability with regard to student performance. If the charter school does not meet state requirements, it could be closed.

Charter Schools

FEDERAL ROLE IN EDUCATION

The federal government influences public education through its funding powers and the enforcement of constitutional rights.

Unlike state constitutions, the U.S. Constitution is silent regarding education; hence, individuals do not have an inherent federally protected right to an education.[7] The Constitution, however, does confer basic rights on individuals, and school personnel must respect these rights. Furthermore, Congress exerts control over the use of federal education aid and regulates other aspects of schools through legislation enacted pursuant to its constitutionally granted powers.

---

[6]Under the Chicago School Reform Act, 105 ILL. COMP. STAT. 5/34-2.2(c) (2012), the local school council is authorized to appoint a principal without school board approval. Under Kentucky's Education Reform Act, KY. REV. STAT. § 160.345(2)(h) (2012), superintendents must forward all principal applicants who meet statutory requirements to the site-based school council, not simply the ones the superintendent recommends and supports, Young v. Hammond, 139 S.W.3d 895 (Ky. 2004). Massachusetts's Education Reform Act, MASS. GEN. LAWS ch. 71, § 59B (2012), lodges the responsibility for hiring and firing of teachers and other building personnel with school principals under the supervision of the superintendent.

[7]San Antonio Indep. Sch. Dist. v. Rodriguez, 411 U.S. 1 (1973).

United States Constitution

A constitution is a body of precepts providing the system of fundamental laws of a nation, state, or society. The U.S. Constitution establishes a separation of powers among the executive, judicial, and legislative branches of government. These three branches form a system of checks and balances to ensure that the intent of the Constitution is respected. The Constitution also provides a systematic process for altering the document, if deemed necessary. Article V stipulates that amendments may be proposed by a two-thirds vote of each house of Congress or by a special convention called by Congress on the request of two-thirds of the state legislatures. Proposed amendments then must be ratified by three-fourths of the states to become part of the Constitution.

The U.S. Constitution is the supreme law in this nation; state authority over education must be exercised in a manner consistent with its provisions. All federal constitutional mandates affect public education to some degree; the provisions discussed below have had the greatest impact on public school policies and practices.

General Welfare Clause.   Under Article I, Section 8 of the Constitution, Congress has the power "to lay and collect taxes, duties, imposts and excises, to pay the debts and provide for the common defense and general welfare of the United States." In 1937, the Supreme Court declared that it will not interfere with the discretion of Congress in its domain unless Congress exhibits a clear display of arbitrary power.[8]

Using the general welfare rationale, Congress has enacted legislation providing substantial federal support for research and instructional programs in areas such as science, mathematics, reading, special education, vocational education, career education, and bilingual education. Congress also has provided financial assistance for the school lunch program and for services to meet the special needs of various groups of students, such as the educationally and culturally disadvantaged. In addition, the federal government, in passing the Children's Internet Protection Act, attempted to protect the welfare of minors by policing the suitability of materials made available electronically.[9]

Commerce Clause.   Congress is empowered to "regulate commerce with foreign nations, among the several states, and with Indian tribes" under Article I, Section 8, Clause 3 of the Constitution. Safety, transportation, and labor regulations enacted pursuant to this clause have affected the operation of public schools. Traditionally, courts have favored a broad interpretation of "commerce" and an expanded federal role in regulating commercial activity to ensure national prosperity. The Court has provided limitations on the reach of the Commerce Clause as well. In *United States v. Lopez*, the Supreme Court invalidated the federal Gun Free School Zones Act of 1990, finding that a law to regulate guns in a school zone was not "economic activity" and had no substantial effect on interstate commerce.[10]

[8]Helvering v. Davis, 301 U.S. 619, 644–45 (1937).

[9]20 U.S.C. § 9134(f) (2012).

[10]514 U.S. 549, 561 (1995).

Obligation of Contracts Clause. Article I, Section 10 of the Constitution stipulates that states cannot enact any law impairing the obligation of contracts. Administrators, teachers, and noncertified personnel are protected from arbitrary dismissals by contractual agreements. The judiciary often is called on to evaluate the validity of a given contract or to assess whether a party has breached its contractual obligations.

Constitutional Amendments that Relate to School Law

First Amendment. **The Bill of Rights, comprising the first ten amendments to the U.S. Constitution, safeguards individual liberties against governmental encroachment.** The most preciously guarded of these liberties are contained in the First Amendment's protection of speech, press, assembly, and religious liberties. The religion clauses have evoked a number of lawsuits challenging government aid to and regulation of nonpublic schools and contesting public school policies and practices as advancing religion or impairing free exercise rights. Cases involving students' rights to express themselves and to distribute literature have been initiated under First Amendment guarantees of freedom of speech and press. Moreover, teachers' rights to academic freedom and to speak out on matters of public concern have precipitated numerous lawsuits. The right of assembly has been the focus of litigation involving student clubs and employees' rights to organize and engage in collective bargaining.

Fourth Amendment. This amendment guarantees the right of citizens "to be secure in their persons, houses, papers, and effects against unreasonable searches and seizures." It safeguards individuals against arbitrary government intrusions and has frequently appeared in educational cases involving drug-testing programs and searches of students' lockers, cars, and persons. A few cases also have involved alleged violations by school officials of school employees' Fourth Amendment rights.

Fifth Amendment. In part, the Fifth Amendment provides that no person shall be "compelled in any criminal case to be a witness against himself, nor be deprived of life, liberty, or property without due process of law; nor shall private property be taken for public use, without just compensation." Several cases have addressed the application of the self-incrimination clause in instances where teachers have been questioned by superiors about their activities outside the school.

Eighth Amendment. The Eighth Amendment prohibits cruel and unusual punishment and has been at issue in some corporal punishment cases.[11]

Ninth Amendment. The Ninth Amendment stipulates that "the enumeration in the Constitution, of certain rights, shall not be construed to deny or disparage others retained by the people." This amendment has appeared in educational litigation in which teachers have asserted that their right to personal privacy outside the classroom is protected

---

[11]*But see* Ingraham v. Wright, 430 U.S. 651 (1977) (finding that Eighth Amendment's prohibition of cruel and unusual punishment does not apply to school personnel who use force when disciplining students).

as an unenumerated right. Furthermore, grooming regulations applied to teachers and students have been challenged as infringing on personal rights retained by the people under this amendment.

Thirteenth Amendment. The Thirteenth Amendment prohibits involuntary servitude and has been invoked by parents contesting public schools' community service requirements.

Fourteenth Amendment. **The Fourteenth Amendment, adopted in 1868, is the most widely invoked constitutional provision in school litigation since it specifically addresses state action.** The Fourteenth Amendment contains two important clauses: the Equal Protection Clause and the Due Process Clause. The Equal Protection Clause provides that no state shall "deny to any person within its jurisdiction, the equal protection of the laws." It has been interpreted to mean that similarly situated individuals must be treated the same. For example, in *Brown v. Board of Education*, African American students were not being treated similarly to white students. This clause has been significant in school cases involving alleged discrimination based on race, national origin, sex, and ethnic background. Also, school finance litigation often has been based on the Equal Protection Clause, although with very little success.[12]

In addition, the Due Process Clause has played an important role in school litigation. The federal judiciary has identified both procedural and substantive components of due process guarantees. *Procedural due process* ensures fundamental fairness if the government threatens an individual's life, liberty, or property interests. Minimum procedures required by the U.S. Constitution are a notice of the charges, an opportunity to refute the charges, and a hearing that is conducted fairly. For example, before a tenured teacher is dismissed, the teacher must be afforded certain procedural rights. In comparison, *substantive due process* requires that state action be based on a valid objective with means reasonably related to attaining the objective. In essence, substantive due process shields the individual against arbitrary governmental action that impairs life, liberty, or property interests. Property rights are legitimate expectations of entitlement created through state laws, regulations, or contracts. Compulsory school attendance laws confer on students a legitimate property right to attend school, and the granting of tenure gives teachers a property entitlement to continued employment. Liberty rights include interests in one's reputation and fundamental rights related to marriage, family matters, and personal privacy.

Also, the Supreme Court has interpreted Fourteenth Amendment liberties as incorporating the personal freedoms contained in the Bill of Rights.[13] Thus, the first ten amendments, originally directed toward the federal government, have been applied to state actions as well. Although the principle of "incorporation" has been criticized, Supreme Court precedent supports the notion that the Fourteenth Amendment restricts state interference with fundamental constitutional liberties. **The incorporation principle is particularly important in school litigation since education is a state function; claims that public school policies or practices impair personal freedoms (e.g., First Amendment free speech guarantees) are usually initiated through the Fourteenth Amendment.**

---

[12] *See, e.g.*, San Antonio Indep. Sch. Dist. v. Rodriguez, 411 U.S. 1 (1973).

[13] *See, e.g.*, Cantwell v. Connecticut, 310 U.S. 296, 303 (1940); Gitlow v. New York, 268 U.S. 652, 666 (1925).

✗ Doesn't apply to private schools

Since the Fourteenth Amendment protects personal liberties against unwarranted state interference, private institutions, including private schools, are not subject to these restrictions. For private school policies and practices to be challenged successfully under the Fourteenth Amendment, there must be sufficient governmental involvement in the private school to constitute "state action."[14] To date, this has not occurred, although the Supreme Court may have opened the window for possible future inclusion when it determined that state athletic associations (typically private corporations) are entwined with state government and therefore are involved in state action.[15]

Federal Legislation

Congress is empowered to enact laws to translate the intent of the U.S. Constitution into actual practices. **Laws reflect the will of the legislative branch of government, which, theoretically, in a democracy represents the citizenry.** Because the states have sovereign power regarding education, the federal government's involvement in public schools has been one of indirect support, not direct control.

Funding Laws. The most comprehensive law offering financial assistance to schools, the Elementary and Secondary Education Act of 1965 (ESEA), in part supplied funds for compensatory education programs for economically disadvantaged students attending public and nonprofit private schools. With the passage of ESEA, federal aid to education doubled, and the federal government's contribution increased steadily until reaching 9.8 percent of total public education revenue in 1980. The federal share then declined to the 6 to 7 percent range for a period of time, but by 2011–2012, it exceeded 10 percent.[16]

Congress and federal administrative agencies have exerted considerable influence in shaping public school policies and practices through categorical funding laws and their accompanying administrative regulations. Individual states or school districts have the option of accepting or rejecting such federal assistance, but if categorical aid is accepted, the federal government has the authority to prescribe guidelines for its use and to monitor state and local education agencies to ensure fiscal accountability.

Much of the federal categorical legislation enacted during the 1960s and 1970s provided funds to assist school districts in attaining equity goals and addressing other national priorities. For example, the Bilingual Education Act of 1968 and the Education for All Handicapped Children Act of 1975 (which became the Individuals with Disabilities Education Act of 1990) have provided federal funds to assist education agencies in offering services for students with special needs. Although in the 1980s Congress shifted away from its heavy reliance on categorical federal aid by consolidating some categorical programs into block grants with reduced funding and regulations, aid for economically disadvantaged and English-deficient students and children with disabilities has remained categorical in nature.

---

[14] *See, e.g.*, Rendell-Baker v. Kohn, 457 U.S. 830 (1982).

[15] *See* Brentwood Acad. v. Tenn. Secondary Sch. Athletic Ass'n, 531 U.S. 288 (2001); *see also* Tenn. Secondary Sch. Athletic Ass'n v. Brentwood Acad., 551 U.S. 291 (2007) (finding no due process violation as appropriate procedures were followed, notwithstanding minor procedural irregularities).

[16] U.S. Dep't of Educ., *The Federal Role in Education*, https://www2.ed.gov/about/overview/fed/role.html.

In 2002, President George W. Bush signed into law the No Child Left Behind Act (NCLB), the most comprehensive reform of the ESEA since it was enacted in 1965.[17] This law, directed at improving the performance of public schools, pledges that no child will be left in a failing school. Specifically, the law requires states to implement accountability systems with higher performance standards in reading, mathematics, and science along with annual testing of all students in grades three through eight. Furthermore, assessment data must be categorized by poverty, ethnicity, race, disability, and limited English proficiency. The law greatly expands choices for parents of children attending schools that do not meet state standards. If students are in a school that has been identified as low performing, students must be given the option of attending a better school within the district, including a charter school. For students attending persistently failing schools (i.e., schools that fail to meet the state standards in three of the four preceding years), the school district must permit the students to use federal funds to obtain supplemental educational services (e.g., tutoring, after-school programs, or summer programs) from either public or private providers. Persistently failing schools not only lose funding as students select other schools but also face mandated reconstitution if they do not make adequate yearly progress.

Civil Rights Laws.   In addition to laws providing financial assistance to public schools, Congress has enacted legislation designed to clarify the scope of individuals' civil rights. **Unlike the discretion enjoyed by state and local education agencies in deciding whether to participate in federal funding programs, educational institutions must comply with these civil rights laws.** Some federal antidiscrimination laws are enacted to enforce constitutional rights and have general application. Others apply only to recipients of federal financial assistance. Various federal agencies are charged with monitoring compliance with these laws and can bring suit against noncomplying institutions. Under many civil rights laws, individuals also can initiate private suits to compel compliance and, in some instances, to obtain personal remedies.

Several laws enacted in the latter part of the nineteenth century to protect the rights of African American citizens were seldom the focus of litigation until the mid-twentieth century. Since the 1960s, these laws, particularly 42 U.S.C. § 1983, have been used by students and teachers to gain relief in instances where their federal rights have been violated by school policies and practices. **Section 1983 provides a private right to bring suit for damages against any person who, acting under the authority of state law (e.g., a public school employee) impairs rights secured by the U.S. Constitution and federal laws.**[18] Although § 1983 does not confer specific substantive rights (i.e., it must attach to another federal law and cannot be the basis for suit standing alone), it has been significant in school cases because it allows individuals to obtain damages from school officials and school districts for abridgments of federally protected rights.[19] However, § 1983 cannot be used to

---

[17]20 U.S.C. § 6301 (2012).

[18]School boards as well as school officials are considered "persons" under 42 U.S.C. § 1983 (2012).

[19]*See, e.g.*, Barrett v. Steubenville City Schs., 388 F.3d 967 (6th Cir. 2004) (finding that the superintendent violated the substitute teacher's right to direct the education of his child as protected by the Constitution and § 1983 when the superintendent refused to consider him for a full-time position because his son was enrolled in a parochial school).

enforce federal laws where congressional intent to create private rights is not clearly stated.[20] In addition, § 1981 of the Civil Rights Act of 1866, as amended in 1991, prohibits race or ethnicity discrimination in making and enforcing contracts and in the terms and conditions of contractual relationships and allows for both compensatory and punitive damages.[21] It applies to all public and private schools, regardless of whether they receive federal aid.

Subsequent civil rights laws enacted since the 1960s confer substantive rights to protect citizens from discrimination. The vindication of employees' rights in school settings has generated substantial litigation under Title VII of the Civil Rights Act of 1964, which prohibits employment discrimination on the basis of race, color, sex, religion, or national origin. Modeled in part after Title VII, the Americans with Disabilities Act of 1990 provides specific protections in employment and public accommodations for individuals with disabilities. Additionally, the Age Discrimination in Employment Act of 1967 protects employees over age forty against age-based employment discrimination. Other civil rights laws—such as Title VI of the Civil Rights Act of 1964 (prohibiting discrimination on the basis of race, color, sex, religion, or national origin), Title IX of the Education Amendments of 1972 (barring sex discrimination against participants in education programs), the Rehabilitation Act of 1973 (prohibiting discrimination against otherwise qualified persons with disabilities), and the Age Discrimination Act of 1975 (barring age discrimination in federally assisted programs or activities)—pertain only to institutions with programs that receive federal funds.[22] Courts often have been called on to interpret these acts and their regulations as they apply to educational practices.

Still other federal laws offer protections to individuals in educational settings and place responsibilities on school officials. For example, the Family Educational Rights and Privacy Act guarantees parents access to their children's school records and safeguards the confidentiality of such records. This federal law also applies to both public and private educational recipients of federal financial assistance. Federal laws also protect human subjects in research projects and require parental consent before students participate in federally supported psychiatric or psychological examination, testing, or treatment designed to reveal information in specified sensitive areas.[23] Courts have played an important role in interpreting the protections included in these laws and ensuring compliance with the federal mandates.

Federal Administrative Agencies

Similar to state governments, much of the regulatory activity at the federal level is conducted by administrative agencies. Specifically, after Congress passes a law, federal

---

[20] *See, e.g.*, Gonzaga Univ. v. Doe, 536 U.S. 273 (2002) (finding that Congress did not intend to create privately enforceable rights under the Family Education Rights and Privacy Act); text accompanying note 79, Chapter 4.

[21] 42 U.S.C. § 1981 (2012). The Civil Rights Act of 1991, 42 U.S.C. § 2000e expanded § 1981's protections and strengthened several other civil rights mandates.

[22] The Civil Rights Restoration Act of 1987, 20 U.S.C. § 1681 (2012), amended these four laws to make them applicable to entire institutions if any of their programs receive federal funds. This law was enacted in response to the Supreme Court ruling in *Grove City College v. Bell*, 465 U.S. 555 (1984).

[23] *See* 20 U.S.C. § 1232h (2012); text accompanying note 107, Chapter 4.

administrative agencies issue regulations, which help to provide more clarity to the federal law that was enacted. The U.S. Department of Education is responsible for many regulations. For example, when Congress passed the NCLB Act, the U.S. Department of Education wrote the regulations for this law.

The primary functions of the Department of Education are to coordinate federal involvement in education activities, identify educational needs of national significance, propose strategies to address these needs, and provide technical and financial assistance to state and local education agencies. Regulations promulgated by the Department of Education to implement funding laws have had a significant impact on many schools. The department solicits public comments on proposed regulations, and Congress reviews the regulations to ensure their consistency with legislative intent. The Department of Education administers regulations for more than 100 different programs, ranging from services for Native American students to projects for school dropouts. The Departments of Agriculture, Labor, Defense, Justice, and Health and Human Services administer the remaining educational programs.

Through their regulatory activities, numerous federal agencies influence state and local education policies. For example, the Office for Civil Rights and the Equal Employment Opportunity Commission have reviewed claims of discrimination in public schools and initiated suits against school districts that are not in compliance with civil rights laws. The Environmental Protection Agency also has placed obligations on schools in connection with the maintenance of safe school environments. School districts can face the termination of federal assistance if they do not comply with such federal regulations.

FUNCTION AND STRUCTURE OF THE JUDICIAL SYSTEM

Courts do not initiate laws, but they influence the law by interpreting the meaning of constitutional and statutory provisions.

Judicial decisions are usually cited in conjunction with statutory and constitutional provisions as a major source of educational law (see Figure 1.1). As early as 1835, Alexis de Tocqueville noted that "scarcely any political question arises in the United States that is not resolved, sooner or later, into a judicial question."[24] Courts, however, do not initiate laws as legislative bodies do; courts apply appropriate principles of law to settle disputes. The terms *common law* and *case law* refer to judicially created legal principles that are relied on as precedent when similar factual situations arise.

In the United States there are two court systems: the federal court system and the state court system. Any type of case can be heard in a state court because state courts are courts of general jurisdiction. One way to enter federal court is when there is a federal

[24]ALEXIS DE TOCQUEVILLE, DEMOCRACY IN AMERICA 280 (New York: Alfred A. Knopf, 1960).

FIGURE 1.1   Sources of Law Affecting Public Schools

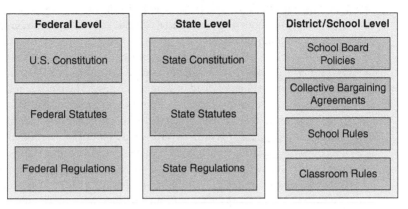

question involved. Thus, if a student was injured on the playground and was filing a negligence lawsuit, it would be filed in state court (there is no federal question involved). If a student was suing under the First Amendment because her right to free speech was denied, she could file in federal court (because of the First Amendment) or in state court (because it is a court of general jurisdiction).

Although most constitutional provisions and statutory enactments never become the subject of litigation, some provisions require judicial clarification. Since federal and state constitutions set forth broad policy statements rather than specific guides to action, courts serve an important function in interpreting such mandates and in determining the legality of various school policies and practices.

The Supreme Court has articulated specific guidelines for exercising the power of judicial review. The Court will not decide hypothetical cases and will not render an opinion on issues in nonadversarial proceedings. A genuine controversy must be initiated by a party with standing and a private right of action to sue (e.g., the right to sue for damages). To achieve such standing, the party must have a "real interest" in the outcome of the case, such as having been adversely affected by the challenged practice. **In applying appropriate principles of law to specific cases, the Court generally follows the doctrine of *stare decisis* (abide by decided cases) and thus relies on precedents established in previous decisions.** On occasion, however, the Court overrules a prior opinion.[25]

Filing a Case

Procedures vary somewhat by type of suit and jurisdiction, but a plaintiff typically initiates a suit by filing a complaint with the appropriate court clerk. After a period of *discovery*, when evidence is gathered, the defendant may submit a *motion to dismiss*, arguing that the

---

[25]For example, in 1954, the Supreme Court in *Brown v. Board of Education*, 347 U.S. 483 (1954), repudiated the long-accepted standard of separate but equal as was supported in *Plessy v. Ferguson*, 163 U.S. 537 (1896), and concluded that separate schools for different racial groups were inherently unequal.

plaintiff has failed to state a legal claim or that the claim is barred by the applicable statute of limitations. Furthermore, either party may request *summary judgment*, noting that the facts of the case are not in dispute and that the party is entitled to judgment based on applicable law. If summary judgment is not granted, the plaintiff's case then is presented.

Success in court is determined by the plaintiff's ability to persuade a judge or jury that he or she (or it) has been wronged and deserves a remedy or by the defendant's ability to show that its action is either allowed or required by law. The parties' persuasive abilities are limited by the availability of creditable, admissible evidence. Notwithstanding the acceptance of a wide range of documentation and testimony, parties should not knowingly present evidence that is *incompetent* (i.e., testifying on a matter for which knowledge or expertise is lacking), *immaterial* (i.e., evidence to prove or disprove a fact that is uncontested), *irrelevant* (i.e., evidence that fails to clarify or be related to the fact or issue in dispute), or *unduly repetitious* (i.e., evidence that adds nothing new and is unnecessarily redundant).

Following a trial court decision or jury verdict, each party then must make the decision whether it is in its best interest to appeal, given the allocation of time and resources. If the original ruling is appealed, the appellate court must accept the trial court's findings of fact unless they are clearly erroneous. The appeals court reviews the written record of the evidence but does not hold a hearing for witnesses to be questioned. The appellate court may accept the trial court's findings of fact but disagree with the conclusions of law. In such instances, the case is usually remanded to the trial court for reconsideration in light of the appropriate legal principles enunciated by the appeals court.

In addition to individual suits,[26] education cases often involve class-action suits brought on behalf of all similarly situated individuals. To be certified as a class action, the suit must satisfy four rules of civil procedure that specify prerequisites to establish class members' commonality of injury and circumstances. If a suit is not properly certified as a class action, and the circumstances of the original plaintiff change (e.g., a student graduates from school before a judgment is rendered), the court may dismiss the suit as moot because the plaintiff is no longer being injured by the contested practice. Various remedies are available through court action. In some suits, a court-ordered injunction is sought to compel school officials to cease a particular action or to command performance of a particular action. Specifically, in offering injunctive relief, a court might issue a preliminary injunction, a temporary restraining order, or a permanent injunction.

Judicial relief can take the form of a declaration that specific rights must be respected. In addition, courts can order personal remedies, such as reinstatement and removal of material from school records. Courts also may award damages and attorneys' fees to compensate individuals for the deprivation of their rights and under certain circumstances may require the payment of punitive damages by state officials if their conduct represents a willful or reckless disregard of protected rights.

In interpreting constitutional and statutory provisions, courts have developed various criteria to evaluate whether the law has been violated. These judicially created standards

---

[26]Most educational litigation involves civil suits, initiated by individuals alleging injury by another private party. Civil suits often involve claims for damages or requests for specific conduct to cease because it impairs the individual's protected rights. In contrast, criminal suits are brought on behalf of society to punish an individual for committing a crime, such as violating compulsory school attendance laws or selling drugs on school grounds.

or "tests" are extremely important and in some instances appear to go beyond the original intent of the constitutional or statutory provision in question. Judicial standards are continually evolving and being refined by courts. The judiciary thus occupies a powerful position in shaping the law through its interpretive powers.

Courts, however, will not intervene in a school-related controversy if the dispute can be settled in a legislative or administrative forum. All state educational systems provide some type of administrative appeals procedure for aggrieved individuals to use in disputes involving internal school operations. Many school controversies never reach the courts because they are settled in these administrative forums. Under most circumstances, courts require such administrative appeals to be exhausted before court action is initiated. For example, before filing a case under the Individuals with Disabilities Education Act (IDEA), certain administrative appeals must be exhausted before the case can be filed in court.

In evaluating the impact of case law, it is important to keep in mind that a judicial ruling applies as precedent within the geographical jurisdiction of the court delivering the opinion. It is possible for two state supreme courts or two federal courts to render conflicting decisions on an issue; nonetheless, such decisions are binding in their respective jurisdictions. Only decisions of the U.S. Supreme Court have national application. See Figure 1.2 to learn how to interpret a case citation.

A case is a written opinion from a judge (or judges). A case can be found in an official reporter or can be accessed by using a database such as LexisNexis or Westlaw. The party filing the lawsuit is known as the plaintiff, and the party defending the lawsuit is known as the defendant. When locating a case, the first page will include the case name and the citation.

Go to www.findlaw.com/casecode, click on U.S. Supreme Court, and put the case citation or case name into the search box. Below is an example of what you will find if you search for *Brown v. Board of Education*, 347 U.S. 483 (1954).

FIGURE 1.2   Finding a Case

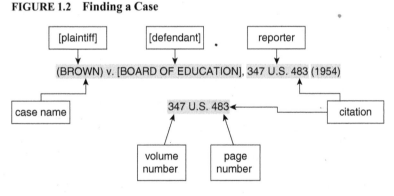

(BROWN ET AL.) v. [BOARD OF EDUCATION OF TOPEKA ET AL.]
APPEAL FROM THE UNITED STATES DISTRICT COURT FOR THE DISTRICT
OF KANSAS. * No. 1.
Argued December 9, 1952. Reargued December 8, 1953.
Decided May 17, 1954.

Note that the plaintiff's and defendant's names will not be in parentheses or brackets in the heading as it will appear on your screen. These have been added here to distinguish between the two. To listen to this case and others, go to http://www.oyez.org.

State Courts

State courts are established pursuant to state constitutional provisions, and the structure of judicial systems varies among states. In contrast to federal courts, which have only those powers granted by the U.S. Constitution, state courts can review most types of controversies unless restricted by state law. State judicial systems usually include trial courts of general jurisdiction, courts of special jurisdiction, and appellate courts. All states have a court of last resort, and decisions rendered by state high courts can be appealed to the U.S. Supreme Court.

In most states, the highest court or the court of last resort is called the supreme court or supreme judicial court. However, in New York and Maryland the highest court is the Court of Appeals, and in West Virginia it is the Supreme Court of Appeals. Courts occupying the next level in the state judicial system below the highest courts usually are referred to as appeals courts or superior courts. State trial courts of general jurisdiction often are called district or circuit courts, but in New York, trial courts are referred to as supreme courts of their respective counties. The most common special jurisdiction courts are juvenile, probate, domestic relations, and small claims. State judges are either elected by the voters or appointed by the governor.

Federal Courts

Article III, Section I, of the U.S. Constitution establishes the Supreme Court and authorizes Congress to create other federal courts as necessary. The federal court system contains courts of special jurisdiction, such as the claims court, tax court, and court of international trade. There are three levels of federal courts of general jurisdiction: district courts, circuit courts of appeal, and the Supreme Court. The number of federal district courts in a state is based on population. Each state has at least one federal district court; many states have two or three; and California, New York, and Texas have four each. Judgments at the district court level are usually presided over by one judge. Generally, only two types of issues can be heard in federal court. The issue must involve a federal question or it must involve parties from different states. In addition, only cases involving $75,000 or more in potential damages may be filed in a federal court.

On the federal appeals level, the nation is divided into twelve geographic circuits, each with its own federal circuit court of appeals.[27] A thirteenth federal circuit court has national jurisdiction to hear appeals regarding specific claims (e.g., customs; copyrights, patents, and trademarks; international trade). Federal circuit courts have from three to twenty-nine judges, depending on the workload of the circuit. A panel of the court (three judges) renders most circuit decisions, but in some instances the majority of the court's judges (en banc) will rehear a case. Although a federal circuit court decision is binding

[27]In 1981, the Fifth Circuit was divided into the Fifth and Eleventh Circuits.

only in the states within that circuit, such decisions often influence other appellate courts when dealing with similar questions. For example, if the Second Circuit ruled that students have a constitutional right to wear campaign T-shirts to school, this decision would apply only to Connecticut, New York, and Vermont, but the decision may influence other appellate courts. The jurisdiction of the federal circuits is as follows:

- First Circuit: Maine, Massachusetts, New Hampshire, Rhode Island, and Puerto Rico
- Second Circuit: Connecticut, New York, and Vermont
- Third Circuit: Delaware, New Jersey, Pennsylvania, and the Virgin Islands
- Fourth Circuit: Maryland, North Carolina, South Carolina, Virginia, and West Virginia
- Fifth Circuit: Louisiana, Mississippi, Texas, and the Canal Zone
- Sixth Circuit: Kentucky, Michigan, Ohio, and Tennessee
- Seventh Circuit: Illinois, Indiana, and Wisconsin
- Eighth Circuit: Arkansas, Iowa, Minnesota, Missouri, Nebraska, North Dakota, and South Dakota
- Ninth Circuit: Alaska, Arizona, California, Idaho, Hawaii, Montana, Nevada, Oregon, Washington, and Guam
- Tenth Circuit: Colorado, Kansas, New Mexico, Oklahoma, Utah, and Wyoming
- Eleventh Circuit: Alabama, Florida, and Georgia
- D.C. Circuit: Washington, D.C.[28]
- Federal Circuit: National jurisdiction on specific claims

The U.S. Supreme Court is, of course, the highest court in the nation. The Supreme Court has the ultimate authority in interpreting federal constitutional guarantees.[29] If the Supreme Court finds a specific practice unconstitutional (e.g., intentional school segregation), this judicial mandate applies nationwide. If the Court, however, concludes that a given activity does not impair federal constitutional guarantees (e.g., corporal punishment in public schools), states and local school boards retain discretion in placing restrictions on the activity. In the latter instances, legal requirements will vary across jurisdictions. U.S. Supreme Court Justices are appointed for life. The President nominates someone for the Court and the Senate must confirm the choice. There are currently nine justices on the Court.

As noted previously, if the judiciary interprets a statutory enactment contrary to legislative intent, the law can be amended to clarify its purpose. Congress has done so with a number of civil rights laws in response to Supreme Court rulings. However, the legislative branch does not have this discretion in connection with constitutional interpretations. If the Supreme Court rules that a federal law conflicts with its interpretation of the U.S. Constitution, the law is invalidated. If Congress persists in its desire for change, a constitutional amendment is required.

The Supreme Court disposes of approximately 5,000 cases a year but renders a written opinion on the merits in less than 5 percent of these cases. The Court often concludes

---

[28]Washington, D.C., has its own federal district court and circuit court of appeals; only federal laws apply in this jurisdiction.

[29]*See* Marbury v. Madison, 5 U.S. (1 Cranch) 137 (1803).

that the topic of a case is not appropriate or of sufficient significance to warrant Supreme Court review. It requires concurrence of at least four justices for a case to be accepted, and denial of review (certiorari) does not infer agreement with the lower court's decision. Since the Supreme Court has authority to determine which cases it will hear, lower courts are left to resolve many issues. Accordingly, precedents regarding some school controversies must be gleaned from federal circuit courts or state supreme courts and may differ from one jurisdiction to another.

At times, an individual need not exhaust state administrative appeals before initiating a federal suit if the abridgment of a federally protected right is involved; however, some federal laws specify administrative procedures that must be pursued before commencing court action (e.g., the IDEA). Suits involving federal issues also may be heard by state courts, and the U.S. Supreme Court may review the interpretation of federal rights by the state judiciary. Individuals have a choice of whether to initiate a federal or state suit in these circumstances, but they cannot relitigate an issue in federal court if they have been denied relief in state court.

Judicial Trends

Traditionally, the federal judiciary did not address educational concerns; fewer than 300 cases involving education were initiated in federal courts prior to 1954.[30] However, starting with the landmark desegregation decision, *Brown v. Board of Education of Topeka* in 1954,[31] federal courts assumed a significant role in resolving educational controversies. At times, courts have taken control of school district operations and have been reluctant to return authority to school boards and educators. Since the 1960s, courts have addressed nearly every facet of the educational enterprise. Much of this judicial intervention has involved the protection of individual rights and the attainment of equity for minority groups.

There has been a notable shift in the posture of the federal judiciary during the past two decades. In the 1960s and early 1970s, federal courts expanded constitutional protections afforded to individuals in school settings, but since the 1980s, the federal judiciary has exhibited more deference to the decisions of the legislative and executive branches and greater reluctance to extend the scope of civil rights. Judicial deference to policy makers nurtures diverse standards across states and local school districts. **When the Supreme Court strikes down a practice under the Constitution, standards become more uniform nationally, but when the Court defers to local boards, standards vary, reflecting local perspectives.** Of course, the composition of the Court has a profound influence on case outcomes.

Although the debate will likely continue over whether courts have the competence to play a key role in shaping educational policies and whether it is legitimate for courts to play such a role, without question, courts do influence school policies. Despite some deceleration in federal litigation, the volume of school cases is still substantial, far outstripping school litigation in any other nation.

---

[30]JOHN HOGAN, THE SCHOOLS, THE COURTS, AND THE PUBLIC INTEREST 11 (Lexington, Mass.: D.C. Heath, 1985).

[31]347 U.S. 483 (1954); *see also* United States v. W. Carroll Parish Sch. Dist., 477 F. Supp. 2d 759 (W.D. La. 2007) (determining that court supervision will be retained until the vestiges of prior race discrimination have been eliminated).

CONCLUSION

Public schools in the United States are governed by a complex body of regulations that are grounded in constitutional provisions, statutory enactments, agency regulations, and court decisions. Since the mid-twentieth century, legislation relating to schools has increased significantly in both volume and complexity, and courts have played an important role in interpreting statutory and constitutional provisions. Although rules made at any level must be consistent with higher authority, administrators and teachers retain considerable latitude in establishing rules and procedures within their specific jurisdictions. So long as educators act reasonably and do not impair the protected rights of others, their actions will be upheld if challenged in court.

School personnel, however, cannot plead "ignorance of the law" as a valid defense for illegal actions.[32] Thus, educators should be aware of the constraints placed on their rule-making prerogatives by school board policies and federal and state constitutional and statutory provisions. Subsequent chapters of this book clarify the major legal principles affecting teachers and students in their daily school activities.

---

[32]*See* Wood v. Strickland, 420 U.S. 308 (1975).

CHAPTER TWO

TORT LIABILITY

Tort law offers civil rather than criminal remedies to individuals for harm caused by the unreasonable conduct of others. A tort is described as a civil wrong, independent of breach of contract, for which relief takes the form of damages. Tort cases primarily involve state law and are grounded in the fundamental premise that individuals are liable for the consequences of their conduct that result in injury to others.[1] Most school tort actions can be grouped into three primary categories: negligence, intentional torts, and defamation.

NEGLIGENCE

To determine whether an educator is negligent in a given situation, courts assess if a reasonably prudent teacher (with the special skills and training associated with that role) would have acted in a similar manner under like conditions.

Negligence is a breach of one's legal duty to protect others from unreasonable risks of harm. The failure to act or an improper act that results in injury or loss to another person can constitute negligence. To establish negligence, an injury must be avoidable by the exercise of reasonable care. Four elements must be present to support a successful claim (see Figure 2.1):

- The defendant has a *duty* to protect the plaintiff.
- The *duty is breached* by the failure to exercise an appropriate standard of care.
- The negligent conduct is the *proximate or legal cause* of the injury.
- An actual *injury* occurs.

[1]Similar claims also have been brought under 42 U.S.C. § 1983 (2012), which entitles individuals to sue persons acting under color of state law for damages in connection with the impairment of federally protected rights.

FIGURE 2.1   Tort Liability
Source: Janet Decker, J.D./Ph.D. and Assistant Professor, Indiana University.

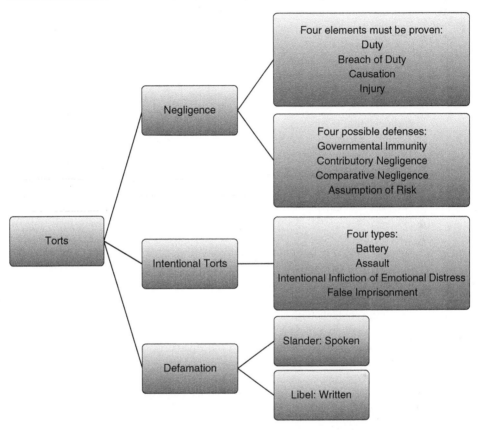

Duty

School officials have a common law duty to anticipate foreseeable dangers and to take necessary precautions to protect students entrusted in their care. Among the specific duties school personnel owe students are the following:

- to give proper instruction;
- to provide adequate supervision;
- to maintain equipment, facilities, and grounds; and
- to warn students of known dangers.

Instruction.   Teachers have a duty to provide students with adequate and appropriate instruction prior to commencing an activity that may pose a risk of harm—the greater the risk, the greater the need for proper instruction.[2] Following such instruction, effort should be made to determine whether the material was heard and understood. Proper instruction was not given to a Nebraska freshman, who was severely burned in a welding course when his flannel shirt ignited.[3] The school failed to make protective leather aprons available to the students, as was recommended for such activities, and the instructor had informed the students simply to wear old shirts. Perhaps most damaging to the district's case was the testimony of the instructor, who stated on four separate occasions that it was not his responsibility to ensure that students wore protective clothing.

[handwritten note in margin: Welding Accident Case]

Supervision.   Although state statutes require educators to provide proper supervision, school personnel are not expected to have every child under surveillance at all times during the school day or to anticipate every possible accident or incident that might occur. Moreover, there is no set level of supervision required under common law for each activity or population. The level of supervision required in any given situation is determined by the aggregate circumstances, including the age, maturity, and prior experience of the students; the specific activity in progress; and the presence of external threats. Accordingly, there may be situations in which no direct supervision is needed, for example, when a nondisruptive student is permitted to leave the classroom to use adjacent restroom facilities in a building with no known dangers,[4] and others where close supervision is prudent (e.g., when students with a history of disruptive behavior are assigned to the same activity), and yet other situations where one-on-one supervision is required (e.g., aquatic exercise class involving students with significant physical disabilities).

In assessing the adequacy of supervision, courts will determine if the events leading up to the injury foreseeably placed the student at risk and whether the injury could have been prevented with proper supervision. For example, the court found the school district liable for negligence because the evidence suggested that the teacher had been on notice about previous problematic behavior in the restroom involving the same students. Students had been playing in the bathroom for four minutes, and during that time, a student was injured after being picked up and dropped on the floor.[5]

Proper supervision is particularly important in settings that pose significant risks to students, such as vocational shops, gymnasiums, science laboratories, and school grounds

---

[2]Some instructional negligence cases have focused on educational malpractice, with students claiming that they are entitled to monetary damages because public schools have not provided them with appropriate instruction. For a discussion of such claims, which have not yet been successful, see MARTHA MCCARTHY, NELDA CAMBRON-MCCABE & SUZANNE ECKES, PUBLIC SCHOOL LAW: TEACHERS' AND STUDENTS' RIGHTS ch. 3 (Upper Saddle River, N.J.: Pearson, 7th ed. 2013).

[3]Norman v. Ogallala Pub. Sch. Dist., 609 N.W.2d 338 (Neb. 2000).

[4]*See, e.g.*, Patel v. Kent Sch. Dist., 648 F.3d 965 (9th Cir. 2011) (finding no teacher liability after unsupervised student was injured while using a bathroom immediately adjacent to the classroom). *But see* Miami-Dade Cnty. Sch. Bd. v. A.N., 905 So. 2d 203 (Fla. Dist. Ct. App. 2005) (affirming jury verdict when the board failed to warn a substitute teacher of the sexually aggressive history of a student; the student was permitted to go to the restroom unsupervised and while in the restroom attacked another student).

[5]Johnson v. Ken-Ton Union Free Sch. Dist. 850 N.Y.S.2d 813 (App. Div. 2008). *But see* Shannea M. v. City of N.Y., 886 N.Y.S.2d 483 (App. Div. 2008) (finding no district liability because there was no notice of prior assaults in the restroom).

where known dangers exist. In these settings, it is critical that school personnel provide both proper instruction and adequate supervision to reduce the likelihood of injury to children and staff. Even when such care is provided, courts acknowledge that accidents will occur. In a New York case, a high school student injured his leg while playing floor hockey in gym class. In ruling for the school district, the court observed that no level of supervision could have prevented the injury.[6]

The school district's duty to supervise also includes the responsibility to protect pupils and employees from foreseeable risks posed by other students or school personnel as well as persons not associated with the district. Depending on the circumstances of a particular case, districts can meet this duty by warning potential victims, increasing the number of supervisory personnel, or providing increased security where assaults, batteries, or other violent acts are reasonably foreseeable. Courts do not expect schools to ensure the safety of students in the event of unforeseeable risks, but they do require that officials respond promptly and professionally when confronted with potentially dangerous circumstances.[7]

When the alleged violator is a school employee, a school district may be held liable under the doctrine of respondeat superior if the school employee committed a tort while performing a job duty.[8] Some courts have rejected claims of school district liability, finding conduct such as battery and sexual assault to represent independent acts outside an individual's scope of employment.[9] Generally, the conduct of the individual violator and not the negligent supervision by the district is the proximate cause of injury. For example, in an Indiana case, the Seventh Circuit found no school district liability for negligent hiring, supervision, or retention because the parents failed to demonstrate that school officials knew that a teacher who had a sexual relationship with their daughter had engaged in such conduct previously.[10]

Notwithstanding the general requirement to provide supervision, there may be times when students pass out of the "orbit of school authority," even though they may remain on school property. This often occurs today, given the wide range of uses of school buildings and the variety of activities. In one such case, an Indiana appeals court found that a district

[6]Odekirk v. Bellmore-Merrick Cent. Sch. Dist., 895 N.Y.S.2d 184 (App. Div. 2009); *see also* Tanenbaum v. Minnesauke Elem. Sch., 901 N.Y.S.2d 102 (App. Div. 2010) (determining that an accident involving a second-grade student who was injured after being pushed in the lunch line could not have been prevented and that school districts should not be found liable when intense supervision could not have prevented the accident).

[7]*Compare* Coleman v. St. Tammany Parish Sch. Bd., 13 So. 3d 644 (La. Ct. App. 2009) (denying school board's motion for summary judgment because it may have been foreseeable that a student would be attacked on the playground at lunchtime; school officials had been on notice that an attack was likely to occur) *with* Brandy B. v. Eden Cent. Sch. Dist. 907 N.Y.S.2d 735 (App. Div. 2010) (finding that a school district had no notice that a student would attack another student and that school personnel did not have specific knowledge to guard against the attack).

[8]Schafer v. Hicksville Union Free Sch. Dist., No. 06-cv-2531, 2011 U.S. Dist. LEXIS 35435 (E.D.N.Y. Mar. 31, 2011).

[9]*See, e.g.,* Acosta-Rodriguez v. City of N.Y., 909 N.Y.S.2d 712 (App. Div. 2010).

[10]Hansen v. Bd. of Tr. of Hamilton Se. Sch. Corp. 551 F.3d 599 (7th Cir. 2008). *But see* C.A. v. William S. Hart Union High Sch. Dist., 270 P.3d 699 (Cal. 2012) (ruling school district was liable for negligence of supervisory personnel who knew or should have known about a counselor's propensity toward sexual harassment).

had no duty to supervise male students who secretly videotaped female lifeguards in their locker room in various stages of undress.[11] The Red Cross lifeguard class, although held in school facilities after school hours, was not part of the public school curriculum, and school employees neither taught nor supervised the course.

Supervision of students en route to and from school also has generated considerable litigation. Over the years, parents have argued that school officials are responsible for their children from the time they leave home until the time they return. The Louisiana Supreme Court found that a school district provided reasonable supervision after a twelve-year-old student was raped on her two and a half-mile walk home from school. State law required the district to provide transportation to students who lived more than one mile from the school. The student in this case was kept after school for a behavior clinic. The district offered to arrange transportation for her, but the student chose to walk home.[12] There is no bright-line test to assist courts in rendering uniform decisions in cases involving students en route to and from school because such a test would place an unrealistic demand on school resources and an unfair burden on personnel. Thus, courts instead focus on whether:

- the events that caused the injury were foreseeable;
- the district had an express or implied duty to provide supervision on and off school grounds both before and after school hours; and
- the child was injured due to a breach of that duty.

Where the district is responsible for providing transportation, officials should ensure that involved staff are properly trained and district procedures are communicated and practiced. Personnel should strictly adhere to transportation requirements, including those related to special licensure; background checks of drivers; vehicle maintenance; driving, loading, and unloading practices; conduct during transport; and criteria for when an aide is to be assigned.[13]

In addition, school officials have a duty to provide supervision during school-sponsored off-campus activities. As with other supervisory roles, school officials accompanying the students need to assess foreseeable risks associated with each activity and be aware of the abilities of participating students.[14] However, when the activity is neither curricular nor school sponsored, liability is less likely, given the difficulty of identifying a continuing duty on the part of school officials to provide supervision. To illustrate, no school district liability was found when a student died in a car accident after attending an off-campus event where alcohol was consumed.[15] The court reasoned that the party was not school related, and the school year had ended prior to the party. In those instances in which districts are not responsible for transporting children to and from school, proper supervision

---

[11]Roe v. N. Adams Cmty. Sch. Corp., 647 N.E.2d 655 (Ind. Ct. App. 1995).

[12]S.J. v. LaFayette Parish Sch. Bd., 41 So. 3d 1119 (La. 2010).

[13]*See, e.g.*, Miloscia v. N.Y.C. Bd. of Educ. 896 N.Y.S.2d 109 (App. Div. 2010) (finding bus driver did not create a dangerous situation when he stopped quickly to avoid an accident, and a student on the bus was injured).

[14]*See* Hansen v. Bath & Tennis Marina Corp., 900 N.Y.S.2d 365 (App. Div. 2010) (determining that it was not foreseeable or preventable when a student burned herself at a school-sponsored event).

[15]Archbishop Coleman F. Carroll High Sch. v. Maynoldi, 30 So. 3d 533 (Fla. Dist. Ct. App. 2010).

still should be provided at the pick-up and drop-off area. Crossing guards should be stationed at nearby intersections for walkers, and assistance should be provided to parents and children to help identify safe routes to and from school.

Moreover, <u>parents need to be informed about the earliest time supervision will be provided before school so that students will not arrive before school personnel. Parents also should be aware of when supervision ends after the school day.</u> Where a student was assaulted by other youths while walking from school, no school district liability was found because the assault occurred thirty minutes after the student left school grounds. The court held that the student was no longer in the custody or control of the school.[16] **As a general rule, school districts are not expected to protect truant and non-attending students** or students who are injured in their homes.[17] This is true for those who never arrive at school as well as for those who leave school grounds during the school day without permission, notwithstanding an appropriate level of surveillance of the school building and grounds as determined by the age and ability of the students. For example, no duty to supervise existed where a high school student was hit by a car after she left school property before the school day to smoke.[18]

Maintenance of Buildings, Grounds, and Equipment.   By law, some states protect frequenters of public buildings from danger to life, health, safety, or welfare. These *safe place statutes* may be used by individuals to obtain damages from school districts for injuries resulting from defective conditions of school buildings and grounds. Furthermore, school officials have a common law duty to maintain facilities and equipment in a reasonably safe condition. Districts can be held liable when they are aware of, or should be aware of, hazardous conditions and do not take the necessary steps to repair or correct the conditions.

The duty to provide reasonable maintenance of facilities does not place an obligation on school personnel to anticipate every possible danger or to be aware of and correct every minor defect as soon as the condition occurs. For example, a Louisiana student was unsuccessful in establishing a breach of duty in connection with an injury she sustained when she slipped and fell in a puddle of liquid on the hallway floor.[19] The state appeals court explained that the presence of liquid on the hallway floor did not automatically create liability; the plaintiff, in failing to demonstrate how long the liquid had been on the floor, had not shown that the school had knowledge of any hazardous condition.

If dangers are known, damages may be awarded when injuries result from unsafe conditions of buildings or grounds. A Michigan student was successful in obtaining damages for the loss of sight in one eye; the injury was sustained while playing in a pile of dirt and sand on the playground after school hours.[20] The area was not fenced, and

---

[16]Pistolese v. William Floyd Union Free Sch. Dist., 895 N.Y.S.2d 125 (App. Div. 2010). *But see* Nash v. Port Wash. Union Free Sch. Dist., 922 N.Y.S.2d 408 (App. Div. 2011) (affirming summary judgment in favor of student who was severely burned while working on science experiment after school).

[17]*See, e.g.*, Maldonado v. Tuckahoe, 817 N.Y.S.2d 376 (App. Div. 2006).

[18]Dalton v. Memminger, 889 N.Y.S.2d 785 (App. Div. 2009).

[19]DeGruy v. Orleans Parish Sch. Bd., 573 So. 2d 1188 (La. Ct. App. 1991).

[20]Monfils v. City of Sterling Heights, 269 N.W.2d 588 (Mich. Ct. App. 1978).

prior to the incident, parents had complained to school officials about "dirt fights" among children. The state appeals court concluded that the school district breached its duty to maintain the school grounds in a safe condition. In contrast, when a student was injured after her thigh hit the net winder on the school district's tennis courts, the court did not find the district negligent in the maintenance of the courts and found no creation of any specific safety hazard.[21]

In addition to maintaining buildings and grounds, school personnel are required to maintain equipment and to use it safely, such as in woodshop, science labs, athletics, or transportation.[22] A Texas appeals court determined that immunity would be waived in part where a five-year-old child fell asleep on her way to school and was locked in the bus for the remainder of the school day. The court reasoned that although the district was immune for its alleged failure to supervise the unloading of the children, the district could be sued for the negligent locking of the door, given that such an act did not qualify as the "operation or use of a motor vehicle" for which immunity is granted.[23]

Warn of Known Dangers.   In nearly all states, courts have recognized either a statutory or common law duty to warn students, parents, and at times educators and staff of known risks they may encounter. This duty has been identified in areas such as physical education and interscholastic sports, vocational education, laboratory science, and other occasions when a student uses potentially dangerous machinery or equipment. Informing, if not warning, students and parents of known dangers is necessary so that they then may assume the usual risk associated with the activity.

In addition to the somewhat traditional warnings connected with sports or the use of equipment, educators, school psychologists, and counselors have a duty to warn when they learn through advising, counseling, or therapy that students intend to harm themselves or others. Those in receipt of such information are required to inform potential victims or to notify parents if the student threatens to self-injure. This requirement supersedes claims of professional ethics, discretion, therapist/client privilege, or confidentiality.

However, school officials will not typically be found liable when the harmful act is unforeseeable (i.e., the threat of suicide was neither explicitly stated nor apparent), even if they knew that a particular student was under stress or seemed depressed or preoccupied. The Ninth Circuit found no school district liability when a student committed suicide at home.[24] The student left school without permission to attend a civil rights rally. When he returned, the vice principal called him dumb and threatened to notify the police. The student was especially worried about being found truant because he was already on probation for bringing a knife to school. Later that night at home, he shot himself. The court observed that the student had the opportunity to appreciate the nature of his actions after he returned to class and that school officials could not be held liable for his decision to take his own life.[25]

[21]Bendig v. Bethpage Union Free Sch. Dist., 904 N.Y.S.2d 731 (App. Div. 2010).

[22]*See, e.g.*, Arteman v. Clinton Cmty. Unit Sch. Dist. No. 15, 740 N.E.2d 47 (Ill. App. Ct. 2000).

[23]Elgin Indep. Sch. Dist. v. R.N., 191 S.W.3d 263, 268 (Tex. App. 2006).

[24]Corales v. Bennett, 567 F.3d 554 (9th Cir. 2009).

[25]*Id*. at 572. *See also* Mixell v. Sch. Admin. Unit No. 33, 972 A.2d 1050 (N.H. 2009) (finding no school district liability when student suicide is considered a deliberate, intentional, and intervening act).

School officials also have a duty to warn employees of known dangers, whether structural, environmental, or human. Accordingly, a Florida court reversed a lower court grant of summary judgment in a case in which district officials failed to warn a teacher about a student's propensity for violence.[26] On remand, to overcome the general rule of workers' compensation[27] immunity, the battered teacher will have to show that the employer engaged in conduct that was substantially certain to result in injury.

Breach of Duty/Standard of Care

Once a duty has been established, the injured individual must show that the duty was breached by the failure of another to exercise an appropriate standard of care.[28] The degree of care teachers owe students is determined by:

- the age, experience, and maturity level of the students;
- the environment within which the incident occurs; and
- the type of instructional or recreational activity.

For example, primary grade students will generally require closer supervision and more detailed and repetitive instructions than high school students, and a class in woodwork will require closer supervision than a class in English literature. Variability in the level of care deemed reasonable is illustrated in a Louisiana case in which a mentally retarded student was fatally injured when he darted into a busy thoroughfare while being escorted with nine other classmates to a park three blocks from the school.[29] The state appellate court noted that the general level of care required for all students becomes greater when children with disabilities are involved, particularly when they are taken away from the school campus. The court found the supervision to be inadequate and the selected route to be less safe than alternate routes. The reasonableness of any given action will be pivotal in determining whether there is liability.

In assessing whether appropriate care has been taken, courts consider whether the defendant acted as a "reasonable person" would have acted under the circumstances. The reasonable person is a hypothetical individual who has:

- the physical attributes of the defendant;
- normal intelligence, problem-solving ability, and temperament;
- normal perception and memory with a minimum level of information and experience common to the community; and
- such superior skill and knowledge as the defendant has or purports to have.

---

[26]Patrick v. Palm Beach Cnty. Sch. Bd., 927 So. 2d 973 (Fla. Dist. Ct. App. 2006), *aff'd mem.*, 50 So. 3d 1161 (Fla. Dist. Ct. App. 2010).

[27]*See, e.g.*, Wyble v. Acadiana Preparatory Sch., 956 So. 2d 722 (La. Ct. App. 2007) (determining that a school employee was eligible for workers' compensation when injured at work while moving a desk; it did not matter that the task was routine rather than an accident).

[28]*See, e.g.*, S.J. v. LaFayette Parish Sch. Bd., 40 So. 3d 1119 (La. 2010).

[29]Foster v. Houston Gen. Ins. Co., 407 So. 2d 759, 763 (La. Ct. App. 1981).

Courts will not assume that a defendant possesses any predetermined physical attributes (e.g., size, strength, agility) but rather will consider each defendant's actual physical abilities and disabilities in determining whether the defendant was responsible in whole or in part for an individual's injury. Accordingly, if a child requires physical assistance to avoid being attacked by another student, a different expectation will exist for a large, physically fit teacher as compared to a small, frail teacher.

Although a defendant's actual physical characteristics and capabilities are used in determining whether his or her conduct was reasonable, that is not the case when considering mental capacity. Courts will assume all adult individuals have normal intelligence, problem-solving ability, and temperament, even when the evidence indicates that they do not possess such attributes.[30] This may initially appear unfair, but any other approach is likely to result in defense claims that are judicially unmanageable. For example, if defendants' own intellect were used, they could argue that consideration should be given to factors such as their inability to make good or quick decisions, lack of perception or concentration, poor attention to detail, confrontational personality, or inability to deal with stress. Trying to determine each person's mental abilities and capabilities would be impractical, if not impossible, given the dearth of valid and reliable assessment instruments or techniques and the ease of those being assessed to misrepresent their abilities.

In an effort to determine whether the defendant acted as a reasonable person, courts also consider whether the defendant had or claimed to have had any superior knowledge or skill. Teachers, who are college graduates and state licensed, are expected to act like reasonable persons with similar education. In addition, any special training an individual has received may affect whether a given act is considered reasonable. To illustrate, a physical education instructor who is a certified lifeguard or a teacher with an advanced degree in chemistry may be held to higher standards of care than others with lesser skills and knowledge when, respectively, a student is drowning or chemicals in a school laboratory are mixed improperly and ignite. In reaching a decision on whether an appropriate standard of care has been provided, courts also determine whether an injured individual was an invitee, licensee, or trespasser, with invitees receiving the greatest level of care and trespassers receiving the least.[31]

Proximate Cause

The plaintiff must demonstrate a causal link between the negligent act and the harm before the defendant can be found liable for negligence.[32] In order to prevail, the plaintiff must show that the defendant's conduct that constituted a breach of duty caused the harm.

There are two types of causation: cause-in-fact and proximate cause. In determining whether a school official's conduct was the cause-in-fact of the student's injury, sometimes courts employ the "but for" test. Under this test, the plaintiff needs to show that "but for" the defendant's act or failure to act there would not have been an injury. With proximate cause, courts decide whether the teacher's action is close enough to the chain of events

---

[30]Dan B. Dobbs, The Law of Torts 284–85 (St. Paul, Minn.: West 2000).

[31]For additional information on invitees, licensees, and trespassers, see Martha McCarthy, Nelda Cambron-McCabe & Suzanne Eckes, Public School Law: Teachers' and Students' Rights ch. 13 (Upper Saddle River, N.J.: Pearson, 7th ed. 2013).

[32]David G. Owen, *The Five Elements of Negligence*, 35 Hofstra L. Rev. 1680–82 (2007).

that caused the harm. For example, there must be a causal connection between the alleged negligent conduct and the resulting injury. The courts might ask whether the incident was foreseeable when making a determination regarding proximate cause.[33]

To illustrate, while playing tag in gym class, a fourth-grade student was unintentionally knocked down by a classmate. He lost two front teeth when a different student tripped over him and caused his face to hit the floor.[34] Affirming the lower court's decision to grant summary judgment in favor of the school district, the appellate court found that the student failed to establish that lack of supervision by the gym teacher and aide was the proximate cause of the injury. Similarly, a New York court ruled that a school district's lack of supervision was not the proximate cause of a student's injuries where a fight, in which the student was injured, occurred in such a short period of time that not even the most intense supervision could have prevented it.[35]

Injury

Legal negligence does not exist unless actual injury is incurred directly by the individual or by the individual's property. Most often, an individual will know of the injury as soon as it occurs; in some instances, however, the individual may not be aware of the injury for many months or even years (e.g., development of asbestosis due to exposure to asbestos twenty years previously). In most states, there is a statute of limitations of one to three years on tort claims, although the actual time can be greater if the limitations period does not begin until the plaintiff reaches the age of majority or becomes aware of the injury.

When students are injured in the school setting, school personnel have a duty to provide reasonable assistance commensurate with their training and experience. Where reasonable treatment is provided, no liability will generally be assessed, even if the treatment later is proven to be inappropriate or inadequate.

Defenses against Negligence

Although tort law is generally addressed in state courts, teachers might find protection against claims of negligence under a federal law. The Paul D. Coverdell Teacher Protection Act, which is included in the No Child Left Behind Act, provides protection to teachers who are "acting within the scope of the teacher's employment or responsibilities to a school" or when the teacher is attempting "to control, discipline, expel, or suspend a student or maintain order or control in the classroom or school."[36]

In addition, there are several defenses available to school districts when employees have been charged with negligence. At times, in an effort to thwart liability claims, districts have identified procedural defects (e.g., the failure to adhere to statutory requirements regarding notice of claim) or have proposed that an individual's injury was caused by uncontrollable events of nature (i.e., an act of God). More commonly, defenses such as immunity, contributory negligence, comparative negligence, and assumption of risk have been asserted.

---

[33]*Id.*

[34]Doyle v. Binghamton City Sch. Dist., 874 N.Y.S.2d 607 (App. Div. 2009).

[35]Keaveny v. Mahopac Cent. Sch. Dist., 897 N.Y.S.2d 222 (App. Div. 2010).

[36]20 U.S.C. § 6736(a) (2012).

Governmental Immunity.   In rare cases in which governmental immunity is comprehensively applied, governmental entities including school districts cannot be sued for any reason. But this defense is available to employees only when state law specifically confers such immunity for acts within the scope of employment, or courts interpret the law to do so.[37] Immunity is seldom comprehensively applied today, as nearly all states have limited its use by considering factors such as whether (1) the claim was related to the maintenance of the school building or property, (2) acts were governmental or proprietary, (3) decisions qualified as discretionary or ministerial, (4) school property was being used for recreational purposes, or (5) the injury was compensable under the state's workers' compensation laws (employees only).[38]

Contributory Negligence.   In states that recognize contributory negligence as a defense, plaintiffs are denied recovery if their actions are shown to have been substantially responsible for the injury; it makes no difference that the defendant was negligent and also partially at fault. In most jurisdictions today, a slight degree of fault will not prevent a plaintiff from prevailing; typically, the contributory negligence must be significant, although it need not be dominant.

In assessing whether contributory negligence exists, children are not necessarily held to the same standard of care as adults. Rather, their actions must be reasonable for persons of similar age, maturity, intelligence, and experience. Many courts make individualized determinations as to whether a minor plaintiff appreciated the risks involved and acted as a reasonable person of like characteristics and abilities. Other courts have established age ranges in an effort to more objectively and uniformly determine whether children have the capacity to contribute to or cause their own injuries.[39] Although courts vary greatly and designated ages may seem arbitrary, the most commonly used ranges are:

- children below the age of seven are considered incapable of negligence;
- children between the ages of seven and fourteen are considered incapable of negligence, but this presumption can be rebutted;[40] and
- students age fourteen and over are generally presumed capable of negligence, although this presumption too can be rebutted.

---

[37]*See, e.g.*, Brown v. Fountain Hill Sch. Dist., 1 S.W.3d 27 (Ark. Ct. App. 1999); Coonse v. Boise Sch. Dist., 979 P.2d 1161 (Idaho 1999).

[38]*Proprietary functions* are those that are only tangentially related to the curriculum, can as easily be performed by the private sector, and often require the payment of a fee (e.g., community use of the pool). *Discretionary functions* are those that require consideration of alternatives, deliberation, judgment, and the making of a decision (e.g., the discretion used in the selection of a new teacher). In contrast, *ministerial functions* are those performed in a prescribed manner, in obedience to legal authority, and without discretion (e.g., procedures used for stopping a school bus at a railroad crossing). *Recreational use* immunity statutes were passed to encourage property and landowners to open their lands and waters for public recreational use. Immunity for injuries incurred while on the property is provided unless the entrant was charged a fee for admission or was injured because of the owner's willful or wanton misconduct.

[39]*See, e.g.*, Berman v. Phila. Bd. of Educ., 456 A.2d 545 (Pa. 1983) (finding that an eleven-year-old student who was injured by a hockey stick after the school failed to provide gear could not be found contributorily negligent).

[40]*See, e.g.*, Clay City Consol. Sch. Corp. v. Timberman, 918 N.E.2d 292 (Ind. 2009) (observing that children between ages seven and fourteen are incapable of negligence in a case involving a thirteen-year-old student who died at basketball practice and was not found to be contributorily negligent).

When adults are injured on school grounds or at school functions, courts will assess the nature of the risk involved and whether such a risk was known to the injured party or reasonably should have been known. An Indiana court upheld a grant of summary judgment where a father fell from backless bleachers while watching his son participate in a basketball game. The court found the plaintiff to be contributorily negligent in that he failed to exercise the degree of care that an ordinary, reasonable, and prudent person in a similar situation would exercise.[41]

Comparative Negligence.   With the comparative model, the plaintiff and/or one or more defendants bear responsibility in proportion to fault. For example, a school district in Wisconsin was found 80 percent liable for an injury sustained by an eighth-grade student while dissecting a plant with a scalpel. The court observed that the teacher had been aware that others had been injured in the past and that she could have done more to avoid this injury.[42] Similarly, an Arizona appeals court upheld a jury verdict where a student was hit by a car when he ran into the street trying to flee another student after he safely exited a school bus on his way home. Liability was apportioned to the injured boy (45 percent), his parents (40 percent), and the district (15 percent) in a $6 million award. Although the school district was not responsible for escorting the child home, school officials were aware of the conduct of the students at the bus stop, a nearby busy street with fast-moving traffic, and the availability of an alternative and safer bus stop.[43]

Assumption of Risk.   This defense can be either express or implied. Express assumption occurs when the plaintiff consents in advance to take his or her chances of injury, given a known danger. On the other hand, *implied assumption* **occurs without an express written or oral agreement, yet it is logically assumed, given the plaintiff's conduct.** For example, implied assumption would exist where spectators at a baseball game elect to sit in unscreened seats; such persons assume the risk of possible injury even if they failed to sign an agreement.

Although inherent risks are associated with athletics or recreation, all participants will not necessarily understand those risks. Understanding risks often is associated with age, maturity, and experience. As a result, school personnel must exercise reasonable care to protect students from unassumed, concealed, or unreasonably high risks. This duty can be met when participation is voluntary and the student is knowledgeable of and assumes the risks associated with the activity. For instance, in Indiana, a football player died following extensive conditioning in hot and humid weather. His mother had signed a release form providing permission for him to participate in organized athletics and acknowledging that injuries and even death may result.[44] The appeals court concluded that the lower court was correct in permitting the admission of the form as part of the district's defense. The athlete

---

[41]Funston v. Sch. Town of Munster, 849 N.E.2d 595 (Ind. 2006).

[42]Heuser v. Cmty. Ins. Corp., 774 N.W.2d 653 (Wis. Ct. App. 2009).

[43]Warrington v. Tempe Elementary Sch. Dist. No. 3, 3 P.3d 988 (Ariz. Ct. App. 1999).

[44]Stowers v. Clinton Cent. Sch. Corp., 855 N.E.2d 739 (Ind. Ct. App. 2006).

had several years of general football experience and in prior years had participated in the conditioning program of the current coach.[45]

However, student athletes assume only those risks that occur during normal participation. For example, in New York, the court found that the student assumed the risk of injury when he landed on a metal cross bar attached to a portable basketball hoop. The court observed that the bar did not create a dangerous condition above the usual dangers of basketball.[46] But students do not assume unknown risks associated with a coach's negligence. Moreover, they are not assuming that they will be exposed to intentional torts or conduct that represents a reckless disregard for the safety of others. Likewise, students do not assume a risk when they are compelled to participate in athletic events.

INTENTIONAL TORTS

School personnel can be liable for intentionally harming others through assault, battery, false imprisonment, or the intentional infliction of mental distress.

Among the more common types of intentional torts are assault, battery, false imprisonment, and intentional infliction of emotional distress. Each of these torts is discussed briefly below.

Assault and Battery

Assault consists of an overt attempt to place another in fear of bodily harm; no actual physical contact need take place. Examples include threatening with words, pointing a gun, waving a knife, or shaking a fist. For there to be an assault, the plaintiff needs to be aware of the threat, and the person committing the assault needs to be perceived as having the ability to carry out the threat. In contrast, **a battery is committed when an assault is consummated. Examples include being shot, stabbed, beaten, or struck.** Actual injury need not result for a battery claim to succeed (e.g., the person could have been punched but not injured due to a comparatively weak blow). For the plaintiff to prevail in either an assault or a battery case, the act must be *intentional*; there is no such thing as a negligent assault or battery.

---

[45]Given the national attention to concussion-related injuries, many school districts and some states are requiring schools to adopt concussion management plans to educate students, parents, and school personnel about concussion prevention and responses. Also, the nation's largest youth football organization has barred some common contact drills to reduce the risk of head injuries. *See, e.g.*, Nat'l Sch. Bds. Ass'n, *Youth Football Organization Adopts New Rules Aimed at Reducing Player Concussions*, LEGAL CLIPS (June 21, 2012), http://legalclips.nsba.org/?p=14941. In addition, school districts are placing restrictions on the length of practice sessions and type of attire worn in preseason football training to avoid heat-related injuries. *See, e.g.*, Elliott Francis, *Coaches Prepare for New Preseason Heat Rules in Maryland* (Aug. 8, 2012), http://wamu.org/news/morning_edition/12/08/08/coaches_prepare_for_new_preseason_heat_rules_in_maryland.

[46]Milea v. Our Lady of Miracles Roman Catholic Church, 736 N.Y.S.2d 84 (App. Div. 2002).

Some school-based assault and battery cases have involved students fighting at school. For example, in Ohio, a student struck another student in the face with a cell phone causing injury.[47] Other assault and battery cases have included the administration of corporal punishment and other forms of discipline that require physical touching. Generally, courts have been reluctant to interfere with a teacher's authority to discipline students and have sanctioned the use of reasonable force to control pupil behavior. The Oregon appeals court ruled that a teacher was not guilty of assault and battery for using force to remove a student from the classroom. After the pupil defiantly refused to leave, the teacher held the student's arms and led him toward the door. The student extricated himself, swung at the teacher, and broke a window, thereby cutting his arm. The court concluded that the teacher used reasonable force with the student and dismissed the assault and battery charges.[48] In contrast, a Louisiana student was successful in obtaining damages.[49] The pupil had sustained a broken arm when a teacher shook him, lifted him against the bleachers in the gymnasium, and then let him fall to the floor. The court reasoned that the teacher's action was unnecessary either to discipline the student or to protect himself. Although comparatively uncommon, school personnel may initiate battery suits against students who injure them.[50]

Self-defense often has been used to shield an individual from liability for alleged battery. **An individual need not wait to be struck to engage in defensive acts, although reasonable grounds must exist to substantiate that harm is imminent.** The "test" in such cases is to determine whether the defendant's conduct was that in which a reasonable person may have engaged given the circumstances. Consideration should be given to the magnitude of the existing threat, possible alternatives to physical contact, and the time frame available to make a decision (i.e., whether the defendant acted instantaneously or had time for contemplation and deliberation). Even where contact is justified, the defendant must use only force that is reasonably necessary for self-protection. Furthermore, if the alleged aggressor is disarmed, rendered helpless, or no longer capable of aggressive behavior, the defendant may not take the opportunity to engage in revenge or to punish.

In addition to self-defense, individuals accused of battery also may claim that they were acting in the defense of others. This type of tort defense is of particular importance in a school setting where educators often are called on to separate students who are fighting or to come to the aid of someone being attacked. Most jurisdictions not only permit such action on behalf of others but also consider it to be a responsibility or duty of educators, assuming good faith and the use of reasonable and necessary force.

---

[47]Watkins v. New Albany Plain Local Schs., No. 2:08-cv-134, 2011 U.S. Dist. LEXIS 55322 (S.D. Ohio May 23, 2011).

[48]Simms v. Sch. Dist. No. 1, 508 P.2d 236 (Or. Ct. App. 1973); *see also* Frame v. Comeaux, 735 So. 2d 753 (La. Ct. App. 1999) (finding no battery when a substitute teacher grabbed a confrontational eighth-grade student by the arm and escorted him out of the room—the student had been talking during a test).

[49]Frank v. Orleans Parish Sch. Bd., 195 So. 2d 451 (La. Ct. App. 1967).

[50]In addition, some negligence suits are filed by school personnel against their districts when they have been battered at work. In most cases, however, courts have found that the incidents were unforeseen and that no special duty existed on the part of the district to prevent the battery. *See, e.g.*, Genao v. Bd. of Educ., 888 F. Supp. 501 (S.D.N.Y. 1995) (finding the school district had not established a special duty to protect the teacher in several incidents involving battery).

False Imprisonment

False imprisonment results when physical action, verbal command, or intimidation is used to restrain or detain persons against their will. All restrictions on the freedom of movement or the effort to enter or exit will not qualify as false imprisonment. For example, the court found no false imprisonment where a student was placed for seven minutes in a holding cell in a county detention facility for continually disrupting a tour of the building—the student's behavior jeopardized the safety of the children and disrupted an otherwise orderly environment.[51] Also, a student who was taken out of class to be questioned by the principal and a magistrate judge regarding sexual activities on the Internet could not claim false imprisonment.[52]

To be falsely imprisoned, one need not be incarcerated; walls, locks, or physical force are not required. Rather, imprisonment can result from being placed in a closet, room, corner, automobile, or even a circle in the middle of a football field; it can occur when confined to an entire building or when forced to accompany another person on a walk or a trip. The taking of a purse, car keys, or other property with the intent to detain the person also may qualify as imprisonment. Tone of voice, body language, and what was reasonably understood or even implied from the defendant's conduct will be considered.

In false imprisonment cases, the plaintiff must be aware of the restraint but does not have to show damages beyond the confinement itself. Accordingly, any time children are unjustifiably restrained against their will, tied or taped to chairs, or bound and gagged, the tort of false imprisonment (as well as other possible violations) may be claimed. For example, a school district's motion for summary judgment was denied when a student with special needs was confined to a very small time-out room. In examining his false imprisonment claim against the district, the record reflected that the student's confinement violated New York law.[53] The plaintiff successfully demonstrated that school personnel intended to confine him, the student was aware of the confinement, and the confinement was not otherwise privileged.

Although there are times when the use of physical restraints may be necessary, educators need to document the circumstances requiring such actions and provide a narrative explaining why restraint is an appropriate and reasoned response to the behavior. Where explanations are insufficient, liability will be possible, if not probable.

Intentional Infliction of Mental or Emotional Distress

A tort claim of intentional infliction of mental distress is available to individuals who have experienced severe mental anguish. This claim, however, does not provide a remedy for every trivial indignity, insult, incidence of bad manners, annoyance, or sexist or racist comment, even if disturbing to the plaintiff.

Some forms of communication can result in an assault claim (e.g., a threat to strike another) or defamation suit (e.g., an unfounded claim that a teacher has been sexually

---

[51]Harris *ex rel.* Tucker v. Cnty. of Forsyth, 921 F. Supp. 325 (M.D.N.C. 1996).

[52]Howard v. Yakovac, No. CV04-202-S-EJL, 2006 U.S. Dist. LEXIS 27253 (D. Idaho May 2, 2006).

[53]Schafer v. Hicksville Free Sch. Dist., No. 06-cv-2531, 2011 U.S. Dist. LEXIS 35435 (E.D.N.Y. Mar. 31, 2011).

involved with students). Other communications might provide a basis for discrimination suits under federal laws (e.g., sexual or racial harassment). **For the conduct to result in intentional infliction of mental or emotional distress under tort law, it must be flagrant, extreme, or outrageous; it must go beyond all possible bounds of decency and be regarded as atrocious and utterly intolerable in civilized society.**[54] No reasonable person should be expected to endure such conduct (e.g., severe and extreme acts of stalking, harassment, and assault). Moreover, in most instances, the conduct must be prolonged and recurring since single acts seldom meet the necessary threshold.

Given the difficulty of meeting this stringent standard, it is not surprising that few school-based intentional infliction of emotional distress claims succeed. Unsuccessful claims include a school supervisor who was callous and offensive when he ridiculed a subordinate's speech impediment;[55] a teacher making a false report against a student for misconduct;[56] teachers refusing to use a student's nickname, Boo, that also has drug connotations;[57] and a school administrator sending a letter to parents and students indicating that a teacher who had made racially offensive remarks was returning to work following a ten-day suspension.[58] None of these cases were found to have met the necessary threshold to qualify as outrageous or extreme.

In contrast, an Illinois federal district court supported parents' claim of intentional infliction of mental distress against a teacher who had sexually abused their first-grade children.[59] The court noted that the teacher's conduct toward the students was extreme and outrageous. Parents may also file such claims against the district if they suffered mental anguish as a result of their child's injury. For example, a parent was successful in an intentional infliction of emotional distress claim when the school released the student to an unauthorized person, and the student was kidnapped.[60]

DEFAMATION

Individuals can receive damages for written or spoken injury to their reputations, presuming, of course, that the statements are false.

---

[54]*See* Ott v. Edinburgh Cmty. Sch. Corp., 189 F. App'x 507 (7th Cir. 2006) (concluding that a former coach was not defamed, nor did statements made about him rise to the level of outrageousness that would cause mental or emotional distress, when a school board member disclosed to the superintendent that the coach had a criminal record).

[55]Shipman v. Glenn, 443 S.E.2d 921 (S.C. Ct. App. 1994).

[56]Mikell v. Sch. Admin. Unit No. 22, 972 A.2d 1050 (N.H. 2009).

[57]Phillips v. Lincoln Cnty. Sch. Dist., 984 P.2d 947 (Or. Ct. App. 1999); *see also* Green v. San Diego Unified Sch. Dist., 226 F. App'x 677 (9th Cir. 2007) (determining that defendant's conduct was neither extreme nor outrageous, and plaintiff failed to meet the standard for emotional distress).

[58]Elstrom v. Indep. Sch. Dist. No. 270, 533 N.W.2d 51 (Minn. Ct. App. 1995).

[59]Doe v. White, 627 F. Supp. 2d 905 (C.D. Ill. 2009); *see also* M.S. v. Seminole Cnty. Sch. Bd., 636 F. Supp. 2d 1317 (M.D. Fla. 2009) (denying defendant's motion for summary judgment, the court found that a teacher who had physically abused a student with autism could be held liable for her outrageous behavior).

[60]Ramirez v. Escondido Unified Sch. Dist., No. 11cv1823, 2012 U.S. Dist. LEXIS 26138 (S.D. Cal. Feb. 29, 2012).

Most tort actions have involved claims for damages that were due to physical or mental injuries, but plaintiffs also have claimed injury to their reputations in the form of defamation.[61] School districts may be liable for the defamatory acts of their employees, but only when they are engaged in school district work and their conduct is within the scope of their authority.[62] Otherwise, claims may be filed only against the individual responsible for the alleged defamation. ***Slander* is the term generally associated with spoken defamation (but also includes sign language), whereas *libel* often is used to refer to written defamation (but also includes pictures, statues, motion pictures, and conduct carrying a defamatory imputation—e.g., hanging a person in effigy).**[63] In determining whether defamation has occurred, courts will consider whether:

- the targeted individual was a private or public person;
- the communication was false;
- the expression qualified as opinion or fact; and
- the comment was privileged.

Private and Public Persons

To prevail in a defamation case, private individuals need prove only that a false publication by the defendant was received and understood by a third party and that injury resulted. Receipt of potentially defamatory information that is not understood (e.g., receiving an unintelligible encrypted message on a computer, hearing Morse code over a radio, receiving a phone call in an unknown language) cannot adversely affect the plaintiff's reputation, dignity, or community standing and does not qualify as defamation. Individuals considered public figures or officials additionally must show that the publication was made with either malice or a reckless disregard for the truth. Definitions vary considerably by state, but public figures generally are those who are known or recognized by the public (e.g., professional athletes, actors), whereas public officials are those who have substantial control over governmental affairs (e.g., politicians, school board members).

The trend in recent years has been to broaden the class of public officials and figures, but it is fortunate for teachers that the vast majority of courts have not found them to be "public," in large part because their authority typically is limited to students.[64] Some courts, however, have found school administrators and coaches to be either public officials or figures.[65]

---

[61]*See, e.g.,* Draker v. Schreiber, 271 S.W.3d 318 (Tex. App. 2008) (dismissing vice principal's causes of action against two students who had created mock Myspace profiles that included personal information and sexual references about her).

[62]*See, e.g.,* Henderson v. Walled Lake Consol. Schs., 469 F.3d 479 (6th Cir. 2006) (finding that a coach's slanderous comments were not made within the scope of his authority as a soccer coach).

[63]DOBBS, *supra* note 30.

[64]McCutcheon v. Moran, 425 N.E.2d 1130 (Ill. App. Ct. 1981). *But see* Elstrom v. Indep. Sch. Dist. No. 270, 533 N.W.2d 51 (Minn. Ct. App. 1995) (concluding that a teacher was a public official).

[65]*See, e.g.,* Jordan v. World Publ'g Co., 872 P.2d 946 (Okla. Ct. App. 1994) (principal). *But see* O'Connor v. Burningham, 165 P.3d 1214 (Utah 2007) (determining that a coach was not a public official as school athletics did not affect in any material way the civic affairs of a community).

This does not mean that all administrators and coaches, even within the same jurisdiction, will qualify as public persons; such a determination is made on an individual basis and is dependent on the role, responsibility, degree of notoriety, and authority of the specific individual.

Veracity of Statements

In assessing defamation claims, courts also consider whether a statement is true or false. If the statement is found to be true, or at least substantially true, judgment will generally be for the defendant, assuming that critical facts have not been omitted, taken out of context, or otherwise artificially juxtaposed to misrepresent.[66] Educators must be particularly careful, however, when discussing students and must avoid making comments in bad faith that will result in liability. For example, if a teacher were to comment in class that a particular female student was a "slut," the comment would qualify as defamation per se.[67] In such cases, no proof of actual harm to reputation is required.

In addition to proving a communication to be false, the individual must show that he or she was the subject addressed. Interestingly, the individual's identity need not be clear to all third parties (i.e., readers, viewers, or hearers of the defamation); so long as at least one third party can identify the individual, the claim is actionable, even though the individual is not mentioned by name. Furthermore, the defamatory content need not be explicit; it may be implied or may be understood only by third parties with additional information.

Fact versus Opinion

Most opinions receive constitutional protection, particularly when public figures or officials are involved or the issue is one of public concern. **To qualify as opinion, the communication must not lend itself to being realistically proven as true or false and must be communicated in such a way as to be considered a personal perspective on the matter.**[68] For example, when a teacher made professional recommendations that were included in a special education student's Individual Education Program (IEP), the court did not find it to be defamation. The statements were opinions and not facts or false statements.[69] Parents may express critical opinions about a teacher (verbally or in writing) and may submit such opinions to a principal or school board.[70] Moreover, parents may even express negative views directly to the teacher, assuming that the expression does not amount to "fighting words"[71]

---

[66]Determining whether something is true can be difficult, as perspectives and standards will vary.

[67]*See, e.g.,* Smith v. Atkins, 622 So. 2d 795 (La. Ct. App. 1993).

[68]*Compare* Milkovich v. Lorain Journal Co., 497 U.S. 1 (1990) (observing that statements made by a newspaper about a high school wrestling coach implied that the coach committed perjury in a judicial proceeding; because the statements could be proven true or false, they did not qualify as opinion) *with* Maynard v. Daily Gazette Co., 447 S.E.2d 293 (W. Va. 1994) (holding that a former athletic director was not defamed by an editorial identifying him as one of several parties responsible for the poor graduation rates of athletes; statements expressed in the newspaper were constitutionally protected opinions regarding topics of public interest).

[69]Luo v. Baldwin Free Sch. Dist., No. 10-cv-1985, 2011 U.S. Dist. LEXIS 26836 (E.D.N.Y. Mar. 15, 2011).

[70]Ansorian v. Zimmerman, 627 N.Y.S.2d 706 (App. Div. 1995).

[71]"Fighting words" are, by their nature, likely to result in an immediate breach of the peace and do not qualify as First Amendment protected speech. *See* text accompanying note 6, Chapter 5.

or qualify as an assault. Notwithstanding these examples, allegations that "the teacher sold drugs to a student" or that "the superintendent stole school funds" are factual statements capable of being substantiated and therefore may qualify as defamation unless proven true.

Privilege

Whether a communication qualifies as "privileged" also may affect whether defamation is supported. Statements that are considered *absolutely privileged* cannot serve as a basis for defamation under any circumstance, even if they are false and result in injury.[72] An absolute privilege defense has been selectively applied in cases involving superintendents and school board members, although it is less common in education than qualified privilege. For example, the North Dakota Supreme Court held that a board member's statements at a school board meeting about a superintendent were absolutely privileged.[73] Similarly, a New York court held that a superintendent's written reprimand to a coach for failure to follow regulations in the operation of the interscholastic athletic program was protected by absolute privilege.[74]

Communication between parties with qualified[75] or conditional privilege also may be immune from liability if made in good faith. But, conditional privilege may be lost if actual malice exists (i.e., a person made a defamatory statement that was known to be false, acted with a high degree of awareness of probable falsity, or entertained serious doubts as to whether the statement was true). Qualified privilege has been supported in administrators' rating of school personnel,[76] a board member commenting on the suspension of a student for marijuana possession,[77] and a teacher informing school officials about the inappropriate conduct of another teacher during a school trip.[78]

DAMAGES

Tort suits for damages may be filed against school districts and the individuals responsible for the injury.

Damages in tort suits can be either **compensatory** or **punitive**, and many include attorneys' fees that are typically calculated as a percent of the total award (often one-third if the case settles prior to trial and 40 percent if the case is tried). **Compensatory damages include**

---

[72]*See, e.g.*, Gallegos v. Escalon, 993 S.W.2d 422 (Tex. App. 1999).

[73]Rykowsky v. Dickinson Pub. Sch. Dist. No. 1, 508 N.W.2d 348 (N.D. 1993).

[74]Santavicca v. City of Yonkers, 518 N.Y.S.2d 29 (App. Div. 1987).

[75]Qualified immunity may shield government officials from liability when they are accused of violating an individual's constitutional rights.

[76]*See, e.g.*, Malia v. Monchak, 543 A.2d 184 (Pa. Commw. Ct. 1988).

[77]Morrison v. Mobile Cnty. Bd. of Educ., 495 So. 2d 1086 (Ala. 1986).

[78]Rocci v. Ecole Secondaire MacDonald-Cartier, 755 A.2d 583 (N.J. 2000).

past and future economic loss, medical expenses, and pain and suffering. These awards are intended to make the plaintiff whole, at least to the degree that money is capable of doing so. If a plaintiff's previous injury has been aggravated, the defendant is generally liable only for the additional loss.

Although damages vary by state, it is common to cap awards for intangibles (e.g., pain, suffering, loss of consortium, mental anguish) but not to cap damages for actual loss. When plaintiffs prevail, it is important to note that school district assets are not subject to execution, sale, garnishment, or attachment to satisfy the judgment. Instead, judgments are paid from funds appropriated specifically for that purpose, acquired through revenue bonds, or available because of insurance. If sufficient funds are not forthcoming, it is common for states to require fiscal officers to certify the amount of unpaid judgment to the taxing authority for inclusion in the next budget. When the amounts are significant, many states permit districts to pay installments (at times up to ten years) for payment of damages that do not represent actual loss.

Furthermore, in most states, educators can be sued individually unless they are "save harmlessed" by their school district. Under save harmless provisions, the school district agrees to provide legal representation and pay any resulting liability. When educators are not "save harmlessed" and do not have personal insurance coverage, their personal assets (e.g., cars, boats, bank accounts) may be attached, their wages may be garnished, and a lien may be placed on their property. Where a lien is filed, the property may not be sold until the debt is satisfied. Moreover, debtors are not permitted to transfer ownership to avoid attachment (i.e., this would represent *fraudulent conveyance*).

Finally, punitive damages are awarded to punish particularly wanton or reckless acts and are in addition to actual damages. The amount is discretionary with the jury and is based on the circumstances, behaviors, and acts. Unlike the calculation of actual damages, the debtor's financial worth may be a factor in determining punitive amounts. When jury verdicts are seemingly out of line, the court may reduce (remittitur) or increase (additur) the amount where either passion or prejudice is a factor.

CONCLUSION

All individuals, including educators, are responsible for their actions and can be liable for damages if they intentionally or negligently cause injury to others. Educators have a responsibility to act reasonably, but some negligent conduct is likely to occur. Consequently, educators should be knowledgeable about their potential liability under applicable state laws and should ensure that they are either protected by their school districts or have adequate insurance coverage for any damages that might be assessed against them.

Moreover, school personnel should refrain from intentionally injuring others, engaging in assaultive behaviors, detaining students for inappropriate reasons, or participating in conduct that ultimately may result in the emotional distress of another. Educators also should be cautious when sharing information about colleagues or students as the dissemination of incorrect or confidential information may result in liability.

POINTS TO PONDER

1. During a faculty meeting, a high school principal mentioned that one of the teachers in the building had been arrested for shoplifting and that extra precautions should be taken to safeguard personal belongings. However, the principal failed to mention that although the teacher had been arrested, evidence was inadequate to support her conviction and she had been released soon after her arrest. The principal did not mention the teacher by name, but his comments about the make and model of her car left no doubt as to her identity. Her reputation was tarnished, and her personal relationships were adversely affected. She sued the principal, claiming defamation of character. Is she likely to win? Explain.

2. A secondary school principal directed a student teacher in social studies to supervise a chemistry class because the regular science teacher was ill. During lab, a student was injured in an explosion. The parents of the injured child sued the principal and the school district. Are the parents likely to prevail in this suit? Explain your reasoning.

3. A physical education instructor required a student to climb a thirty-foot rope in physical education class even though the student informed the teacher that he was afraid of heights (a fact that also was part of his school record). After the instructor threatened the student with corporal punishment, he climbed the rope, but fell when about halfway up. He was not injured, but sued the instructor and the district, claiming negligence. Will he succeed in this claim? Why or why not?

4. While on the school bus, two students got into an altercation over loud radio music. The male radio owner refused to turn off or even turn down the music. As a result, a female student informed him that if the music was not turned off, the radio would be destroyed and he would be struck. Numerous passengers overheard the conversation. The radio owner was a large, athletic, eighteen-year-old male; the confronting student was a small, frail, twelve-year-old female. She had no special martial arts skills and did not give the impression that she was capable of carrying out the threat. The male student sued the female, claiming assault. Will he succeed in his claim? Why or why not?

CHAPTER THREE

CHURCH/STATE RELATIONS

Efforts to identify the appropriate relationship between government and religion have generated substantial controversy in our nation, and since the mid-twentieth century, schools have provided the battleground for some of the most volatile disputes. This chapter provides an overview of the constitutional framework, the evolution of legal activity, and the current status of church/state relations involving education.

CONSTITUTIONAL FRAMEWORK

The First Amendment's Establishment Clause is used primarily to challenge governmental *advancement* of religion, whereas Free Exercise Clause claims usually challenge secular government regulations that allegedly impair the practice of religious beliefs.

The First Amendment to the United States Constitution stipulates in part that "Congress shall make no law respecting an establishment of religion or prohibiting the free exercise thereof." Although this amendment was directed toward the *federal* government, the Fourteenth Amendment, adopted in 1868, specifically placed restrictions on *state* action impairing personal rights. **In the twentieth century, the Supreme Court recognized that the fundamental concept of "liberty" in the Fourteenth Amendment incorporates First Amendment guarantees and safeguards these rights against state interference.**[1] **Because education is primarily a state function, most church/state controversies involving schools have been initiated through the Fourteenth Amendment.**

In the first major Establishment Clause decision, *Everson v. Board of Education*, the Supreme Court in 1947 reviewed the history of the First Amendment and concluded that the Establishment Clause (and its Fourteenth Amendment application to states) means:

> Neither a state nor the Federal Government can set up a church. Neither can pass laws which aid one religion, aid all religions, or prefer one religion over another. . . . In the words of Jefferson, the clause against establishment of religion by law was intended to erect "a wall of separation between church and state."[2]

[1]*See* Cantwell v. Connecticut, 310 U.S. 296, 303 (1940).

[2]330 U.S. 1, 15–16 (1947) (quoting Reynolds v. United States, 98 U.S. 145, 164 (1878)).

Thomas Jefferson's wall was used widely by the federal judiciary for more than thirty years following *Everson*, even though this phrase does not appear in the First Amendment.

In a 1971 case, *Lemon v. Kurtzman*, the Supreme Court articulated a three-part test to assess Establishment Clause claims. **To withstand scrutiny under the *Lemon* test, government action must (1) have a secular purpose, (2) have a primary effect that neither advances nor impedes religion, and (3) avoid excessive governmental entanglement with religion.** This test was used consistently in Establishment Clause cases involving school issues until 1992. However, Supreme Court Justices increasingly have voiced dissatisfaction with this test,[3] and few recent Supreme Court Establishment Clause rulings have relied solely on *Lemon*. Support for church/state separation may be waning, even in school cases where the separationist doctrine has been the strongest.

The current Supreme Court seems to favor an *endorsement* standard under which governmental action will be struck down if an objective observer would view it as having the purpose or effect of endorsing or disapproving religion. And on occasion, the Supreme Court has applied a *coercion* test, which bases an Establishment Clause violation on whether there is direct or indirect governmental coercion on individuals to profess a faith.[4] Some lower courts are attempting to cover all bases by reviewing government action under the *Lemon* test, the endorsement standard, and the coercion test (see Figure 3.1).

Whereas the Establishment Clause is used primarily to challenge governmental advancement of religion, lawsuits under the Free Exercise Clause usually focus

FIGURE 3.1   Judicial Standards to Evaluate Challenged Government Action under the Establishment Clause

The government actions or practices will violate the Establishment Clause if they:	
■ Have a religious (sectarian) purpose ■ Advance or impede religion ■ Create excessive government entanglement with religion	*Lemon Test*
■ Have a purpose or effect endorsing or disapproving religion	*Endorsement Test*
■ Place direct or indirect government coercion on individuals to profess a faith	*Coercion Test*

[3]*See* Lamb's Chapel v. Ctr. Moriches Union Free Sch. Dist., 508 U.S. 384, 398 (1993) (Scalia, J., concurring) (comparing the *Lemon* standard to a "ghoul" that rises from the dead "after being repeatedly killed and buried").

[4]*See* Lee v. Weisman, 505 U.S. 577 (1992).

on secular (nonreligious) government regulations alleged to interfere with religious practices. To evaluate free exercise claims, the judiciary traditionally applied a balancing test including an assessment of whether practices dictated by a sincere and legitimate religious belief were impeded by the government action and, if so, to what extent. Finding such an impairment, the judiciary evaluated whether the government action served a compelling interest justifying the burden imposed on the exercise of religious beliefs. Even with such a compelling interest, the judiciary still required the government to attain its objectives through the means least burdensome on free exercise rights.

In the most significant school case involving a free exercise claim, *Wisconsin v. Yoder*, the Supreme Court exempted Amish children from compulsory school attendance upon successful completion of eighth grade.[5] Although noting that the assurance of an educated citizenry ranks at the pinnacle of state functions, the Court nonetheless concluded that parents' rights to practice their legitimate religious beliefs outweighed the state's interest in mandating two additional years of formal schooling for Amish youth. The Court cautioned, however, that its ruling was limited to the Amish who offer a structured vocational program to prepare their youth for a cloistered agrarian community rather than mainstream American society.

In a 1990 decision, the Supreme Court modified this balancing test, ruling that the government does not have to demonstrate a compelling interest to defend a criminal law that burdens the free exercise of religious beliefs. Distinguishing this case from *Yoder's* combination of free exercise rights and parental rights, the Court majority concluded that without such a "hybrid" situation, individuals cannot rely on the Free Exercise Clause to be excused from complying with a valid criminal law prohibiting specific conduct.[6]

Courts not only apply different criteria to assess claims under the Free Exercise and Establishment Clauses; they also impose different remedies for violations of the two clauses. **If government activity abridges the Establishment Clause, the unconstitutional activity must cease. Where government action is found to impair the Free Exercise Clause, accommodations to enable individuals to practice their religious beliefs may be required, but the secular policy or program would not have to be eliminated.**

Troublesome church/state controversies involve competing claims under the Free Exercise and Establishment Clauses because there is an inherent tension between the two provisions. The controversies become even more complex when Free Speech Clause protections are implicated. This tension among First Amendment guarantees has complicated the judiciary's task in assessing claims regarding the role of religion in public schools and government relations with sectarian schools.

RELIGIOUS INFLUENCES IN PUBLIC SCHOOLS

Devotionals sponsored by public schools violate the Establishment Clause, whereas *private* religious expression is protected by the Free Exercise and Free Speech Clauses.

---

[5]406 U.S. 205 (1972).

[6]Emp't Div. v. Smith, 494 U.S. 872 (1990) (upholding the termination of employees who ingested peyote at a religious ceremony of the Native American Church).

In two precedent-setting decisions in the early 1960s, the Supreme Court prohibited public schools from sponsoring daily prayer and Bible reading, concluding that such activities advance religion in violation of the Establishment Clause, and students' voluntary participation was irrelevant.[7] The fact that daily devotional activities were conducted under the auspices of the public school was sufficient to abridge the First Amendment.[8] However, these rulings have not resolved some issues pertaining to religious influences in public education. Is the Establishment Clause violation lessened if students rather than teachers initiate the devotional activities or if religious observances are occasional rather than daily? Can religious speech be distinguished from other types of speech in applying restrictions? These and other issues are addressed below in connection with silent prayer statutes; school-sponsored versus private devotionals; religious displays, music, and holiday observances; proselytization in the classroom; and equal access for religious expression and groups.

Silent Prayer Statutes

Students have a free exercise right to engage in *private* devotional activities in public schools so long as they do not interfere with regular school activities. Indeed, it would be difficult to monitor whether students were engaging in silent prayer. Controversies have focused on state laws or school board policies that condone silent devotionals, thus placing the stamp of public school approval on such activities.

In 1985, the Supreme Court rendered its first and only opinion to date on this issue in *Wallace v. Jaffree*, invalidating a 1981 Alabama silent prayer law under the Establishment Clause.[9] The Court majority concluded that the only logical reason for adding the phrase "or voluntary prayer" to Alabama's silent meditation law was to encourage students to pray. But the Court indicated that laws calling for silent meditation or prayer in public schools without a legislative intent to impose prayer might withstand scrutiny under the Establishment Clause. Therefore, **the constitutionality of laws authorizing a moment of silence for prayer or meditation in public schools, which currently are on the books in a majority of the states, must be resolved on a case-by-case basis, and courts have rejected most recent challenges to such laws.**

For example, the Eleventh Circuit upheld termination of a high school teacher for refusing to comply with Georgia's law that requires each public school teacher to conduct a minute of quiet reflection at the opening of the school day.[10] The Fourth Circuit also

---

[7]Sch. Dist., Abington Twp. v. Schempp, 374 U.S. 203 (1963); Engel v. Vitale, 370 U.S. 421 (1962).

[8]Federal appellate courts recently have struck down devotional activities at school board meetings as well. *See* Doe v. Indian River Sch. Dist., 653 F.3d 256 (3d Cir. 2011); Joyner v. Forsyth Cnty., 653 F.3d 341 (4th Cir. 2011) (distinguishing board meetings where students might be present from permissible prayers in legislative sessions, which the Supreme upheld in *Marsh v. Chambers*, 463 U.S. 783 (1983)).

[9]472 U.S. 38 (1985), *aff'g* 705 F.2d 1526 (11th Cir. 1983).

[10]Bown v. Gwinnett Cnty. Sch. Dist., 112 F.3d 1464 (11th Cir. 1997); *see also* No Child Left Behind (NCLB) Act of 2001, 20 U.S.C. § 6061 (2012) (specifying that no federal funds can be appropriated under the Act to be used for policies that prevent voluntary prayer and meditation in public schools).

endorsed a Virginia silent prayer statute, reasoning that a time for quiet reflection is a good management strategy to calm students.[11] And the Fifth Circuit in 2009 rejected a challenge to a similar Texas law, finding that it did not promote or inhibit religion.[12] The following year, the Seventh Circuit ruled that unlike the Alabama law challenged in *Wallace*, an Illinois law making a moment of silence at the beginning of the school day mandatory in all public schools was designed for the secular purpose of preparing students for a day of learning; the court emphasized that religion was not mentioned during the legislative debate on the bill.[13] Given these rulings, it appears that silent prayer provisions are not vulnerable to being invalidated under the Establishment Clause unless they represent a clear intent to have children pray in public schools.

School-Sponsored versus Private Devotionals

The most controversial issues currently revolve around what constitutes *private* religious expression in public schools. Such private expression does not trigger Establishment Clause restrictions because it is not sponsored by the public school.

***Weisman* and Its Progeny.**   The Supreme Court's 1992 decision in *Lee v. Weisman* generated a wave of legislative activity pressing the limits of the Establishment Clause. The divided Court struck down a Rhode Island school district's policy that permitted principals to invite clergy members to deliver invocations and benedictions at middle and high school graduation ceremonies.[14] The Court majority reasoned that the policy had a coercive effect; students felt peer pressure to participate in the devotionals that were conducted at the school-sponsored graduation ceremony; students should not have to make a choice between attending their graduation ceremony and respecting their religious convictions.

Negative reactions to this ruling resulted in school authorities and students finding creative strategies to include prayers in graduation ceremonies.[15] Because of the prohibition on *school-sponsored* religious activities, most post-*Weisman* controversies have involved *student-led* devotionals. **In some school districts, the graduation ceremony has been designated as a forum for student expression, so students' messages (including religious references) are not subject to review and do not bear the stamp of school approval.** The Ninth Circuit endorsed an Idaho school district's policy that prohibited school authorities from censoring students' graduation speeches and allowed student speakers (chosen by academic standing) to select a poem, reading, song, prayer, or any

---

[11]Brown v. Gilmore, 258 F.3d 265, 270 (4th Cir. 2001).

[12]Croft v. Governor of Tex., 562 F.3d 735 (5th Cir. 2009).

[13]Sherman v. Koch, 623 F.3d 501 (7th Cir. 2010), *cert. denied*, 132 S. Ct. 92 (2011).

[14]505 U.S. 577 (1992).

[15]Some districts responded to *Weisman* by reinstating baccalaureate services, which had not been held for many years; students, churches, or other groups can rent space from the public school district to conduct such religious services that are not sponsored by the public school district, and school employees can participate in such private religious services. *See, e.g.*, Allen v. Sch. Bd., 782 F. Supp. 2d 1304 (N.D. Fla. 2011).

other presentation of their choice.[16] Finding the ceremony a forum for student expression, the court reasoned that the student speakers were selected based on secular criteria and were not advised to include devotionals in their remarks.

In two other Ninth Circuit cases, however, the appeals court upheld school districts in barring proselytizing graduation speeches that students had submitted to their principals for review in accordance with school policy. Unlike the first case, school authorities in these districts clearly maintained control of the graduation ceremony. Thus, the court found censorship of the proposed religious speeches appropriate to avoid an Establishment Clause violation.[17] **The central consideration seems to be whether the school has explicitly created a forum for student expression in the graduation ceremony or has retained control over students' graduation speeches.**

Student Elections to Authorize Prayers.   Especially volatile controversies surround having students decide by election to include student-led devotionals in graduation ceremonies and other school activities. Federal appellate courts have differed regarding the constitutionality of such elections.[18]

In a 2000 decision, *Santa Fe Independent School District v. Doe*, the Supreme Court found an Establishment Clause violation in a Texas school district's policy authorizing student-led devotionals before public school football games.[19] The controversial policy, and an identical graduation policy, authorized two elections—one to determine whether to have invocations and the second to select the student to deliver them. The Supreme Court limited its ruling to the football game policy, noting that such events occur more often than the graduation ceremony, involve a more diverse age span of students, and cannot be justified to solemnize sporting events. **The Court majority declared that student-led expression at a school event on school property and representing the student body under the supervision of school personnel could not be considered private speech.**[20] The degree

---

[16]Doe v. Madison Sch. Dist. No 321, 147 F.3d 832 (9th Cir. 1998), *vacated and remanded*, 177 F.3d 789, 792 (9th Cir. 1999) (en banc) (vacating the panel decision because the plaintiff had graduated, but the contested policy remained in force); *see also* Griffith v. Butte Sch. Dist. No. 1, 244 P.3d 321, 334 (Mont. 2010) (finding that the school district violated a student's speech rights by not allowing her to make "passing references" to her religious faith in her valedictory speech that did not represent the school).

[17]*See* Lassonde v. Pleasanton Unified Sch. Dist., 320 F.3d 979 (9th Cir. 2003); Cole v. Oroville Union High Sch. Dist., 228 F.3d 1092 (9th Cir. 2000); *see also* A.M. v. Taconic Hills Cent. Sch. Dist., No. 12-753-cv, 2013 WL 342680 (2d Cir. Jan. 30, 2013) (finding that the school's Establishment Clause concern justified not allowing a student to include a blessing in her speech at the middle school's "moving up" ceremony); Corder v. Lewis Palmer Sch. Dist. No. 38, 566 F.3d 1219 (10th Cir. 2009) (upholding the school's decision to require a student to publicly apologize for making a religious valedictory speech that had not been approved; her speech was school sponsored and subject to the principal's review).

[18]*Compare* ACLU of N.J. v. Black Horse Pike Reg'l Bd. of Educ., 84 F.3d 1471 (3d Cir. 1996) *with* Jones v. Clear Creek Indep. Sch. Dist., 930 F.2d 416 (5th Cir. 1991), *vacated and remanded*, 505 U.S. 1215 (1992), *on remand*, 977 F.2d 963 (5th Cir. 1992).

[19]530 U.S. 290 (2000), *aff'g* 168 F.3d 806 (5th Cir. 1999).

[20]*Santa Fe*, 530 U.S. at 310. The Court emphasized that it is necessary to carefully review the history and context of the challenged action in determining its facial validity. *Id.* at 317; *see also* Doe v. Elmbrook Sch. Dist., 658 F.3d 710 (7th Cir. 2011), *rev'd en banc*, 687 F.3d 840 (7th Cir. 2012) (finding an Establishment Clause violation in a public school holding its graduation ceremony in a church with a large cross over the dais and religious banners and staffed information booths displaying proselytizing literature in the lobby).

of school involvement gave the impression that the devotionals at issue represented the school, leading the Court to conclude that the practice had a sham secular purpose and entailed both perceived and actual endorsement of religion. **Noting that the purpose of the Bill of Rights is to shield certain subjects from the political process, the Court held that the Establishment Clause infraction cannot be eliminated by delegating decisions to students.** But the Court also emphasized that only state sponsorship of devotionals violates the Establishment Clause; nothing in the Constitution prohibits public school students from voluntarily praying at school.

Post–*Santa Fe* Rulings.   The *Santa Fe* decision did not resolve what distinguishes protected private religious expression from unconstitutional school-sponsored devotionals. Indeed, some post–*Santa Fe* federal appellate rulings represent an expansive stance regarding the reach of the Free Speech Clause in protecting students' private religious expression in public schools. For example, the Eleventh Circuit reaffirmed two pre–*Santa Fe* rulings in which it upheld a school district's policy authorizing seniors to select graduation speakers who could choose religious content[21] and lifted an injunction that had prohibited students from expressing religious views in most public school settings in an Alabama district.[22] The appeals court declared that the Establishment Clause does not *require* and the Free Speech Clause does not *permit* suppressing student-initiated religious expression in public schools or relegating it to whispers or behind closed doors. The Eleventh Circuit reasoned that school censorship of *private* student religious expression abridges the First Amendment, emphasizing that all student religious speech in public schools should not be equated with expression *representing* the school.[23]

In light of *Santa Fe* and its progeny, courts will review the legislative history of school district policies to ascertain whether there has been a pattern of efforts to infuse devotionals in the public schools. **Student religious expression may be considered private if truly student initiated, but the *Santa Fe* decision casts doubt on the legality of holding student elections to determine whether student-led devotionals will be included in school-sponsored activities.**

Religious Displays, Music, and Holiday Observances

The display of religious documents, the observance of religious holidays, and the use of religious music in public schools also remain controversial. In 1980, the Supreme Court declined to hear an appeal of a decision allowing religious holiday observances and the temporary display of religious symbols in public education,[24] but a week later, in *Stone v. Graham*, the divided Court struck down a Kentucky law calling for the posting of the

---

[21]Adler v. Duval Cnty. Sch. Bd., 206 F.3d 1070 (11th Cir. 2000) (en banc), *vacated and remanded*, 531 U.S. 801 (2000), *reinstated on remand*, 250 F.3d 1330 (11th Cir. 2001).

[22]Chandler v. James, 180 F.3d 1254 (11th Cir. 1999), *vacated and remanded*, 530 U.S. 1256 (2000), *reinstated on remand sub nom.* Chandler v. Siegelman, 230 F.3d 1313 (11th Cir. 2000).

[23]*Chandler*, 230 F.3d at 1315.

[24]Florey v. Sioux Falls Sch. Dist. 49-5, 619 F.2d 1311 (8th Cir. 1980).

Ten Commandments in public school classrooms.[25] In the first case, the historical and cultural significance of Christmas convinced the Eighth Circuit that the prudent and objective observance of this holiday in public schools does not serve to advance religion, despite religious songs such as *Silent Night* being sung and the nativity scene being displayed.[26]

In contrast, the five-member Supreme Court majority in *Stone* was not persuaded that the Ten Commandments' historical and cultural significance justified posting this religious document in public schools. The majority held that the purpose behind the Kentucky legislation was to advance a particular religious faith in violation of the Establishment Clause; the constitutional impairment was not neutralized because the copies were purchased with private donations.

However, disputes over religious displays have continued. The Supreme Court rendered companion decisions in 2005 with different outcomes pertaining to displays of the Ten Commandments on government property.[27] In 2009, the Supreme Court sided with city officials in barring the Summum religious organization from displaying its seven principles in a Utah city park even though the Ten Commandments are displayed. The Court reasoned that decisions about displaying privately donated monuments represents government speech that is exempt from First Amendment scrutiny.[28] Thus, the city is not obligated by the First Amendment to honor other requests simply because it has allowed a donated Ten Commandments monument to be placed in the park. School displays of the Ten Commandments were not at issue in these cases, but the Court indicated that *Stone v. Graham* still has precedential value. Nonetheless, displays of the Ten Commandments in school districts continue to generate challenges.[29]

Other religious displays have been controversial in public schools. Courts have supported school authorities in removing religious pictures, murals, and banners from public schools.[30] However, the Tenth Circuit upheld the Las Cruces school district's use of the

---

[25]449 U.S. 39 (1980).

[26]*Florey*, 619 F.2d at 1314.

[27]*See* Van Orden v. Perry, 545 U.S. 677 (2005) (upholding the long-standing display of a Ten Commandments monument with other monuments on the Texas state capitol grounds to pay tribute to the state's history); McCreary Cnty., Ky. v. ACLU, 545 U.S. 844 (2005) (striking down the display of framed copies of the Ten Commandments in two Kentucky county courthouses; finding that attempts to add secular items to the displays did not eliminate their initial religious purpose).

[28]Pleasant Grove City v. Summum, 555 U.S. 460 (2009). *But see* Red River Freethinkers v. City of Fargo, 679 F. 3d 1015 (8th Cir. 2012) (finding that a city's denial of a companion monument while retaining the Ten Commandments on public grounds implicated the Establishment Clause; remanding the case for additional consideration of the expression issue).

[29]Schools' displays in Pennsylvania, Tennessee, and Virginia recently have been controversial. *See* Freedom from Religion Found. v. Connellsville Area Sch. Dist., No. 12-1406, 2013 U.S. Dist. LEXIS 31 (W.D. Pa. Mar. 7, 2013) (allowing challenge to monument with inscriptions, including the Ten Commandments, that is displayed at the entrance to a Pennsylvania public school, to proceed to discovery stage); Nat'l Sch. Bds. Ass'n, *Tennessee District Votes to Erect Display of Historic Documents Including Ten Commandments*, LEGAL CLIPS (Jan. 31, 2013), http://legalclips.nsba.org/?p=18047; Nat'l Sch. Bds. Ass'n, *Federal Court Approves Settlement in Suit over Virginia District's Ten Commandments Display*, LEGAL CLIPS (July 12, 2012), http://legalclips.nsba. org/?p=15186.

[30]*See, e.g.*, Bannon v. Sch. Dist., 387 F.3d 1208 (11th Cir. 2004); Gernetzke v. Kenosha Unified Sch. Dist. No. 1, 274 F.3d 464 (7th Cir. 2001); Ahlquist v. City of Cranston, No. 11-138L, 840 F. Supp. 2d 507 (D.R.I. 2012).

city's symbol of three crosses in a sculpture and on district maintenance vehicles, given that the city's name means "the crosses" and the absence of any religious motives.[31] Also, a federal district court in New Jersey found that inclusion of religious holidays, such as Christmas and Hanukkah, on school district calendars was designed to broaden students' sensitivity toward religious diversity and their knowledge of the role of religion in the development of civilization.[32]

The use of religious music in public school programs has generated recent controversy. The Ninth Circuit endorsed a Washington principal's decision to prohibit a school woodwind ensemble's choice of *Ave Maria* as its graduation performance piece; the decision did not inhibit religion or free expression under the First Amendment.[33] The Third Circuit also rejected a challenge to a school board policy that prohibited the performance of celebratory religious music in school concerts and programs as not inhibiting religion or impairing students' rights to receive information and ideas.[34] This represents somewhat of a change in judicial posture, because in several earlier cases, courts had upheld school districts' justifications for allowing choirs to perform religious music.[35]

Religious displays, music, and holiday observances are destined to remain controversial. The Supreme Court has condoned the use of public funds or property for certain religious displays in several decisions outside the school domain,[36] but **courts seem likely to continue to strike down the display of sectarian documents in public schools and to uphold school boards' restrictions on religious music. Yet, the objective recognition of religious holidays will presumably withstand judicial scrutiny so long as particular faiths are not compromised.**

Proselytization in the Classroom

Because teachers and other school personnel are working with a vulnerable captive audience in public schools, their actions have been scrutinized to ensure that classrooms are not

---

[31]Weinbaum v. Las Cruces, 541 F.3d 1017 (10th Cir. 2008); *see also* Skoros v. City of New York, 437 F.3d 1 (2d. Cir. 2007) (holding that the city's holiday display policy for public schools promoted respect and tolerance for diverse holiday customs; a reasonable observer would not view the display of a Jewish menorah and Muslim star and crescent as advancing religious beliefs or interfering with parental rights to direct the upbringing of their children).

[32]Clever v. Cherry Hill Twp. Bd. of Educ., 838 F. Supp. 929 (D.N.J. 1993); *see also* Guyer v. Sch. Bd., 634 So. 2d 806 (Fla. Dist. Ct. App. 1994) (holding that the display of witches at Halloween does not promote a nontheistic religion or give an impression that the public school endorses Wicca).

[33]Nurre v. Whitehead, 580 F.3d 1087 (9th Cir. 2009), *cert. denied*, 130 S. Ct. 1937 (2010). Dissenting from the Supreme Court's denial of review, Justice Alito asserted that "a reasonable reading of the Ninth Circuit's decision is that it authorizes school administrators to ban any controversial student expression at any school event attended by parents because of the importance of the event for participating students." *Id.* at 1940.

[34]Stratechuk v. Bd. of Educ., 587 F.3d 597 (3d Cir. 2009), *cert. denied*, 131 S. Ct. 72 (2010).

[35]*See, e.g.*, Bauchman v. W. High Sch., 132 F.3d 542 (10th Cir. 1997); Florey v. Sioux Falls Sch. Dist. 49-5, 619 F.2d 1311 (8th Cir. 1980).

[36]For citations and further explanation of these cases, see Martha McCarthy, Nelda Cambron-McCabe & Suzanne Eckes, Public School Law: Teachers' and Students' Rights ch. 2 (Upper Saddle River, N.J.: Pearson, 7th ed. 2014).

used as a forum to indoctrinate sectarian beliefs. Federal appellate courts have enjoined teacher-initiated devotionals in the classroom and ordered teachers to:

- remove religiously oriented books from a classroom library and refrain from silently reading the Bible during school hours;[37]
- stop using religious references in delivering the instructional program;[38]
- cover a proselytizing shirt ("Jesus 2000, J2K") at school;[39]
- remove a classroom display of news articles promoting Christianity and a poster publicizing the National Day of Prayer;[40] and
- remove religious banners from the classroom.[41]

In these decisions, courts recognized that **educators cannot use their positions of power and prestige in public schools to influence their students' religious beliefs.**

The Ninth Circuit also rejected a charter school's challenge to Idaho's ban on the inclusion of sectarian texts in public schools, concluding that the ban was designed to avoid religious inculcation. The court reasoned that the school curriculum represents government speech, not private expression, and the policy does not violate the Establishment or Equal Protection Clauses.[42] Several years earlier, the Third Circuit ruled that a coach kneeling and bowing his head when his team engaged in locker-room prayer abridged the Establishment Clause.[43] In another Third Circuit case, the court backed a school district in prohibiting a parent from reading the Bible to her child's kindergarten class because the parent represented the school.[44] Moreover, courts have upheld the dismissal of teachers who disregarded selected aspects of the curriculum that conflicted with their religious values.[45] **Public school educators enjoy a constitutional right to their religious beliefs, but they do not have a right to freely express those beliefs to their students.**

The words "under God," which were added to the Pledge of Allegiance to the American flag in 1954, also have been challenged as unconstitutionally proselytizing students.

---

[37]Roberts v. Madigan, 921 F.2d 1047 (10th Cir. 1990) (enjoining the school board, however, from removing the Bible from the school library, noting its literary and historical significance).

[38]Marchi v. Bd. of Coop. Educ. Servs., 173 F.3d 469 (2d Cir. 1999).

[39]Downing v. W. Haven Bd. of Educ., 162 F. Supp. 2d 19 (D. Conn. 2001).

[40]Lee v. York Cnty. Sch. Div., 484 F.3d 687 (4th Cir. 2007) (holding that the expression was curricular in nature, so it constituted an employment dispute and not protected expression).

[41]Johnson v. Poway Unified Sch. Dist., 658 F.3d 954 (9th Cir. 2011), *cert. denied*, 132 S. Ct. 1807 (2012).

[42]Nampa Classical Acad. v. Goesling, 447 F. App'x 776 (9th Cir. 2011), *cert. denied*, 132 S. Ct. 1795 (2012).

[43]Borden v. Sch. Dist. of Twp. of E. Brunswick, 523 F.3d 153 (3d Cir. 2008) (noting that the coach had engaged in many years of prayer activities with the high school football team, so a reasonable observer would conclude that his silent activities endorsed religion).

[44]Busch v. Marple Newton Sch. Dist., 567 F.3d 89 (3d Cir. 2009), *cert. denied*, 558 U.S. 1158 (2010).

[45]*See, e.g.*, Palmer v. Bd. of Educ., 603 F.2d 1271 (7th Cir. 1979) (upholding dismissal of a kindergarten teacher who refused to teach about patriotic holidays and historical figures for religious reasons); *see also* Grossman v. S. Shore Pub. Sch. Dist., 507 F. 3d 1097 (7th Cir. 2007) (upholding dismissal of a school counselor for unilaterally deciding, based on her religious beliefs, to provide students with information on abstinence only rather than on other forms of birth control).

More than four-fifths of the states have laws or policies specifying that the Pledge will be said in public schools, and many of these provisions were enacted or amended since the terrorist attacks on September 11, 2001.[46] As discussed later, students have a right to opt out of the Pledge based on their religious or philosophical beliefs,[47] but the Ninth Circuit attracted national attention in 2002 when it declared that the phrase "under God" could not be said in public schools because it endorses a belief in monotheism in violation of the Establishment Clause.[48] The appellate panel emphasized that the words "under God" had been inserted in the Pledge to promote religion rather than to advance the legitimate secular goal of encouraging patriotism. The Supreme Court reversed the Ninth Circuit's decision in 2004 without addressing the constitutional claim in *Elk Grove Unified School District v. Newdow*. The Court majority reasoned that under California law, the noncustodial parent, Newdow, lacked standing to challenge his daughter's participation in the Pledge.[49]

Other courts have not been sympathetic to challenges to "under God" in the Pledge. Prior to the *Newdow* decision, the Seventh Circuit rejected an Establishment Clause challenge to an Illinois law requiring students to recite the Pledge, concluding that the "ceremonial deism" in the Pledge "has lost through rote repetition any significant religious content."[50] More recently, the First Circuit ruled that the New Hampshire statute requiring time for daily teacher-led recitation of the Pledge of Allegiance did not violate the Establishment Clause.[51] Also, the Fifth Circuit rejected a challenge to a Texas law requiring recitation of the Texas Pledge of Allegiance that was amended to add the phrase, "one state under God," reasoning that a patriotic observance could acknowledge the existence of a religious belief without unconstitutionally favoring that belief.[52] And a Ninth Circuit panel in 2010 by a two-to-one vote upheld inclusion of "under God" in the Pledge, which was the opposite of the earlier panel's split decision.[53] The Supreme Court is not likely to strike down the inclusion of "under God" in the Pledge recited in public schools, and if it were to do so, a strong negative political reaction could be assured.

Although school personnel cannot proselytize students, the Supreme Court has emphasized that it is permissible, even desirable, to teach the Bible and other religious documents from a literary, cultural, or historical perspective.[54] More than 2,000 public

---

[46]*See* ProCon.org., *State Requirements on Pledge of Allegiance in Schools* (Oct. 24, 2008), http://undergod.procon.org/view.resource.php?resourceID=000074.

[47]*See* W. Va. State Bd. of Educ. v. Barnette, 319 U.S. 624 (1943); *infra* text accompanying note 91.

[48]Newdow v. U.S. Cong., 292 F.3d 597 (9th Cir. 2002), *opinion amended and superseded by* 328 F.3d 466 (2003), *rev'd sub nom.* Elk Grove Unified Sch. Dist. v. Newdow, 542 U.S. 1 (2004).

[49]*Id.*, 542 U.S. at 17–18.

[50]Sherman v. Cmty. Consol. Sch. Dist. 21, 980 F.2d 437, 446 (7th Cir. 1992); *see also* Myers v. Loudoun Cnty. Sch. Bd., 251 F. Supp. 2d 1262, 1268 (E.D. Va. 2003), *aff'd*, 418 F.3d 395 (4th Cir. 2005) (finding the Pledge's reference to God "theologically benign" and further ruling that nonparticipating students were not punished, even though recitation of the Pledge was part of a citizenship reward program).

[51]Freedom from Religion Found. v. Hanover Sch. Dist., 626 F.3d 1 (1st Cir. 2010).

[52]Croft v. Perry, 624 F.3d 157 (5th Cir. 2010).

[53]Newdow v. Rio Linda Union Sch. Dist., 597 F.3d 1997 (9th Cir. 2010). There is some sentiment that the widespread negative response to the 2002 Ninth Circuit decision influenced the court's position reversal.

[54]*See* Sch. Dist., Abington Twp. v. Schempp, 374 U.S. 203, 225 (1963).

schools across thirty-eight states use the Bible as a textbook for courses on "the Bible as Literature," supported by the National Council on Bible Curriculum in Public Schools, and about 540 additional schools offer an elective high school course using the textbook, *The Bible and Its Influence*, sponsored by the Bible Literacy Project.[55]

Yet in some courses, the line is not clear between teaching about religion and instilling religious tenets. Numerous Bible study courses, particularly at the elementary school level, have been challenged as ploys to advance sectarian beliefs. Courts have carefully evaluated curricular materials and even reviewed videotapes of lessons to determine whether such instruction fosters a particular creed. Courts have struck down programs in which private groups have controlled the hiring and supervision of personnel or the selection of curricular materials. While most challenges have involved instruction pertaining to the Bible and the Christian faith, the Ninth Circuit upheld a school's use of role-playing to teach seventh-grade world history students about Islam, reasoning that learning about the five pillars of Islam did not entail the practice of a religion.[56]

Some controversies over proselytization in the classroom have not challenged teachers' activities but have entailed requests for students to include sectarian materials in their presentations, artwork, or other school assignments. In most of these cases, the schools have prevailed in denying the students' requests. For example, the Sixth Circuit upheld a school district's prohibition on an elementary school student showing in class a videotape of herself singing a proselytizing religious song, concluding that student projects can be censored to ensure that the school is not viewed as endorsing religious content.[57] The same court backed a junior high school teacher who gave a student a zero on a report because the student had cleared a different topic with the teacher but then wrote her report on the life of Jesus Christ.[58] One judge observed that the student might have raised a legitimate free speech issue if the assignment had been to write an opinion piece on any topic of personal interest, and religious content had been rejected.[59]

In contrast to the above cases, the Second Circuit found viewpoint discrimination in a teacher's refusal to display one poster and censorship of a replacement poster because of religious content depicted by a kindergarten student asked to portray what he had learned about the environment. The court reasoned that blatant viewpoint discrimination is not allowed even in a nonpublic forum.[60] And some states have enacted or are

---

[55]*See* Nat'l Council on Bible Curriculum in Pub. Schs., *It's Coming Back . . . and It's Our Constitutional Right* (Jan. 2012), http://www.bibleinschools.net; The Bible Literacy Project, *Public School Bible Textbook Now in More than 540 Schools in 43 States* (Feb. 2012), http://www.bibleliteracy.org/site.

[56]Eklund v. Byron Union Sch. Dist., 154 F. App'x 648 (9th Cir. 2005).

[57]DeNooyer v. Merinelli, 12 F.3d 211 (6th Cir. 1993). *But see* O.T. *ex rel.* Turton v. Frenchtown Elementary Sch. Dist., 465 F. Supp. 2d 369 (D.N.J. 2006) (upholding student's right to sing a religious song in the school talent show, which was viewed as a limited public forum; the student was not conveying the school's message in her performance).

[58]Settle v. Dickson Cnty. Sch. Bd., 53 F.3d 152 (6th Cir. 1995).

[59]*Id.* at 159 (Batchelder, J., concurring).

[60]Peck v. Baldwinsville Cent. Sch. Dist., 426 F.3d 617 (2d Cir. 2005) (remanding for further consideration of the free expression issue but ruling that the lower court properly dismissed the Establishment Clause claim). *But see* C.H. v. Oliva, 226 F.3d 198 (3d Cir. 2000) (finding no constitutional violation in connection with refusal to let a student read a Bible story to classmates or in the removal of the student's religious poster from the school hallway, but remanding the case to allow plaintiffs an opportunity to substantiate a viable complaint regarding the poster).

considering laws that protect students' decisions to use religious materials in completing class assignments. To illustrate, in 2007, Texas enacted a law allowing religious beliefs to be expressed in homework, artwork, and other assignments, and stipulating that students should not be rewarded or penalized because of the religious content of their work.[61] Two years later, Arizona enacted legislation that prohibits public schools from discriminating against students or parents on the basis of religious viewpoint or expression; students cannot be penalized or rewarded for including religious content or views in class assignments.[62] Thus, although students usually have not been successful in challenging school requirements under the First Amendment, state law may protect their use of religious materials in school assignments.

Equal Access for Religious Expression and Groups

In the 1960s and 1970s, it often was assumed that the Establishment Clause demanded that religious speech be barred from government forums. More recently, however, the Supreme Court has reasoned that **singling out religious views for differential treatment compared with other *private* expression would be unconstitutional viewpoint discrimination, which abridges the Free Speech Clause.**[63]

Equal Access Act. The Free Speech Clause was augmented in 1984 by the Equal Access Act (EAA), under which federally funded secondary schools that have established a limited open forum for student groups to meet during noninstructional time cannot deny school access to noncurriculum student-led groups based on the religious, philosophical, or political content of their meetings (see Figure 3.2).[64] In 1990, the Supreme Court in *Board of Education of Westside Community Schools v. Mergens* rejected an Establishment Clause challenge to the EAA, recognizing the law's secular purpose of preventing discrimination against religious and other types of private student expression.[65] **The Court distinguished government speech promoting religion that is prohibited by**

---

[61]Religious Viewpoints Anti-Discrimination Act, Tex. Educ. Code Ann. § 25.151 (2012).

[62]Students' Religious Liberties Act, Ariz. Rev. Stat. § 15-110 (2012). South Carolina adopted a similar law in 2010, Religious Viewpoints Anti-discrimination Act, S.C. Code Ann. § 59-1-435 (2012). Also, the U.S. Department of Education's *Policy Guidance* stipulates that students may express their religious views in their homework, artwork, and other written and oral assignments, despite some contrary judicial rulings. U.S. Dep't of Educ., *Guidance on Constitutionally Protected Prayer in Public Elementary and Secondary Schools* (Feb. 7, 2003), http://www2.ed.gov/policy/gen/guid/religionandschools/prayer_guidance.html.

[63]*See* Widmar v. Vincent, 454 U.S. 263 (1981) (finding no Establishment Clause violation in providing student religious group's access to a forum created for student expression on state-supported college campuses). *But see* Christian Legal Soc'y v. Martinez, 130 S. Ct. 2971 (2010) (upholding the Hastings Law School's denial of official recognition to a student religious group that did not comply with the university's nondiscrimination policy).

[64]20 U.S.C. §§ 4071–4074 (2012).

[65]496 U.S. 226, 249 (1990).

FIGURE 3.2   The Equal Access Act, 20 U. S. C. §§ 4071–4074 (2012)

Sec. 801(a) It shall be unlawful for any public secondary school which receives federal financial assistance and which has a limited open forum to deny equal access or a fair opportunity to, or discriminate against, any students who wish to conduct a meeting within that limited open forum on the basis of the religious, political, philosophical, or other content of the speech at such meetings.

(b) A public secondary school has a limited open forum whenever such school grants an offering to or opportunity for one or more noncurriculum related student groups to meet on school premises during noninstructional time.

(c) Schools shall be deemed to offer a fair opportunity to students who wish to conduct a meeting within its limited open forum if such school uniformly provides that

    (1) the meeting is voluntary and student-initiated;

    (2) there is no sponsorship of the meeting by the school, the government, or its agents or employees;

    (3) employees or agents of the school or government are present at religious meetings only in a nonparticipatory capacity;

    (4) the meeting does not materially and substantially interfere with the orderly conduct of educational activities within the school; and

    (5) nonschool persons may not direct, conduct, control, or regularly attend activities of student groups.

the Establishment Clause from private religious expression protected by the Free Speech and Free Exercise Clauses.[66] In subsequent cases, federal appellate courts have ruled that the EAA:

- prevails over state constitutional provisions requiring greater separation of church and state than demanded by the Establishment Clause;[67]
- authorizes student religious meetings during lunch if that is considered noninstructional time;[68]
- authorizes student religious groups to require certain officers to be Christians to preserve the spiritual content of their meetings;[69] and
- requires student religious groups to be provided equal access to fund-raising activities, school bulletin boards, and other resources available for student clubs.[70]

Although there are limits on the reach of the EAA, this federal law codified for secondary students the concept of equal access and equal treatment of religious expression that currently guides First Amendment litigation as well. Indeed, given recent broad interpretations of the Free Speech Clause in requiring equal treatment of private religious expression in public schools, there is some sentiment that the EAA may no longer be needed.

---

[66]*Id.* at 250.

[67]Ceniceros v. Bd. of Trs., 106 F.3d 878 (9th Cir. 1997); Garnett v. Renton Sch. Dist. No. 403, 987 F.2d 641 (9th Cir. 1993).

[68]*Ceniceros*, 106 F.3d 878.

[69]Hsu v. Roslyn Union Free Sch. Dist. No. 3, 85 F.3d 839 (2d Cir. 1996). *But see* Truth v. Kent Sch. Dist., 524 F3d 957 (9th Cir. 2008) (upholding a school district's denial of recognition to a student Bible club that denied voting membership to students who did not pledge to abide by the Bible).

[70]Prince v. Jacoby, 303 F.3d 1074 (9th Cir. 2002).

School Access for Community Groups. **The EAA applies *only* to secondary students, so community religious groups desiring public school access during noninstructional time must rely on First Amendment protections.** Since the early 1990s, the Supreme Court has made some definitive pronouncements about protecting private religious expression from viewpoint discrimination. In *Lamb's Chapel v. Center Moriches Union Free School District*, the Court held that if secular community groups are allowed to use the public school after school hours to address particular topics (e.g., family life, child rearing), a sectarian group desiring to show a film series addressing these topics from a religious perspective cannot be denied public school access.[71]

Subsequently, the Supreme Court delivered a seminal decision, *Good News Club v. Milford Central School*, allowing a private Christian organization to hold its meetings in a New York public school after school hours.[72] The Milford School District had denied the Good News Club's request under its community-use policy that allows civic and recreational groups to use the school, but not for religious purposes, contending that the club affiliated with the Child Evangelism Fellowship was engaging in prohibited religious worship and instruction. Disagreeing with the school district and the lower courts, the Supreme Court in *Milford* held that the school district's policy discriminated against religious viewpoints in violation of the Free Speech Clause.

Under the *Milford* ruling, if a public school establishes a limited forum for community meetings during noninstructional time, it cannot bar religious groups, even though elementary students attending the school are the central participants in the devotional activities. The Court did not find a danger that the community would perceive the Good News Club's access as school district endorsement of religion. In subsequent cases, lower courts have allowed community religious groups to display literature on a table during back-to-school night, permitted flyers about sectarian meetings to be sent home with students, required fees to be waived for religious meetings if other clubs received such waivers, and enjoined a school district from dropping the Good News Club from its after-school enrichment program.[73] The Eighth Circuit even ruled that a teacher could participate in meetings of the Good News Club held at the elementary school where she taught.[74] Whether school districts can deny requests for religious groups to hold weekly services in public schools is not completely clear.[75]

[71]508 U.S. 384 (1993).

[72]533 U.S. 98 (2001); *see also* Whitson v. Knox Cnty. Bd. of Educ., 468 F. App'x 532 (6th Cir. 2012) (holding that a school district did not violate a student's free speech right to participate in student-led Bible study during recess since students were free to engage in any activity they desired while on the playground).

[73]*See, e.g.*, Child Evangelism Fellowship (CEF) v. Minneapolis Special Sch. Dist. No. 1, 690 F.3d 996 (8th Cir. 2012); CEF v. Montgomery Cnty. Pub. Schs., 457 F.3d 376 (4th Cir. 2006); CEF v. Stafford Twp. Sch. Dist., 386 F.3d 514 (3d Cir. 2004), *on remand*, No. 02-4549 (MLC), 2006 U.S. Dist. LEXIS 62966 (D.N.J. Sept. 5, 2006).

[74]Wigg v. Sioux Falls Sch. Dist. 49-5, 382 F.3d 807 (8th Cir. 2004).

[75]*See* Bronx Household of Faith v. Bd. of Educ., 650 F.3d 30 (2d Cir. 2011) (distinguishing the permissible use of school facilities by religious groups from impermissible weekly religious services in public schools), *cert. denied*, 132 S. Ct. 816 (2011). *But see* Bronx Household of Faith v. Bd. of Educ., 855 F. Supp. 2d 44 (S.D.N.Y. 2012) (allowing the weekly religious services because the school district's policy discriminated among religions).

Distribution of Religious Literature and Gifts.   The Supreme Court has not directly addressed the distribution of religious literature in public schools, and lower courts have rendered a range of opinions on this topic. Courts consistently have ruled that school personnel cannot give students Bibles or other religious materials, and most courts have prohibited religious sects, such as the Gideons, from coming to the school to distribute materials to captive public school audiences.[76]

Many recent controversies have focused on student requests to distribute religious publications. Like meetings of student-initiated religious groups, these requests pit Free Speech Clause protections against Establishment Clause restrictions.[77] **Some courts addressing PK–12 controversies have applied the "equal access" concept in concluding that the same legal principles govern students' distribution of religious and non-religious literature.** For example, the Third Circuit held that a student's distribution of a flyer about a religious event did not pose a school disruption so could not be prohibited.[78] Also, an Arkansas federal district court awarded a preliminary injunction to allow student distribution of flyers advertising a church party because all organizations but churches had been allowed to distribute flyers at the public school.[79]

Conflicting opinions have been rendered regarding student distribution of gifts with religious messages to classmates. The Third Circuit sided with school officials in prohibiting elementary school students from distributing pencils and candy canes with religious messages during classroom holiday parties because of the difficulty young children would have in distinguishing school sponsorship from the private religious expression.[80] The Sixth Circuit also upheld a principal's refusal to allow a student to "sell" pipe cleaner candy cane ornaments with religious messages at a simulated marketplace; the principal's decision to prevent use of this activity to advance religious beliefs was based on legitimate educational concerns.[81]

Yet in a long-running suit, the Fifth Circuit ruled in 2011 that two principals likely abridged the rights of students who were not allowed to distribute religious-themed candy canes and pencils with religious messages to classmates, finding viewpoint discrimination against private religious speech.[82] However, the court held that the principals were entitled to qualified immunity because decisions pertaining to student religious speech and the "murky waters of the Establishment Clause" are far from clear; the "general state of the law in this area is abstruse, complicated, and subject to great debate among jurists."[83]

---

[76]*See, e.g.*, Roark v. S. Iron R-1 Sch. Dist., 573 F.3d 556 (8th Cir. 2009); Doe v. Duncanville Indep. Sch. Dist., 70 F.3d 402 (5th Cir. 1995); Berger v. Rensselaer Cent. Sch. Corp., 982 F.2d 1160 (7th Cir. 1993).

[77]*See* Rosenberger v. Rector & Visitors, 515 U.S. 819 (1995) (ruling that religious material must be treated like other material in student-initiated publications subsidized by the university).

[78]K.A. v. Pocono Mountain Sch. Dist., K.A. v. Pocono Mountain Sch. Dist., 710 F.3d 99 (3d Cir. 2013).

[79]Wright v. Pulaski Cnty. Special Sch. Dist., 803 F. Supp. 2d 980 (E.D. Ark. 2011).

[80]Walz v. Egg Harbor Twp. Bd. of Educ., 342 F.3d 271 (3d Cir. 2003) (concluding that reasonable accommodations were made in that religious materials could be distributed before and after school and during recess).

[81]Curry v. Hensinger, 513 F.3d 570 (6th Cir. 2008).

[82]Morgan v. Swanson, 659 F.3d 359 (5th Cir. 2011), *cert. denied*, 132 S. Ct. 2740 (2012); *see also* Pounds v. Katy Indep. Sch. Dist., 730 F. Supp. 2d 636 (S.D. Tex. 2010) (holding that religious messages could not be treated differently from other messages on greeting cards with student artwork for a school fundraiser).

[83]*Morgan*, 659 F.3d at 382.

Even private expression is subject to reasonable time, place, and manner regulations. For example, school policies requiring students to give the principal advance notice of the distribution of materials are permissible. In 2009, the Fifth Circuit upheld content-neutral regulations that restricted where students could distribute materials during noninstructional time, reasoning that the school district had a legitimate interest in providing a focused learning environment for students.[84] Whereas reasonable restrictions can be imposed on *how* material is distributed, school districts cannot place a blanket ban on student distribution of religious literature.

ACCOMMODATIONS FOR RELIGIOUS BELIEFS

Religious exemptions from school observances and assignments will be upheld so long as they do not interfere with the management of the school or the excused student's progress.

In addition to challenging sectarian influences in public schools, some students have asserted a right to accommodations so they can practice their religious beliefs. Conflicts have arisen over release-time programs for religious education and religious exemptions from secular school observances and activities.

Release-Time Programs

Although the Supreme Court has struck down the practice of using public school classrooms for clergy to provide religious training to public school students during the instructional day, the Court has recognized that the school can accommodate religion by releasing students to receive such religious training off public school grounds.[85] The Second Circuit found that a school district's release-time program did not endorse Christianity over other religions or violate the rights of nonparticipating students by directing religious criticism toward them,[86] and a release-time program was even upheld in a Virginia school district where students received an hour of religious instruction each week in a mobile unit parked at the edge of school property.[87] Courts have not been persuaded that offering a single choice of attending religious classes or remaining in the public school advances religion or that nonparticipating pupils are denied their state-created right to an education because academic instruction ceases during the release-time period.

---

[84]Morgan v. Plano Indep. Sch. Dist., 589 F.3d 740 (5th Cir. 2009), *cert. denied*, 130 S. Ct. 3503 (2010); *see also* Victory Through Jesus Sports Ministry v. Lee's Summit R-7 Sch. Dist., 640 F.3d 329 (8th Cir. 2011) (upholding a policy limiting distribution of a religious group's flyers to one time at the beginning of the school year).

[85]*Compare* Zorach v. Clauson, 343 US. 306 (1952) *with* McCollum v. Bd. of Educ., 333 U.S. 203 (1948).

[86]Pierce v. Sullivan W. Cent. Sch. Dist., 379 F.3d 56 (2d Cir. 2004).

[87]Smith v. Smith, 523 F.2d 121 (4th Cir. 1975). It appears that programs in which all students are released early from school one day a week would be easier to defend constitutionally because students would not be restricted to either remaining at the public school or attending sectarian classes.

In a Utah case, the Tenth Circuit held that time spent by public school students in a release-time program at a Mormon seminary could be counted toward satisfying compulsory school attendance and in calculating the school's state aid.[88] However, the court enjoined the school's practice of awarding high school credit for the secular aspects of daily instruction received at the seminary because the monitoring required would unconstitutionally entangle school officials with the church. In contrast, the Fourth Circuit more recently upheld a South Carolina school district's release-time program that awards students academic credit, pursuant to state law, for attending off-campus religious instruction.[89]

Even though the release-time concept has been judicially endorsed, courts have ruled that a few programs have violated the Establishment Clause. For example, an Indiana federal district court enjoined a nondenominational Christian release-time program that was held in a trailer parked in the school's parking lot because such religious instruction on school grounds during school hours conveyed a message of religious support and endorsement.[90]

Religious Exemptions from Secular Activities

Courts have required school districts to accommodate reasonable, but not excessive, absences for students to practice their religious beliefs. More prevalent than requests for religious absences are requests for students to be excused from public school activities and requirements that allegedly impair the practice of their religious tenets. In evaluating whether school authorities must honor such requests, courts have attempted to balance parents' interests in directing the religious upbringing of their children against the state's interest in ensuring an educated citizenry.

Observances.   Courts have relied on the First Amendment in striking down required student participation in certain public school observances. In the landmark case, *West Virginia State Board of Education v. Barnette*, the Supreme Court ruled in 1943 that students could not be required to pledge their allegiance to the American flag in contravention of their religious beliefs,[91] overturning a precedent established by the Court only three years earlier.[92]

Nonetheless, controversy still surrounds the nature of required exemptions from the Pledge. Courts have struck down laws or policies requiring students to stand during the Pledge reasoning, that such a requirement coerces students to participate, but conflicting rulings have been rendered regarding the legality of mandatory parental notification of

---

[88]Lanner v. Wimmer, 662 F.2d 1349 (10th Cir. 1981).

[89]Moss v. Spartanburg Cnty. Sch. Dist. No. 7, 683 F.3d 599 (4th Cir. 2012), *cert. denied*, 133 S. Ct. 623 (2012).

[90]H.S. v. Huntington Cnty. Cmty. Sch. Corp., 616 F. Supp. 2d 863 (N.D. Ind. 2009); *see also* Doe v. Shenandoah Cnty. Sch. Bd., 737 F. Supp. 913 (W.D. Va. 1990) (granting a temporary restraining order against weekday religious education classes being held in buses—almost identical to public school buses—parked in front of the school, with instructors going into the school to recruit students).

[91]319 U.S. 624 (1943).

[92]Minersville Sch. Dist. v. Gobitis, 310 U.S. 586 (1940).

nonparticipating students.[93] Furthermore, the Eleventh Circuit concluded that paddling a student because he silently raised his fist in protest during the Pledge of Allegiance was an unwarranted infringement on expression rights.[94] Of course, students who opt not to participate can be disciplined if they create a disturbance while others are reciting the Pledge.

The Supreme Court has not directly addressed teachers' free exercise rights in connection with patriotic observances in public schools, but it is generally assumed that teachers, like students, have a First Amendment right to refuse to pledge allegiance as a matter of personal conscience. Teachers, however, cannot use their religious beliefs to deny students the opportunity to engage in this observance. If a school district requires the Pledge to be recited daily, teachers must make provisions for this observance in their classrooms. As discussed previously, whether "under God" can be said in the Pledge at all in public schools has been controversial, but to date, courts have not concluded that the contested phrase turns this patriotic observance into a prayer.[95]

Curriculum Components. Religious exemptions also have been sought from components of the curriculum. Whereas teachers cannot assert a free exercise right to disregard aspects of the state-prescribed curriculum, the judiciary has been more receptive to students' requests for exemptions from instructional requirements. Students, unlike teachers, are compelled to attend school, and for many, this means a public school. Accordingly, the judiciary has been sensitive to the fact that certain public school policies may have a coercive effect on religious practices. In balancing the interests involved, courts consider:

- the extent to which the school requirement burdens the exercise of sincere religious beliefs;
- the governmental justification for the requirement; and
- alternative means available to meet the state's objectives.

School authorities must have a compelling justification to deny students an exemption from a requirement that impairs the exercise of sincere religious beliefs.

Most requests for religious exemptions are handled at the classroom or school level and do not evoke legal controversies. When they have generated litigation, students often have been successful in securing religious exemptions from instructional activities, such as drug education, sex education, coeducational physical education, dancing instruction, officers' training programs, and specific course assignments where alternatives can satisfy the instructional objectives. Although individual children have been excused, the secular activities themselves have not been disturbed. For example, public schools often allow students to opt out of sex education instruction or require parental consent for children to participate in such instruction.

---

[93]*See, e.g.*, Frazier v. Winn, 535 F.3d 1279 (11th Cir. 2009) (holding that a student could not be forced to participate or stand during the Pledge, but upholding the state law provision requiring parental notification of non-participating students); Circle Sch. v. Pappert, 381 F. 3d 172 (3rd Cir. 2004) (holding that a parental notification provision in state law abridged the First Amendment).

[94]Holloman v. Harland, 370 F.3d 1252 (11th Cir. 2004) (noting that he was protesting the public chastisement of a classmate for not reciting the Pledge).

[95]*See supra* text accompanying notes 49–53.

Religious exemptions have not been honored if considered unnecessary to accommodate the practice of religious tenets or if the exemptions would substantially disrupt the school or students' academic progress or pose a safety hazard. In an illustrative case, the Second Circuit rejected a parent's request for his son to be exempted from a Connecticut school district's mandatory health curriculum, finding such attendance rationally related to the legitimate governmental goal of providing students important health information.[96] However, the student was allowed to be excused from certain lessons found offensive. In a widely publicized 1987 case, the Sixth Circuit rejected fundamentalist Christian parents' request that their children be excused from exposure to the basal reading series used in elementary grades.[97] The appeals court reasoned that the readers did not burden the students' exercise of their religious beliefs, because the students were not required to profess a creed or perform religious exercises. Courts also have denied religious exemptions for student athletes if an excusal from specific regulations might pose a safety risk or interfere with the management of athletic teams.[98]

As discussed in Chapter 4, conservative parents' organizations have secured federal and state laws allowing students to be excused from public school activities and components of the curriculum for religious and other reasons. A New Hampshire law enacted in 2011 allows parents to secure alternative assignments for any that they find objectionable.[99] Thus, parents may be able to use federal or state legislation to secure exemptions for their children, even if they cannot substantiate that particular instructional activities impair free exercise rights.

■ ■ ■ ■ ■

RELIGIOUS CHALLENGES TO THE SECULAR CURRICULUM

Most lawsuits claiming that components of the public school curriculum (e.g., evolution) advance an antitheistic religious belief have not succeeded.

Although courts often have been receptive to requests for individual exemptions from specific public school activities, **the judiciary has not been inclined to allow the restriction of the secular curriculum to satisfy parents' religious preferences.** The Supreme Court has recognized that "'the state has no legitimate interest in protecting any or all religions from views distasteful to them.'"[100]

Challenges to the public school curriculum raise complex questions involving what constitutes religious beliefs and practices that are subject to First Amendment protections and restrictions. **In protecting the free exercise of beliefs, the Supreme Court has adopted an expansive view toward religion, but it has not yet found an Establishment**

[96]Leebaert v. Harrington, 332 F.3d 134 (2d Cir. 2003).

[97]Mozert v. Hawkins Cnty. Bd. of Educ., 827 F.2d 1058 (6th Cir. 1987).

[98]*See, e.g.*, Menora v. Ill. High Sch. Ass'n, 683 F.2d 1030 (7th Cir. 1982).

[99]N.H. Rev. Stat. Ann § 186:11 (2012); *see* Chapter 4 for a discussion of the federal laws.

[100]Epperson v. Arkansas, 393 U.S. 97, 107 (1968) (quoting Joseph Burstyn, Inc. v. Wilson, 343 U.S. 495, 505 (1952)).

Clause violation in connection with claims that public school instruction advances a nontheistic creed. However, several courts have suggested that secular religions should be subject to the same Establishment Clause standards applied to theistic religions, and the Third Circuit ruled that public school instructional modules in transcendental meditation unconstitutionally advanced a nontraditional religious belief (the Science of Creative Intelligence).[101] Also, the Ninth Circuit held that a nonprofit group had standing to proceed with an Establishment Clause challenge to magnet and charter schools using Waldorf methods that are guided by the spiritual science of anthroposophy.[102]

The Origin of Humanity

Instruction pertaining to the origin of human life has generated continuing legal disputes. Historically, several states by law barred the teaching of evolution because it conflicted with the biblical account of creation. In the famous *Scopes* "monkey trial" in the 1920s, the Tennessee Supreme Court upheld such a law, prohibiting the teaching of any theory that denies the Genesis version of creation or suggests "that man has descended from a lower order of animals."[103] However, the United States Supreme Court in 1968 struck down an Arkansas anti-evolution statute under the Establishment Clause, concluding that evolution is science (not a secular religion), and a state cannot restrict student access to such information simply to satisfy religious preferences.[104]

Almost two decades later, the Supreme Court in 1987 invalidated a Louisiana statute that mandated "equal time" for creation science and evolution and required school boards to make available curriculum guides, teaching aids, and resource materials on creation science.[105] **Reasoning that creationism is not science, the Court concluded that the law was intended to discredit scientific information and advance religious beliefs in violation of the Establishment Clause.** The Court did not accept the argument that the law promoted academic freedom and reasoned that it actually inhibited teachers' discretion to incorporate scientific theories about the origin of humanity into the curriculum. In subsequent cases, federal appellate courts have ruled that school districts:

- can require instruction in evolution;
- cannot make teachers issue a disclaimer that instruction in evolution is not meant to dissuade students from the biblical account; and
- cannot put stickers in biology texts warning that evolution is a theory that should be critically assessed.[106]

[101]Malnak v. Yogi, 592 F.2d 197 (3d Cir. 1979).

[102]PLANS v. Sacramento City Unified Sch. Dist., 319 F.3d 504 (9th Cir. 2003).

[103]Scopes v. Tennessee, 289 S.W. 363, 364 (Tenn. 1927).

[104]*Epperson*, 393 U.S. 97.

[105]Edwards v. Aguillard, 482 U.S. 578 (1987).

[106] *See, e.g.*, Selman v. Cobb Cnty. Sch. Dist., 390 F. Supp. 2d 1286, 1312 (N.D. Ga. 2005), *vacated with instructions for the district court to conduct new evidentiary proceedings*, 449 F.3d 1320 (11th Cir. 2006); Freiler v. Tangipahoa Parish Bd. of Educ., 185 F.3d 337 (5th Cir. 1999); Peloza v. Capistrano Unified Sch. Dist., 37 F.3d 517 (9th Cir. 1994); Webster v. New Lenox Sch. Dist. No. 122, 917 F.2d 1004 (7th Cir. 1990).

Part of the recent controversy has focused on teaching intelligent design (ID), which supporters distinguish from creationism because the ID doctrine contends that human beings are too complex to have evolved randomly by natural selection, but it does not mention God. In 2005, a Pennsylvania federal district court struck down a school board's requirement that administrators must read a statement that evolution is a theory and must refer students to a book explaining ID as an alternative theory. The court reasoned that the policy was a ploy to infuse religious beliefs into the public school science curriculum.[107]

Nonetheless, disputes over teaching evolution and alternative theories persist in legislative and judicial forums. There has been political activity at the school district or state level pertaining to such instruction in forty states during the past decade.[108] In 2010, a teacher's termination was upheld for violating the Texas Education Agency's policy calling for school personnel to remain neutral toward creationism because she forwarded an e-mail message to fellow teachers and to science organizations advertising a speech of an opponent of the Biblical account.[109] The next year, the Ninth Circuit overturned a lower court decision in part, holding that a teacher who allegedly made negative remarks about religion generally and about creationism specifically in an advanced placement history course was entitled to qualified immunity because of the unsettled nature of the law.[110]

Other Challenges

Allegations are being made that other components of the public school curriculum violate the Establishment Clause because they advance "secular humanism" or "New Age theology," which critics claim disavows God and exalts humans as masters of their own destinies. In addition to evolution, central targets have been sex education, values clarification, and outcome-based education, but few aspects of the curriculum have remained untouched by such claims. Inclusion of the popular *Harry Potter* series in public school libraries has been challenged because the books deal with wizardry and magic that allegedly advance the occult/satanism.[111]

Even courts that have considered nontheistic creeds to be "religions" for First Amendment purposes have not ruled that challenged public school courses and materials advance such creeds. In a 1987 case, the Eleventh Circuit reversed an Alabama federal judge's conclusion that a school district's use of several dozen home economics, history, and social studies books unconstitutionally advanced secular humanism, finding instead

---

[107]*See* Kitzmiller v. Dover Area Sch. Dist., 400 F. Supp. 2d 707, 747 (M.D. Pa. 2005). The board members who championed the policy were voted out of office, and the policy was rescinded before the court's decision was rendered. *See* Martha McCarthy, *Instruction About the Origin of Humanity: Legal Controversies Evolve*, 203 EDUC. L. REP. 453 (2006).

[108]For information on recent controversies across states, see "News," Nat'l Ctr. for Science Educ., http://www.ncseweb.org/pressroom.asp?branch=statement.

[109]Comer v. Scott, 610 F.3d 929 (5th Cir. 2010).

[110]C.F. v. Capistrano Unified Sch. Dist., 654 F.3d 975 (9th Cir. 2011), *cert. denied*, 132 S. Ct. 1566 (2012).

[111]*See* Elizabeth Kennedy, *The Harry Potter Controversy* (Apr. 2012), http://childrensbooks.about.com/cs/censorship/a/banharry.htm; text accompanying note 8, Chapter 4.

that the books instilled in students values such as "independent thought, tolerance of diverse views, self-respect, maturity, self-reliance, and logical decision-making."[112]

The Eighth Circuit also ruled that a Missouri teacher's contract was not renewed for impermissible reasons after she sent a "magic rock" home with each student, with a letter indicating that the rock is "special and unique, just like you!"[113] The court found community complaints that the letter and rock advanced New Ageism to be the basis for the board's action rather than the asserted concerns about the teacher's grading practices. The Second Circuit similarly found no unconstitutional advancement of a nontheistic religion in celebrating Earth Day or in role playing as part of a drug prevention program using peer facilitators.[114] However, it ruled that one teacher's assignment for students to construct images of a Hindu deity abridged the First Amendment and that making worry dolls amounted to preference of superstition over religion in violation of the Establishment Clause.

Sex education classes have been particularly susceptible to charges that an antitheistic faith is being advanced, but courts consistently have found that the challenged courses do not denounce Christianity and instead present public health information that furthers legitimate educational objectives.[115] The judiciary has ruled that the Establishment Clause precludes the state from barring sex education simply to conform to the religious beliefs of some parents. But, courts have acknowledged that students have a free exercise right to be excused from sex education classes if such instruction conflicts with their sectarian beliefs.[116]

Conflicting rulings have been rendered regarding the rights at stake regarding curricular materials designed to promote tolerance for alternative lifestyles. The First Circuit held that an elementary school curriculum encouraging respect for gay persons and same-sex marriage did not abridge the free exercise rights of students or parental rights to direct the upbringing of their children.[117] A Kentucky federal district court similarly rejected a parental challenge to mandatory diversity training (including respect for homosexuality) for middle and high school students. However, the Sixth Circuit, while finding that the diversity training did not promote or condemn any religious beliefs, reversed and remanded this case for additional proceedings regarding whether the policy chilled student expression of contrary views.[118]

---

[112]Smith v. Bd. of Sch. Comm'rs, 827 F.2d 684, 692 (11th Cir. 1987) (also rejecting the contention that the mere omission of Christian religious facts in the curriculum represented unconstitutional hostility toward theistic beliefs), *rev'g* 655 F. Supp. 939 (S.D. Ala. 1987).

[113]Cowan v. Strafford R-VI Sch. Dist., 140 F.3d 1153, 1156 (8th Cir. 1998); *see also* text accompanying note 48, Chapter 10.

[114]Altman v. Bedford Cent. Sch. Dist., 245 F.3d 49 (2d Cir. 2001).

[115]*See, e.g.*, Fields v. Palmdale Sch. Dist., 447 F.3d 1187 (9th Cir. 2006) and text accompanying note 111, Chapter 4. Abstinence programs also have been controversial. *See* ACLU v. Foster, No. 02-1440, 2002 U.S. Dist. LEXIS 13778 (E.D. La. July 25, 2002) (instructing state officials to ensure that federal funds are not used to promote religious beliefs under the Governor's Program on Abstinence); Coleman v. Caddo Parish Sch. Bd., 635 So. 2d 1238 (La. Ct. App. 1994) (ordering changes in some parts of a school district's abstinence program that included some erroneous information and promoted Christian doctrine).

[116]*See, e.g.*, Brown v. Hot, Sexy & Safer Prods., 68 F.3d 525 (1st Cir. 1995).

[117]Parker v. Hurley, 514 F.3d 87 (1st Cir. 2008) (dismissing state law claims without prejudice so such claims could be reinstituted in state courts); *see* text accompanying note 9, Chapter 4.

[118]Morrison v. Bd. of Educ., 419 F. Supp. 2d 937 (E.D. Ky. 2006), *rev'd and remanded*, 507 F.3d 494 (6th Cir. 2007).

Although courts have not condoned parental attacks on various aspects of the public school curriculum that allegedly conflict with their religious values, more difficult legal questions are raised when policy makers support curriculum restrictions for religious reasons. Because courts show considerable deference to legislatures and school boards in educational matters, conservative parent organizations have pressed for state and federal legislation and school board policies barring certain content from public schools.

STATE AID TO PRIVATE SCHOOLS

The Supreme Court is likely to uphold government aid to religious schools that benefits primarily the child or goes to sectarian schools because of parents' choices.

In addition to disputes over the place of religion in public schools, government relations with private—primarily religious—schools have generated a substantial amount of First Amendment litigation. Unquestionably, parents have a legitimate interest in directing the upbringing of their children, including their education. **In 1925, the Supreme Court afforded constitutional protection to private schools' rights to exist and to parents' rights to select private education as an alternative to public schooling.**[119] Yet the Court also recognized that the state has a general welfare interest in mandating school attendance and regulating private education to ensure an educated citizenry, considered essential in a democracy.

Some litigation has involved conflicts between the state's exercise of its *parens patriae* authority to protect the well-being of children and parental interests in having their children educated in settings that reinforce their religious and philosophical beliefs. If the government interferes with parents' child-rearing decisions, it must show that the intervention is necessary to protect the child or the state. Courts have upheld minimum state requirements for private schools (e.g., prescribed courses, personnel requirements), but the recent trend has been toward imposing outcome measures, such as requiring private school students to participate in statewide testing programs.

About 11 percent of all PK–12 students in the United States are enrolled in private schools, but this ratio could change if additional government aid flows to private education. Despite the fact that thirty-seven states specifically prohibit the use of public funds for sectarian purposes, about three-fourths of the states provide some public aid to private school students, including those attending sectarian schools. The primary types of aid are for transportation services, the loan of textbooks, state-required testing programs, special education for children with disabilities, and counseling services. Several of the most significant Supreme Court decisions interpreting the Establishment Clause have pertained to the use of public funds for private, primarily sectarian, education.

[119]Pierce v. Soc'y of Sisters, 268 U.S. 510 (1925).

Aid for Student Services

The Supreme Court's support of religious accommodations in terms of allowing government support for parochial school students has been consistent since 1993, with some evidence of the accommodationist trend much earlier. Indeed, the "child-benefit" doctrine has been used to justify government aid for transportation and secular textbooks for parochial school students since the mid-twentieth century.[120]

In 1993, the Supreme Court found no Establishment Clause violation in publicly supporting sign-language interpreters in parochial schools,[121] signaling a paradigm shift toward the use of public school personnel in sectarian schools. The Court in *Zobrest v. Catalina Foothills School District* reasoned that the aid is going to the child as part of a federal government program that distributes funds neutrally to qualifying children with disabilities under federal law. The child is the primary recipient of the aid, and the school receives only incidental benefits.

Subsequently, in *Agostini v. Felton*, the Supreme Court removed the prohibition it had announced twelve years earlier on public school personnel providing remedial instruction in religious schools.[122] In both *Zobrest* and *Agostini*, the Court rejected the notion that the Establishment Clause lays down an "absolute bar to the placing of a public employee in a sectarian school."[123]

The Supreme Court in *Mitchell v. Helms* found no Establishment Clause violation in using federal aid to purchase instructional materials and equipment for student use in sectarian schools.[124] Specifically, under a federal law providing support for disadvantaged students, the ruling allows the use of public funds for computers, other instructional equipment, and library books in religious schools. The plurality reasoned that religious indoctrination or subsidization of religion could not be attributed to the government when aid, even direct aid, is:

- distributed based on secular criteria;
- available to religious and secular beneficiaries on a nondiscriminatory basis; and
- allowed to flow to religious schools only because of private choices of parents.[125]

The plurality emphasized that the constitutional standard is whether the aid itself would be appropriate for a public school to receive and is distributed in an even-handed manner—conditions it concluded were satisfied by the aid in *Helms*. Six Justices agreed that prior Supreme Court rulings barring state aid in the form of providing maps, slide projectors,

---

[120]*See* Bd. of Educ. v. Allen, 392 U.S. 236 (1968) (finding no Establishment Clause violation in a state law requiring public school districts to loan secular textbooks to all secondary students, including those attending parochial schools); Everson v. Bd. of Educ., 330 U.S. 1 (1947) (rejecting an Establishment Clause challenge to the use of public funds to provide transportation services for nonpublic school students).

[121]Zobrest v. Catalina Foothills Sch. Dist., 509 U.S. 1 (1993).

[122]521 U.S. 203 (1997).

[123]*Agostini*, 521 U.S. at 223–24; *Zobrest*, 509 U.S. at 13.

[124]530 U.S. 793 (2000).

[125]*Id.* at 809–14.

auxiliary services, and other instructional materials and equipment to sectarian schools were no longer good law.[126]

There are very few rulings left that reflect the Supreme Court's separationist stance regarding state aid to nonpublic schools. In fact, the Supreme Court seems to have dismantled most of the decisions rendered during the heyday of applying the stringent *Lemon* test in the 1970s, when it struck down various types of public assistance to private schools.

It must be remembered, however, that simply because courts have interpreted the Establishment Clause as allowing various types of public aid for nonpublic school students does not mean that states *must* use public funds for these purposes if support for transportation, textbooks, and other services in nonpublic schools conflicts with state law. In 2004, the Supreme Court delivered a significant decision, *Locke v. Davey*, upholding states' discretion to adopt more stringent antiestablishment provisions than demanded by the First Amendment.[127] The Court endorsed the state of Washington's prohibition on using state scholarships for college students to pursue pastoral degrees. The Court reasoned that simply because such aid is *permitted* by the Establishment Clause[128] does not mean it is *required* by the Free Exercise Clause. The Supreme Court held that the Washington constitutional provision was intended to keep schools free from sectarian control, rejecting the contention that it emanated from religious bigotry as a so-called Blaine Amendment.[129]

Most of the state constitutional provisions that preclude the use of public funds for religious purposes are more restrictive than the Establishment Clause. The *Locke* decision has provided an impetus for an increase in state litigation as the limits of similar antiestablishment provisions are tested in other states.

Aid to Encourage Educational Choice

Tax-relief measures for private school tuition and educational vouchers have received considerable attention in legislative forums to make private schooling a viable choice for more families. The primary justification for such measures is that the aid flows to religious schools only because of private choices of parents.

Tax-Relief Measures.   Tax benefits in the form of deductions or credits for private school expenses have been proposed at both state and federal levels. Although Congress has not yet endorsed federal income tax credits for private school tuition, several states have enacted tax-relief provisions for educational expenses. The central constitutional question is whether such measures advance religion in violation of the Establishment Clause because the primary beneficiaries are parents of parochial school children and ultimately religious institutions.

In 1983, the Supreme Court upheld a Minnesota tax-benefit program allowing parents of public or private school students to claim a limited state income tax deduction for

---

[126]*Id.* at 835–36, *overturning* Wolman v. Walter, 433 U.S. 229 (1977); Meek v. Pittenger, 421 U.S. 349 (1975).

[127]540 U.S. 712 (2004).

[128]*See* Witters v. Wash. Dep't of Servs., 474 U. S. 481 (1986).

[129]*Locke*, 540 U.S. at 724 n.7 (finding that Washington's constitutional prohibition on the use of public funds for religious worship, exercise, or instruction was *not* modeled on a failed constitutional amendment proposed by former House Speaker James Blaine in 1875, which allegedly reflected anti-Catholic sentiment).

tuition, transportation, and secular textbook expenses incurred for each elementary or secondary school dependent. The Court majority in *Mueller v. Allen* found the Minnesota law "vitally different" from an earlier New York provision, which violated the Establishment Clause by bestowing tax benefits *only* on private school patrons.[130]

In 2011, the Supreme Court rejected a challenge to Arizona's tax benefit program allowing citizens to claim a tax credit for contributions to private student tuition organizations (STOs) that provide scholarships for students to attend private schools.[131] The Supreme Court concluded that taxpayers did not have standing to raise an Establishment Clause challenge to the program because it did not involve state funds. Despite the fact that the vast majority of STOs are religiously affiliated and can restrict their scholarships to particular sectarian schools, **the Court nonetheless suggested that state-created tax-relief programs involving private entities to distribute the funds will not likely be vulnerable to Establishment Clause challenges.** However, most efforts to provide state tax relief for educational expenses have been defeated when placed before the voters, possibly because of the significant impact of such policies on state revenues.

Vouchers. The debate continues over the merits of various voucher models under which public funds would flow to private schools based on parental choices. A number of New England states have had de facto voucher plans for years; school districts without high schools provide a designated amount for high school tuition in neighboring public school districts or independent private schools that the families select. Yet very few other plans were adopted until the mid-1990s, and not until 1999 did Florida become the first state to implement a statewide voucher plan allowing students attending failing public schools to use government vouchers in qualified public or private schools of their choice. Also, several urban districts have adopted state-funded voucher plans for disadvantaged youth, and privately funded scholarships are available for students to attend private schools in many cities nationally.[132]

In 2002, the Supreme Court in *Zelman v. Simmons-Harris* resolved the conflict among lower courts regarding the application of the First Amendment to the participation of religious schools in state-funded voucher programs. In this five-to-four ruling, the Court rejected an Establishment Clause challenge to a scholarship program that gives choices to economically disadvantaged families in the Cleveland City School District through vouchers that can be used toward tuition at participating public or private schools.[133] The Supreme Court relied heavily on the fact that parents—not the government—make the decision for the scholarship funds to flow to private schools. Considering the program religiously neutral and representing "true private choice" among public and private options, the Court found no Establishment Clause violation, even though 96 percent of participating students attend religious schools.[134]

---

[130]463 U.S. 388, 398 (1983) (contrasting Comm. for Pub. Educ. & Religious Liberty v. Nyquist, 413 U.S. 756 (1973)).

[131]Ariz. Christian Sch. Tuition Org. v. Winn, 131 S. Ct. 1436 (2011).

[132]In 1990, Milwaukee established the first state-funded voucher program for disadvantaged students. Privately funded scholarships for children to attend nonpublic schools also have become increasingly popular. *See* Children's Scholarship Fund (2013), http://www.scholarshipfund.org/drupal1.

[133]536 U.S. 639 (2002).

[134]*Id.* at 649.

Since voucher programs do not present federal constitutional issues, their legality will be determined on the basis of state law. The Milwaukee and Cleveland programs have been endorsed by state courts,[135] but some other programs have not fared well when challenged under state education clauses or state prohibitions on the use of public funds for religious purposes. In 2006, the Florida Supreme Court relied on the state constitution's education clause, similar to provisions in many other states, to invalidate the statewide voucher program for students attending deficient public schools.[136] The court interpreted the legislature's duty to provide for a uniform system of public schools as requiring all schools that receive state aid to satisfy the same standards. The court reasoned that the Florida voucher program unconstitutionally diverted public funds into separate, nonuniform, private systems that compete with and reduce funds for public education.

The Colorado Supreme Court also invalidated a pilot voucher program for low-income students attending low-performing schools, concluding that the program violated the "local control" clause of the state constitution by taking away districts' discretion in spending funds for instruction.[137] In addition, federal and state courts have upheld Maine's law that excludes religious schools from the state's tuition reimbursement program for high school students in districts that do not operate public high schools.[138] As discussed, the Supreme Court's 2004 *Locke* decision recognized that states can adopt more stringent antiestablishment measures than included in the First Amendment without exhibiting hostility toward religion, thereby strengthening the state grounds for challenging voucher programs.[139]

Despite recent judicial setbacks, several states are considering voucher proposals, and some programs have been adopted. Arizona, Florida, Georgia, Louisiana, and Ohio have established voucher programs for children with disabilities to attend private schools.[140] Since 2010, voucher bills have been introduced in thirteen states, and Indiana and Louisiana have adopted the most comprehensive programs, with relaxed eligibility criteria for students to use state funds to attend private schools.[141]

Voucher proposals will likely continue to be enacted and challenged, and their legality will depend primarily on state courts' interpretations of state constitutional provisions. Indeed, instead of a national policy, we soon may have fifty standards regarding the legality

---

[135]*See* Simmons-Harris v. Goff, 711 N.E.2d 203 (Ohio 1999); Jackson v. Benson, 578 N.W.2d 602 (Wis. 1998).

[136]Bush v. Holmes, 919 So. 2d 392, 398 (Fla. 2006) (interpreting FLA. CONST. art. IX, § 1(a)).

[137]Owens v. Colo. Congress of Parents, Teachers, & Students, 92 P.3d 933 (Colo. 2004). Florida, Georgia, Kansas, Montana, and Virginia have provisions similar to Colorado's "local control" clause.

[138]Eulitt v. Me. Dep't of Educ., 386 F.3d 344 (1st Cir. 2004); Strout v. Albanese, 178 F.3d 57 (1st Cir. 1999); Anderson v. Town of Durham, 895 A.2d 944 (Me. 2006); *see also* Kimery v. Broken Arrow Pub. Schs., No. 11-CV-0249-CVE-PJC, 2011 U.S. Dist. LEXIS 77871 (N.D. Okla. July 18, 2011) (issuing a stay of Oklahoma's law providing vouchers for special needs students pending an investigation of complaints that the aid impermissibly flows to sectarian institutions).

[139]*See* Locke v. Davey, 540 U.S. 712 (2004); *supra* text accompanying note 127.

[140]Christine Samuels, *Oklahoma Students with Disabilities Get Voucher Program*, EDUC. WK. BLOG (June 9, 2010), http://blogs.edweek.org/edweek/speced/2010/06/oklahoma_gets_new_voucher_prog.html

[141]*See* Meredith v. Pence, 984 N.E.2d 1213 (Ind. 2013) (rejecting a challenge to Indiana's voucher program under the state constitution's education clause and its prohibition on use of public funds for religious purposes); Louisiana Federation of Teachers v. State, Nos. 2013-CA-0120, 2013-CA-0232, 2013-CA-0350, 2013 WL 1878913 (La. May 7, 2013) (striking down the state's use of the public school funding formula to support vouchers for private school tuition).

of school vouchers. And if such measures to increase parental choice result in a significant increase in the number of children attending private schools, this could have a significant impact on support for public education in our nation.

CONCLUSION

Since the early 1960s, church/state controversies have generated a steady stream of education litigation, and there are no signs of diminishing legal activity in this domain. The principle that the First Amendment demands wholesome governmental neutrality toward religion has been easier to assert than to apply. Some lawsuits have involved claims under the Free Exercise Clause, but most school cases have focused on interpretations of Establishment Clause prohibitions.

From the 1960s through the mid-1980s, the federal judiciary seemed more committed to enforcing Establishment Clause restrictions in elementary and secondary school settings than elsewhere. Since the mid-1980s, however, there seems to be greater acceptance of government accommodation of religion, especially in terms of public funds flowing to religious schools. Also, religious influences and accommodations in public schools have become more common. The Free Speech Clause increasingly seems to prevail over Establishment Clause restrictions in protecting religious expression in public education, and the metaphor of separation of church and state seems to have been replaced by the concepts of equal access for religious groups and expression. But there are inconsistencies across decisions, and Establishment Clause jurisprudence remains far from clear.

POINTS TO PONDER

1. Some courts have emphasized that for student-initiated devotional activities in public school to be upheld, prayers must be nonsectarian. Can a prayer be nonsectarian, or is the term "nonsectarian prayer" an oxymoron?

2. A student who attended the middle school was killed in an automobile accident. The next day, a classmate asks you if she can lead the class in saying a prayer for the deceased student. What would be your response, and why?

3. The majority of the senior class engaged in a recitation of the Lord's Prayer five minutes before the high school graduation ceremony. School authorities did not lead the prayer, and although they had heard rumors that the student-initiated recitation was planned, they had not been officially informed. Did this activity represent the school? Did it violate an injunction prohibiting school personnel from authorizing, conducting, sponsoring, or intentionally permitting prayers during the graduation ceremony?

4. High school students have requested that their religious club be allowed to hold meetings in the public school during lunch when other student groups are allowed to meet. They also have asked for access to student activity funds to promote their meetings and distribute religious materials, because other student groups can use such funds to support their activities. What would be your response, and why?

5. Is "a wall of separation between church and state" still the guiding metaphor? If not, what has replaced it?

CHAPTER FOUR

INSTRUCTIONAL ISSUES

Although U.S. citizens have no federal constitutional right to a public education, each state constitution places a duty on its legislature to provide for free public schooling, thus creating a state entitlement (property right) for all children to be educated at public expense.[1] Substantial litigation has resulted from the collision of state interests in providing for the welfare of all citizens and individual interests in exercising constitutional and statutory rights. This chapter focuses on legal mandates pertaining to various requirements and rights associated with the public school instructional program.

THE SCHOOL CURRICULUM

States and local school boards control the public school curriculum, but they must respect federal constitutional guarantees.

The federal government influences the curriculum through funds it provides for particular initiatives, such as reading instruction in early grades, but such influence is quite limited. In contrast, state legislatures have plenary or complete power over education and thus broad authority to impose curriculum mandates.

Requirements and Restrictions

A few state constitutions include specific curriculum mandates, but more typically, the legislature is given responsibility for curricular determinations. Most states mandate instruction pertaining to the Federal Constitution; American history; English; mathematics; and health, drug, character, and physical education. Some state statutes specify what subjects

---

[1]*See* Goss v. Lopez, 419 U.S. 565 (1975); text accompanying note 20, Chapter 8. For a discussion of compulsory education and exceptions, residency requirements, home education, and related issues, see MARTHA MCCARTHY, NELDA CAMBRON-MCCABE & SUZANNE ECKES, PUBLIC SCHOOL LAW: TEACHERS' AND STUDENTS' RIGHTS ch. 3 (Upper Saddle River, N.J.: Pearson, 7th ed. 2014).

will be taught in which grades, and many states have detailed legislation pertaining to vocational education, bilingual education, and special services for children with disabilities. State laws usually stipulate that local school boards must offer the state-mandated minimum curriculum, which they may supplement unless there is a statutory prohibition. In about half of the states, local school boards are empowered to adopt courses of study, but often they must secure approval from the state board of education to do so. Building on state standards, a national initiative was launched in 2010 to develop common core state standards, which are designed to provide a clear understanding of what students nationally are expected to learn at each grade level and to reflect the knowledge and skills that individuals need for success in college and careers.[2]

Despite states' latitude in curricular matters, some legislative attempts to impose curriculum restrictions have impaired federal constitutional rights. The first curriculum case to reach the Supreme Court involved a 1923 challenge to a Nebraska law that prohibited instruction in a foreign language to any public or private school student who had not successfully completed the eighth grade.[3] The state high court had upheld the dismissal of a private school teacher for teaching the subject of reading in German to elementary school students. In striking down the statute, the Supreme Court reasoned that the teacher's right to teach, the parents' right to engage him to instruct their children, and the children's right to acquire useful knowledge were protected liberties under the Due Process Clause of the Fourteenth Amendment.

The Supreme Court on occasion has ruled that other curriculum decisions violate constitutional rights. The Court held in 1968 that under the First Amendment, states cannot bar public school instruction—teaching about evolution—simply because it conflicts with certain religious views.[4] Yet **courts will not interfere with instructional decisions made by state and local education agencies, unless the decisions are clearly arbitrary or impair constitutional rights.** For example, federal appellate courts have rejected allegations that mandatory community service requirements for students force expression of altruistic values in violation of the First Amendment, entail involuntary servitude prohibited by the Thirteenth Amendment, or impair parents' Fourteenth Amendment rights to direct the upbringing of their children.[5] Also, the Supreme Court in 2011 declined to review a decision in which the First Circuit held that revisions in the state's curriculum guide constituted government speech related to the school curriculum so did not implicate the First Amendment.[6] In this case, Turkish groups unsuccessfully challenged politically motivated changes in the guide addressing teaching about genocide and human rights. School authorities also have discretion in establishing standards for pupil performance and

---

[2]The District of Columbia and forty-six states have adopted these standards in language arts, and forty-five states have adopted them in mathematics. *See* Andrew Ujifusa, *New Tests Put States on Spot*, EDUC. WK., June 8, 2012, at 1, 24; Council for Chief State Sch. Officers & Nat'l Governors Ass'n, *Common Core State Standards Initiative* (2012), http://www.corestandards.org.

[3]Meyer v. Nebraska, 262 U.S. 390 (1923).

[4]Epperson v. Arkansas, 393 U.S. 97 (1968); *see* text accompanying notes 100, 104, Chapter 3.

[5]*See, e.g.*, Herndon v. Chapel Hill-Carrboro City Bd. of Educ., 89 F.3d 174 (4th Cir. 1996); Immediato v. Rye Neck Sch. Dist., 73 F.3d 454 (2d Cir. 1996).

[6]Griswold v. Driscoll, 616 F.3d 53 (1st Cir. 2010), *cert. denied*, 131 S. Ct. 1006 (2011).

imposing other instructional requirements, such as prerequisites and admission criteria for particular courses, so long as such criteria are not arbitrary and do not disadvantage certain groups of students.

In addition to having authority over the content of the public school curriculum, states also have the power to specify textbooks and to regulate the method by which such books are obtained and distributed. Typically, the state board of education or a textbook commission adopts a list of acceptable books, and local school boards then select specific texts from the list. However, in some states, such as Colorado, almost complete authority is delegated to local boards to make textbook selections. Courts will not interfere with textbook decisions unless the established procedures are not followed or overtly biased materials are adopted.

Censorship of Instructional Materials

Attempts to remove books from classrooms and libraries and to tailor curricular offerings and methodologies to particular religious and philosophical values have led to constitutional challenges. Although most people agree that schools transmit values, little consensus exists regarding *which* values should be transmitted or *who* should make this determination.

Parental Challenges. Some civil rights and consumer groups have challenged public school materials and programs as allegedly promoting racism, sexism, or bad health habits for students. But most of the challenges come from conservative parent groups, alleging that the use of instructional activities and materials considered immoral and anti-Christian impairs parents' rights to control their children's course of study in public schools.[7] As discussed in Chapter 3, courts have endorsed requests for specific children to be excused from selected course offerings (e.g., sex education) that offend their religious beliefs, so long as the exemptions do not impede the students' academic progress or the management of the school. Challenges to the courses themselves, however, have not found a receptive judiciary.

To date, courts have not allowed mere parental disapproval of instructional materials to dictate the public school curriculum. Federal appellate courts have been unsympathetic to claims that reading series or individual novels used in public schools conflict with Christian doctrine and advance an antitheistic creed, finding the challenged materials to be religiously neutral and related to legitimate educational objectives.[8] Although

---

[7]Some of the best-known conservative groups are the American Coalition for Traditional Values, the Christian Coalition, Citizens for Excellence in Education, Concerned Women for America, the Eagle Forum, and Focus on the Family. In addition to these conservative citizen organizations, a new type of advocacy group is having a significant impact on the instructional program. These organizations (e.g., Education Reform Now, Stand for Children, Students First, and Democrats for Education Reform) focus on raising standards for teacher evaluation (based in part on evidence of student learning), implementing higher standards for students, and increasing educational options for families.

[8]*See, e.g.*, Monteiro v. Tempe Union High Sch. Dist., 158 F.3d 1022 (9th Cir. 1998); Fleischfresser v. Dirs. of Sch. Dist. 200, 15 F.3d 680 (7th Cir. 1994); Smith v. Sch. Bd. of Sch. Comm'rs, 827 F.2d 684 (11th Cir. 1987); text accompanying note 112, Chapter 3. The Harry Potter books received the most challenges overall during the past decade. *See* Molly Driscoll, *10 Most Challenged Books on the American Library Association's 2011 List*, CHRISTIAN SCIENCE MONITOR (Apr. 9, 2012), http://www.csmonitor.com/Books/chapter-and-verse/2012/0409/10-most-challenged-books-on-the-American-Library-Association-s-2011-list.

many challenges have religious overtones, some simply assert parents' rights to determine their children's education. The First Circuit rejected parents' claim that the school district was liable for subjecting their children to a mandatory AIDS-awareness assembly that featured a streetwise, comedic approach to the topic. The appeals court observed that "if all parents had a fundamental constitutional right to dictate individually what the schools teach their children, the schools would be forced to cater a curriculum for each student whose parents had genuine moral disagreements with the school's choice of subject matter."[9] The Ninth Circuit subsequently held that the Oregon law restructuring public schools to impose a rigorous academic program and student assessments did not abridge speech rights or "freedom of the mind," because nothing in the law compelled students to adopt state-approved views.[10] And the same court dismissed African American parents' complaint that their daughter suffered psychological injuries due to being required to read two literary works that contained repeated use of the word "nigger."[11]

Sometimes school districts have *not* prevailed if it is shown that they acted arbitrarily or in violation of parents' or students' protected rights. For example, a Maryland federal district court enjoined implementation of a school district's pilot sex education program, reasoning that additional investigation was needed to determine if the materials on "sexual variation" constituted viewpoint discrimination by presenting only the perspective that homosexuality is natural and a morally correct lifestyle. The curriculum subsequently was revised and approved by the school board with the directive that teachers must convey that sexual orientation is an innate characteristic.[12]

Censorship by Policy Makers. Although courts have not been receptive to challenges to school boards' curricular decisions simply because some materials or courses offend the sensibilities of specific students or parents, the legal issues are more complicated when policy makers themselves (e.g., legislators, school board members) support the censorship activity. Bills calling for instructional censorship have been introduced in Congress and numerous state legislatures, and policies have been proposed at the school board level to eliminate "objectionable" materials from public school classrooms and libraries. **The Supreme Court has recognized the discretion of school boards to make decisions that reflect the "legitimate and substantial community interest in promoting respect for authority and traditional values, be they social, moral, or political."**[13] Thus, the judiciary

[9]Brown v. Hot, Sexy & Safer Prods., 68 F.3d 525, 534 (1st Cir. 1995); *see also* Parker v. Hurley, 514 F.3d 87 (1st Cir. 2008) (finding no constitutional violation in a program teaching respect for homosexuality and same-sex marriages); Mooney v. Garcia, 143 Cal. Rptr. 3d 195 (Ct. App. 2012) (rejecting parental request to be on the school board agenda to object to a student-sponsored "Rainbow Day" diversity observance at an individual school), *review denied,* No. H037233, 2012 Cal. LEXIS 9128 (Cal. Sept. 26, 2012).

[10]Tennison v. Paulus, 144 F.3d 1285, 1287 (9th Cir. 1998).

[11]*Monteiro*, 158 F.3d 1022 (remanding for further proceedings, however, regarding allegations that school personnel failed to respond to complaints of a racially hostile environment in violation of Title VI of the Civil Rights Act of 1964).

[12]Citizens for a Responsible Curriculum v. Montgomery Cnty. Pub. Schs., No. AW 05 1194, 2005 U.S. Dist. LEXIS 8130, at *3 (S.D. Md. May 5, 2005); Citizens for a Responsible Curriculum v. Montgomery Cnty. Pub. Schs., No. 284980 (Md. Cir. Ct. Jan. 31, 2008) (upholding the revised curriculum).

[13]Bd. of Educ. v. Pico, 457 U.S. 853, 864 (1982).

has been reluctant to interfere with school boards' prerogatives in selecting and eliminating instructional materials, unless a board flagrantly abuses its authority. To illustrate, the Eleventh Circuit allowed the Miami-Dade School Board to remove from elementary school libraries the book *Vamos a Cuba!* along with twenty-three other books in a series about life in other countries. The appellate court concluded that the board's action was constitutionally sound because evidence showed that the books were removed for factual inaccuracies and not because of impermissible viewpoint discrimination.[14]

Courts generally have upheld school boards' authority in determining curricular materials and offerings, but some specific censorship activities have been invalidated. Courts have intervened if the censorship of library selections has clearly been motivated by a desire to suppress particular viewpoints or controversial ideas in violation of the First Amendment. The Fifth Circuit remanded a case for a trial to determine whether a Louisiana school board was unconstitutionally suppressing ideas in removing from school libraries all copies of *Voodoo & Hoodoo*, which traces the development of African tribal religion and its evolution in African American communities in the United States.[15] Also, an Arkansas federal district court found insufficient justification for a school district's policy requiring parental permission for students to check out specific library books allegedly dealing with witchcraft and the occult, concluding that the policy stigmatized the targeted books and abridged students' First Amendment rights to have access to the materials without parental permission.[16]

Despite considerable activity in lower courts, the Supreme Court has rendered only one decision involving censorship in public schools. This case, *Board of Education v. Pico*,[17] unfortunately did not provide significant clarification regarding the scope of school boards' authority to restrict student access to particular materials, with seven of the nine Supreme Court Justices writing separate opinions. In *Pico*, the school board removed certain books from junior high and high school libraries, in spite of the contrary recommendation of a committee appointed to review the books. The Supreme Court narrowly affirmed the appellate court's remand of the case for a trial because of irregularities in the removal procedures and unresolved factual questions regarding the school board's motivation. However, even the three Justices endorsing the notion that students have a protected right to receive information recognized the broad authority of school boards to remove materials that are vulgar or educationally unsuitable so long as they used regular and unbiased procedures. The *Pico* plurality also emphasized that the controversy involved *library* books, which are not required reading for students, noting that school boards "might well defend their claim of absolute discretion in matters of *curriculum* by reliance upon their duty to inculcate community values."[18]

---

[14]ACLU v. Miami-Dade Cnty. Sch. Bd., 557 F.3d 1177 (11th Cir. 2009).

[15]Campbell v. St. Tammany Parish Sch. Bd., 64 F.3d 184 (5th Cir. 1995).

[16]Counts v. Cedarville Sch. Dist., 295 F. Supp. 2d 996 (W.D. Ark. 2003).

[17]474 F. Supp. 387 (E.D.N.Y. 1979), *rev'd and remanded*, 638 F.2d 404 (2d Cir. 1980), *aff'd*, 457 U.S. 853 (1982).

[18]*Id.*, 457 U.S. at 869 (emphasis added). Following the Supreme Court's decision, the school board voted to return the controversial books to the school libraries, thus averting the need for a trial regarding the board's motivation for the original censorship.

Further strengthening the broad discretion of school authorities in curriculum-related censorship was the landmark 1988 Supreme Court decision involving students' free speech rights, *Hazelwood School District v. Kuhlmeier*.[19] The Court declared that public school authorities can censor student expression in school-sponsored activities to ensure that the expression is consistent with educational objectives. Relying on *Hazelwood*, the Eleventh Circuit upheld a Florida school board's decision to ban a humanities textbook because it included Aristophanes' *Lysistrata* and Chaucer's *The Miller's Tale*, which board members considered vulgar. Although not addressing the wisdom of the board's decision, the court deferred to the board's discretion in curricular matters.[20]

Specific issues may change, but controversies surrounding the selection of materials for the public school library and curriculum will likely persist, reflecting the basic tension between instilling community values in students and exposing them to new ideas. School boards would be wise to establish procedures for reviewing objections to course content and library materials *before* a controversy arises. Criteria used to acquire and eliminate instructional materials should be clearly articulated and educationally defensible. **Once a process is in place to evaluate complaints relating to the instructional program, school boards should follow it carefully, as courts will show little sympathy when a school board ignores its own established procedures.**

Electronic Censorship. Some recent censorship activity has focused on the electronic frontier. It was estimated in 2011 that approximately 95 percent of American teenagers went online, and 74 percent owned computers.[21] In addition to issues addressed in Chapter 5 regarding students' postings on the Internet, concerns are being raised about adults electronically transmitting sexually explicit and other harmful material to minors. With schools and parents increasingly making online services accessible to students, children are vulnerable to sexual predators via the Internet. Many states as well as the federal government have enacted measures to restrict minors' access to harmful electronic postings.

The only federal law that has survived a First Amendment challenge is the Children's Internet Protection Act (CIPA), which received Supreme Court endorsement in 2003.[22] This law requires libraries and school districts receiving technology funds to monitor student Internet use and to implement technology protection measures that safeguard students from access to harmful content.[23] The Supreme Court reasoned that CIPA places a condition on the use of federal funds, which poses a small burden for library patrons, and the law does not penalize those posting materials on the Internet.[24]

In implementing the required Internet safety plans, most school districts are relying on filtering software and thus delegating to private companies the decisions concerning

---

[19]484 U.S. 260 (1988). See text accompanying note 16, Chapter 5, for a discussion of this case.

[20]Virgil v. Sch. Bd., 862 F.2d 1517 (11th Cir. 1989).

[21]*See* Pew Internet & American Life Project, *Demographics of Teen Internet Users* (July 2011), http://www.pewinternet.org/Trend-Data-%28Teens%29/Whos-Online.aspx.

[22]United States v. Am. Library Ass'n, 539 U.S. 194 (2003).

[23]20 U.S.C.§ 9134(f) (2012); 47 U.S.C. § 254(h)(5) (2012).

[24]*Am. Library Ass'n*, 539 U.S. 194.

what materials are appropriate for their students. Some fear that measures such as CIPA will have a chilling effect on schools using computer networks to enhance instructional experiences for students. For example, a Missouri federal district court in 2012 enjoined a school district's use of filtering software that blocked websites with resources directed toward lesbian, gay, bisexual, and transgender youth, reasoning that the publishers of the websites and students would likely prevail in their First Amendment claim.[25] The competing government and individual interests affected by legislative restrictions on information distributed electronically will undoubtedly generate additional litigation.

Academic Freedom

The concept of academic freedom historically was applied to postsecondary education and embodied the principle that faculty members should be free from government controls in conducting research and imparting knowledge to students. **Public school teachers have asserted a similar right to academic freedom, but courts have not extended the protections found in higher education to public elementary and secondary schools.** Although reasoning that teachers possess academic interests, courts have refrained from establishing precise legal principles in this domain. Instead, courts have balanced teachers' interests in academic freedom against school boards' interests in ensuring an appropriate instructional program and efficient school operations.

Curriculum Content.   Public school teachers do not have a right to determine the content of the instructional program. Recognizing that the state, as employer, controls the curriculum, the Ninth Circuit rejected a vagueness challenge to California legislation holding teachers personally liable for actual damages if they willfully refuse to teach predominantly in English.[26] The court concluded that in the vast majority of instances, teachers would clearly know when they were dispensing instruction that would be subject to the language restriction.

Despite the state's legal authority to impose such curricular restrictions, state law often delegates to local school boards considerable authority to make instructional decisions. Several courts have declared that school boards are not legally obligated to accept teachers' curricular recommendations in the absence of a board policy to that effect. To illustrate, the Fifth Circuit held that teachers cannot assert a First Amendment right to substitute their own supplemental reading list for the officially adopted list without securing administrative approval.[27] And the Fourth Circuit ruled that a high school teacher did not have complete discretion to select the plays performed by her acting class students, recognizing school officials' legitimate pedagogical interests in regulating the curriculum.[28]

More recently, a New York federal district court upheld a school district's decision to not renew a probationary teacher's contract after she used an icebreaker exercise in a

---

[25]Parents, Families, & Friends v. Camdenton R-III Sch. Dist., 853 F. Supp. 2d 888 (W.D. Mo. 2012).

[26]Cal. Teachers Ass'n v. State Bd. of Educ., 271 F.3d 1141 (9th Cir. 2001).

[27]Kirkland v. Northside Indep. Sch. Dist., 890 F.2d 794 (5th Cir. 1989).

[28]Boring v. Buncombe Cnty. Bd. of Educ., 136 F.3d 364 (4th Cir. 1998).

human reproduction lesson where she asked the students to sketch the male reproductive system. The court reasoned that the teacher could have explained the reproductive system in a more appropriate way.[29] In another New York case, a federal district court upheld reassignment of a teacher to nonclassroom duties because during a health course lesson on HIV transmission, the teacher had students identify slang words for body parts or bodily fluids that she wrote on the blackboard and then identified acceptable equivalents. The court granted the school district's motion for summary judgment, holding that the teacher's classroom speech did not relate to a matter of public concern and that school officials may regulate use of vulgar terms in the classroom.[30]

Teachers are not permitted to ignore or omit prescribed course content under the guise of academic freedom. To exemplify, the Seventh Circuit upheld a school board's dismissal of a kindergarten teacher who, for religious reasons, refused to teach patriotic topics.[31] The Supreme Court of Washington found no First Amendment impairment in a school board prohibiting two teachers from team teaching a history course, finding it within the board's discretion to require teachers to cover course content in a conventional manner.[32] Also, the Third Circuit held that a teacher could not assert a First Amendment right to disregard school board instructions and continue using a classroom management technique, Learnball, that gave students responsibility for establishing class rules and grading procedures.[33] And the Supreme Court of Colorado upheld a policy requiring administrative review of "controversial learning resources," noting the district's legitimate pedagogical interest in shaping its secondary school curriculum.[34]

Educators are not legally vulnerable when they are teaching the prescribed curriculum, even though their superiors instruct them to honor requests from school patrons.[35] For example, the Sixth Circuit ruled in favor of a teacher who was teaching a life science course in compliance with the school board's directives, finding that community protests did not justify school authorities placing restrictions on his course content that was consistent with the course objectives.[36] More recently, after a Maine teacher received several complaints about his curriculum from members of a Christian church, the school board ordered the teacher to refrain from teaching certain social science subjects pertaining to

[29]Kirby v. Yonkers Sch. Dist., 767 F. Supp. 2d 452 (S.D.N.Y. 2011).

[30]Kramer v. N.Y. City Bd. of Educ., 715 F. Supp. 2d 335 (E.D.N.Y. 2010).

[31]Palmer v. Bd. of Educ., 603 F.2d 1271 (7th Cir. 1979).

[32]Millikan v. Bd. of Dirs., 611 P.2d 414, 418 (Wash. 1980).

[33]Murray v. Pittsburgh Bd. of Educ., 919 F. Supp. 838 (W.D. Pa. 1996), aff'd mem., 141 F.3d 1154 (3d Cir. 1998).

[34]Bd. of Educ. v. Wilder, 960 P.2d 695, 702 (Colo. 1998) (upholding termination of a teacher for showing his high school class portions of a movie that included nudity, profanity, and graphic violence; also rejecting the teacher's due process claim since sufficient notice of the policy had been provided); infra text accompanying note 38.

[35]It should also be noted that school counselors may discuss controversial issues in confidence with counselees and provide information as well as referrals. For example, counselors can provide factual information on the legal status of abortions, but they cannot urge or coerce students to have an abortion. See Arnold v. Bd. of Educ., 880 F.2d 305 (11th Cir. 1989), on remand, 754 F. Supp. 853 (S.D. Ala. 1990).

[36]Stachura v. Truszkowski, 763 F.2d 211 (6th Cir. 1985), rev'd and remanded on other ground (compensatory damages) sub nom. Memphis Cmty. Sch. Dist. v. Stachura, 477 U.S. 299 (1986); see text accompanying note 44, Chapter 10.

prehistoric times and Greek, Roman, and Asian history. The teacher challenged the board's action, and the district court denied the board's request for summary judgment, reasoning that the teacher was threatened with termination for teaching "non-Christian" ancient history. The court emphasized that classrooms cannot be used to promote Christian ideology.[37]

Teaching Strategies.   State laws and school board policies establish the basic contours of the curriculum, but teachers retain some discretion in choosing *relevant strategies* to convey prescribed content. In reviewing school board restrictions on teachers' classroom activities, the judiciary considers several factors, such as:

- whether teachers have been provided adequate notice that use of specific teaching methodologies or materials will result in disciplinary action;
- relevance of the method to the course of study and age and maturity of the students;
- support of the method by the profession;
- threat of disruption posed by the method; and
- impact of the strategy on community norms.

A primary consideration in reviewing the legitimacy of classroom activities is whether instructional strategies are related to course objectives. Relevancy applies also to the age and maturity of the students; a controversial topic appropriate for high school students would not necessarily be suitable for elementary and junior high pupils. Relevance has been found lacking in several cases in which teachers have shown R-rated movies to public school students.[38] Also, the Eighth Circuit upheld termination of a teacher who willfully violated board policy by permitting her students to use profanity in their creative writing assignments.[39]

Teachers, however, cannot be forced to discontinue instructionally relevant activities solely because of parental displeasure. The Fifth Circuit ruled that a teacher's use of a simulation to teach about post–Civil War U.S. history was related to legitimate educational objectives, and therefore dismissal for refusing to stop using the simulation impaired the teacher's academic rights.[40] Relevancy was established in the Sixth Circuit case discussed previously in which the court ordered reinstatement of the teacher who was teaching his life science course in conformance with board-approved objectives.[41]

Among the factors courts examine in assessing restrictions on classroom instruction is whether a teacher's action poses a threat of disruption to the operation of the school. To illustrate, an Oregon federal district court found a school board's policy banning all political speakers from the high school unreasonable on several grounds, including the fact that

---

[37]Cole v. Me. Sch. Admin. Dist. No. 1, 350 F. Supp. 2d 143 (D. Me. 2004).

[38]*See, e.g.*, Fowler v. Bd. of Educ., 819 F.2d 657 (6th Cir. 1987); Borger v. Bisciglia, 888 F. Supp. 97 (E.D. Wis. 1995); Bd. of Educ. v. Wilder, 960 P.2d 695, 702 (Colo. 1998).

[39]Lacks v. Ferguson Reorganized Sch. Dist. R-2, 147 F.3d 718 (8th Cir. 1998); *see also* Oleske v. Hilliard City Sch. Dist., 764 N.E.2d 1110 (Ohio Ct. App. 2001) (upholding dismissal of a teacher who told dirty jokes to middle school students and referred to another teacher by a derogatory name).

[40]Kingsville Indep. Sch. Dist. v. Cooper, 611 F.2d 1109 (5th Cir. 1980).

[41]Stachura v. Truszkowski, 763 F.2d 211 (6th Cir. 1985); *supra* text accompanying note 36.

no disruptions had occurred or could be anticipated from political discussions.[42] However, an Illinois federal district court recognized that a school board does not necessarily have to show that instructional materials actually caused a disruption to justify nonrenewal of a teacher's contract. Materials may be considered inappropriate for classroom use (e.g., an R-rated film with vulgarity and sexually explicit scenes), despite the fact that students "quietly acquiesce" to their use.[43]

Courts have been protective of school boards' authority to design the curriculum to reflect community values. A New York appeals court held that a teacher, who defied warnings that use of certain materials and sexual words in classroom discussions offended community mores, had no First Amendment grounds to challenge his reprimand.[44] Yet, if a particular strategy is instructionally relevant and supported by the profession, it likely will survive judicial review even though it might disturb some school patrons.

COPYRIGHT COMPLIANCE

School personnel must comply with the federal copyright law; some copyrighted materials may be used for instructional purposes without the publisher's permission if fair use guidelines are followed.

Educators extensively use published materials and various other media in the classroom, and as a general rule, teachers should assume material is copyrighted unless it explicitly states that it is in the public domain.[45] Although the law grants the owner of a copyright exclusive control over the protected material, courts since the 1800s have recognized exceptions to this control under the doctrine of *fair use*. The fair use doctrine cannot be precisely defined, but the judiciary frequently has described it as the "privilege of people other than the copyright owner to use the copyrighted material in a reasonable manner without . . . consent, notwithstanding the monopoly granted to the owner."[46]

Congress incorporated the judicially created fair use concept into the 1976 revisions of the Copyright Act. In identifying the purposes of the fair use exception, Congress specifically noted teaching. **The exception provides needed flexibility for teachers but**

[42]Wilson v. Chancellor, 418 F. Supp. 1358 (D. Or. 1976).

[43]Krizek v. Bd. of Educ., 713 F. Supp. 1131, 1141 (N.D. Ill. 1989); *see also* Solmitz v. Me. Sch. Admin. Dist. No. 59, 495 A.2d 812 (Me. 1985) (upholding a school board's cancellation of a Tolerance Day program for legitimate safety concerns over bomb threats received).

[44]*In re* Arbitration Between Bernstein & Norwich City Sch. Dist., 726 N.Y.S.2d 474 (App. Div. 2001).

[45]*See generally* Authors Guild v. Google, 770 F. Supp. 2d 666 (S.D.N.Y. 2011) (emphasizing that copyright is conferred the moment of creation and that the copyright symbol is no longer required); *see also* Kirtsaeng v. John Wiley & Sons, Inc., 133 S. Ct. 1351 (2013) (holding that copyrighted materials legitimately purchased abroad could be resold in the United States for a profit; the Copyright Act was not intended to place a geographic restriction on the resale of lawfully purchased materials).

[46]Shepard v. Miler, No. 2:10-1863, 2010 U.S. Dist. LEXIS 136504, at *11 (E.D. Cal. Dec. 14, 2010).

does *not* exempt them from copyright infringements. The following factors are used in assessing whether copying specific material constitutes fair use or an infringement:

- the purpose and character of the use, including whether such use is of a commercial nature or is for nonprofit educational purposes;
- the nature of the copyrighted work;
- the amount and substantiality of the portion used in relation to the copyrighted work as a whole; and
- the effect of the use upon the potential market for or value of the copyrighted work.[47]

To clarify fair use pertaining to photocopying from books and periodicals, the House and Senate conferees incorporated in their conference report a set of classroom guidelines developed by a group representing educators, authors, and publishers.[48] These guidelines are only part of the legislative history of the Copyright Act and do not have the force of law, but they have been widely used as persuasive authority in assessing the legality of reproducing printed materials in the educational environment. The guidelines permit making single copies of copyrighted material for teaching or research but are quite restrictive on the use of multiple copies. **To use multiple copies of a work, the tests of brevity, spontaneity, and cumulative effect must be met** (see Figure 4.1). Furthermore, the guidelines do not permit copying to substitute for anthologies or collective works or to replace consumable materials such as workbooks.

Publishers have taken legal action to ensure compliance with these guidelines. The Sixth Circuit held that a commercial copy shop violated the fair use doctrine in the reproduction of course packets for faculty at the University of Michigan. The copy shop owner argued that such reproduction of multiple copies for classroom use is a recognized statutory exemption. The appellate court disagreed, reasoning that the sale of multiple copies for commercial, not educational, purposes destroyed the publisher's potential licensing revenue, contained creative material, and involved significant portions of the copyrighted publications (as much as 30 percent of one work).[49] This ruling does not prevent faculty from using course packets or anthologies in the classroom, but it requires them to seek permission from publishers and the possible payment of fees prior to photocopying.

The fair use doctrine and congressional guidelines have been strictly construed in educational settings. Although materials reproduced for the classroom meet the first factor in determining fair use—educational purpose—the remaining factors also must be met. The Ninth Circuit held that fair use was not met in a teacher's use of a copyrighted booklet to make a learning activity packet used for the same purpose as the protected booklet.[50] The

---

[47]17 U.S.C. § 107 (2012). Teachers' ideas might be excluded from copyright protection if the idea constitutes a "work for hire." Works that are created as part of the employment relationship can be considered a work for hire, and the employer is considered the author unless the parties have expressly agreed to another arrangement. 17 U.S.C. § 201(b) (2012).

[48]U.S. Copyright Office, *Circular 21: Reproduction of Copyrighted Works by Educators and Librarians* (2009), http://www.copyright.gov/circs/circ21.pdf.

[49]Princeton Univ. Press v. Mich. Document Servs., 99 F.3d 1381 (6th Cir. 1996).

[50]Marcus v. Rowley, 695 F.2d 1171 (9th Cir. 1983).

FIGURE 4.1   Copyright Guidelines for Not-for-Profit Educational Institutions: Multiple Copies

Each copy must include the copyright notice and meet the following criteria:

Brevity

- For poems, not more than 250 words can be copied.
- For prose, a complete article of less than 2,500 words or an excerpt of not more than 1,000 words or 10 percent of the work, whichever is less, can be copied.
- Copies of illustrations can be one chart, graph, diagram, drawing, cartoon, or picture per book or periodical.

Spontaneity

- The copying is initiated by the individual teacher (not an administrator or supervisor).
- The inspiration to use the material occurs in such a manner that does not reasonably permit a timely request for permission.

Cumulative effect

- The copies are for use in one course.
- Not more than one short poem, article, or two excerpts can be copied from a given source or author during one class term.
- Multiple copying in a term is limited to nine instances.

The following practices are prohibited:

- Copying cannot substitute for compilations or collective works.
- Consumable works cannot be copied (e.g., workbooks, standardized tests).
- The same items cannot be copied from term to term.
- Copying cannot replace the purchase of books or periodicals.

absence of personal profit on the part of the teacher did not lessen the violation. Furthermore, half of the packet was a verbatim copy of the copyrighted material, and the copying did not meet the guideline of spontaneity in that it was reproduced several times over two school years.

An Illinois federal district court ruled that a Chicago teacher and editor of a newspaper called *Substance* committed a copyright violation against the Chicago school board by publishing its copyrighted tests used to assess educational levels of high school freshmen and sophomores. The tests were clearly marked with the copyright notice and included a warning that the material could not be duplicated. In dismissing the teacher's affirmative defenses, the court ruled that he did not possess a First Amendment right to publish the copyrighted tests because the Copyright Act limits First Amendment freedoms, and publication of the material did not fall within the fair use guidelines.[51]

Rapid developments in instructional technology pose a new set of legal questions regarding use of videotapes, digital video disks, and computer software. Recognizing the need for guidance related to recording material, Congress issued guidelines for educational use in 1981.[52] These guidelines specify that recording must be made at the request of the

[51]Chi. Sch. Reform Bd. v. Substance, 79 F. Supp. 2d 919 (N.D. Ill. 2000).

[52]Guidelines for Off-Air Recording of Broadcast Programming for Educational Purposes, Cong. Rec. § E4751 (daily ed. Oct.14, 1981).

teacher, and the material must be used for relevant classroom activities only once within the first ten days of recording. Additional use is limited to instructional reinforcement or evaluation, and the tape or disk must be erased after forty-five calendar days. A New York federal district court held that a school system violated the fair use standards by extensive off-air taping and replaying of entire television programs.[53] The taping interfered with the producers' ability to market the tapes and films. In a subsequent appeal, the school system sought permission for temporary taping; however, because of the availability of these programs for rental or lease, even temporary recording violated fair use by interfering with the marketability of the films.[54]

Recording television broadcasts on home video recorders for later classroom use may constitute copyright infringement if the above off-air taping guidelines are not followed. The Supreme Court ruled that personal video recording for the purpose of "time shifting" is a legitimate, unobjectionable purpose, posing minimal harm to marketability.[55] However, **home recording for broader viewing by students in the classroom would be beyond the purposes envisioned by the Supreme Court and would necessitate careful adherence to the guidelines for limited use.**

Under 1980 amendments to the copyright law, software was included as protected intellectual property.[56] It is clear from the amended law that only one duplicate or backup copy can be made of the master computer program to ensure a working copy of the program if the master copy is damaged. Application of the fair use exception does not alter this restriction for educators. Although duplicating multiple copies would be for educational purposes, other factors of fair use would be violated. The software is readily accessible for purchase, programs can only be duplicated in their entirety, and copying substantially reduces the potential market.

In spite of the amendments, publishers continue to be concerned about illegal copying of computer software in the school environment. Limited school budgets and high costs have led to abuse of copyrighted software. In 1999, the school board of the Los Angeles Unified School District settled a significant case of software piracy in its schools.[57] An investigation by a group of software companies discovered more than 1,400 copies of software, such as Microsoft Word and Adobe Photoshop, allegedly being used without authorization. The school district denied the violation but settled to avoid the costs of a trial.

A question not answered by the copyright law but plaguing schools is the legality of multiple use of a master program. That is, can a program be loaded on many computers in a laboratory for simultaneous use, or can a program be modified for use in a network of microcomputers? Again, application of the fair use concept would indicate that multiple use is not permissible. The most important factor is that the market for the educational

---

[53]Encyclopedia Britannica Educ. Corp. v. Crooks, 542 F. Supp. 1156 (W.D.N.Y. 1982).

[54]Encyclopedia Britannica Educ. Corp. v. Crooks, 558 F. Supp. 1247 (W.D.N.Y. 1983).

[55]Sony Corp. v. Universal City Studios, 464 U.S. 417 (1984).

[56]17 U.S.C. § 117 (2012).

[57]*L.A. School Board Settles Software Copyright Suit*, 27 SCH. L. NEWS 2 (Mar. 5, 1999). The case was settled for $300,000 plus an additional $1.5 million for a task force to monitor software usage over a three-year period.

software would be greatly diminished. Several students using the master program one at a time (serial use), however, would appear not to violate the copyright law. **To acquire broad use of particular software, school systems must either purchase multiple copies or negotiate site license agreements with the publishers.**

As schools are developing their capacity to take advantage of the Internet, copyright law also is evolving. Congress amended the law in 1998 with the Digital Millennium Copyright Act, reinforcing that an individual's copyright is secured when the work is created and "fixed in any tangible medium of expression."[58] In 2002, greater clarity was provided for educators regarding the use of digital media in distance education with the enactment of the Technology, Education, and Copyright Harmonization (TEACH) Act.[59] The Act gives accredited nonprofit educational institutions more flexibility in using the Internet to distribute copyrighted materials in distance education programs. Basically, **the Act allows copyrighted materials to be used in distance education courses in the same way they can be used in regular classrooms.**

Case law clearly indicates that the Internet is not immune from the basic principles of copyright law; material that is created on the Internet or produced in a different format and then converted for use on the Internet is entitled to full legal protections. For example, in 2001 the Ninth Circuit imposed an injunction against Napster Corporation and its distribution of a file-sharing program that allowed individuals to download music files.[60] More recently, the Supreme Court found that two software companies, presenting themselves as "alternatives" to Napster, infringed the rights of songwriters, music publishers, and motion picture studios who had brought suit to prevent unauthorized use of their protected property. Like Napster, the challenged software companies distributed free software products that allowed individuals to share electronic files through peer-to-peer networks, so the companies were "liable for the resulting acts of infringement by third parties."[61] Although the file-sharing software had some lawful uses, its primary purpose was to share copyrighted files, which made the software companies culpable.

Extraordinary technological advances have given teachers and their school systems the means to access a wide range of instructional materials and products, but many of them are protected by the federal copyright law that restricts unauthorized reproduction. **Because violation of the law can result in school district and educator liability, school boards should adopt guidelines to prohibit infringement and alert individuals of unlawful practices.**[62]

---

[58]17 U.S.C. § 1201 (2012).

[59]17 U.S.C. § 110 (2012).

[60]A&M Records v. Napster, 239 F.3d 1004 (9th Cir. 2001).

[61]Metro-Goldwyn-Mayer Studios v. Grokster, Ltd., 545 U.S. 913, 919 (2005) (remanding the case to the district court for a trial).

[62]*See* 17 U.S.C. § 511(a) (2012). In response to several appellate court decisions holding that under the Eleventh Amendment states and their agents were not subject to federal suits for copyright infringements, Congress amended the copyright law (Copyright Remedy Clarification) specifically abrogating immunity. *See also* BV Eng'g v. UCLA, 858 F.2d 1394 (9th Cir. 1988); Richard Anderson Photography v. Brown, 852 F.2d 114 (4th Cir. 1988).

■ ■ ■ ■ ■

STUDENT PROFICIENCY TESTING

Courts have recognized that an educated citizenry is an appropriate government goal, and the establishment of minimum performance standards to give value to a high school diploma is a rational means to attain that goal.

The concept of performance assessment is not new, but the use of proficiency tests as a condition of grade promotion or the receipt of a high school diploma has a relatively brief history. In 1976, only four states had enacted student proficiency testing legislation. Now, **all states have laws or administrative regulations pertaining to statewide performance testing programs, and more than half of the states condition receipt of a high school diploma on passing a test.** Given the state's authority to establish academic standards, including mandatory examinations, the judiciary traditionally has been reluctant to interfere with assessments of pupil performance.[63]

Recently, other forms of performance assessment, such as portfolios, have received attention, but standardized tests continue to be used in most school districts. Annual student testing is strongly supported by the federal government. Indeed, the No Child Left Behind (NCLB) Act:

- mandates annual testing in grades three through eight in reading and math and in science at certain grade intervals;
- requires high school students to take a general test in core subjects at least once; and
- ties federal assistance and sanctions for schools to student test scores.[64]

High-stakes assessments shape the instructional program, and states increasingly are evaluating educators' performance based on their students' test scores. Not surprisingly, claims are being made that teachers are limiting classroom activities to material covered on the tests and/or unfairly coaching students for the exams. For example, substantial publicity surrounded the test-score tampering controversy in Atlanta that in 2013 resulted in the indictments of thirty-five teachers and administrators, including the former superintendent of the Atlanta Public Schools, Beverly Hall.[65]

Although the state's authority to evaluate student performance has not been questioned, specific high-stakes assessment programs have been legally challenged as impairing students' rights to fair and nondiscriminatory treatment. In a case still widely cited as

---

[63]*See* Hurd v. Hansen, 230 F. App'x 692 (9th Cir. 2007) (holding that a teacher's grading decision did not violate a student's equal protection or substantive due process rights).

[64]20 U.S.C. § 6301 (2012).

[65]*See* Don Campbell, *Lessons from Atlanta School Cheating Scandal*, USA TODAY (Apr. 7, 2013), http://www.usatoday.com/story/opinion/2013/04/07/-atlanta-school-cheating-scandal-column/2044107/. *See also* Buck v. Lowndes Cnty. Sch. Dist., 761 So. 2d 144 (Miss. 2000) (upholding nonrenewal of teachers' contracts for noncompliance with testing procedures that resulted in a reduction in the district's accreditation level).

establishing the legal standards, *Debra P. v. Turlington*, the Fifth Circuit in 1981 recognized that by making schooling mandatory, Florida created a property interest—a valid expectation that students would receive diplomas if they passed required courses.[66] **This state-created property right to an education requires sufficient notice of conditions attached to high school graduation and a fair opportunity to satisfy them before a diploma can be withheld.** The court found that thirteen months was insufficient notice of the test requirement and further held that the state may have administered a fundamentally unfair test covering material that had not been taught in Florida schools. The appeals court also enjoined the state from using the test as a diploma prerequisite for four years to provide time for the vestiges of prior school segregation to be removed and to ensure that all minority students subjected to the requirement started first grade under desegregated conditions. However, the court concluded that continued use of the test to determine remediation needs was constitutionally permissible, noting that the disproportionate placement of minority students in remedial programs per se without evidence of intentional discrimination does not abridge the Equal Protection Clause.

On remand, the district court ruled that the injunction should be lifted, and the appeals court affirmed this decision in 1984.[67] By presenting considerable evidence, including curriculum guides and survey data, the state convinced the judiciary that the test was instructionally valid in that it covered material taught to Florida students. Also, data showed that only students who entered school under desegregated conditions would be subjected to the diploma sanction. Furthermore, there had been significant improvement among African American students during the six years the test was administered.

Other courts have reiterated the principles established in *Debra P.* and have reasoned that despite evidence of higher minority failure rates, such testing and remediation programs are effectively addressing the effects of prior discrimination.[68] Yet courts have not agreed as to whether individual rights are abridged when students are not allowed to participate in graduation exercises because they failed the statewide proficiency examination used as a prerequisite to receipt of a diploma.[69]

A California appeals court rejected a claim that students in an economically challenged community were entitled to diplomas because they had passed all of the required

---

[66]474 F. Supp. 244 (M.D. Fla. 1979), *aff'd in part, vacated in part*, 644 F.2d 397 (5th Cir. 1981).

[67]Debra P. v. Turlington, 564 F. Supp. 177 (M.D. Fla. 1983), *aff'd*, 730 F.2d 1405 (11th Cir. 1984). The Fifth Circuit was divided into the Fifth and Eleventh Circuits while this case was in progress.

[68]*See, e.g.*, GI Forum v. Tex. Educ. Agency, 87 F. Supp. 2d 667 (W.D. Tex. 2000). Courts also have upheld the practice of conditioning grade promotion on test scores. *See, e.g.*, Parents Against Testing Before Teaching v. Orleans Parish Sch. Bd., 273 F.3d 1107 (5th Cir. 2001); Bester v. Tuscaloosa City Bd. of Educ., 722 F.2d 1514 (11th Cir. 1984); Sandlin v. Johnson, 643 F.2d 1027 (4th Cir. 1981). States increasingly are requiring students to pass a reading test in third grade before being promoted to fourth grade; thirteen states adopted such requirements in 2012. *See* Nat'l Sch. Bds. Ass'n, *States Adopting Laws Requiring Third Graders to Pass Reading Test or Face Retention*, LEGAL CLIPS (Mar. 14, 2013), http://legalclips.nsba.org/?p=18686.

[69]*Compare* Williams v. Austin Indep. Sch. Dist., 796 F. Supp. 251 (W.D. Tex. 1992) (holding that the graduation ceremony can be reserved for students meeting all requirements, assuming that appropriate notice and instruction are provided) *with* Crump v. Gilmer Indep. Sch. Dist., 797 F. Supp. 552 (E.D. Tex. 1992) (requiring a Texas school to permit students who failed the exam but satisfied other graduation requirements to take part in the graduation ceremony, even though they will not receive their diplomas until they pass the test).

courses but had not been provided adequate educational resources to pass the state's high school exit examination. The court found use of the test as a diploma sanction integral to the goal of raising academic standards in the state's schools.[70] States and school districts have unsuccessfully asserted that the federal government must provide the funds necessary to devise and administer tests, improve test scores, and train teachers before requiring schools to comply with requirements under the NCLB Act.[71]

Administering proficiency tests to children with limited mastery of English and to children with disabilities has been controversial. After school districts and others challenged California's failure to make appropriate testing accommodations under the NCLB for students with limited English proficiency, the parties reached a settlement under which the U.S. Department of Education changed its classification of schools needing improvement to allow more accommodations for non-English speakers.[72]

Courts in general have ruled that the state does not have to alter its academic standards for students with disabilities; such children can be denied grade promotion or a diploma if they do not meet the specified standards.[73] A child with mental disabilities may be given the option of not taking a proficiency examination if the team planning the individualized education program (IEP) concludes that there is little likelihood of the child mastering the material covered on the test. Children excused from the test requirement usually are awarded certificates of school attendance instead of diplomas. Yet such children cannot be denied the *opportunity* to satisfy requirements (including tests) for promotion or a diploma.

The Seventh Circuit has suggested that children with disabilities may need earlier notice of a proficiency test requirement than other students to ensure an adequate opportunity for the material on the test to be incorporated into their IEPs.[74] Although students with disabilities are entitled to special accommodations in the administration of examinations

[70]O'Connell v. Valenzuela, 47 Cal. Rptr. 3d 147 (Ct. App. 2006) (recognizing that if students receive diplomas without demonstrating mastery of basic skills, they will not be provided the remediation they need to be productive workers and citizens); *see also* Valenzuela v. O'Connell, No. JCCP-4468 (Cal. Super. Ct. Aug. 13, 2007) (approving a settlement agreement that calls for legislation providing two years of academic assistance to students who do not pass the exam).

[71]*See, e.g.*, Connecticut v. Duncan, 612 F.3d 107 (2d Cir. 2010), *cert. denied*, 131 S. Ct. 1471 (2011); Sch. Dist. v. Sec'y of U.S. Dep't of Educ., 584 F.3d 253 (6th Cir. 2009), *cert. denied*, 130 S. Ct. 3385 (2010). The Supreme Court's recent decision in *National Federation of Independent Business v. Sebelius*, 132 S. Ct. 2566 (2012) (holding in part that states cannot be threatened with loss of Medicaid funding if they refuse to expand Medicaid coverage), may encourage challenges to education spending laws, such as the NCLB Act.

[72]Coachella Valley Unified Sch. Dist. v. California, 98 Cal. Rptr. 3d 9 (Ct. App. 2009) (denying a writ of mandamus and declaratory relief where the State Board of Education did not abuse its discretion in developing a testing system).

[73]*See, e.g.*, Brookhart v. Ill. State Bd. of Educ., 697 F.2d 179 (7th Cir. 1983); Anderson v. Banks, 540 F. Supp. 761 (S.D. Ga. 1982); Bd. of Educ. v. Ambach, 457 N.E.2d 775 (N.Y. 1983).

[74]*Brookhart*, 697 F.2d at 187. *But see* Rene v. Reed, 751 N.E.2d 736 (Ind. Ct. App. 2001), *transfer denied*, 774 N.E.2d 506 (Ind. 2002) (reasoning that three years' notice of the test requirement as a prerequisite to a diploma was sufficient for children with disabilities, given ample opportunities to receive remediation and retake the exam). See Chapter 7 for a discussion of federal and state protections of children with disabilities.

FIGURE 4.2   High-Stakes Proficiency Testing Programs

Proficiency tests used as a prerequisite to high school graduation will survive legal challenges if:

- students are advised upon entrance into high school of test requirements as a prerequisite to graduation;
- students have the opportunity to be adequately prepared for the tests;
- tests are not intentionally discriminatory and do not perpetuate the effects of past school segregation;
- students who fail are provided remedial opportunities and the chance to retake the examinations; and
- children with disabilities and English language deficiencies receive appropriate accommodations.

to ensure that their knowledge, rather than their disability, is being assessed (e.g., braille tests), they are not entitled to accommodations that would jeopardize the validity of the graduation test, such as reading to the student a test measuring reading comprehension.[75] The types of accommodations required for graduation tests remain controversial, especially when accommodations that are part of the student's IEP for classroom instruction are denied for high-stakes tests.[76]

Specific proficiency testing programs will likely continue to be challenged on constitutional and statutory grounds. Educators would be wise to keep in mind the points listed in Figure 4.2.

INSTRUCTIONAL PRIVACY RIGHTS

Parents are entitled to review their children's records and instructional materials and to have personal information kept confidential.

The protection of students' privacy rights has become an increasingly volatile issue in political forums. The Supreme Court has recognized that the U.S. Constitution protects a zone of personal privacy, requiring a compelling justification for governmental action that impairs privacy rights, including the right to have personal information kept confidential. A Texas federal district court ruled in 2011 that a student had a substantive due process right to challenge school authorities' disclosure of her sexual orientation to her mother. The court reasoned that the school's action was not taken to protect the student, but to retaliate for alleged rumors the student had started about the high school softball coach.[77]

---

[75]*See Rene*, 751 N.E.2d 736. The Office for Civil Rights in the U.S. Department of Education has reasoned that states can deny use of reading devices to accommodate children with disabilities on graduation exams, even though their IEPs allow use of such devices. *See* Ala. Dep't of Educ., 29 Individuals with Disabilities Educ. L. Rep. (LRP) 249 (1998).

[76]*See* Smiley v. Cal. Dep't of Educ., 53 F. App'x 474 (9th Cir. 2002) (dissolving the parts of the lower court's injunction pertaining to required test waivers and alternative assessments for children with disabilities as not ripe for adjudication).

[77]Wyatt v. Kilgore Indep. Sch. Dist., No. 6:10-cv-674, 2011 WL 6016467 (E.D. Tex. Nov. 30, 2011).

The same year, a parent was unsuccessful in asserting that she had a constitutional right to obtain information about her children from their school.[78] Because her ex-husband had primary physical custody of the children, the Eighth Circuit ruled that the mother had no valid constitutional claim to the requested information.

State and federal laws additionally place dual duties on the government—to protect the public's right to be informed about government activities and to protect the personal privacy of individuals. Often there is a tension between these two legitimate government interests. Laws also have been enacted to protect students from mandatory participation in research projects and instructional activities designed to reveal personal information in sensitive areas. This section provides an overview of legal developments pertaining to students' privacy rights in instructional matters.

Student Records

Due to widespread dissatisfaction with educators' efforts to ameliorate abuses associated with student record-keeping practices, Congress enacted the Family Educational Rights and Privacy Act (FERPA) in 1974.[79] **FERPA stipulates that federal funds may be withdrawn from any education agency or institution that (1) fails to provide parents access to their child's education records or (2) disseminates such information (with some exceptions) to third parties without parental permission.** Upon reaching the age of majority, students may exercise the rights previously guaranteed to their parents.[80] FERPA was amended in 1992 to allow the release of records for purposes of law enforcement, which includes school districts' security units, and again in 1998 to specify that records related to discipline for crimes of violence or sex crimes were excluded from FERPA protection.[81] In 2009, the Department of Education issued changes in FERPA rules stipulating that FERPA can apply to alumni records as well as those of current students, and in 2011, the definition of education programs was broadened to cover any programs primarily involved in the provision of education, including early childhood, elementary and secondary, postsecondary, special education, job training, career and technical, and adult education.[82]

After reviewing a student's permanent file, the parent or eligible student can request amendments to any information thought to be inaccurate, misleading, or in

---

[78]Schmidt v. Des Moines Pub. Schs., 655 F.3d 811 (8th Cir. 2011).

[79]20 U.S.C. § 1232g (2012); 34 C.F.R. §§ 99.1–99.67 (2012). Parents are not entitled to *free* copies of their children's records, but they do have a right to have them interpreted.

[80]The Family Policy Compliance Office was created to investigate alleged FERPA violations. 20 U.S.C. § 1232g(g). For a discussion of FERPA protections, see Student Press Law Ctr., *FERPA and Access to Public Records* (2011), http://www.splc.org/pdf/ferpa_wp.pdf.

[81]*See* 34 C.F.R. § 99.8; U.S. Dep't of Educ., *Addressing Emergencies on Campus* (June 2011), http://www2.ed.gov/policy/gen/guid/fpco/pdf/emergency-guidance.pdf.

[82]*See* 34 C.F.R. §§ 99.3, 99.35; *see also* Souffrance v. Doe, 968 N.E.2d 477 (Ohio 2012) (holding that FERPA precluded releasing records with the identities of students who had used particular school computer terminals during specific times; although the individuals no longer were students, they were students when the records were created and originally maintained).

violation of the student's protected rights. If school authorities decide that an amend-ment is not warranted, the parent or eligible student must be advised of the right to a hear-ing and of the right to place in the file a personal statement specifying objections to the hearing officer's decision. Education officials should assume that a parent is entitled to exercise rights under FERPA unless state law or a court order bars a parent's access to his or her child's records under specific circumstances. Joint custodial parents must be given equal access to education information about their child.

Individuals can file a complaint with the U.S. Department of Education if they believe a school district exhibits a custom or practice of violating FERPA provisions. The remedy for FERPA violations is the withdrawal of federal funds, and the Department of Education has enforcement authority. Some school districts have been advised to remedy their practices to conform to FERPA, but to date, no district has lost federal funds for noncompliance.

The Department of Education functioned without direction from the Supreme Court until 2002 when the Court rendered two FERPA decisions. **In *Gonzaga University v. Doe*, the Court held that individuals cannot bring damages suits for FERPA violations because the law does not create privately enforceable rights; Congress must create such rights in unambiguous terms.**[83] The Supreme Court further ruled that since FERPA contains no rights-creating language, the law cannot be enforced through individual dam-ages suits based on the deprivation of federal rights.[84] The Court reiterated that FERPA has an aggregate rather than individual focus, and the remedy for violations is the denial of fed-eral funds to schools that exhibit a policy or practice of noncompliance. School personnel were relieved that the Court did not authorize private suits for damages to enforce FERPA, because such a ruling would have provided a significant incentive for parents to challenge student record-keeping practices in court.

In the second 2002 Supreme Court ruling, *Owasso Independent School District v. Falvo*, the Court reversed the Tenth Circuit's conclusion that peer grading practices vio-late FERPA.[85] **The Supreme Court concluded that peer graders are not "maintain-ing" student records under FERPA**, and even though students may call out the scores in class, they are not "acting for" the educational institution.[86] There may be educational reasons for not having students grade each others' work, but given the *Falvo* ruling, there is no FERPA barrier.

Under FERPA, education records are files, documents, and other materials that contain information identifying a student and are maintained by the education

---

[83]536 U.S. 273 (2002) (overturning an award of damages to a student for an alleged FERPA violation in connec-tion with a private university's release to the state education department of an unsubstantiated allegation of sexual misconduct, which resulted in the student being denied an affidavit of good moral character required to become a public school teacher).

[84]*Id.* at 285; *see* Civil Rights Act of 1871, § 1 (codified at 42 U.S.C. § 1983 (2012)). For a discussion of damages remedies available under this federal law, see text accompanying note 109, Chapter 12.

[85]233 F.3d 1203 (10th Cir. 2000), *rev'd and remanded*, 534 U.S. 426 (2002), *on remand*, 288 F.3d 1236 (10th Cir. 2002) (granting summary judgment in favor of defendant school district and administrators).

[86]*Owasso*, 534 U.S. at 433. Although peers can call out scores, students' grades cannot be posted or disseminated in any manner that allows individual students to be identified (e.g., by name or listed in alphabetical order).

agency.[87] In 2009, the Department of Education broadened the definition of education records, specifying that schools can deny requests for records even with identifiable information removed if the records could be linked to a particular student by someone in the school community with inside knowledge.[88] Once identifying information is removed (redacted), it ceases to be an education record and may then be subject to disclosure under state open records or freedom-of-information laws.[89] The Tenth Circuit concluded that school personnel could advise the parents of harassment and assault victims regarding how they dealt with the perpetrator; disclosures to parents of victims and to witnesses of the playground assaults did not comprise an education record that would implicate FERPA.[90]

A student's records can be released to school employees authorized to review such information and to officials of a school where the student is transferring if the parents or eligible student are notified or if the sending institution has given prior notice that it routinely transfers such records. Students' records must be disclosed when subpoenaed by a grand jury or law enforcement agency, and schools may disclose information pursuant to other court orders or subpoenas if a reasonable effort is made to notify the parent or eligible student. The Sixth Circuit ruled that records related to substitute teachers' use of corporal punishment must be disclosed in a suit challenging the use of this disciplinary technique because FERPA does not prevent discovery of such records.[91]

Identifiable information also can be disclosed to appropriate authorities or to advocacy groups if necessary to protect the health or safety of the student or others.[92] For example, the Seventh Circuit ruled that the Wisconsin Department of Public Instruction must provide names of students in connection with a state-designated advocacy agency's investigation of alleged abuse or neglect without first obtaining parental consent because the need to investigate suspected abuse or neglect can outweigh privacy interests.[93]

Personal notes pertaining to pupil progress that are kept by educators and shared only with substitute teachers are not considered education records that must be made available to parents. To illustrate, a California federal district court ruled that e-mail messages about students stored on individual teachers' computers were not

---

[87]20 U.S.C. § 1232g(a)(4)(A). According to the Student Press Law Center, *supra* note 80, a document must not simply mention a student, but the information must be *about* the student to be protected by FERPA.

[88]34 C.F.R. § 99.3.

[89]Student Press Law Ctr., *supra* note 80.

[90]Jensen v. Reeves, 3 F. App'x 905 (10th Cir. 2001); *see also* Lindeman v. Kelso Sch. Dist. No. 458, 172 P.3d 329 (Wash. 2007) (holding that a videotape recorded on the school bus for safety reasons was not a record maintained for students, so it did not qualify as exempt from public disclosure under state law).

[91]Ellis v. Cleveland Mun. Sch. Dist., 455 F.3d 690 (6th Cir. 2006); *see also* People v. Owens, 727 N.Y.S.2d 266 (Sup. Ct. 2001) (finding no FERPA violation in prosecution based in part on records subpoenaed from educational institutions).

[92]*See, e.g.*, Disability Law Ctr. v. Anchorage Sch. Dist., 581 F.3d 936 (9th Cir. 2009) (ruling that advocacy organization could have access to personally identifiable information about students with disabilities as part of its investigation of alleged violations of the Developmental Disabilities Assistance and Bill of Rights Act); Doe v. Woodford Cnty. Bd. of Educ., 213 F.3d 921 (6th Cir. 2000) (upholding disclosure to coach of information that student was a hemophiliac and carrier of hepatitis B); 34 C.F.R. § 99.36.

[93]Disability Rights Wis., Inc. v. Wis. Dep't of Pub. Instruction, 463 F.3d 719 (7th Cir. 2006).

education records because they were not maintained by the school.[94] Private notes, however, become education records and are subject to legal specifications once they are shared, even among educators who have a legitimate need for access to such information.

Under FERPA, certain public directory information, such as students' names, addresses, dates and places of birth, major fields of study, e-mail addresses, pictures, and degrees and awards received, can be released without parental consent.[95] Any educational agency releasing such data must give public notice of the specific categories it has designated as "directory" and must allow a reasonable period of time for parents to inform the agency that any or all of this information on their child should not be released without their prior consent. Directory data about a student cannot be released if accompanied by other personally identifiable information unless it is among the specified exceptions to the general rule against nonconsensual disclosure.

Students' privacy rights do not preclude federal and state authorities from having access to data needed to audit and evaluate the effectiveness of publicly supported education programs so long as collected in a way that prevents the disclosure of personally identifiable information. However, FERPA was amended in 2001 in accordance with the provisions of the USA PATRIOT (Uniting and Strengthening America by Providing Appropriate Tools Required to Intercept and Obstruct Terrorism) Act[96] to give institutions permission to disclose, without parental or student consent, personally identifiable information to representatives of the U.S. Attorney General based on an order from a court of competent jurisdiction in connection with investigations of terrorism crimes.[97] A provision of the No Child Left Behind Act also requires public secondary schools to provide military recruiters with access to personal contact information for every student, although parents can request that their children's records be withheld.[98]

Composite information on pupil achievement and discipline can be released to the public so long as individual students are not personally identified. Disciplinary information (number of occurrences and when they occurred without identifiable data) *must* be released to the media under some state open records laws.[99] But personally identifiable data cannot be released under FERPA, and state law may be more restrictive. For example, a Florida appeals court ruled that discipline forms and surveillance video tapes about incidents on school buses could not be disclosed to a television station even with

---

[94]S.A. v. Tulare Cnty. Office of Educ., No. CV F 08-1215 LJO GSA, 2009 WL 3216322 (Sept. 24, 2009); *see also* Easton Area Sch. Dist. v. Baxter, 35 A.3d 1259 (Pa. Commw. Ct. 2012) (holding that personal e-mails of board members and the superintendent that did not document a transaction or school district activity were not records subject to disclosure under the state's right-to-know law, but FERPA does not shield disclosure of the records of district transactions or activities so long as personally identifiable information is redacted).

[95]For a complete list of directory items, see 34 C.F.R. § 99.3. In 2011, the Department of Education clarified that students may be allowed to wear badges or other types of identification at school without abridging FERPA if the IDs cannot be used to access education records without a password or PIN.

[96]18 U.S.C. § 2332b(g)(5)(B) (2012).

[97]20 U.S.C. § 1232g(j) (2012). Schools are required to record such disclosures in students' permanent files.

[98]20 U.S.C. § 1232h(c)(4)(a)(i) (2012).

[99]*See e.g.*, Hardin Cnty. Schs. v. Foster, 40 S.W.3d 865 (Ky. 2001); Bd. of Trs. v. Cut Bank Pioneer Press, 160 P.3d 482 (Mont. 2007)

personally identifying information redacted, because Florida law goes further than FERPA in preventing the release of such information.[100]

FERPA cannot be used by parents to assert a right to review faculty evaluations used to determine which students will be given academic honors, such as membership in the National Honor Society.[101] Also, students cannot rely on FERPA to challenge teachers' grading procedures, other than whether grades were accurately calculated and recorded.[102] The Fourth Circuit ruled that FERPA does not entitle students to see an answer key to exams to check the accuracy of their grades, because the key is not part of students' education records.[103]

Other federal laws provide additional protections regarding the confidentiality and accessibility of student records.[104] Many states also have enacted legislation addressing the maintenance and disclosure of student records. Both state and federal privacy laws recognize certain exceptions to "access and disclosure" provisions, such as a teacher's daily notes discussed previously.

Since Congress, state legislatures, and the judiciary have indicated a continuing interest in safeguarding students' privacy rights in connection with school records, school boards would be wise to reassess their policies to ensure they are adhering to federal and state laws.[105] School personnel should use some restraint, however, before purging information from student files. Pertinent material that is necessary to provide continuity in a student's instructional program *should* be included in a permanent record and be available for use by authorized personnel. It is unfortunate that school personnel, fearing federal sanctions under FERPA, have deleted useful information—along with material that should be removed—from student records. The mere fact that information in a student's file is negative does not imply that the material is inappropriate. Public school officials have a *duty* to record true, factual information about students and to communicate such information to schools where students are transferring, including institutions of higher learning.

---

[100]WFTV v. Sch. Bd., 874 So. 2d 48 (Fla. Dist. Ct. App. 2004); *see also* K.L. v. Evesham Twp. Bd. of Educ., 32 A.3d 1136 (N.J. Super. Ct. App. Div. 2011) (holding that notes prepared by school personnel concerning bullying incidents would not have to be released to the public under the state's open records law; confidentiality concerns were overriding).

[101]*See, e.g.*, Moore v. Hyche, 761 F. Supp. 112 (N.D. Ala. 1991); Price v. Young, 580 F. Supp. 1 (E.D. Ark. 1983); Becky v. Butte-Silver Bow Sch. Dist. 1, 906 P.2d 193 (Mont. 1995).

[102]*See, e.g.*, Tarka v. Cunningham, 917 F.2d 890 (5th Cir. 1990); *see also* Hurd v. Hansen, 230 F. App'x 692 (9th Cir. 2007) (finding no violation of a student's due process and equal protection rights in a teacher's award of a "C" grade to the student).

[103]Lewin v. Cooke, 28 F. App'x 186 (4th Cir. 2002).

[104]*See, e.g.*, Individuals with Disabilities Education Act, 20 U.S.C. § 1415(b)(1) (2012) (protecting the right of parents to examine all school records maintained on their children with disabilities); Children's Online Privacy Protection Act of 1998, 15 U.S.C. § 6501 (2012) (requiring operators of websites that collect or maintain personal information about the website visitors to obtain parental consent before such information is collected on children under thirteen).

[105]*See* L.S. v. Mt. Olive Bd. of Educ., 765 F. Supp. 2d 648 (D.N.J. 2011) (finding a school social worker and special education instructor liable for violating a high school student's federal and state privacy rights by intentionally disclosing to classmates his confidential psychiatric evaluation that was not properly redacted).

Pupil Protection and Parental Rights Laws

Congress and state legislatures have enacted laws to protect family privacy in connection with school research activities and treatment programs. Under federal law, human subjects are protected in research projects supported by federal grants and contracts in any private or public institution or agency.[106] **Informed consent must be obtained before placing subjects at risk of being exposed to physical, psychological, or social injury as a result of participating in research, development, or related activities.** All education agencies are required to establish review committees to ensure that the rights and welfare of all subjects are adequately protected.

Several amendments to the General Education Provisions Act, most notably the 1978 Hatch Amendment, require all instructional materials in federally assisted research or experimentation projects to be made available for inspection by parents of participating students. Under the more recent Protection of Pupil Rights Amendment, parents must be allowed to review in advance all instructional materials in programs administered by the Department of Education, and such **federally assisted programs cannot require students, without prior written parental consent, to be subjected to surveys or evaluations that reveal information pertaining to personal beliefs, behaviors, and family relationships.**[107] The department is charged with reviewing complaints under this law; if an educational institution is found in violation and does not comply within a reasonable period, federal funds can be withheld.

Parents have not been successful in using these provisions to require parental consent for a student to be seen by a school counselor,[108] to challenge use of certain questions in the statewide student assessment program,[109] or to negate surveying elementary students about their attitudes and behaviors so long as the data are reported only in the aggregate.[110] The Ninth Circuit declared that parents do not have a free-standing fundamental right, or a right encompassed by any other fundamental right, to prevent the school from providing elementary school students with important information pertaining to psychological barriers to learning.[111] Proclaiming that "schools cannot be expected to accommodate the personal, moral, or religious concerns of every parent,"[112] the court found the school's psychological survey to be a reasonable way to advance legitimate state interests.

---

[106]42 U.S.C. § 289 (2012); 45 C.F.R. §§ 46.101–46.124 (2012).

[107]20 U.S.C. § 1232h (2012). The sensitive areas pertain to students' or their parents' political affiliations; mental or psychological problems; sexual behavior or attitudes; illegal, antisocial, or demeaning behavior; critical appraisals of family members; legally recognized privileged relationships; religious practices or beliefs; and income. Parents must be notified at least annually of their rights under this law.

[108]Newkirk v. E. Lansing Pub. Schs., No. 91-CV563, 1993 U.S. Dist. LEXIS 13194 (W.D. Mich. Aug. 19, 1993), *aff'd mem.*, 57 F.3d 1070 (6th Cir. 1995).

[109]Triplett v. Livingston Cnty. Bd. of Educ., 967 S.W.2d 25 (Ky. Ct. App. 1997).

[110]C.N. v. Ridgewood Bd. of Educ., 430 F.3d 159 (3d Cir. 2005).

[111]Fields v. Palmdale Sch. Dist., 427 F.3d 1197, 1206 (9th Cir. 2005) (citing Brown v. Hot, Sexy & Safer Prods., 68 F.3d 525, 533–34 (1st Cir. 1995)).

[112]*Fields*, 427 F.3d at 1206.

There is concern among educators that the federal pupil protection requirements and similar provisions being considered or enacted by many states that allow parents to seek alternative assignments for instruction they find offensive will cause certain instructional activities to be dropped. Although these measures are couched in terms of protecting students' privacy rights by granting them *exemptions* from particular instructional activities, if a significant number of exemptions are requested, the instructional activity may be eliminated from the curriculum.

CONCLUSION

Issues pertaining to the public school instructional program will continue to generate legal activity, both legislative mandates and judicial challenges to such requirements. Student testing practices are likely to remain controversial, especially the instruments being designed to assess mastery of the common core standards. The state and its agents enjoy considerable latitude in regulating various aspects of the public school instructional program, but requirements cannot impair students' constitutional rights. School authorities must be able to substantiate that there is an overriding public interest to be served if school policies or practices abridge students' or parents' protected rights.

Although teachers do not have a right to control the public school curriculum, they have some discretion to select relevant instructional strategies that are supported by the profession. Educators always should ensure that their instructional activities match course objectives and that they respect federal copyright requirements and students' privacy rights.

POINTS TO PONDER

1. A school board decided to eliminate several books from the English curriculum, including *The Learning Tree, The Adventures of Huckleberry Finn*, and *The Catcher in the Rye*, because of parental complaints. Several teachers contend that they have a right to use these books in their classes because the books relate to course objectives, and their use is supported by the profession. How would the court rule, and why?

2. A school district has a policy stipulating that students cannot be promoted from third to fourth grade or from seventh to eighth grade until they demonstrate on proficiency tests that they have mastered specified skills. Parents of children who were not promoted at both grade levels based on test passage have brought suit alleging that the use of test scores in this manner violates their children's protected rights. What will the court consider in assessing this claim? Will the parents prevail?

3. Is this notation appropriate for a student's permanent record? If not, how would you change it?

   Sam is an extremely troubled child who comes from a broken home. He is lazy, and his work is spotty. He hangs around with the wrong crowd and always seems to be in trouble. He is bright enough to do the assigned work, but he does not seem to apply himself.

4. A school distributed an anonymous survey asking students about their attitudes and behaviors. The students and their parents were informed that participation was completely voluntary and that no student's responses could be identified, but parents were not asked to give written permission for their children to participate. Parents claimed that the survey violated the federal Protection of Pupil Rights Amendment. How should the court rule?

5. A middle school teacher taped several television movies on the Disney Channel to show to her classes. She has shown the movies the past two semesters. Is this protected as fair use? Is there a copyright violation?

CHAPTER FIVE

STUDENT EXPRESSION, ASSOCIATION, AND APPEARANCE

Students continue to test the limits of their personal freedoms in public schools, frequently colliding with educators' efforts to maintain an appropriate school environment. This chapter addresses students' substantive rights regarding First Amendment freedoms of speech and press and closely related association rights.

FREEDOM OF SPEECH AND PRESS

Students have the right to express nondisruptive ideological views at school, but restrictions can be placed on their expression that represents the school.

The First Amendment, as applied to the states through the Fourteenth Amendment, restricts *governmental* interference with citizens' free expression rights, which are perhaps the most preciously guarded individual liberties. **The government, including public school boards, must have a compelling justification to curtail citizens' expression, even of unpopular viewpoints.**[1] The First Amendment also shields the individual's right to remain silent when confronted with an illegitimate government demand for expression, such as mandatory participation in saluting the American flag in public schools.[2] But free speech guarantees apply only to conduct that constitutes expression. **Where conduct is meant to communicate an idea that is likely to be understood by the intended audience, it is considered expression for First Amendment purposes.**[3]

---

[1]*See, e.g.*, Texas v. Johnson, 491 U.S. 397 (1989) (upholding political protesters' right to burn the American flag). Yet free expression rights can be restricted. As Justice Holmes noted about a century ago, freedom of speech does not allow an individual to yell "fire" in a crowded theater when there is no fire. Schenck v. United States, 249 U.S. 47, 52 (1919).

[2]*See* W. Va. State Bd. of Educ. v. Barnette, 319 U.S. 624 (1943); text accompanying note 91, Chapter 3.

[3]For a discussion of these requirements, see *Johnson*, 491 U.S. at 404. In the school context, see, e.g., *Jarman v. Williams*, 753 F.2d 76 (8th Cir. 1985) (holding that social and recreational dancing in public schools is not expression that enjoys First Amendment protection).

Even if specific conduct qualifies as expression, it is not assured constitutional protection. **The judiciary has recognized that defamatory,[4] obscene,[5] and inflammatory[6] communications are outside the protective arm of the First Amendment.** In addition, as discussed below, lewd and vulgar comments and expression that promote illegal activity for minors are not protected in the public school context. Also, commercial expression, although constitutionally protected, has not been afforded the same level of First Amendment protection as has speech intended to convey a particular point of view.[7]

Where protected expression is at issue, an assessment of the type of forum the government has created for expressive activities has been important in determining whether the expression can be restricted. The Supreme Court has recognized that public places, such as streets and parks, are traditional public forums for assembly and communication where content-based restrictions cannot be imposed unless justified by a compelling government interest.[8] In contrast, expression can be confined to the governmental purpose of the property in a nonpublic forum, such as a public school. **Content-based restrictions are permissible in a nonpublic forum to ensure that expression is compatible with the intended governmental purpose, provided that regulations are reasonable and do not entail viewpoint discrimination.[9]**

The government can create a limited public forum for expression on public property that otherwise would be considered a nonpublic forum and reserved for its governmental function. For example, a student activities program held after school might be established as a limited forum for student expression. A limited forum can be restricted to a certain class of speakers (e.g., students) and/or to specific categories of expression (e.g., noncommercial

---

[4]For a discussion of spoken and written defamation in the school setting, see section entitled "Defamation" in Chapter 2.

[5]The judiciary has held that individuals cannot claim a First Amendment right to voice or publish obscenities, although there is no bright-line rule regarding what expression falls in this category. *See* Miller v. California, 413 U.S. 15, 24 (1973) (identifying the following test to distinguish obscene material from constitutionally protected material: "(a) whether 'the average person, applying contemporary community standards' would find that the work, taken as a whole, appeals to the prurient interests; (b) whether the work depicts or describes, in a patently offensive way, sexual conduct specifically defined by the applicable state law; and (c) whether the work, taken as a whole, lacks serious literary, artistic, political, or scientific value") (citations omitted). The Supreme Court has recognized the government's authority to adjust the definition of obscenity as applied to minors. *See, e.g.,* Ginsberg v. New York, 390 U.S. 629 (1968) (upholding a state law prohibiting the sale to minors of magazines depicting female nudity).

[6]Courts have differentiated fighting words and other expression that agitate, threaten, or incite an immediate breach of peace from speech that conveys ideas and stimulates discussion. *See infra* text accompanying notes 28–37 for a discussion of litigation pertaining to student expression considered inflammatory or threatening.

[7]Bd. of Trs. v. Fox, 492 U.S. 469 (1989). Courts generally have also upheld regulations prohibiting sales and fund-raising activities in public schools as justified to preserve schools for their educational function and to prevent commercial exploitation of students.

[8]Cornelius v. NAACP Legal Def. & Educ. Fund, 473 U.S. 788 (1985); Perry Educ. Ass'n v. Perry Local Educators' Ass'n, 460 U.S. 37 (1983).

[9]*Cornelius*, 473 U.S. at 800. Some speech in public schools, such as that related to the curriculum, is considered government speech that is not subject to First Amendment analysis. *See* Nelda Cambron-McCabe, *When Government Speaks: An Examination of the Evolving Government Speech Doctrine*, 274 EDUC. L. REP. 753–73 (2012).

speech).[10] Otherwise, expression in a limited forum is subject to the same protections that govern a traditional public forum.

Legal Principles

This section reviews the four Supreme Court decisions that have established the legal principles governing student expression rights in public schools. Application of these principles is addressed in subsequent sections.

In 1969, the Supreme Court rendered its landmark decision, *Tinker v. Des Moines Independent School District*, the Magna Carta of students' expression rights.[11] In *Tinker*, three students were suspended from school for wearing black armbands to protest the Vietnam War. Hearing about the planned silent protest, the school principals met and devised a policy forbidding the wearing of armbands at school. Concluding that the students were punished for expression that was not accompanied by any disorder or disturbance, the Supreme Court ruled that "undifferentiated fear or apprehension of disturbance is not enough to overcome the right to freedom of expression."[12]

Tinker standard → In *Tinker*, the Supreme Court echoed statements made in an earlier federal appellate ruling: **A student may express opinions on controversial issues in the classroom, cafeteria, playing field, or any other place, so long as the exercise of such rights does not "materially and substantially interfere with the requirements of appropriate discipline in the operation of the school" or collide with the rights of others.**[13] The Supreme Court emphasized that educators have the authority and duty to maintain discipline in schools, but they must consider students' constitutional rights as they exert control.

Fraser → The Supreme Court did not decide another student expression case until 1986. In a significant opinion, *Bethel School District No. 403 v. Fraser*, the Supreme Court granted school authorities considerable latitude in censoring lewd, vulgar, and indecent student expression. Overturning the lower courts, the Supreme Court upheld disciplinary action against a student for using a sexual metaphor in a nomination speech during a student government assembly.[14] Concluding that the sexual innuendos were offensive to both teachers

---

[10]*See* R.O. *ex rel.* Ochshorn v. Ithaca City Sch. Dist., 645 F.3d 533, 539 (2d Cir. 2011) (noting that in a limited forum, school authorities can restrict speech in a viewpoint-neutral manner that is reasonable in light of the forum's purpose), *cert. denied*, 132 S. Ct. 422 (2011); *infra* text accompanying note 24.

[11]393 U.S. 503 (1969).

[12]*Id.* at 508.

[13]*Id.* at 509 (quoting Burnside v. Byars, 363 F.2d 744, 749 (5th Cir. 1966)). Debate surrounds whether the two prongs of this standard are independent guarantees or linked, in that evidence of a disruption is required for the expression to collide with others' rights. *See* Martha McCarthy, *Curtailing Student Expression: Is a Link to a Disruption Required?* 38 J. Law & Educ. 607–21 (2009).

[14]478 U.S. 675 (1986). Throughout his speech, Fraser employed a sexual metaphor to refer to the candidate, using such phrases as "he's firm in his pants … his character is firm," "a man who takes his point and pounds it in," "he doesn't attack things in spurts—he drives hard, pushing and pushing until finally he succeeds," and "a man who will go to the very end—even the climax, for each and every one of you." *Id.* at 687 (Brennan, J., concurring). Fraser was suspended for two days and disqualified as a candidate for commencement speaker. However, he did eventually deliver a commencement speech, so his claim that the disqualification violated due process rights was not reviewed by the appellate court.

and students, **the Court majority held that the school's legitimate interest in protecting the captive student audience from exposure to lewd and vulgar speech justified the disciplinary action.**

The Court in *Fraser* reiterated that speech protected by the First Amendment for adults is not necessarily protected for children, reasoning that in the public school context, the sensibilities of fellow students must be considered. The majority recognized that an important objective of public schools is the inculcation of fundamental values of civility and that the school board has the authority to determine what manner of speech is appropriate in classes or assemblies.[15]

Only two years after *Fraser*, the Court rendered a seminal decision further limiting, but not overturning, the reach of *Tinker*. In *Hazelwood School District v. Kuhlmeier*, the Court held that **school authorities can censor student expression in school publications and other school-related activities so long as the censorship decisions are based on legitimate pedagogical concerns.**[16] At issue in *Hazelwood* was a high school principal's deletion of two pages from the school newspaper because of the content of articles on divorce and teenage pregnancy and fears that individuals could be identified in the articles.

Rejecting the assertion that the school newspaper had been established as a public forum for student expression, the Court declared that only with school authorities' clear *intent* do school activities become a public forum.[17] The Court drew a distinction between a public school's *toleration* of private student expression, which is constitutionally required under some circumstances, and its *promotion* of student speech that represents the school. Reasoning that student expression appearing to bear the school's imprimatur can be censored, the Court acknowledged school authorities' broad discretion to ensure that such expression occurring in school publications and all school-sponsored activities (including extracurricular) is consistent with educational objectives. The Court's expansive interpretation of what constitutes school-sponsored expression has narrowed the circumstances under which students can prevail in First Amendment claims.

Almost two more decades passed before the Supreme Court rendered its fourth decision pertaining to public school student expression rights. In 2007, the Court in *Morse v. Frederick* held that given the special circumstances in public schools, **students can be disciplined for expression reasonably viewed as promoting or celebrating illegal drug use; incitement to lawless conduct is not required.**[18] *Morse* focused on a banner containing the phrase, "BONG HITS 4 JESUS," which Joseph Frederick and some friends unfurled across the street from their school as the Olympic torch relay passed by. The Supreme Court reasoned that the students were under the school's control when they were allowed to cross the street and watch the torch relay because it was a school-authorized event supervised by school personnel.

[15]*Id.* at 683 (rejecting also the contention that the student had no way of knowing that his expression would evoke disciplinary action; teachers' admonitions that his planned speech was inappropriate and violated a school rule provided adequate warning).

[16]484 U.S. 260 (1988), *on remand*, 840 F.2d 596 (8th Cir. 1988).

[17]*Id.*, 484 U.S. at 267.

[18]551 U.S. 393 (2007).

Reversing the Ninth Circuit, the Supreme Court majority emphasized the importance of deterring drug use by students and concluded that Frederick's action violated the school board's policy of prohibiting expression advocating the use of illegal substances.[19] The Court declared that its earlier *Fraser* decision stands for the proposition that considerations beyond the *Tinker* disruption standard are appropriate in assessing student expression in public schools. However, a majority of the Justices declined to extend school authorities' discretion to the point that they can curtail any student expression they find "plainly offensive" or at odds with the school's "educational mission."[20] All Justices agreed that students can be disciplined for promoting the use of illegal drugs, but they differed regarding whether the banner at issue actually did so.

Lower courts have rendered a range of decisions in applying these legal principles articulated by the Supreme Court. Some of these rulings are reviewed below in connection with school-sponsored expression; threats and other inflammatory expression; prior restraints versus punishment after the fact; anti-harassment and anti-bullying provisions; electronic expression; and time, place, and manner restrictions. For the questions that must be answered in assessing student expression rights, see Figure 5.1.

School-Sponsored Expression

During the 1970s and early 1980s, many courts broadly interpreted the circumstances under which limited forums for student expression were created in public schools. School-sponsored newspapers often were considered such a forum, and accordingly, courts held that articles on controversial subjects such as the Vietnam War, abortion, and birth control could not be barred from these publications, placing the burden on school authorities to justify prior administrative review of both school-sponsored and nonsponsored literature.

However, since *Hazelwood,* expression appearing to bear the school's imprimatur can be censored for pedagogical reasons. The *Tinker* standard applies *only* to protected *private* expression, and some lower courts have broadly interpreted student expression that might be perceived as representing the school.[21] Relying on *Hazelwood*, the Ninth Circuit rejected Planned Parenthood's claim that a school district's denial of its request to advertise in school newspapers, yearbooks, and programs for athletic events violated free speech

---

[19]*Id.* All of the Justices concurred that the principal should not be held liable for violating clearly established law, and Justice Breyer thought the decision should have focused only on this issue. *See id.* at 425–33 (Breyer, J., concurring in part and dissenting in part).

[20]*See Morse*, 551 U.S. at 423. Justices Alito and Kennedy emphasized that this decision is restricted to the promotion of illegal drug use and does not extend to censorship of expression on social or political issues that may be viewed as inconsistent with the school's mission. *Id.* at 422 (Alito, J., joined by Kennedy, J., concurring).

[21]In response to *Hazelwood*, a number of state legislatures considered, and several enacted, laws granting student editors of school-sponsored papers specific rights in determining the content of their publications. As of 2012, ten states (Arkansas, California, Colorado, Illinois, Iowa, Kansas, Oregon, Massachusetts, Pennsylvania, and Washington) had laws or state board of education regulations in this regard. *See* Student Press Law Ctr., *State Legislation* (Mar. 2012), http://www.splc.org/knowyourrights/statelegislation.asp.

FIGURE 5.1   Assessing Student Expression Rights

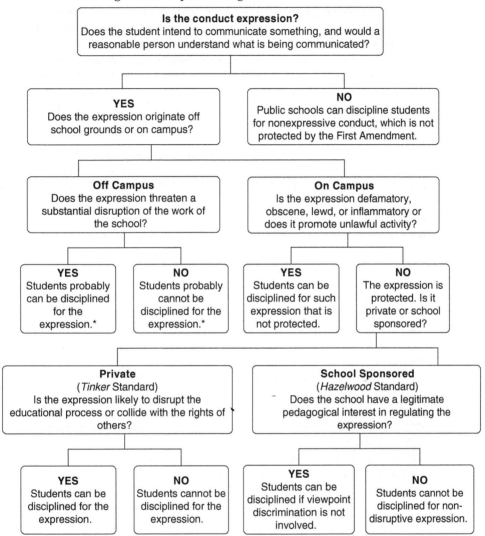

*The Supreme Court has not clarified whether standards beyond *Tinker's* disruption standard apply to off-campus student expression.

rights, concluding that the school district could bar advertisements inconsistent with its educational mission.[22] The Eighth Circuit similarly relied on *Hazelwood* in upholding a principal's decision to disqualify a student council candidate who handed out condoms with stickers bearing his campaign slogan ("Adam Henerey, the Safe Choice"), noting that *Hazelwood* grants school authorities considerable discretion to control student expression

[22]Planned Parenthood v. Clark Cnty. Sch. Dist., 887 F.2d 935, 942 (9th Cir. 1989), *rehearing en banc*, 941 F.2d 817 (9th Cir. 1991).

in school-sponsored activities.[23] More recently, the Second Circuit applied *Hazelwood* in ruling that school authorities were justified in prohibiting students from running a lewd, sexually explicit cartoon in the school-sponsored paper, as the decision was reasonably related to legitimate pedagogical concerns. Even though students wrote the paper's content, its operation was supervised by the faculty advisor, so the paper was not considered a limited forum for student expression.[24]

Courts have reasoned that the school has the right to disassociate itself from controversial expression that conflicts with its mission and have considered school-sponsored activities to include student newspapers supported by the public school, extracurricular activities sponsored by the school, school assemblies, and classroom activities. **The key consideration is whether the expression is viewed as bearing the school's imprimatur; only under such circumstances is *Hazelwood*'s broad deference to school authorities triggered.**

Ironically, since *Hazelwood*, student expression in underground (not school-sponsored) student papers distributed at school enjoys greater constitutional protection than does expression in school-sponsored publications. The former is considered private expression governed by the *Tinker* principle, whereas the latter represents the school and is subject to censorship under *Hazelwood*. As discussed in Chapter 3, most courts have treated the distribution of religious literature by secondary students like the distribution of other material that is not sponsored by the school.

There are limits, however, on school authorities' wide latitude to censor student expression that bears the public school's imprimatur. For example, **blatant viewpoint discrimination in a nonpublic forum abridges the First Amendment.**[25] And even if viewpoint discrimination is not involved, censorship actions in a nonpublic forum still must be based on legitimate pedagogical concerns. A Michigan federal district court found no legitimate pedagogical reason to remove from the school newspaper a student's article on a pending lawsuit alleging that school bus diesel fumes constituted a neighborhood nuisance.[26]

Furthermore, a school-sponsored publication might be considered a forum for student expression under certain circumstances. In a Massachusetts case, school authorities had given students editorial control of school publications, so independent decisions of the students could not be attributed to school officials. In this situation, the student editors of the school newspaper and yearbook rejected advertisements from a parent who was a leading opponent of the district's condom-distribution policy. The First Circuit concluded that school officials, who had recommended that the students publish the ads, could not be held liable for the students' decisions because the student editors were not state actors.[27]

---

[23]Henerey v. City of St. Charles Sch. Dist., 200 F.3d 1128 (8th Cir. 1999).

[24]R.O. *ex rel.* Ochshorn v. Ithaca City Sch. Dist., 645 F.3d 533 (2d Cir. 2011) (holding also that school authorities could bar distribution on campus of an independent student publication with the same cartoon, which was considered lewd and vulgar and thus not protected), *cert. denied*, 132 S. Ct. 422 (2011).

[25]*See, e.g.*, Searcey v. Harris, 888 F.2d 1314 (11th Cir. 1989) (placing the burden on school authorities to justify viewpoint discrimination against a peace activist group that was not allowed to display its literature on school premises or participate in career day when military recruiters were allowed such access).

[26]Dean v. Utica Cmty. Schs., 345 F. Supp. 2d 799 (E.D. Mich. 2004) (ruling that the censorship was based on the superintendent's disagreement with the views expressed about the lawsuit against the school district).

[27]Yeo v. Town of Lexington, 131 F.3d 241 (1st Cir. 1997).

Threats and Other Inflammatory Expression

The U.S. Supreme Court has not addressed the application of the First Amendment to alleged threats made by students toward classmates or school personnel, but there is a growing body of lower court litigation. In determining if a true threat has been made, courts consider a number of factors, such as:

- reactions of the recipient and other listeners;
- whether the maker of the alleged threat had made similar statements to the victim in the past;
- if the utterance was conditional and communicated directly to the victim; and
- whether the victim had reason to believe that the speaker would engage in violence.[28]

In an illustrative case, the Fifth Circuit held that a student's notebook, outlining a pseudo-Nazi group's plan to commit a "Columbine shooting," constituted a "terroristic threat" that was not protected by the First Amendment.[29] The Eleventh Circuit similarly ruled that a student's story about shooting her math teacher was a threat of violence; her suspension was justified because she shared the story with another student.[30] Citing *Morse,* the court reasoned that disciplining students for threats of violence is even more important than curtailing their promotion of illegal drug use.[31]

Also finding a threat, the Eighth Circuit reversed the lower court and upheld expulsion of a student for writing a letter indicating he was going to rape and murder his former girl-friend. The court was convinced that the writer intended to communicate the threat because he shared the letter with a friend whom he assumed would give it to his former girlfriend.[32] In 2011, the same court found a true threat in a student's online instant message sent from home to a classmate in which he mentioned getting a gun and shooting other students at school.[33] The serious statements were communicated to a third party, and combined with the speaker's admitted depression and access to weapons, the appeals court reasoned that school authorities did not need to wait until the threat was carried out before taking action.

Utterances can be considered inflammatory, and thus unprotected, even if *not* found to be true threats or fighting words. The Ninth Circuit ruled that a student could be subject to emergency expulsion, with a hearing occurring afterward, for writing a poem about someone who had committed multiple murders in the past and decided to kill himself for fear of murdering others.[34] The poem was not considered a true threat or to contain fighting words. The Wisconsin Supreme Court similarly held that school authorities had more

---

[28]United States v. Dinwiddie, 76 F.3d 913 (8th Cir. 1996).

[29]Ponce v. Socorro Indep. Sch. Dist., 508 F.3d 765, 767 (5th Cir. 2007).

[30]Boim v. Fulton Cnty. Sch. Dist., 494 F.3d 978 (11th Cir. 2007).

[31]*Id.* at 984 (citing Morse v. Frederick, 551 U.S. 393 (2007)).

[32]Doe v. Pulaski Cnty. Special Sch. Dist., 306 F.3d 616 (8th Cir. 2002).

[33]D.J.M. v. Hannibal Pub. Sch. Dist. # 60, 647 F.3d 754 (8th Cir. 2011).

[34]LaVine v. Blaine Sch. Dist., 257 F.3d 981 (9th Cir. 2001) (holding, however, that the placement and maintenance of negative documentation in the student's file after he was readmitted to school and the concern about harm had subsided went beyond the district's documentation needs).

than enough reason to suspend a student for his creative writing assignment, describing a student removed from class for being disruptive (as he had been) who returned the next day to behead his teacher.[35] But the court found no true threat that would justify prosecution of the student for disorderly conduct.

The Second Circuit in 2011 ruled in favor of school authorities who detained a middle school student to determine if he posed a danger to himself or others and reported his parents to Child and Family Services for possible neglect in connection with an essay he wrote that included discussion of illegal acts, violence, and his own suicide. The court reasoned that school authorities did not violate the student's expression rights or his parents' substantive due process rights by taking precautionary actions.[36] The following year, the same court ruled that school authorities reasonably could forecast a disruption from an elementary school student's picture expressing a desire to blow up the school and its teachers.[37] Upholding the student's six-day suspension, the appeals court reasoned that the student's actual intent and capacity to carry out the threat were irrelevant. **Courts generally seem more inclined to uphold school disciplinary action, in contrast to criminal prosecution, for students' alleged threats or other inflammatory expression.**

Prior Restraints versus Punishment After the Fact

When determined that protected private expression is at issue, courts then are faced with the difficult task of assessing whether restrictions are justified. Under the *Tinker* principle, private expression can be curtailed if it is likely to disrupt the educational process or intrude on the rights of others. For example, bans on wearing buttons at school have been upheld where linked to an interference with the educational process.[38]

The imposition of **prior restraints on student speech must bear a substantial relationship to an important government interest, and any regulation must contain narrow, objective, and unambiguous criteria for determining what material is prohibited and procedures that allow a speedy determination of whether materials meet those criteria.** Recognizing that the Constitution requires a high degree of specificity when imposing restraints on private expression, the Ninth Circuit held that school authorities in a Washington school district could not suspend students for distributing a student paper produced off campus and could not subject the paper's content to prior review under a policy

---

[35]*In re* Douglas D., 626 N.W.2d 725 (Wis. 2001); *see also* S.G. v. Sayreville Bd. of Educ., 333 F.3d 417 (3d Cir. 2003) (upholding suspension of a kindergarten student for saying, "I'm going to shoot you," during a game at recess, which violated the school's prohibition on speech threatening violence and the use of firearms); Wynar v. Douglas Cnty. Sch. Dist., No. 3:09-cv-0626-LRH-VPC, 2011 WL 3512534 (D. Nev. Aug. 10, 2011) (upholding a student's ninety-day expulsion for sending instant messages with assertions that he would do bodily harm toward other students; school personnel could reasonably expect a substantial disruption).

[36]Cox v. Warwick Valley Cent. Sch. Dist., 654 F.3d 267 (2d Cir. 2011) (noting that the student had a history of misbehavior and was on probation and under a behavior contract when the essay was written).

[37]Cuff v. Valley Cent. Sch. Dist., 677 F.3d 109 (2d Cir. 2012).

[38]*See, e.g.*, Guzick v. Drebus, 431 F.2d 594 (6th Cir. 1970) (upholding ban on button soliciting participation in antiwar demonstration); Blackwell v. Issaquena Cnty. Bd. of Educ., 363 F.2d 749 (5th Cir. 1966) (upholding prohibition on students wearing freedom buttons that distracted classmates and disrupted instruction).

that was overbroad.[39] But more recently, the Tenth Circuit endorsed a policy requiring prior approval of all materials distributed at school and upheld administrators in halting an anti-abortion student group's distribution of rubber doll fetuses.[40]

The burden is on school authorities to justify policies requiring administrative approval of unofficial (underground) student publications, but such prior review is not unconstitutional per se. Of course, courts are more inclined to support disciplinary action and confiscation of materials *after* the expression has occurred, if it is considered unprotected (i.e., comments that are libelous, inflammatory, vulgar, or promote illegal activity), threatens a disruption of the educational process, interferes with the rights of others, or represents the school. To illustrate, students can be disciplined after the fact for expression advocating the destruction of school property in publications they distribute at school, even though the anticipated destruction of school property never materializes.[41] Also, the Second Circuit upheld school authorities in sending a student home for allegedly making a racial slur and in denying the student's request to return to school to explain his version of events to classmates, given the significant threat of a disruption. In light of the racial tensions created by the situation and concern for the student's safety, his expulsion for the remainder of the school year was considered reasonable.[42]

Sometimes state law has a bearing on whether students can be disciplined after the fact for their expression. **States can be more protective of students' expression rights, but they cannot drop below federal constitutional minimums.** A California appeals court ruled that a school district violated a student's expression rights when it refused to publish his caustic editorial about immigration. The appeals court held that the expression was not prohibited under the state law that bars student speech inciting others or creating a clear and present danger of disrupting the schools. Noting that the article was politically charged because it suggested that individuals who do not speak English are illegal immigrants and likely to turn to crime, the court did not find the speech so inflammatory that it would incite a disturbance, even though opponents of the expression might cause a disruption.[43]

Courts have condoned disciplinary action against students who have engaged in walkouts, boycotts, sit-ins, or other protests involving conduct that blocks hallways, damages property, causes students to miss class, or interferes with essential school activities in other ways. The Sixth Circuit held that a petition circulated by four football players, denouncing the head coach, justified their dismissal from the varsity football team. The court reasoned that the petition disrupted the team, and athletes are subject to greater restrictions than are applied to the general student body.[44] The Ninth Circuit also ruled

---

[39]Burch v. Barker, 861 F.2d 1149, 1155 (9th Cir. 1988).

[40]Taylor v. Roswell Indep. Sch. Dist., 713 F.3d 25 (10th Cir. 2013).

[41]*See, e.g.*, Boucher v. Sch. Bd., 134 F.3d 821, 828 (7th Cir. 1997) (upholding expulsion of a student for distributing at school an article that contained information about how to disable the school's computer system).

[42]DeFabio v. E. Hampton Union Free Sch. Dist., 623 F.3d 71 (2d. Cir. 2010), *cert. denied*, 131 S. Ct. 1578 (2011).

[43]Smith v. Novato Unified Sch. Dist., 59 Cal. Rptr. 3d 508 (Ct. App. 2007); see *infra* text accompanying note 60 for a discussion of the "hecklers' veto."

[44]Lowery v. Euverard, 497 F.3d 584 (6th Cir. 2007); *see also* Corales v. Bennett, 567 F.3d 554 (9th Cir. 2009) (holding that students could be disciplined for leaving school to engage in a political protest).

that student athletes could be disciplined for protesting actions of the coach by refusing to board the team bus and to play in a basketball game, which substantially disrupted a school activity.[45] However, this court departed from the Sixth Circuit in finding that the students' petition requesting that the coach resign because of derogatory remarks he made toward players was protected speech.

Anti-Harassment and Anti-Bullying Policies

A number of school districts have adopted policies prohibiting expression that constitutes verbal or physical harassment based on race, religion, color, national origin, sex, sexual orientation, disability, or other personal characteristics. Also, forty-nine states and the District of Columbia have anti-bullying provisions that often share similar language with anti-harassment policies.[46] In some of these provisions, the terms "harassment" and "bullying" are used interchangeably, even though "harassment" is associated with specific legal liability under federal civil rights laws that do not apply to bullying.[47]

The public school policies prohibiting bullying and harassment traditionally have not appeared vulnerable to First Amendment challenges, whereas "hate speech" policies have been struck down in municipalities and public higher education. Public schools have been considered a special environment in terms of government restrictions on private expression because of their purpose in educating America's youth and inculcating basic values, such as civility and respect for others with different backgrounds and beliefs.

A growing body of cases interpreting anti-harassment provisions has focused on students displaying Confederate flags, and some courts have upheld restrictions on such displays. In a typical case, the Sixth Circuit in 2010 upheld a student's suspension for wearing clothing depicting the Confederate flag in violation of the school's dress code. The court held that school officials reasonably could forecast a substantial disruption from such displays but noted that a link to a disruption was not required to curtail displays that

---

[45]Pinard v. Clatskanie Sch. Dist. 6J, 467 F.3d 755 (9th Cir. 2006) (remanding the case for a determination of whether the students were impermissibly removed from the basketball team in retaliation for their petition).

[46]As of this writing, Montana is the only state that does not have a law prohibiting bullying, though legislation has been proposed. All but two of the laws prohibit electronic harassment, and sixteen specifically address cyberbullying, *See* Cyberbullying Research Ctr. (Feb. 2013), http://www.cyberbullying.us/cyberbullying-laws. New Jersey's Anti-Bullying Bill of Rights, enacted in 2011, is among the most comprehensive laws in prohibiting bullying, harassment, or intimidation that disrupts the school or interferes with the rights of others. Under the law, each school district must have an anti-bullying specialist, complaints must be investigated within ten days, schools are graded on how they handle such complaints, and school principals can be disciplined for failure to comply with this law. N.J. STAT. ANN. § 18A:37-13 (West 2012).

[47]According to an initiative sponsored by the federal government, peer bullying is a major concern nationally because victims can become depressed, fearful of being at school, and can contemplate suicide. *See* U.S. Dep't of Health & Human Servs., *Who Is at Risk?* (Feb. 2012), http://www.StopBullying.gov. A coalition of religious and educational organizations issued a pamphlet in 2012 to assist school personnel in balancing free expression and school safety concerns. Am. Jewish Comm., *Harassment, Bullying and Free Expression: Guidelines for Free and Safe Public Schools* (Washington, D.C. 2012).

convey racial hostility.[48] The same court previously upheld a school district's ban on students displaying the Confederate flag, again finding the potential for a school disturbance but acknowledging that school authorities could ban this symbol *without* having to forecast a school disruption.[49] The Tenth Circuit also upheld disciplinary action against a Kansas middle school student for drawing a Confederate flag during math class in violation of the school district's anti-harassment policy.[50] The court was persuaded that the school district had reason to believe that the display of the Confederate flag might cause a disruption and interfere with the rights of others because the school district had already experienced some racial incidents related to the Confederate flag.

A few courts, however, have struck down such restrictions on Confederate flag displays. These courts have reasoned that students should prevail in the absence of a link to disruption[51] or if the policies were applied inconsistently. For example, the Sixth Circuit found no evidence that a shirt with a country singer on the front and the Confederate flag on the back, worn to express Southern heritage, would cause a disruption and furthermore questioned whether there may have been viewpoint discrimination in applying the school's prohibition on emblems with racial implications.[52]

Several cases have focused on the conflict between expressing religious views and promoting civil expression; these cases are particularly sensitive because they pit free speech and free exercise guarantees against the school's authority to instill basic values, including respect for others. The Third Circuit struck down a Pennsylvania school district's anti-harassment policy challenged by plaintiffs who feared reprisals for voicing their religious views about moral issues, including the harmful effects of homosexuality.[53] The court found no evidence that the policy was necessary to advance the recognized compelling government interests in maintaining an orderly school and protecting the rights of others. Concluding that the policy was unconstitutionally overbroad, the court reasoned that the policy went beyond expression that could be curtailed under the *Tinker* disruption standard.

Yet most other anti-harassment or anti-bullying policies have not been struck down, even if the students have prevailed on their free speech claims. To illustrate, a year after the Third Circuit decision discussed above, the same court upheld a school district's

---

[48]Defoe v. Spiva, 625 F.3d 324 (6th Cir. 2010), *rehearing denied en banc*, 674 F.3d 505 (6th Cir. 2011), *cert. denied*, 132 U.S. 399 (2011). See also Martha McCarthy, Nelda Cambron-McCabe & Suzanne Eckes, Public School Law: Teachers' and Students' Rights ch 4 (Upper Saddle River, N.J.: Pearson, 2014) for a discussion of additional cases involving Confederate flag displays.

[49]Barr v. Lafon, 538 F.3d 554 (6th Cir. 2008).

[50]West v. Derby Unified Sch. Dist., 206 F.3d 1358 (10th Cir. 2000) (noting that the student had been disciplined numerous times and accused of using racial slurs).

[51]*See, e.g.*, Bragg v. Swanson, 371 F. Supp. 2d 814 (S.D. W. Va. 2005) (overturning disciplinary action against a student for wearing a T-shirt displaying the Confederate flag in observance of his Southern heritage; finding overbroad the policy that prohibited displays of the Rebel flag within the category of racist symbols).

[52]Castorina *ex rel.* Rewt v. Madison Cnty. Sch. Bd., 246 F.3d 536 (6th Cir. 2001); *infra* text accompanying note 92.

[53]Saxe v. State Coll. Area Sch. Dist., 240 F.3d 200 (3d Cir. 2001).

anti-harassment policy enacted to respond to incidents of race-based conflicts and narrowly designed to reduce racially divisive expression. Although finding that the policy as applied violated the students' expression rights in this case, the court voiced approval of the school's anti-harassment provision.[54]

The Ninth Circuit found the second prong of the *Tinker* standard to be controlling when it ruled that a student wearing a T-shirt degrading homosexuality "'collides with the rights of other students' in the most fundamental way."[55] The court reasoned that the school is allowed to prohibit such expression, regardless of the adoption of a valid anti-harassment policy, so long as it can show that the restriction is necessary to prevent the violation of other students' rights *or* a substantial disruption of school activities. **The court disagreed with the suggestion that injurious slurs interfering with the rights of others cannot be barred unless they *also* are disruptive, reasoning that the two *Tinker* prongs are independent restrictions.**[56]

But other courts have applied the *Tinker* disruption standard in ruling that students have a right to express their religious views that denounce homosexuality.[57] The Seventh Circuit found a T-shirt with "Be Happy, Not Gay" to be much less offensive than the expression in the Ninth Circuit case above and not linked to a substantial disruption.[58] Thus, the court ruled that school authorities could not bar students from wearing the shirt because "people in our society do not have a legal right to prevent criticism of their beliefs or for that matter their way of life," reasoning that in the absence of fighting words, schools cannot impair students' free expression rights based on their targets' "hurt feelings."[59] **The court recognized that the expression could not be curtailed based on the hecklers' veto, or those opposing the expression could always stifle speakers simply by mounting a riot.**[60] Yet the court did not enjoin enforcement of the school's rule that prohibited students from making derogatory comments referring to race, ethnicity, religion, gender, sexual orientation, or disability. Since the Supreme Court has not rendered an opinion in these sensitive cases, the collision of religious views and anti-harassment policies seems destined to remain controversial.

[54]Sypniewski v. Warren Hills Reg'l Bd. of Educ., 307 F.3d 243 (3d Cir. 2002) (upholding the policy but ordering the phrase banning speech that "creates ill will" to be eliminated as reaching some protected expression). See *infra* text accompanying note 90 for a discussion of the application of the policy.

[55]Harper v. Poway Unified Sch. Dist., 445 F.3d 1166, 1178 (9th Cir. 2006) (quoting Tinker v. Des Moines Indep. Sch. Dist., 393 U.S. 503, 508 (1969)), *cert. granted, judgment vacated, and case remanded to dismiss as moot*, 549 U.S. 1262 (2007).

[56]*Harper*, 445 F.3d at 1180; *see also* Kowalski v. Berkeley Cnty. Schs., 652 F.3d 565 (4th Cir. 2011), *cert. denied*, 132 S. Ct. 1095 (2012), *infra* text accompanying note 67.

[57]*See, e.g.*, Nixon v. N. Local Sch. Dist., 383 F. Supp. 2d 965, 971–74 (S.D. Ohio 2005) (rejecting school administrators' assertion that a shirt denigrating homosexuality, Islam, and abortion was "plainly offensive" under *Fraser*; applying *Tinker* instead and finding no disruption or evidence that the expression interfered with the rights of others).

[58]Zamecnik v. Sch. Dist. #204, 636 F.3d 874 (7th Cir. 2011).

[59]*Id.* at 876.

[60]*Id.* at 877.

Electronic Expression

The most volatile current disputes involve Internet expression, particularly pertaining to social networks. These cases are particularly troublesome because students often prepare and disseminate the materials from their homes, but their expression is immediately available to the entire school population and beyond. Although the judiciary has not spoken with a single voice on the First Amendment issues raised in these cases, most courts have applied the *Tinker* disruption standard in assessing Internet expression.[61] With the increasing use of cellular phones and the amount of material posted on Facebook, Myspace, and other social networking sites, legal activity in this arena is bound to increase. A 2011 report indicated that teens on average sent more than 100 text messages per day.[62] And concerns over students sending sexually explicit or suggestive messages electronically are resulting in legislative responses to curtail such "sexting."[63]

Students have prevailed in several challenges to disciplinary actions for the creation of web pages or postings on social networks that have originated from their homes. For example, the full Third Circuit in 2011 rendered decisions favoring students' expression rights in two cases that had generated conflicting decisions by different Third Circuit panels.[64] At issue were mock Myspace profiles of the school principals that were vulgar and linked the principals to drugs, alcohol, sexual abuse, and other degrading activities. **Finding no disruption of the educational process, the appeals court required off-campus expression to be linked to a school disruption to justify disciplinary action.** However, the school policies requiring students to express their ideas in a respectful manner and to refrain from verbal abuse were not found to be overbroad.

Not all courts have agreed with the Third Circuit's stand that a link to a disruption is required for students' off-campus Internet expression to be curtailed. The Second Circuit ruled in favor of school authorities who prevented a student from running for senior class

---

[61]393 U.S. 503, 508 (1969); *supra* text accompanying note 13.

[62]Digital Media & Learning Research Hub, *An Analytical Take on Youth, Social Networking, and Web 2.0: A Few Moments with Amanda Lenhart* (May 2012), http://dmlcentral.net/newsletter/05/2012/analytical-take-youth-social-networking-and-web-20-few-moments-amanda-lenhart.

[63]The National Conference of State Legislatures (NCSL) reported in 2011 that twenty-one states had introduced legislation on sexting, with fourteen requiring youth offenders to register as sex offenders. *See* NCSL, *2011 Legislation Related to "Sexting": 2011 Year-End Summary* (Jan. 23, 2012), http://www.ncsl.org/default.aspx?tabid=22127. *But see* T.V. v. Smith-Green Cmty. Sch. Corp., 807 F. Supp. 2d 767 (N.D. Ind. 2011) (invalidating suspension from extracurricular activities of students who took sexually suggestive pictures of themselves at a slumber party and posted them on the Internet; reasoning that the photos did not constitute child pornography under state law or pose a threat of a school disruption).

[64]Layshock v. Hermitage Sch. Dist., 650 F.3d 205 (3d Cir. 2011), *cert. denied sub nom.* J.S. *ex. rel.* Snyder v. Blue Mountain Sch. Dist., 132 S. Ct 1097 (2012); J.S. *ex. rel.* Snyder v. Blue Mountain Sch. Dist., 650 F.3d 915 (3d Cir. 2011), *cert. denied*, 132 S. Ct. 1097 (2012); *see also* J.C. v. Beverly Hills Unified Sch. Dist., 711 F. Supp. 2d 1094 (C.D. Cal. 2010) (finding a violation of a student's free speech rights in disciplinary action imposed for posting a YouTube video that was disparaging toward a classmate because there was not a sufficient link to a school disruption); R.S. v. Minnewaska Area Sch. Dist., 894 F. Supp. 2d 1128 (D. Minn. 2012) (finding a valid claim that school officials violated a middle school student's free speech rights by disciplining her for Facebook posts critical of a school employee and whoever alerted authorities; Fourth Amendment rights were also implicated by school personnel's search of her Facebook posts against her will).

secretary because of a vulgar blog entry she posted from home that urged others to complain to the school administrators about a change in scheduling an event, Jamfest, an annual battle of the bands concert.[65] The court reasoned that school officials reasonably could conclude that the expression might disrupt student government functions. Also at issue were T-shirts supporting her freedom of speech that students planned to wear to the school assembly where candidates for the class offices were to give their speeches. **Acknowledging that the shirts might be protected under *Tinker* if not linked to a disruption, the court held that the school defendants were entitled to qualified immunity on this claim as well because the rights at issue were not clearly established.**

In 2011, the Fourth Circuit upheld West Virginia school authorities in suspending a student for creating a website primarily used to ridicule a classmate with accusations that she was a slut with herpes. The disciplined student alleged that the suspension violated her free speech rights because the expression was private speech initiated from her home. But the court sided with the school administrators who reasoned that the student had created a "hate website" in violation of the school's policy forbidding "harassment, bullying, and intimidation."[66] The court concluded that the student's website "materially and substantially interferes with the requirements of appropriate discipline in the operation of the school and collides with the rights of others," seeming to rely on both prongs of the *Tinker* standard.[67] The court emphasized that conduct does not have to physically originate in the school building or during the school day to adversely affect the learning environment and the rights of others.

In 2012, the Eighth Circuit also sided with school authorities in declaring that the lower court should not have enjoined the suspension of students for creating a racist and sexist website and blog.[68] Finding the students' punishment appropriate for producing a disruptive website, the court did not address whether the website also collided with the rights of others.

In these cases, **the key determinant of disciplinary action appears to be whether the material created off campus has a direct and detrimental impact on the school.** But since the Supreme Court has refused to review appeals of these decisions, and federal

---

[65]Doninger v. Niehoff, 642 F.3d 334 (2d Cir. 2011); *see also* Wisniewski v. Bd. of Educ., 494 F.3d 34 (2d Cir. 2007) (upholding a semester expulsion of a student for displaying in his instant messaging buddy icon a drawing of a pistol firing at a person's head, with the caption "Kill Mr. VenderMolen," his English teacher); Bell v. Itawamba Cnty. Sch. Bd., 859 F. Supp. 2d 834 (N.D. Miss. 2012) (endorsing disciplinary action against a student for the Internet posting of a vulgar rap song that accused two school coaches of improper contact with female students). *But see* TC v. Valley Cent. Sch. Dist., 777 F. Supp. 2d 577 (S.D.N.Y. 2011) (finding a violation of free speech rights, in addition to racial discrimination, in the suspension of a student who possessed a rap song with offensive lyrics because there was no evidence that the lyrics created a distraction).

[66]Kowalski v. Berkeley Cnty. Schs., 652 F.3d 565, 574 (4th Cir. 2011), *cert. denied*, 132 S. Ct. 1095 (2012). The student originally was suspended for ten days, which was reduced to five days, and she received a ninety-day social suspension from school-related activities.

[67]*Id.* at 572 (quoting Tinker v. Des Moines Indep. Sch. Dist., 393 U.S. 503, 513 (1969)). The Fourth Circuit reasoned that expression interfering with another's rights *creates* the necessary disruption to trigger *Tinker*'s exclusion from constitutional protection.

[68]S.J.W. *ex rel.* Wilson v. Lee's Summit R-7 Sch. Dist., 696 F.3d 771 (8th Cir. 2012).

appellate courts have rendered a range of opinions, school personnel have insufficient guidance as to the application of the First Amendment to electronic expression that originates off school grounds. Given students' preference to communicate electronically and the growing popularity of social networking sites, texting, and blogs, Supreme Court clarification of the First Amendment standard is sorely needed.

The National School Boards Association (NSBA), joined by several other professional education organizations, has argued that the Internet has blurred the line between off-campus and in-school expression. The NSBA has contended that if the expression pertains to members of the school community, it should be considered in-school speech and subject to sanctions, regardless of its origin.[69] In the absence of a Supreme Court ruling, the only consolation for school authorities is that they likely can claim immunity for disciplining students for their electronic expression because the law on this topic is far from clearly established.

Time, Place, and Manner Regulations

Although private expression enjoys greater constitutional protection than does school-sponsored expression, the judiciary consistently has upheld reasonable policies regulating the time, place, and manner of private expression. For example, students can be prohibited from voicing political and ideological views and distributing literature during instructional time. Additionally, to ensure that the distribution of student publications does not impinge upon other school activities, school authorities can ban literature distribution near the doors of classrooms while class is in session, near building exits during fire drills, and on stairways when classes are changing. The Fifth Circuit reasoned that student literature distribution could be prohibited in the cafeteria to maintain order and discipline because ample other opportunities were available for students to distribute their materials at school.[70]

Time, place, and manner regulations, however, must be reasonable, content neutral, and uniformly applied to expressive activities. Also, they cannot restrict more speech than necessary to ensure nondisruptive distribution of materials. School officials must provide students with specific guidelines regarding when and where they can express their ideas and distribute materials. Moreover, literature distribution cannot be relegated to remote times or places either inside or outside the school building, and regulations must not inhibit any person's right to accept or reject literature that is distributed in accordance with the rules. Policies governing demonstrations should convey to students that they have the right to assemble, distribute petitions, and express their ideas under nondisruptive circumstances. If regulations do not precisely inform demonstrators of behavior that is prohibited, the judiciary may conclude that punishment cannot be imposed.

---

[69]Amicus Brief of Nat'l Sch. Bds. Ass'n in Support of Petition for Certiorari, Blue Mountain School District v. Snyder, No. 11-502 (2011). If the Supreme Court would consider student electronic expression to be "in school" so long as it targets the school community, this would resolve the debate over whether *Fraser*'s exclusion of lewd and vulgar expression from constitutional protection applies to Internet expression.

[70]Morgan v. Plano Indep. Sch. Dist., 589 F.3d 740 (5th Cir. 2009), *cert. denied*, 130 S. Ct. 3503 (2010).

STUDENT-INITIATED CLUBS

Public schools can deny access to all noncurriculum student clubs during noninstructional time but cannot discriminate against specific groups based on the content of their meetings.

Free expression and related association rights have arisen in connection with the formation and recognition of student clubs. Freedom of association is not specifically included among First Amendment protections, but the Supreme Court has held that associational rights are "implicit in the freedoms of speech, assembly, and petition."[71] The word *association* refers to the medium through which individuals seek to join with others to make the expression of their own views more meaningful.

Public school pupils have not prevailed in asserting that free expression and association rights shield student-initiated social organizations or secret societies with exclusive membership usually determined by a vote of the clubs' members. In contrast, prohibitions on student-initiated organizations with *open* membership are vulnerable to First Amendment challenge. Even before Congress enacted the Equal Access Act (EAA), it was generally accepted that public school access policies for student meetings must be content neutral and not disadvantage selected groups. **The EAA, enacted in 1984, stipulates that if federally assisted secondary schools provide a limited open forum for noncurricular student groups to meet during noninstructional time, access cannot be denied based on the religious, political, philosophical, or other content of the groups' meetings.**[72] The EAA was championed by the Religious Right, but its protection encompasses far more than student-initiated religious expression.

As discussed in Chapter 3, the Supreme Court in 1990 rejected an Establishment Clause challenge to the EAA in *Board of Education of the Westside Community Schools v. Mergens.*[73] The Court held that if a federally assisted secondary school allows even one noncurricular group to use school facilities during noninstructional time, the EAA guarantees equal access for other noncurricular student groups. Of course, meetings that threaten a disruption can be barred. Moreover, school authorities can decline to establish a limited forum for student-initiated meetings and thus confine school access to student organizations that are an extension of the curriculum, such as drama groups, language clubs, and athletic teams.

Controversies have surfaced over what constitutes a curriculum-related group, since the EAA is triggered only if noncurriculum student groups are allowed school access during noninstructional time. Many of these cases have focused on the Gay-Straight Alliance (GSA). To illustrate, after the Salt Lake City School Board implemented a policy denying school access to all noncurriculum student groups, it rejected the GSA's petition to hold meetings in a public high school. The GSA then asserted that it was related to the

[71]Healy v. James, 408 U.S. 169, 181 (1972).

[72]20 U.S.C. § 4071 (2012). *See* text accompanying note 64, Chapter 3.

[73]496 U.S. 226 (1990) (rejecting the contention that only noncurricular, *advocacy* groups are protected under the EAA).

curriculum and should be treated like other curriculum-related groups. The federal district court ultimately enjoined school authorities from denying access to the student club because it addressed content in the school's history and sociology courses, even though the club's major focus was on the rights of lesbian, gay, bisexual, and transgender (LGBT) persons.[74] Also, the Eighth Circuit addressed a Minnesota school district's distinction between *curricular* student groups that were allowed to use the public address system and other forms of communication and *noncurricular* groups that could not use such communication avenues or participate in fundraising activities or field trips.[75] Concluding that some groups identified as curricular, such as cheerleading and synchronized swimming, were not related to material regularly taught in the curriculum, the court enjoined the district from treating the club, Straights and Gays for Equality, differently from other student groups. Even if agreed that a secondary school has *not* established a limited forum, it still cannot exert viewpoint discrimination against particular curriculum-related groups.

STUDENT APPEARANCE

Restrictions can be placed on student grooming and attire if based on legitimate educational and safety objectives and not intended to suppress expression.

Fads and fashions in hairstyles and clothing have regularly evoked litigation as educators have attempted to exert some control over pupil appearance. Courts have been called upon to weigh students' interests in selecting their hairstyle and attire against school authorities' interests in preventing disruptions and promoting school objectives.

Hairstyle

Considerable judicial activity in the 1970s focused on school regulations governing the length of male students' hair. The Supreme Court, however, refused to hear appeals of these cases, and federal circuit courts reached different conclusions in determining the legality of policies governing student hairstyle. If school officials have offered health or safety reasons for grooming regulations, such as requiring hair nets, shower caps, and other hair restraints intended to protect students from injury or to promote sanitation, the policies typically have been upheld. Furthermore, restrictions on male students' hairstyles at vocational schools have been upheld to create a positive image for potential employers visiting the school for recruitment purposes. Special grooming regulations have been endorsed as

[74]E. High Sch. Prism Club v. Seidel, 95 F. Supp. 2d 1239 (D. Utah 2000).

[75]Straights & Gays for Equality (SAGE) v. Osseo Area Schs., 471 F.3d 908 (8th Cir. 2006); *see also* Pratt v. Indian River Cent. Sch. Dist., 803 F. Supp. 2d 135 (N.D.N.Y. 2011) (finding, among claims of differential treatment based on sexual orientation, a sufficient EAA claim that the school district did not give equal access and benefits to the GSA compared to other student groups). For a discussion of public school access for meetings of community religious groups, including the Good News Club, see text accompanying note 71, Chapter 3.

conditions of participation in extracurricular activities for legitimate health or safety reasons, and, in some instances, to enhance the school's image. Of course, students can be disciplined for hairstyles that cause a disruption, such as hair groomed or dyed in a manner that distracts classmates from instructional activities.

But hairstyle regulations cannot be arbitrary or devoid of an educational rationale. A Texas federal district court ruled that school officials failed to show a valid justification to impair Native American students' protected expression right to wear long hair that posed no disruption.[76] More recently, the Fifth Circuit relied on a Texas law protecting religious liberties in ruling that a school district violated a Native American student's rights to express his religious beliefs by requiring him to wear one long braid tucked in his shirt or a bun on top of his head instead of wearing his two long braids in plain view.[77]

Attire

Although public school students' hair length has subsided as a major subject of litigation, other appearance fads have become controversial as students have asserted a First Amendment right to express themselves through their attire at school. Some courts have distinguished attire restrictions from hair regulations because clothes, unlike hair length, can be changed after school. Even in situations where students' rights to govern their appearance have been recognized, the judiciary has upheld restrictions on attire that is immodest, disruptive, unsanitary, or promotes illegal behavior.

If school authorities can link particular attire to gang activities or other school violence, restrictions likely will be upheld. A Nebraska federal district court in 2012 supported school authorities in suspending students for wearing bracelets and T-shirts with the phrase, "Julius RIP" (rest in peace) in remembrance of their friend who had been shot at his apartment complex allegedly for gang-related reasons.[78] The court agreed with school authorities that the attire could be banned in the interest of safety because it might trigger violence at the school. Two years earlier, a West Virginia federal district court upheld a student's suspension for writing a slogan on his hands about freeing a classmate who was accused of shooting a police officer. The court agreed with school officials' prediction that the expression would contribute to gang-related disturbances.[79]

Some recent controversies have addressed school prohibitions on students wearing cancer awareness bracelets with the message, "I love Boobies (Keep a Breast)." School authorities have argued that the bracelets are vulgar and can be banned under *Fraser*. But a Pennsylvania federal district court found no evidence that these bracelets were linked to a disruption and did not consider the word "boobies" to be vulgar in this context, so it granted a preliminary injunction against the school district's ban on wearing the bracelets.[80]

---

[76]Ala. & Coushatta Tribes v. Trs., 817 F. Supp. 1319 (E.D. Tex. 1993), *remanded per curiam*, 20 F.3d 469 (5th Cir. 1994).

[77]A.A. v. Needville Indep. Sch. Dist., 611 F.3d 248 (5th Cir. 2010).

[78]Kuhr v. Millard Pub. Sch. Dist., No. 8:09CV363, 2012 U.S. Dist. LEXIS 56189 (D. Neb. Apr. 23, 2012).

[79]Brown v. Cabell Cnty. Bd. of Educ., 714 F. Supp. 2d 587 (S.D. W. Va. 2010).

[80]B.H. v. Easton Area Sch. Dist., 827 F. Supp. 392 (E.D. Pa. Apr. 12, 2011).

Dress Codes. Under the principle established in *Fraser*, lewd and vulgar expression is outside the protective arm of the First Amendment. Thus, **indecent attire can be curtailed regardless of whether the attire would meet the *Tinker* test of threatening a disruption.** For example, an Idaho federal district court held that a school could prevent a student from wearing a T-shirt that depicted three high school administrators drunk on school grounds, noting that the student had no free expression right to portray administrators in a fashion that would undermine their authority and compromise the school's efforts to educate students about the harmful effects of alcohol.[81] A Georgia federal district court also upheld the suspension of a student who wore a T-shirt with the phrases "kids have civil rights too" and "even adults lie."[82] The court ruled that wearing the shirt was the last incident in a series of disruptions justifying the student's suspension.

A few courts have upheld dress codes that prohibit male students from wearing earrings, rejecting the assertion that jewelry restrictions must be applied equally to male and female students. In an illustrative case, an Illinois federal district court found the school district's ban on male students wearing earrings rationally related to the school's legitimate objective of inhibiting the influence of gangs, as earrings were used to convey gang-related messages.[83] Also, while acknowledging the absence of a gang-related justification, an Indiana appeals court nonetheless upheld a school district's ban on male students wearing earrings in elementary schools as advancing legitimate educational objectives and community values supporting different attire standards for males and females.[84]

In a New Mexico case, the federal district court upheld a student's suspension for wearing "sagging" pants in violation of the school's dress code.[85] Rejecting the student's contention that his attire conveyed an African-American cultural message, the court noted that "sagging" pants could as easily be associated with gang affiliation or simply reflect a fashion trend among adolescents. The Seventh Circuit found no First Amendment right for gifted students to wear a T-shirt they had designed that depicted in a satirical manner a physically disabled child with the word "gifties." The students wore their shirt to protest the election to select a class shirt, which they alleged was rigged because school authorities did not like their design.[86]

In one of the most expansive interpretations of *Fraser*, the Sixth Circuit upheld a school district's decision to prohibit students from wearing Marilyn Manson T-shirts.

---

[81]Gano v. Sch. Dist. No. 411, 674 F. Supp. 796 (D. Idaho 1987); *see also* Madrid v. Anthony, 510 F. Supp. 2d 425 (S.D. Tex. 2007) (upholding a ban on students, who were mostly Hispanic, wearing T-shirts with the statement "We Are Not Criminals" to protest pending immigration legislation; school authorities instituted the ban to curb the escalating racial tension in the school that threatened student safety).

[82]Smith v. Greene Cnty. Sch. Dist., 100 F. Supp. 2d 1354 (M.D. Ga. 2000).

[83]Olesen v. Bd. of Educ., 676 F. Supp. 820 (N.D. Ill. 1987); *see also* Barber v. Colo. Indep. Sch. Dist., 901 S.W.2d 447 (Tex. 1995) (upholding earring as well as hair-length restrictions applied only to male students).

[84]Hines v. Caston Sch. Corp, 651 N.E.2d 330 (Ind. Ct. App. 1995). *But see* McMillen v. Itawamba Cnty. Sch. Dist., 702 F. Supp. 2d 699 (N.D. Miss. 2010) (upholding a female student's right to wear a tuxedo to the prom and bring her girlfriend as her date).

[85]Bivens *ex rel.* Green v. Albuquerque Pub. Schs., 899 F. Supp. 556 (D.N.M. 1995), *aff'd mem.*, 131 F.3d 151 (10th Cir. 1997).

[86]Brandt v. Bd. of Educ., 480 F.3d 460 (7th Cir. 2007).

The appeals court agreed with school authorities that the shirts were offensive, promoted destructive conduct, and were counter to the school's efforts to denounce drugs and promote human dignity and democratic ideals.[87] The court held that under *Fraser*, schools can prohibit student expression that is inconsistent with its basic educational mission even though such speech might be protected by the First Amendment outside the school environment.

Several restrictive dress codes have received judicial endorsement. The Fifth Circuit upheld a dress code prohibiting any clothing with printed words except for school logos as content neutral.[88] Also upholding a restrictive dress code as reasonable to create unity and focus attention on learning, the Sixth Circuit found no violation of a student's free expression rights, her right to wear clothes of her choice, or her father's right to control his daughter's attire.[89]

However, **like hairstyle regulations, school authorities must have an educational rationale for attire restrictions, such as enhancing learning or preventing class disruptions.** The Third Circuit struck down a prohibition on wearing T-shirts with the comedian Jeff Foxworthy's "red-neck sayings" as not sufficiently linked to racial harassment or other disruptive activity.[90] A student also prevailed in wearing a T-shirt depicting three black silhouettes holding firearms with "NRA" and "Shooting Sports Camp" superimposed over the silhouettes. School authorities asked the student to change the shirt, contending that it conflicted with the school's mission of deterring violence. Applying *Tinker* instead of *Fraser*, the Fourth Circuit held that the student's free expression rights were overriding because the shirt was not disruptive and did not promote gun use.[91]

In addition, dress codes must not be discriminatorily enforced. In a case mentioned previously, the Sixth Circuit ordered a school district to reconsider suspensions of two students who refused to change or turn inside out T-shirts with a country singer on the front and the Confederate flag on the back.[92] School authorities asserted that the shirts violated the school's dress code prohibiting clothing or emblems that contain slogans or words depicting alcohol or tobacco or have illegal, immoral, or racist implications, but the court found no indication of racial tension in the school or that the shirt would likely lead to a disruption. There also was evidence that the dress code had been selectively enforced in a viewpoint-specific manner; students had been allowed to wear shirts celebrating Malcolm X. Thus, the court remanded the case to determine if the students' First Amendment rights had been violated.

---

[87]Boroff v. Van Wert City Bd. of Educ., 220 F.3d 465 (6th Cir. 2000); *see also* Dariano v. Morgan Hill Unified Sch. Dist., 822 F. Supp. 2d 1037 (N.D. Cal. 2011) (rejecting First Amendment challenge to dress code that barred American flag emblems where there had been conflicts between Hispanic and Caucasian students).

[88]Palmer *ex rel.* Palmer v. Waxahachie Indep. Sch. Dist., 579 F.3d 502 (5th Cir. 2009), *cert. denied*, 558 U.S. 1111 (2010).

[89]Blau v. Ft. Thomas Pub. Sch. Dist., 401 F.3d 381 (6th Cir. 2005); *see also* Long v. Bd. of Educ., 121 F. Supp. 2d 621 (W.D. Ky. 2000), *aff'd mem.*, 21 F. App'x 252 (6th Cir. 2001) (upholding a restrictive student dress code devised by a Kentucky school-based council that limits the colors, materials, and type of clothing allowed, and bars logos, shorts, cargo pants, jeans, and other specific items; the court found legitimate safety justifications and no intent to suppress free speech).

[90]Sypniewski v. Warren Hills Reg'l Bd. of Educ., 307 F.3d 243 (3d Cir. 2002); *supra* text accompanying note 54.

[91]Newsom v. Albemarle Cnty. Sch. Bd., 354 F.3d 249 (4th Cir. 2003).

[92]Castorina *ex rel.* Rewt v. Madison Cnty. Sch. Bd., 246 F.3d 536 (6th Cir. 2001). Most courts, however, have upheld restrictions on Confederate flag displays under anti-harassment policies, finding no viewpoint discrimination; *see supra* text accompanying note 48.

Additionally, students cannot be disciplined for expressing their disagreement with a dress code in a nondisruptive manner. Applying *Tinker*, the Eighth Circuit ruled that students had a First Amendment right to wear black armbands to protest the district's student apparel policy.[93]

The Second Circuit relied on *Tinker* in protecting a student's right to wear a shirt expressing political views; the shirt depicted George W. Bush negatively (i.e., calling him "Chicken Hawk in Chief" and linking him to drinking, taking drugs, and being a crook and draft dodger).[94] Reasoning that simply because the expression is in poor taste is not sufficient grounds to curtail students' expression rights, the appeals court concluded that student expression would have to contain sexual innuendos or profanity to be censorable as plainly offensive under *Fraser*. Since neither was at issue, the court applied the *Tinker* disruption standard and found that the controversial shirt was not linked to any disruption.

Student Uniforms. Many attire controversies might be avoided if public school students were required to wear uniforms as they do in many countries. **Voluntary and mandatory student uniforms increasingly are being adopted by school districts nationally, especially those in urban settings.**[95] Advocates assert that student uniforms eliminate gang-related attire, reduce violence and socioeconomic distinctions, and improve school climate by placing the emphasis on academics rather than fashion fads. And the line is not always clear between restrictive dress codes and student uniforms.

Courts have upheld uniform policies so long as there are waivers for those opposed to uniforms on religious or philosophical grounds and provisions are made for students who cannot afford the uniforms.[96] Courts have not been persuaded that any rights are violated because a stigma is associated with exercising the First Amendment right to be exempt from uniform requirements.[97]

Since the federal judiciary has recognized that public schools can impose restrictive dress codes and even mandate uniforms for students, perhaps this is depressing challenges to attire regulations. Nonetheless, school officials would be wise to ensure that they have a legitimate educational justification for any grooming or dress restrictions. Policies designed to protect students' health and safety, reduce violence and discipline problems, and enhance learning usually will be endorsed. Given the current student interest in tattoos, body piercings, and other fashion fads and school authorities' concerns about attire linked to gangs and violence, controversies over student appearance in public schools seem likely to persist.

---

[93]Lowry *ex rel.* Crow v. Watson Chapel Sch. Dist., 540 F.3d 752 (8th Cir. 2008). *But see* Hardwick v. Heyward, No. 4:06-cv-1042-TLW, 2012 U.S. Dist. LEXIS 31438 (D.S.C. Mar. 8, 2012) (holding that a student could not protest the ban on Confederate flag displays with a shirt depicting the flag, although other nondisruptive "protest" shirts would be allowed).

[94]Guiles v. Marineau, 461 F.3d 320, 322 (2d Cir. 2006).

[95]*See* Erik Hayden, *No Uniform Solution*, Pacific Standard (Nov. 23, 2009), http://www.miller-mccune.com/culture-society/no-uniform-solution-5609/.

[96]*See, e.g.*, Jacobs v. Clark Cnty. Sch. Dist., 526 F.3d 419 (9th Cir. 2008); Canady v. Bossier Parish Sch. Bd., 240 F.3d 437 (5th Cir. 2001); Littlefield v. Forney Indep. Sch. Dist., 268 F.3d 275 (5th Cir. 2001); Frudden v. Pilling, 842 F. Supp. 2d 1265 (D. Nev. 2012); Derry v. Marion Cmty. Schs., 790 F. Supp. 2d 839 (N.D. Ind. 2008).

[97]*See, e.g.*, Wilkins v. Penns Grove-Carneys Point Reg'l Sch. Dist., 123 F. App'x 493 (3d Cir. 2005).

CONCLUSION

Student expression and association rights have generated a significant amount of school litigation. In the late 1960s and early 1970s, the federal judiciary expanded First Amendment protections afforded to students following the Supreme Court's landmark *Tinker* decision. Yet the reach of the *Tinker* standard was narrowed somewhat after the Supreme Court ruled in *Fraser* and *Hazelwood* that lewd or vulgar speech and attire are not protected by the First Amendment and that school authorities can censor student expression that appears to represent the school. The Supreme Court in *Morse* again restricted use of the disruption standard if expression can be viewed as promoting or celebrating illegal activity. *Tinker* has not been overturned, but it governs more limited circumstances than was true in the 1970s.

Students do not need to rely solely on constitutional protections because federal and state laws, most notably the Equal Access Act, also protect students' expression and association rights. And *Tinker* has been revitalized as the primary standard used in First Amendment challenges to anti-harassment and anti-bullying policies and electronic expression. Important questions persist regarding whether school authorities can discipline students for vulgar and hurtful electronic expression that originates from their homes but can reach the entire school community instantaneously. Judicial criteria to weigh the competing interests of students and school authorities under statutory and constitutional provisions continue to be refined.

POINTS TO PONDER

1. Students opposed to the United States' military involvement in the Middle East organized several activities to protest the government's policy. The students:

   a. distributed flyers condemning the war to classmates at school;
   b. posted flyers on school bulletin boards that announced an antiwar rally to be held after school;
   c. led students in walking out of a school assembly to meet with protesting adults who were holding a rally across from the school; and
   d. held a rally in front of the county courthouse after school.

   Could school authorities legally curtail any of these activities? Which activities implicate students' First Amendment rights?

2. Students developed a newspaper in their homes and distributed it at a local store. The articles were critical of school administrators and contained vulgar language. Can school authorities discipline the students for their expression? Would your conclusion be different if the paper were distributed over the Internet?

3. A high school allows a chess club to meet in a classroom after school. Three other student clubs—the Gay-Straight Alliance, the Fellowship of Christian Athletes, and the Young Neo-Nazis—have asked for similar privileges. Must each of these groups be provided school access? Why or why not?

4. A school-based council has decided to adopt a policy requiring students to wear uniforms. What features should the policy include to survive a legal challenge?

5. Students wore T-shirts condemning homosexuality. Can school authorities ban such attire? Why or why not?

CHAPTER SIX

STUDENT CLASSIFICATIONS

It might appear from a literal translation of the word *equality* that once a state establishes an educational system, all students must be treated in the same manner. Courts, however, have recognized that individuals are different and that equal treatment of unequals can have negative consequences. Accordingly, valid classification practices, designed to enhance the educational experiences of children by recognizing their unique needs, generally have been accepted as a legitimate prerogative of educators. While educators' authority to classify students has not been seriously contested, the bases for certain classifications and the procedures used to make distinctions among students have been the focus of substantial litigation.[1]

LEGAL CONTEXT

The Equal Protection Clause of the Fourteenth Amendment to the U.S. Constitution is often at issue when school districts attempt to classify students based on race, native language, ability and achievement, age, sex, and sexual orientation.[2]

The Equal Protection Clause states in part that no state shall deny to any person within its jurisdiction equal protection of the laws. This applies to subdivisions of states, including school districts, and it requires that similarly situated individuals be treated the same. (See overview of Fourteenth Amendment, Figure 6.1.) As a result, equal protection claims often arise if a government law or policy creates a classification

---

[1]Some charter schools recently have been accused of stratifying students by race, sex, language, sexual orientation, and ability. Specifically, the increased flexibility that charter schools have to experiment within public education gives charter school leaders more power than traditional public school leaders to shape their educational communities. Some charter schools seek to serve a specific population of students, which may result in a more stratified student body.

[2]For information on classifications based on achievement and age, see MARTHA MCCARTHY, NELDA CAMBRON-MCCABE & SUZANNE ECKES, PUBLIC SCHOOL LAW: TEACHERS' AND STUDENTS' RIGHTS ch. 5 (Upper Saddle River, N.J.: Pearson, 7th ed. 2013).

FIGURE 6.1   Fourteenth Amendment

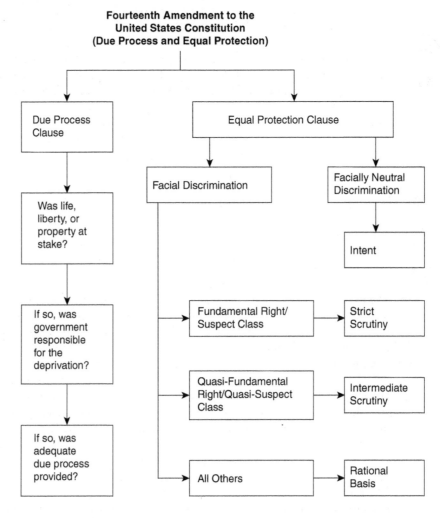

that advantages or disadvantages one group over another. When examining a government policy, courts apply three different levels of scrutiny (i.e., strict, intermediate, and rational basis scrutiny) for different classes of people and if different interests are at stake.

For example, the government must have a compelling interest for any policy that treats students differently based on race, which is a suspect classification. National origin and alienage are also considered suspect classifications. Intermediate scrutiny is applied to challenged classifications based on sex.[3] This standard requires that the policy have an important governmental interest and that it be substantially related to advancing significant

---

[3]Miss. Univ. for Women v. Hogan, 458 U.S. 718 (1982).

governmental objectives. Where any other classification or form of discrimination is present (e.g., disability, age, sexual orientation), courts apply rational basis scrutiny. All that is required under this level of review is that some rational basis was used in the state's decision. This is a very low threshold and is generally met with relative ease. Thus, under the Equal Protection Clause, it would be much more difficult to open a public school that serves only Latino students than it would be to open a public school that serves only gay students. The school serving only Latino students would need to demonstrate a compelling government interest in segregating students by race and that the classification serves a necessary interest. The school serving only gay students would need to show simply a legitimate governmental objective with a rational relationship between the means and the ends.

CLASSIFICATIONS BASED ON RACE

The Supreme Court has declared that separate schools based on race are inherently unequal.

The most prevalent reason for classifying students according to race has been to establish or perpetuate racially segregated schools. Widespread racial segregation in educational institutions existed in this country from the colonial period well into the twentieth century. Even after the adoption of the Fourteenth Amendment in 1868, most schools remained segregated either pursuant to state constitution or statute, local ordinance, district policy or practice, or court interpretation, and were seldom equal. When such practices were challenged, courts generally mandated only that children be provided with access to public education. Despite laws and policies to racially integrate student bodies, some school districts remain highly segregated. In addition to traditional public schools, charter schools have also been accused of racially segregating students.[4]

Plessy and *Brown*

Perhaps the most infamous case supporting the "separate but equal" interpretation was *Plessy v. Ferguson* in 1896, in which the Supreme Court upheld racial segregation of passengers in railroad coaches as required by Louisiana law.[5] Although "separate but equal" case law and state statutes were common 75 to 100 years before *Plessy*, nevertheless *Plessy* most often is mentioned today when the standard is discussed.

In the early 1950s, the time appeared ripe to attack the "separate but equal" policy directly in elementary and secondary schools because of some success in higher

---

[4]SUZANNE ECKES, *Charter School Legislation's Impact on Diversity, in* THE CHARTER SCHOOL EXPERIMENT: EXPECTATIONS, EVIDENCE AND IMPLICATIONS (Christopher Lubienski & Peter Weitzel eds., Harvard Education Press 2010).

[5]163 U.S. 537 (1896); *see also* Bolling v. Sharpe, 347 U.S. 497 (1954) (invalidating school segregation in Washington, D.C., under the Fifth Amendments' Due Process Clause because the Fourteenth Amendment does not apply in that jurisdiction).

education cases.[6] This occurred in 1954 when the Supreme Court combined cases from four states—Kansas, South Carolina, Virginia, and Delaware.[7] **In the landmark decision, collectively called *Brown v. Board of Education*, Chief Justice Warren, writing for a unanimous Court, declared education to be "perhaps the most important function of state and local governments"[8] and repudiated the separate but equal doctrine, stipulating that racially segregated public schools were "inherently unequal."[9]**

Because of the significant impact of this decision and the difficulty in fashioning an immediate remedy, the Supreme Court delayed an implementation decree for one year, soliciting friend-of-the-court briefs[10] regarding strategies to integrate school districts. Then, in 1955 in *Brown II*, the Court concluded that the conversion from dual to unitary districts must occur "with all deliberate speed,"[11] although it gave little guidance as to what specific time frame was required or to what extent integration was mandated. As a result, states varied widely in their efforts to comply.

De Jure and De Facto Segregation

Despite the *Brown* mandate to end unconstitutional segregation, for more than a decade, little progress was made in integrating schools. The Supreme Court was forced to react to some blatant violations, such as state officials' efforts to physically block the desegregation of schools in Little Rock[12] and an attempt to avoid integration by closing public schools in one Virginia county, while maintaining public schools in other counties in the state.[13] But confusion remained as to whether *Brown* required affirmative action to integrate schools or only the removal of state laws authorizing school segregation.

Then, in a trilogy of cases in 1968, the Supreme Court announced that school officials in systems that were segregated by law in 1954 had an affirmative duty to take whatever steps were necessary to convert to unitary school systems and to eliminate the effects of past discrimination.[14] Furthermore, the Court declared that desegregation remedies would be evaluated based on their effectiveness in dismantling dual school systems. **Thus, the notion of state neutrality was transformed into a requirement of affirmative state action to desegregate; the mere removal of barriers to school integration was not sufficient.**

---

[6]*See* McLaurin v. Okla. State Regents for Higher Educ., 339 U.S. 637 (1950); Sweatt v. Painter, 339 U.S. 629 (1950); Sipuel v. Bd. of Regents, 332 U.S. 631 (1948) (per curiam); Missouri *ex rel*. Gaines v. Canada, 305 U.S. 337 (1938).

[7]Brown v. Bd. of Educ., 98 F. Supp. 797 (D. Kan. 1951); Briggs v. Elliott, 98 F. Supp. 529 (E.D.S.C. 1951), *vacated and remanded*, 342 U.S. 350 (1952), *on remand*, 103 F. Supp. 920 (E.D.S.C. 1952); Davis v. Cnty. Sch. Bd., 103 F. Supp. 337 (E.D. Va. 1952); Gebhart v. Belton, 87 A.2d 862 (Del. Ch. 1952), *aff'd*, 91 A.2d 137 (Del. 1952).

[8]347 U.S. 483, 493 (1954) (Brown I).

[9]*Id*. at 495.

[10]Friend-of-the-court (*amicus curiae*) briefs are provided by nonparties to inform or perhaps persuade the court.

[11]Brown v. Bd. of Educ., 349 U.S. 294, 301 (1955) (Brown II).

[12]Cooper v. Aaron, 358 U.S. 1 (1958).

[13]Griffin v. Cnty. Sch. Bd., 377 U.S. 218 (1964).

[14]*See* Green v. Cnty. Sch. Bd., 391 U.S. 430 (1968); Raney v. Bd. of Educ., 391 U.S. 443 (1968); Monroe v. Bd. of Comm'rs, 391 U.S. 450 (1968).

In one of these 1968 cases, *Green v. County School Board*, the Court reviewed a freedom-of-choice plan adopted by a small district in Virginia. During the three-year period immediately following implementation, no Caucasian children enrolled in the historically African American school, while only a few African American children enrolled in the historically Caucasian school. The district contended that any resulting segregation was due to the choices of individuals, not to government action, and was therefore permissible; the Supreme Court disagreed. As a result, the district was ordered to come forward with a new plan that promised "realistically to work and to work now."[15] In addition, **the Court ruled that school authorities must eliminate the racial identification of schools in terms of the *composition of the student body, faculty, and staff; transportation; extracurricular activities; and facilities.*** These six elements still are used today and are referred to in the aggregate simply as the *Green* criteria.

In 1971, additional direction was provided when the Supreme Court ruled in *Swann v. Charlotte-Mecklenburg Board of Education* that the elimination of invidious racial distinctions may be sufficient in connection with transportation, support personnel, and extracurricular activities, but that more was necessary in terms of constructing facilities and making faculty and student assignments.[16] The Court endorsed the practice of assigning teachers on the basis of race until faculties were integrated and declared that new schools must be located so that the dual school system would not be perpetuated or reestablished.

Correcting racial imbalance among student populations, however, was more difficult. For the vestiges of segregation to be eliminated, the school district had to achieve racial balance in a sufficient number of schools, although every school did not have to reflect the racial composition of the school district as a whole. The presence of a small number of predominantly one-race schools in the district did not necessarily mean that it continued to practice state-imposed segregation, but the burden of proof was placed on school officials to establish that such schools were not the result of present or past discriminatory action. To achieve the desired racial balance, the Court suggested pairing or consolidating schools, altering attendance zones, and using racial quotas, but rejected the practice of assigning students to the schools nearest their homes if doing so failed to eliminate de jure segregation. The Court also endorsed the use of reasonable busing as a means to integrate schools, yet qualified that endorsement by noting that the soundness of any transportation plan must be evaluated based on the time involved, distance traveled, and age of the students.

By applying the criteria established in *Green* and *Swann*, substantial desegregation was attained in southern states during the 1970s. Where unconstitutional segregation was found, federal courts exercised broad power in ordering remedies affecting student and staff assignments, curriculum, school construction, personnel practices, and budgetary allocations. This judicial activity was augmented also by threats from the former Department of Health, Education, and Welfare to terminate federal funds to school districts not complying with Title VI of the Civil Rights Act of 1964.[17] Title VI, like the Fourteenth Amendment, requires the integration only of de jure segregated school districts.

[15]*Green*, 391 U.S. at 439.

[16]402 U.S. 1 (1971).

[17]42 U.S.C. §§ 2000d–2000d-7 (2012).

Since the Supreme Court carefully limited its early decisions to states and school districts with a long history of school segregation by official policy, questions remained regarding what type of evidence—other than explicit legislation requiring school segregation—was necessary to establish unconstitutional de jure segregation. **De jure segregated schools are those where the separation of the races is required by law or the result of other action by the state or its agents. De facto segregation occurs by practice (e.g., families choosing to live in a particular neighborhood).**

During this time, there was a debate about what factors would distinguish unlawful de jure segregation from permissible de facto segregation. Answers to this debate began to evolve in *Keyes v. School District No. 1, Denver*, in which the Supreme Court in 1973 held **that if "no statutory dual system has ever existed, plaintiffs must prove not only that segregated schooling exists but also that it was brought about or maintained by intentional state action."**[18] Some federal courts have assumed that a presumption of unlawful purpose can be established if the natural, probable, and foreseeable results of public officials' acts perpetuate segregated conditions,[19] while others have required evidence that policy makers actually harbored a desire to segregate.[20] Although courts vary in the processes they use to determine whether school districts are guilty of discriminatory intent, they often consider:

- the impact of the disputed governmental act;
- the history of discriminatory official action;
- procedural and substantive departures from norms generally followed; and
- discriminatory statements made publicly or in legislative or administrative sessions.

If intent is proven, courts then are responsible for fashioning appropriate remedies, but when allegations of discriminatory intent are not supported, no action on the part of the district is required. Moreover, **school districts that either have no history of unlawful segregation or have become unitary while under court supervision will not be responsible for correcting any future racial imbalance they have not created.**[21]

Fashioning Appropriate Remedies

Because each desegregation case involves a combination of unique circumstances and violations, it is not surprising that each remedy to address segregation also is unique and at times requires:

- rezoning and redistricting;[22]
- providing thematic magnet schools;

[18]413 U.S. 189, 198 (1973).

[19]*See, e.g.*, Arthur v. Nyquist, 573 F.2d 134 (2d Cir. 1978).

[20]*See, e.g.*, Vill. of Arlington Heights v. Metro. Hous. Dev. Corp., 429 U.S. 252 (1977).

[21]Pasadena City Bd. of Educ. v. Spangler, 427 U.S. 424 (1976).

[22]*See* Milliken v. Bradley, 433 U.S. 267, 280–81 (1977) (Milliken II) (finding that an interdistrict remedy may include only those districts that were guilty of de jure segregation).

- developing new curricular offerings and specialized learning centers;
- providing compensatory education programs, bilingual/bicultural programs, and counseling and career guidance services;
- closing, reopening, renovating, or constructing schools;
- busing students;[23] or
- hiring, transferring, or retraining current staff.

Basically, courts have considerable discretion in requiring districts and states to take steps to remedy unconstitutional school segregation, and costs often have seemed irrelevant.

Rezoning and the Closing, Reopening, or Construction of Schools.   Although some-times politically unpopular, the rezoning of schools often was the fastest, least expensive, and simplest way to integrate students. Because of a long history of gerrymandering boundary lines with the intent to segregate, many school boundaries during the 1950s and 1960s had little to do with geographic barriers (e.g., rivers, hills); safety issues (e.g., location of busy roads, factories); or the size, location, or dispersion of the student population. As a result, significant integration often has resulted through the simple use of good-faith redistricting and/or, in fairly narrow circumstances, the creation of new or consolidated school districts.[24]

In addition, early in the twentieth century, many school districts were able to remain or become segregated by strategically locating new schools; downsizing or closing existing buildings; or operating schools that were overenrolled, often requiring the use of mobile units or temporary classrooms. Just as these methods were used to segregate, they also have been used to integrate. Where there has been a history of de jure segregation, it is common to require adjustments in building use and to determine site selection of future schools, at least in part, on the impact that their locations will have on the effort to integrate.

Busing.   Contributing to the cost and controversy was the use of busing to accomplish integration when other alternatives had not succeeded. Even though busing is admittedly effective at achieving student integration, it also represents a significant expense; is inefficient in the use of student time; and is an unpopular option with many students, parents, taxpayers, and voters of all races. Consequently, several bills to limit the authority of federal courts to order the busing of students have been introduced in Congress. Foremost among these were provisions included in Title IV of the Civil Rights Act of 1964[25] and the Equal Educational Opportunities Act (EEOA) of 1974.[26] Title IV provides technical assistance in the preparation, adoption, and implementation of desegregation plans; gives direction in the operation of training institutes to improve the ability of educators to deal effectively

---

[23]*See* N.C. State Bd. of Educ. v. Swann, 402 U.S. 43 (1971) (striking down a state law forbidding the busing of students to create racially balanced schools). *But see* Crawford v. Bd. of Educ., 458 U.S. 527 (1982) (upholding a state constitutional amendment in California that permitted busing only when de jure segregation was present).

[24]Newburg Area Council v. Bd. of Educ., 510 F.2d 1358 (6th Cir. 1974).

[25]42 U.S.C. §§ 2000c–2000c-9 (2012).

[26]20 U.S.C. § 1701 (2012).

with special education problems occasioned by desegregation; and places limitations on court-ordered busing. The EEOA prohibits public schools from denying equal educational opportunities to students based on their race, color, sex, or national origin; purports that the neighborhood is the appropriate basis for determining public school assignment; and stipulates that busing may be used only in situations where the intent to segregate is established.

Moreover, state busing limitation measures have generated litigation. In 1971, the Supreme Court in *North Carolina State Board of Education v. Swann* struck down a state law forbidding the busing of students to create racially balanced schools. The Court concluded that the provision unconstitutionally restricted the discretion of local school authorities to formulate plans to eliminate dual school systems.[27] Furthermore, the Court reasoned that busing was one of the truly effective remedies to racially integrate students.

Achieving Unitary Status

Federal courts have found numerous school systems guilty of having engaged in de jure segregation and have fashioned a variety of remedies. Some orders required only a few years to demonstrate compliance, while others continue to exist today, even though the original decisions may have been rendered in the 1950s, 1960s, or 1970s. Such lengthy supervision has usurped the traditional roles of trained and licensed school administrators, elected school boards, and state legislatures regarding funding, facilities, personnel, and curriculum. Although federal judges generally lack the knowledge and expertise to properly administer schools or to make curricular or instructional decisions, on occasion they assumed control of these matters and then retained it for decades, even when compliance seemingly had occurred. With key decisions in the early 1990s, however, the Supreme Court provided complying school districts with a means to an end.

Specifically, in *Board of Education v. Dowell*, the Supreme Court concluded that **the federal judiciary should terminate supervision of school districts where school boards have complied with desegregation mandates in good faith and have eliminated vestiges of past discrimination "to the extent practicable."**[28] Then, in *Freeman v. Pitts*, the Supreme Court held that a district court must relinquish its supervision and control over those aspects of a school system in which there has been compliance with a desegregation decree even if other aspects of the decree have not been met. Through this approach, the Court sought to restore to state and local authorities control over public schools at the earliest possible date and noted that "[p]artial relinquishment of judicial control . . . can be an important and significant step in fulfilling the district court's duty to return the operations and control of schools to local authorities."[29] To guide the lower courts in determining whether supervision should be removed, the Court identified three questions:

- Has there been full and satisfactory compliance with the decree in those aspects of the system where supervision is to be withdrawn?

---

[27]402 U.S. 43 (1971). *But see* Crawford v. Bd. of Educ., 458 U.S. 527 (1982) (upholding a state constitutional amendment in California that permitted busing only when de jure segregation was present).

[28]498 U.S. 237, 249–50 (1991).

[29]503 U.S. 467, 489 (1992).

- Is the retention of judicial control necessary or practicable to achieve compliance with the decree in other facets of the school system?
- Has the district demonstrated a good faith commitment to the court's entire decree and relevant provisions of federal law?

Finally, in 1995, the Supreme Court ruled in *Missouri v. Jenkins* that the elimination of racial disparities was not required for granting unitary status unless the plaintiffs can demonstrate that the disparity relates directly to prior segregation.[30] With guidance from the *Dowell*, *Freeman*, and *Jenkins* decisions, numerous districts have been able to show that they have achieved a unitary operation.

Postunitary Transfer and School Assignment

Litigation will not end simply because the school district has achieved unitary status and has initially been relieved of judicial control and supervision. Any decision that may even potentially result in racial imbalance, whether de jure or de facto, is likely to be challenged. Accordingly, **the placement of a new school or the creation of a new school district will foreseeably be scrutinized,**[31] **as will policies regarding school transfer, initial school assignment, open enrollment, or charter schools.** However, a transfer policy that results in only an insignificant change in minority-majority enrollment within the district will not typically justify reasserting judicial supervision.[32]

Furthermore, students have challenged school district policies that were designed and administered to maintain the racial balance accomplished through years of court supervision, integrate de facto segregated communities, or achieve the goal of a diverse student body. In such instances, students generally were permitted to enroll in schools where their race was a minority or otherwise underrepresented, but not vice versa, which has been challenged. Guidance for lower courts began to emerge in 2003 when the Supreme Court, in *Grutter v. Bollinger*,[33] permitted a law school to consider race as one of several factors in determining the composition of its first-year class. In denying the Caucasian plaintiff's race-based Fourteenth Amendment claim, the Court majority identified a compelling interest (i.e., the benefits derived from a diverse student body) and reasoned that the school's admission procedures were sufficiently narrowly tailored not to adversely affect the rights of rejected Caucasian applicants.

Additional guidance within the K–12 context was provided in a 2007 Supreme Court decision, *Parents Involved in Community Schools v. Seattle School District No. 1*. The plurality opinion identified an Equal Protection Clause violation where both the Seattle,

---

[30]515 U.S. 70 (1995).

[31]*See, e.g.*, Anderson v. Canton Mun. Separate Sch. Dist., 232 F.3d 450 (5th Cir. 2000).

[32]United States v. Texas, 457 F.3d 472 (5th Cir. 2006).

[33]539 U.S. 306 (2003). Since *Grutter*, Michigan voters amended the state constitution to prohibit the consideration of race in making admissions decisions. MICH. CONST. art. I, § 26. However, the state ban was overturned as unconstitutional by the Sixth Circuit in 2012. *See* Coal. to Defend Affirmative Action v. Regents of the Univ. of Mich., 701 F.3d 466 (6th Cir. 2012), *cert. granted sub nom.* Schuette v. Coal. to Defend Affirmative Action, No. 12-168, 2013 U.S. LEXIS 2504 (U.S. Mar. 25, 2013).

Washington, and Jefferson County, Kentucky, school districts considered race to determine school assignment once residence and availability of space were considered.[34] Seattle had never been found guilty of de jure segregation or been subjected to court-ordered desegregation, though Jefferson County had its court order dissolved in 2000 after it had eliminated the vestiges of prior segregation to the greatest extent practicable.

The Court reasoned that each district's diversity plan relied on race in a nonindividualized mechanical way even though other means were available to address integration goals of the de facto segregated communities. The plans were neither race neutral nor narrowly tailored. Guidelines issued in December 2011 by the U.S. Department of Justice and the U.S. Department of Education provide assistance to both public PK–12 schools and universities when developing student assignment plans that consider race.[35] The guidelines offer examples of what is permissible when school districts are trying to achieve a higher level of student diversity. The Supreme Court will decide another case involving race-conscious admissions, *Fisher v. University of Texas*, which could provide further guidance in this area.[36]

Race as a Factor in Admission to Private Schools

When private schools use race as a factor to determine admission, only Title VI and 42 U.S.C. § 1981 at the federal level will apply, in addition to any related state laws or local ordinances. Title VI forbids race discrimination but applies only to those schools that receive federal financial assistance. On the other hand, § 1981 prohibits both race and ethnicity discrimination in entering into and fulfilling contracts and requires compliance of all public and private schools, regardless of whether they qualify as recipients of federal aid. The seminal case applying this law to a private education setting is *Runyon v. McCrary*, in which the Supreme Court held that § 1981 was violated when private school administrators rejected all applicants to their school who were not Caucasian.[37] The Court concluded that the practice violated the right to contract due to race, and purported that its ruling violated neither parents' privacy rights nor their freedom of association.

Notwithstanding, the Ninth Circuit in 2006 found no § 1981 violation where a private school in Hawaii founded by the descendants of King Kamehameha I denied admission to an applicant because he was not of Hawaiian ancestry.[38] In rendering its decision permitting continued use of race in making admission decisions and distinguishing the present case from *Runyon*, the court reasoned that the preference was remedial in nature in that it was targeted to assist native Hawaiian students who were performing less well academically than all other classes of students. Additionally, the court held that when Congress reenacted § 1981 in 1991, it likely intended to allow the operation of Kamehameha schools in Hawaii.

---

[34]551 U.S. 701 (2007) (aggregating claims from Parents Involved in Cmty. Sch. v. Seattle Sch. Dist. No. 1, 426 F.3d 1162 (9th Cir. 2005) and McFarland v. Jefferson Cnty. Pub. Schs., 416 F.3d 513 (6th Cir. 2005)).

[35]U.S. Dep't of Justice & U.S. Dep't of Educ., *Guidance on the Voluntary Use of Race to Achieve Diversity and Avoid Racial Isolation in Elementary and Secondary Schools* (2011), http://www.justice.gov/crt/about/edu/documents/guidanceelem.pdf.

[36]*See* No. 11-345 (argued Oct. 10, 2012).

[37]427 U.S. 160 (1976).

[38]Doe v. Kamehameha Schs., 470 F.3d 827 (9th Cir. 2006).

The next decade should continue to provide ample case law dealing with strategies designed to remedy past discrimination and to promote racial diversity in schools. Future cases are likely to be similar to those litigated over the past few years.

Race Discrimination and Matriculated Students

Although there are a number of laws that prohibit race discrimination in educational settings, there is no doubt that discrimination continues, though it is likely to be more subtle and therefore more difficult to prove than in prior years. Such discrimination has been alleged in such areas as the assignment to ability-based courses or programs (e.g., gifted, advanced, developmental);[39] athletic eligibility;[40] racial profiling;[41] academic dismissal from special programs;[42] sexual harassment and molestation;[43] the creation of a hostile environment;[44] and the like. More recent controversies have focused on the overrepresentation of minority students in school disciplinary matters, but little litigation has been generated in this area.[45]

Claims of racial discrimination also have been at issue in cases involving school mascots. In these cases, courts have addressed school mascots that are considered offensive to Native Americans. In one case, three Native American students and their mother contended that the school district's use of the Indian logo as a mascot was racially discriminatory. A Wisconsin appellate court did not find the logo to be discriminatory because it did not depict a negative stereotype.[46] The court further reasoned that the logo did not portray any particular tribe. Given these controversies, it is not surprising that the Oregon State Board of Education recently decided to ban Native American–themed mascots in schools.[47]

Even though there are only a limited number of cases reported with regard to racial discrimination involving matriculated students, it is still prudent for school officials to establish a written policy prohibiting race and other forms of impermissible discrimination, inform educators and staff of their individual responsibilities, promptly and thoroughly

---

[39]See, e.g., Hobson v. Hansen, 269 F. Supp. 401 (D.D.C. 1967), aff'd sub nom. Smuck v. Hobson, 408 F.2d 175 (D.C. Cir. 1969).

[40]See, e.g., Allen-Sherrod v. Henry Cnty. Sch. Dist., 248 F. App'x 145 (11th Cir. 2007).

[41]See, e.g., Carthans v. Jenkins, No. 04 C 4528, 2005 U.S. Dist. LEXIS 23294 (N.D. Ill. Oct. 6, 2005).

[42]See, e.g., Brewer v. Bd. of Trs. of Univ. of Ill., 479 F.3d 908 (7th Cir. 2007) (finding no discrimination and identifying no comparable student of another race who had ever been retained with a grade point average lower than plaintiff's who did not have extraordinarily compelling circumstances).

[43]Doe v. Smith, 470 F.3d 331 (7th Cir. 2006).

[44]Qualls v. Cunningham, 183 F. App'x 564 (7th Cir. 2006) (finding no support for the claim that school officials had created a racially hostile environment that caused plaintiff to receive poor grades and ultimately resulted in his academic dismissal).

[45]See Russ Skiba, Suzanne Eckes & Kevin Brown, African American Disproportionality in School Discipline: The Divide Between Best Evidence and Legal Remedy, 54 N.Y.L. SCH. L. REV. 1071 (2010) (finding that students of color are disproportionately represented in school discipline matters, but few recent cases involve this issue).

[46]Munson v. State Superintendent of Pub. Instruction, 577 N.W.2d 387 (Wis. Ct. App. 1998) (unpublished).

[47]Kim Murphy, Home of the Braves No More: Oregon Bans Native American Mascots, L.A. TIMES (May 18, 2012), http://articles.latimes.com/2012/may/18/nation/la-na-nn-native-mascots-20120518.

investigate claims of impropriety, conduct fair and impartial hearings, and determine an appropriate response (e.g., suspension of a student, termination of an employee) for those who have engaged in discriminatory behavior.

CLASSIFICATIONS BASED ON IMMIGRATION STATUS OR NATIVE LANGUAGE

School districts may not discriminate against students based on their immigrant status, and they have the responsibility to remove English-language barriers that impede equal participation of non-English-speaking students.

In addition to claims of racial discrimination, allegations have been made that public schools are discriminating against classes of students because of their immigration status or native language. With regard to immigration status, courts have generally ruled that public schools are obligated to educate school-age children who are residents, meaning they live in the district with their parents or legal guardian. In an important 1982 decision, *Plyler v. Doe*, the Supreme Court held that school districts could not deny a free public education to resident children whose parents had entered the country illegally.[48] Recognizing the individual's significant interest in receiving an education, the Court ruled that classifications affecting access to education must be substantially related to an important governmental objective to satisfy the Equal Protection Clause. The Court found that Texas's asserted interest in deterring aliens from entering the country illegally was not important enough to deny students an opportunity to be educated.

Despite this decision, states continue to consider and enact provisions that place obligations on schools to identify illegal immigrants and to notify state authorities regarding undocumented students. Although these laws do not specifically bar the education of such students at public expense, which Texas was not allowed to do in *Plyler*, the required identification of undocumented students is viewed as a deterrent to these children enrolling in public schools. In 2012, the Eleventh Circuit blocked implementation of such a provision in an Alabama law as violating the equal protection rights of the affected children.[49] A few months earlier, the Supreme Court struck down several parts of the Arizona immigration law as intruding on the federal government's responsibilities to regulate immigration, but upheld the part allowing police officers to verify the immigration status of those being arrested.[50] The Arizona law has no student identification provision, and whether states can require public schools to identify undocumented students has not yet been addressed by the Supreme Court. However, it is clear that such children cannot be denied a public education.

[48]457 U.S. 202 (1982).

[49]*See* United States v. Alabama, 691 F.3d 1269 (11th Cir. 2012).

[50]Arizona v. United States, 132 S. Ct. 2492 (2012).

With regard to native language, among the numerous identifiable "classes" of students in American schools are "linguistic minorities," some of whom have been denied an adequate education due to the failure of the school district to address their language differences through appropriate instruction. Educators may use bilingual education or other appropriate methods that assist English Language Learners (ELLs) in classrooms in which English is the primary language of instruction; school districts have the responsibility to remove English language barriers that impede equal participation of non-English-speaking students.

The rights of linguistic minorities are protected by the Fourteenth Amendment, Title VI of the Civil Rights Act of 1964, and the Equal Educational Opportunities Act of 1974 (EEOA).Title VI stipulates that "[n]o person in the United States shall, on the ground of race, color, or national origin, be excluded from participation in, be denied the benefits of, or be subjected to discrimination under any program or activity receiving [f]ederal financial assistance from the Department of Education."[51] Additionally, this statute requires compliance throughout a school district if *any* activity is supported by federal funds (e.g., special education). Discrimination against linguistic minorities is considered a form of national origin discrimination and is therefore prohibited by Title VI.

Moreover, the Equal Educational Opportunities Act (EEOA) of 1974 requires public school systems to develop appropriate programs for limited English proficient (LEP) students.[52] The Act mandates in part that "[n]o state shall deny equal educational opportunity to an individual on account of his or her race, color, sex, or national origin, by . . . the failure by an educational agency to take appropriate action to overcome language barriers that impede equal participation by its students in its instructional program."[53]

In the first U.S. Supreme Court decision involving the rights of LEP students, *Lau v. Nichols,* Chinese children asserted that the San Francisco public schools failed to provide for the needs of non-English-speaking students. The Supreme Court agreed with the students and held that the lack of sufficient remedial English instruction violated Title VI. The Court reasoned that equality of treatment was not realized merely by providing students with the same facilities, textbooks, teachers, and curriculum, and that requiring children to acquire English skills on their own before they could hope to make any progress in school made "a mockery of public education."[54] The Court emphasized that "basic English skills are at the very core of what these public schools teach," and, therefore, "students who do not understand English are effectively foreclosed from any meaningful education."[55]

Lower courts have also addressed important issues involving the rights of English language learners. A federal district court, in assessing compliance of the Denver public schools, concluded that **the law does not require a full bilingual education program for every LEP student but does place a duty on the district to take action to eliminate barriers that prevent LEP children from participating in the educational program**. A good

---

[51]42 U.S.C. § 2000d (2012). Regulations may be found at 34 C.F.R. § 100 (2012).

[52]20 U.S.C. § 1701 (2012).

[53]20 U.S.C. § 1703(f) (2012).

[54]Lau v. Nichols, 414 U.S. 563, 566 (1974).

[55]*Id.*

faith effort is inadequate. What is required, according to the court, is an effort that "will be reasonably effective in producing intended results."[56] In the absence of such an effort in the Denver public schools, an EEOA violation was found. Although a transitional bilingual program was selected by district personnel, it was not being implemented effectively, primarily due to poor teacher training, selection, and assignment.

California has generated a significant amount of case law involving the instruction of non- and limited English-speaking students. Many suits have attacked Proposition 227, which requires that all children in public schools be taught English through "sheltered English immersion" (SEI).[57] This approach requires the use of specially designed materials and procedures where "nearly all" classroom instruction is in English. In most instances, the law requires school districts to abandon their use of bilingual education. Notwithstanding the prior use of bilingual programming, immigrant children within the state had experienced a high dropout rate and were low in English literacy. Only those children who already possess good English language skills or those for whom an alternate course of study would be better suited may be excused from the SEI initiative. Even then, twenty or more exempted students per grade level are required before an alternative program such as bilingual education must be provided.

In *Horne v. Flores*, the Supreme Court provided further guidance in this area when it held that states and local educational authorities have wide latitude in determining which programs and techniques they will implement to meet their obligations under the Equal Educational Opportunity Act.[58] The state of Arizona was ultimately given relief from a decree related to an ELL program. The Court looked beyond funding for ELL instruction and determined that obligations under the original decree had been satisfied in other ways.

Another type of national origin/language discrimination was alleged in Kansas where the principal and several teachers prohibited students from speaking Spanish while on school grounds.[59] The student argued that the school district created a hostile environment based on national origin and race under Title VI. Overruling an earlier decision which granted the school district's motion for summary judgment, the court found that the student had established a prima facie case against the school district. In light of the significant growth of Hispanic and other populations immigrating to the United States, expect more litigation in this area.

---

[56]Keyes v. Sch. Dist. No. 1, 576 F. Supp. 1503, 1520 (D. Colo. 1983); *see also* Gomez v. Ill. State Bd. of Educ., 811 F.2d 1030, 1043 (7th Cir. 1987) (finding selection of transitional bilingual education was appropriate, but it had not been effectively implemented). *But see* Teresa P. v. Berkeley Unified Sch. Dist., 724 F. Supp. 698 (N.D. Cal. 1989) (holding school district's bilingual and ESL program was based on sound theory and appropriately implemented).

[57]Other states have passed similar ballot initiatives. For example, Arizona passed Proposition 203 in 2000 (ARIZ. REV. STAT. ANN. § 15-751(5) (2012)), and Massachusetts passed Question 2 in 2002 (MASS. GEN. LAWS ch. 386, § 1 (2012)) (amending ch. 71A).

[58]557 U.S. 433 (2009).

[59]Rubio v. Turner Unified Sch. Dist. No. 202, 523 F. Supp. 2d 1242 (D. Kan. 2007).

CLASSIFICATIONS BASED ON SEX[60]

Students are protected against discrimination based on sex, including sexual harassment by educators and peers.

Classifications and discriminatory treatment based on sex in public education are as old as public education itself, as the first public schools and colleges primarily served only males. When women eventually were allowed to enroll, programs for them were typically segregated and inferior. Over the years, sex equality in public schools has improved, but at times, classifications based on sex have limited both academic as well as extracurricular activities for females. Aggrieved parties often turn to federal courts to vindicate their rights. In most cases, plaintiffs allege a violation of either the Fourteenth Amendment or Title IX of the Education Amendments of 1972.[61] Under Title IX, educational recipients of federal financial assistance are prohibited from discriminating, excluding, or denying benefits because of sex.[62]

In addition, Title IX has been interpreted to prohibit retaliation against both students and staff who themselves are not the target of intentional discrimination but are adversely treated due to their advocacy roles. The Supreme Court addressed this issue in 2005 in *Jackson v. Birmingham Board of Education*, where a teacher/coach was removed from his coaching position, allegedly due to his complaints about the treatment of the girls' basketball team (i.e., not receiving equal funding, equal access to equipment and facilities, and so forth).[63] The Court reasoned that discriminatory treatment against advocates was impliedly prohibited by Title IX and remanded the case for a determination of whether the coach's advocacy was in fact the motivating factor in his removal.

Interscholastic Sports

Sex discrimination litigation involving interscholastic sports has focused on two primary themes: the integration of single-sex teams and the unequal treatment of males and females. Although courts will issue injunctions to correct discriminatory conduct where it is found, they will not award monetary damages unless the school receives actual notice of the violation and then is shown to be deliberately indifferent to the claim.[64]

---

[60]"Sex" generally refers to having male or female reproductive systems, whereas "gender" generally refers to social identity related to one's sex.

[61]20 U.S.C. § 1681 (2012).

[62]If aid is received by any program or activity within the school system, compliance must be demonstrated district-wide. Also, although Title IX does not include a specific statute of limitations, courts have elected to borrow the relevant limitations period for personal injury. *See, e.g.,* Stanley v. Trs. of Cal. State Univ., 433 F.3d 1129 (9th Cir. 2006) (identifying the appropriate limitations period to be one year).

[63]544 U.S. 167 (2005).

[64]Grandson v. Univ., 272 F.3d 568 (8th Cir. 2001).

Single-Sex Teams.   One of the more controversial issues involving high school athletics is the participation of males and females together in contact sports (e.g., wrestling, rugby, ice hockey, football, basketball, and other sports that involve physical contact). Title IX explicitly permits separation of students by sex within contact sports. However, individual school districts can determine whether to allow coeducational participation in contact sports in their efforts to provide equal athletic opportunities for males and females.[65] Where integration is either permitted or required in a contact sport, each athlete must receive a fair, nondiscriminatory opportunity to participate.

A New York federal district court reviewed a student's claim that she was not allowed to try out for the junior varsity football squad in violation of the Fourteenth Amendment.[66] The school district was unable to show that its policy of prohibiting mixed competition served an important governmental objective, as is required under intermediate scrutiny. In rejecting the district's assertion that its policy was necessary to ensure the health and safety of female students, the court noted that no female student was given the opportunity to show that she was as fit, or more fit, than the weakest male member of the team. A Wisconsin federal district court similarly ruled that female students have the constitutional right to compete for positions on traditionally male contact teams, declaring that once a state provides interscholastic competition, such opportunities must be provided to all students on equal terms.[67]

In addition to the controversies regarding coeducational participation in contact sports, there have been numerous challenges to policies denying integration of males and females in noncontact sports. **Title IX regulations explicitly require recipient districts to allow coeducational participation in those sports that are available only to one sex, presuming that athletic opportunities for that sex have been historically limited.** Thus, females tend to succeed in their claims, whereas males tend to fail.[68]

Fewer Sports Opportunities for Females.   Although athletic opportunities for females have significantly increased since passage of Title IX in 1972, equal opportunity has not been achieved within all school districts. The Office for Civil Rights' Policy Interpretation requires that for schools to be in compliance, they should (1) provide interscholastic sports opportunities for both sexes in terms of numbers of participants that are substantially proportionate to the respective enrollments of male and female students, (2) show a history of expanding sports programs for the underrepresented sex, or (3) provide enough opportunities to match the sports interests and abilities of the underrepresented sex.[69] Given such financial constraints, equality of athletic opportunities for males and females often has been achieved either by reducing the number of sports traditionally available for males[70] or by lowering the

[65]Elborough v. Evansville Cmty. Sch. Dist., 636 F. Supp. 2d 812 (W.D. Wis. 2009).

[66]Lantz v. Ambach, 620 F. Supp. 663 (S.D.N.Y. 1985); *see also* Adams v. Baker, 919 F. Supp. 1496 (D. Kan. 1996) (upholding female student's right under the Fourteenth Amendment to participate in wrestling).

[67]Leffel v. Wis. Interscholastic Athletic Ass'n, 444 F. Supp. 1117 (E.D. Wis. 1978).

[68]*See, e.g.,* Williams v. Sch. Dist., 998 F.2d 168 (3d Cir. 1993); Croteau v. Fair, 686 F. Supp. 552 (E.D. Va. 1988).

[69]U.S. Dep't of Educ. Office for Civil Rights' 1979 *Policy Interpretation*, 44 Fed. Reg. 71,413 (Dec. 11, 1979).

[70]*See, e.g.,* Chalenor v. Univ. of N.D., 291 F.3d 1042 (8th Cir. 2002); Boulahanis v. Bd. of Regents, 198 F.3d 633 (7th Cir. 1999); Miami Univ. Wrestling Club v. Miami Univ., 195 F. Supp. 2d 1010 (S.D. Ohio 2001).

number of participants on boys' teams (e.g., football) to provide generally equal opportunities for males and females.[71] Also, efforts have been made to disguise the existing inequity (e.g., double counting participants in women's indoor and outdoor track, but not double counting men in fall/spring events such as track, golf, and tennis) to avoid taking corrective action.

At times, female athletes have expressed an insufficient interest in a given sport to have it approved by the state athletic association. In a Kentucky case, high school athletes claimed a Title IX violation when the state athletic association refused to approve females' interscholastic fast-pitch softball. The association's decision was based on its policy of not sanctioning a sport unless at least 25 percent of its member institutions demonstrated an interest in participation. Since only 17 percent had indicated an interest, approval was denied. In the original hearing on this controversy, the Sixth Circuit had held that the 25 percent requirement did not violate the Equal Protection Clause because the facially neutral policy was not proven to entail intentional discrimination.[72] The case then was remanded and later appealed. The court again found no Title IX violation and further concluded that grouping sports by sex did not violate federal law.

The U.S. Department of Education issued a "Dear Colleague" letter in 2008 to provide further guidance to schools regarding how athletic opportunities are counted for Title IX compliance.[73] The letter outlines factors that may be considered in determining whether an institution has complied with Title IX. It stresses that the Office for Civil Rights will evaluate each institution on a case-by-case basis to allow flexibility in offering sports that align with the specific interests of the student body. Despite attempts to further explain the law, litigation in both PK–12 and higher education will likely continue as schools attempt to achieve greater sex equity.[74]

Academic Programs

Allegations of sex bias in public schools have not been confined to athletic programs. Differential treatment of males and females in academic courses and schools also has generated litigation.[75] **Because the "separate but equal" principle has been applied in cases alleging a Fourteenth Amendment violation, public school officials are required to show an exceedingly persuasive justification for classifications based on sex that are used to segregate the sexes or exclude either males or females from academic programs.**

[71]Neal v. Bd. of Trs., 198 F.3d 763 (9th Cir. 1999).

[72]Horner v. Ky. High Sch. Athletic Ass'n, 43 F.3d 265 (6th Cir. 1994).

[73]U.S. Dep't of Educ., *Dear Colleague Letter: Athletic Activities Counted for Title IX Compliance* (Sept. 17, 2008), http://www2.ed.gov/about/offices/list/ocr/letters/colleague-20080917.pdf.

[74]*See, e.g.*, Equity in Athletics, Inc. v. Dep't of Educ., 639 F.3d 91 (4th Cir. 2011) (finding nonprofit organization failed to show that the three-part test violated the Equal Protection Clause); Pederson v. La. State Univ., 213 F.3d 858 (5th Cir. 2000) (concluding that university had violated Title IX by failing to accommodate the interests and abilities of female athletes); Cohen v. Brown Univ., 101 F.3d 155 (1st Cir. 1996) (rejecting university's claim that female students were less interested in sports); Parker v. Franklin Cnty. Cmty. Sch. Corp., 667 F.3d 910 (7th Cir. 2012) (remanding case to determine if scheduling girls' basketball games on weeknights instead of weekend nights like the boys' games amounted to discrimination under Title IX).

[75]Gossett v. Oklahoma, 245 F.3d 1172 (10th Cir. 2001).

The Third Circuit held that the operation of two historically sex-segregated pub-lic high schools (one for males, the other for females) in which enrollment is voluntary and educational offerings are essentially equal, is permissible under the Equal Protection Clause, Title IX, and the Equal Educational Opportunities Act of 1974.[76] Noting that Phila-delphia's sex-segregated college preparatory schools offered functionally equivalent pro-grams, the court concluded that the separation of the sexes was justified because youth might study more effectively in sex-segregated high schools. The court emphasized that the female plaintiff was not compelled to attend the sex-segregated academic school; she had the option of enrolling in a coeducational school within her attendance zone. Further-more, the court stated that her petition to attend the male academic high school was based on personal preference rather than on an objective evaluation of the offerings available in the two schools. Subsequently, an equally divided United States Supreme Court affirmed this decision without delivering an opinion. Interestingly, in another case, which involved the same Philadelphia school as the *Vorchheimer* case, three female students were denied admission at the all-male Philadelphia high school.[77] In this case, a common pleas court in Pennsylvania did not find the public school for the girls and the public school for the boys to be substantially similar. Some of the alleged inequities between the two schools included a "Bachelor of Arts" degree instead of a typical high school diploma, smaller class sizes, a larger building, and more books and computers at the boys' school. As a result of some of the inequities, the court held that the female students must be admitted to the all-male school.

Detroit school officials did not prevail in their attempt to segregate inner-city, African American male students to address more effectively these students' unique educational needs. Three African American male academies (preschool to fifth grade, sixth to eighth grade, and high school) were proposed. The three-year experimental academies were designed to offer an Afrocentric curriculum, emphasize male responsibility, provide mentors, offer Saturday classes and extended classroom hours, and provide individual counseling. No comparable program existed for females, although school authorities indicated that one would be forthcoming. The district court issued a preliminary injunction prohibiting the board from opening the academies, given the likelihood that the practice violated the Equal Protection Clause.

In a higher education case with PK–12 implications, the Supreme Court in 1982 struck down a nursing school's admission policy that restricted admission in degree pro-grams to females without providing comparable opportunities for males.[78] The Court found no evidence that women had ever been denied opportunities in the field of nursing that would justify remedial action by the state. In applying intermediate scrutiny, the Court con-cluded that the university failed its burden of showing that the facially discriminatory sex classification served an important governmental objective or that its discriminatory means were substantially related to the achievement of those objectives.

---

[76]Vorchheimer v. Sch. Dist., 532 F.2d 880 (3d Cir. 1976), *aff'd mem. by equally divided court*, 430 U.S. 703 (1977).

[77]Newberg v. Bd. of Pub. Educ., 26 Pa. D. & C.3d 682 (C.P. Phila. Cnty. 1983).

[78]Miss. Univ. for Women v. Hogan, 458 U.S. 718 (1982).

Similarly, the U.S. Supreme Court addressed male-only admissions policies in *United States v. Virginia*. The Court held that the state had violated the Fourteenth Amendment in failing to provide equal opportunities for women in the area of military training when they were denied admission at the Virginia Military Institute.[79] A new program at a private, women-only institution would never be able to approach the success, quality, and prestige associated with that provided at VMI.

In 2006, the U.S. Department of Education issued new regulations that permit school districts to offer voluntary public single-sex classrooms and schools.[80] These regulations were a result of language included in the No Child Left Behind Act of 2001, which encourages school districts to experiment with public single-sex education programs.[81] Under Title IX regulations, coeducational schools must offer equal educational opportunities to both sexes, and enrollment in a single-sex class should be completely voluntary. Specifically, non-vocational public single-sex schools are permitted, but a substantially similar coeducational school or single-sex school for students of the other sex must be available. Also, one of two objectives must be satisfied before implementing a single-sex educational program. The program must (1) improve the educational achievement of a recipient's students through an established policy to provide diverse educational opportunities or (2) meet the particular, identified educational needs of a recipient's students.[82] As a result of these amendments, many school districts have begun to experiment with single-sex educational programs. For example, although only three single-sex public education programs existed in the United States in 1995,[83] by 2010, there were roughly 500 schools offering some single-sex classes in forty states[84] and ninety single-sex public schools nationally.[85]

Recent litigation involves the amended Title IX regulations as well as the Equal Protection Clause in combination with other claims arising out of state law. In these legal challenges, the female students generally argue that school officials have failed to demonstrate an "exceedingly persuasive" justification for creating single-sex educational programs.[86] The outcomes of these cases have been mixed.

---

[79]518 U.S. 515 (1996).

[80]Title IX Regulations, 34 C.F.R. § 106.34 (2012).

[81]No Child Left Behind Act § 5131(a)(23)–c (2012).

[82]Title IX Regulations (2006); 34 C.F.R. §106.34(b)(1)(i)(A) & (B) (2012).

[83]Diane Schemo, *Change in Federal Rules Backs Single-Sex Public Education*, N.Y. TIMES, Oct. 25, 2006, at A1.

[84]Tamar Lewin, *Single-Sex Education is Assailed in Report*, N.Y. TIMES, Sept., 23, 2011, at A19.

[85]Meagan Patterson & Erin Pahlke, *Student Characteristics Associated with Girls' Success in a Single-Sex School*, 65 SEX ROLES 737 (2010).

[86]*See, e.g.*, Doe v. Vermilion Parish Sch. Bd., 421 F. App'x 366 (5th Cir. 2011) (denying school district's motion to dismiss because students provided sufficient evidence that single-sex program may be harmful); Doe v. Wood Cnty. Bd. of Educ., 888 F. Supp. 2d 771 (S.D. W. Va. 2012) (granting students' request for preliminary injunction prohibiting school district from operating single-sex classes). *But see* A.N.A. v. Breckinridge Cnty. Bd. of Educ., 833 F. Supp. 2d 673 (W.D. Ky. 2011) (finding that female students did not suffer an injury when school district offered optional single-sex classes).

Sexual Harassment of Students

Title IX and the Equal Protection Clause of the Fourteenth Amendment also have been applied in sex-based claims of sexual harassment and abuse of students. Under the Equal Protection Clause, students have the right to be free from harassment on an equal basis with all other students, while Title IX prohibits discrimination on the basis of sex. Historically, charges of sexual harassment against school districts generally were dismissed. But in 1992, the Supreme Court rendered *Franklin v. Gwinnett County Public Schools*, involving a female student's allegations that a coach initiated sexual conversations, engaged in inappropriate touching, and had coercive intercourse with her on school grounds on several occasions. The Court held that Title IX prohibited the sexual harassment of students and that damages could be awarded where appropriate.[87] Since *Gwinnett*, numerous other cases—with mixed results—have been filed by current and former students alleging hostile environment,[88] student-to-student harassment,[89] sexual involvement and abuse of students by school staff,[90] and same sex harassment.[91] With *Gwinnett* as a starting point, two similar but slightly different standards have evolved: one for employee-to-student harassment and the other for student-to-student harassment.

Employee-to-Student Harassment.   In 1998, the Supreme Court provided further guidance in *Gebser v. Lago Vista Independent School District* regarding the liability of school districts when students are harassed by school employees.[92] In this case, a high school student and a teacher were involved in a relationship that had not been reported to the administration until the couple was discovered having sex and the teacher was arrested. The district then terminated the teacher's employment, and the parents sued under Title IX. On appeal, the Supreme Court held that to be liable, the district had to have *actual notice* of the harassment. The Court reasoned that allowing recovery of damages based on either respondeat superior or constructive notice (i.e., notice that is inferred or implied) would be inconsistent with the objective of the Act, as liability would attach even though the district had no actual knowledge of the conduct or an opportunity to take action to end the harassment.[93] Accordingly, **for there to be an award of damages, an official who has the authority to address the alleged discrimination must have *actual knowledge* of the inappropriate conduct and then fail to ameliorate the problem. Moreover, the failure to respond must amount to *deliberate indifference* to the discrimination.** In the instant case, the plaintiff did not

---

[87]503 U.S. 60 (1992).

[88]*See, e.g.,* Jennings v. Univ. of N.C., 444 F.3d 255 (4th Cir. 2006).

[89]*See, e.g.,* Estate of Brown v. Ogletree, No. 11-cv-1491, 2012 U.S. Dist. LEXIS 21968 (S.D. Tex. Feb. 21, 2012); Price v. Scranton, 11-0095, 2012 U.S. Dist. LEXIS 1651 (M.D. Pa. Jan. 6, 2012).

[90]*See, e.g.,* Blue v. Dist. of Columbia, 850 F. Supp. 2d 16 (D.D.C. 2012).

[91]*See, e.g.,* Shrum v. Kluck, 249 F.3d 773 (8th Cir. 2001); Martin v. Swartz Cmty. Schs., 419 F. Supp. 2d 967 (E.D. Mich. 2006).

[92]524 U.S. 274 (1998).

[93]*See* Henderson v. Walled Lake Consol. Schs., 469 F.3d 479 (6th Cir. 2006) (observing that even if administrators had notice that a female soccer player was involved in a relationship with her coach, such awareness did not establish notice that the plaintiff, another member of the team, had been exposed to a hostile environment).

argue that actual notice had been provided, and the district's failure to promulgate a related policy and grievance procedure failed to qualify as deliberate indifference.

In subsequent litigation, courts have assessed who is an "appropriate official" with authority to act, what constitutes "actual knowledge," and what substantiates "deliberate indifference." *Gebser* did not identify which individuals in the school district must have knowledge.[94] Without deciding whether a principal possesses this authority, several courts have assumed, for the purpose of analyzing claims, that principals have the power to remedy abuse.[95] To illustrate, the Eleventh Circuit concluded that a principal's knowledge of the harassment was sufficient and that he was an appropriate person because of his authority to take corrective measures.[96]

Questions also have arisen concerning notice of sexual harassment or abuse. Evidence indicating a potential or theoretical risk has not been equated with actual knowledge. The Third Circuit warned that "a 'possibility' cannot be equated with a 'known act.'"[97] The Eighth Circuit noted that the principal was unaware of the high school basketball coach having a sexual relationship with a student. Although the coach had sent inappropriate text messages to several female players, the court did not find the messages to have provided the principal with actual notice of the specific relationship. Further, when the victim's mother asked the principal if something was going on between her daughter and the coach, the court observed that the parent's question did not constitute actual notice.[98] The Eleventh Circuit, however, reasoned that a principal's knowledge of a teacher's alleged touching and propositions to students provided sufficient notice.[99] A few courts have addressed whether other school officials, in addition to school principals, have the power to respond to abuse. For example, the Eighth Circuit stated that "we do not hold that guidance counselors and school teachers are never 'appropriate persons' for the purposes of finding a school district liable for discrimination under Title IX," but in this particular case, they had not been vested with sufficient authority to address the harassment.[100]

To counter claims of deliberate indifference, school officials must show that they took action on complaints. For example, a principal was not found to be deliberately indifferent because he contacted his superior and took corrective measures by asking the counselor to interview the student, the accused teacher, and other possible witnesses.[101]

[94]*See* Warren v. Reading Sch. Dist., 278 F.3d 163 (3d. Cir. 2002) (remanding for a determination of who may qualify as an "appropriate person" to receive actual notice under the *Gebser* standard; a criminally prosecuted male teacher was fired because of his sexual involvement with male students).

[95]*See, e.g.*, Davis v. Dekalb Cnty. Sch. Dist., 233 F.3d 1367 (11th Cir. 2000); Doe v. Dallas Indep. Sch. Dist., 220 F.3d 380 (5th Cir. 2000); Flores v. Saulpaugh, 115 F. Supp. 2d 319 (N.D.N.Y. 2000).

[96]Doe v. Sch. Bd., 604 F.3d 1248 (11th Cir. 2010).

[97]Bostic v. Smyrna Sch. Dist., 418 F.3d 355, 361 (3d Cir. 2005); *see also* N.R. Doe v. St. Francis Sch. Dist., 694 F.3d 869 (7th Cir. 2012) (finding that staff suspicions of inappropriate relationship between a teacher and a student did not qualify as actual knowledge).

[98]Doe v. Flaherty, 623 F.3d 577 (8th Cir. 2010); *see also* Blue v. Dist. of Columbia, 850 F. Supp. 2d 16 (D.D.C. 2012) (finding that appropriate person lacked knowledge of student's sexual relationship with teacher).

[99]Doe v. Sch. Bd. of Broward Cnty., 604 F.3d 1248 (11th Cir. 2010).

[100]Plamp v. Mitchell Sch. Dist. No. 172, 565 F.3d 450, 459 (8th Cir. 2009).

[101]Davis v. Dekalb Cnty. Sch. Dist., 233 F.3d 1367 (11th Cir. 2000).

Although these actions may have appeared insufficient and did not prevent the teacher from sexually molesting students, the court found the relevant fact to be that the principal did not act with deliberate indifference. It should be noted, however, that school districts that "shuffle" abusive teachers to other districts might generate legal challenges.[102]

Also of relevance in hostile environment cases where school personnel are allegedly involved is the fact that, at least for younger children, the behavior does not have to be "unwelcome," as it does in Title VII (Civil Rights Act of 1964) employment cases.[103] The Seventh Circuit reviewed a case where a twenty-one-year-old male kitchen worker had a consensual sexual relationship with a thirteen-year-old middle school female.[104] The court noted that under Indiana criminal law, a person under the age of sixteen cannot consent to sexual intercourse and that children may not even understand that they are being harassed. To rule that only behavior that is not unwelcome is actionable would permit violators to take advantage of impressionable youth who voluntarily participate in requested conduct. Moreover, if welcomeness were an issue properly before the court, the children bringing the suits would be subject to intense scrutiny regarding their degree of fault.

Student-to-Student Harassment.   Educators must be in control of the school environment, including student conduct, and eliminate known dangers and harassment. Not all harassment will be known, however, and not all behavior that is offensive will be so severe as to violate Title IX. Also, for student-to-student harassment to be actionable, the behavior must be unwelcome. Further clarification regarding liability associated with student-to-student harassment was provided in 1999 when the Supreme Court in *Davis v. Monroe County Board of Education*[105] proposed a two-part test: (1) whether the board acted with deliberate indifference to known acts of harassment and (2) whether the harassment was so severe, pervasive, and objectively offensive that it effectively barred the victim's access to an educational opportunity or benefit.[106]

The *Davis* Court remanded the case to determine whether these standards were met. The plaintiff's daughter had allegedly been subjected to unwelcome sexual touching and rubbing as well as sexual talk. On one occasion, the violating student put a doorstop in his pants and acted in a sexually suggestive manner toward the plaintiff. Ultimately, the youth was charged with and pled guilty to sexual battery for his misconduct. The victim and her mother notified several teachers, the coach, and the principal of these incidences. No disciplinary action was ever taken other than to threaten the violating student with possible sanctions.

Since the *Davis* decision, courts have addressed several cases involving peer harassment under Title IX. In these cases, plaintiffs sometimes have difficulty proving that school

---

[102]*See, e.g.,* Doe-2 v. McLean Cnty. Unit Dist. No. 5, 593 F.3d 507, 517 (7th Cir. 2010); Shrum v. Kluck, 249 F.3d 773 (8th Cir. 2001).

[103]J.F.K. v. Troup Cnty. Sch. Dist., 678 F.3d 1254 (11th Cir. 2012).

[104]Mary M. v. N. Lawrence Cmty. Sch. Corp., 131 F.3d 1220 (7th Cir. 1997).

[105]526 U.S. 629 (1999).

[106]*See* Bruneau v. S. Kortright Cent. Sch. Dist., 163 F.3d 749 (2d Cir. 1998) (affirming lower court's determination that offensive behavior of male students against a female student did not qualify as harassment or adversely affect her education).

officials had actual knowledge of the harassment or acted with deliberate indifference. For example, when a cheerleader claimed that she had been harassed by another cheerleader, the school official was not found to have acted with deliberate indifference because he took the action that was required under the school's harassment policy.[107] Specifically, the principal created a formal report outlining the investigation and actions taken to prevent further harassment. He removed the alleged perpetrator from the plaintiff's sixth period class and took other efforts to keep the two students apart. As noted, plaintiffs also need to demonstrate that they were denied educational benefits as a result of the harassment. In a Sixth Circuit case, although a mother outlined that the harassment her daughter experienced at school was pervasive, she failed to explain how the incidents deprived her daughter access to educational opportunities and benefits.[108] Some plaintiffs have struggled to demonstrate that the harassment is sufficiently severe or pervasive.[109] Interestingly, courts have found that "pervasiveness" may be established under Title IX by a one-time sexual assault.[110] Thus, if the conduct is quite egregious, it does not have to be repeated to abridge Title IX.

Neither Eleventh Amendment immunity[111] nor the claim that the violator was engaged in First Amendment protected free speech may be used as defenses to Title IX actions.[112] As a result, damages awards[113] are available from educational institutions receiving federal funds, although not from those persons who were directly responsible for the harassment.[114] Also, plaintiffs can allege that they are entitled to damages under § 1983 for a violation of their federal constitutional or statutory rights.[115] Of course, violators can be sued directly under state tort law for sexual battery or intentional infliction of emotional distress,[116] and criminal charges may be filed against perpetrators where force is used or minors

---

[107]Sanches v. Carrolton-Farmers Branch Indep. Sch. Dist., 647 F.3d 156 (5th Cir. 2011); *see also* Long v. Murray Cnty. Sch. Dist., No. 4:10-CV-00015, 2012 U.S. Dist. LEXIS 86155 (N.D. Ga. May 21, 2012) (concluding that administrators were not deliberately indifferent toward harassment because they had disciplined the harassers, and they took steps to prevent harm).

[108]Pahssen v. Merrill Cmty. Sch. Dist., 668 F.3d 356 (6th Cir. 2012), *cert. denied*, No. 12-8, 2012 U.S. LEXIS 6437 (Oct. 1, 2012).

[109]McSweeney v. Bayport Bluepoint Cent. Sch. Dist., 864 F. Supp. 2d 240 (E.D.N.Y. 2012) (holding that incidents involving a book being dropped on a finger and other threats were not severe or pervasive, nor were they based on sex or gender); *see also* Wolfe v. Fayetteville, 648 F.3d 860 (8th Cir. 2011) (finding that name-calling does not amount to sex-based harassment under Title IX unless motivated by hostility toward a person's sex).

[110]Doe T.Z. v. City of N.Y., 634 F. Supp. 2d 263 (E.D.N.Y. 2009); S.S. v. Alexander, 177 P.3d 724 (Wash. Ct. App. 2008).

[111]*See, e.g.*, Franks v. Ky. Sch. for the Deaf, 142 F.3d 360 (6th Cir. 1998).

[112]*See, e.g.*, Cohen v. San Bernardino Valley Coll., 883 F. Supp. 1407 (C.D. Cal. 1995), *aff'd in part, rev'd in part, remanded*, 92 F.3d 968 (9th Cir. 1996).

[113]*See, e.g.*, Doe v. E. Haven Bd. of Educ., 200 F. App'x 46 (2d Cir. 2006) (affirming award of $100,000 to a victim of student-to-student harassment; finding officials deliberately indifferent to the harassment, taunting, and name-calling following plaintiff's rape). However, it is unlikely that punitive awards are available under Title IX. *See* Schultzen v. Woodbury Cent. Cmty. Sch. Dist., 187 F. Supp. 2d 1099 (N.D. Iowa 2002).

[114]*See, e.g.*, Hartley v. Parnell, 193 F.3d 1263 (11th Cir. 1999).

[115]*See, e.g.*, Fitzgerald v. Barnstable Sch. Comm., 555 U.S. 246 (2009).

[116]*See, e.g.*, Johnson v. Elk Lake Sch. Dist., 283 F.3d 138 (3d Cir. 2002).

are involved. In 2011, the U.S. Department of Education issued further guidance related to the harassment of students.[117] The Department explained that, in addition to prohibiting harassment based on sex, Title IX also prohibits gender-based harassment, including hostility based on sex or sex stereotyping and harassing conduct that is not sexual in nature.

Also, the Department of Education's Revised Sexual Harassment Guidance states that "sexual harassment directed at gay or lesbian students that is sufficiently serious to limit or deny a student's ability to participate in or benefit from the school's program constitutes sexual harassment prohibited by Title IX under the circumstances of this guidance."[118] In recent years, several cases have been filed under Title IX that have addressed same-sex or gender-based harassment or harassment based on perceived sexual orientation.[119] Students have generally been successful in demonstrating that these claims are covered by Title IX.

The high volume of sexual harassment litigation will likely continue. Even when administrators deal with claims of sexual harassment in timely and effective ways, parents still may file suit. They will be understandably angry that their child has been subjected to inappropriate behavior and will be looking for someone to blame, if not pay.

CONCLUSION

A basic purpose of public education is to prepare students for postsecondary life, regardless of their innate characteristics. Accordingly, courts and legislatures have become increasingly assertive in guaranteeing that students have the chance to realize their capabilities while in school. Arbitrary classification practices that disadvantage certain groups are not tolerated. Conversely, valid classifications, applied in the best interests of students, are generally supported. Indeed, some legal mandates require the classification of certain students to ensure that they receive instruction appropriate to their needs.

Sex-based classification schemes and discrimination are likely to continue to be heavily litigated, particularly involving harassment and sports opportunities. Also, the number of cases that claim native language discrimination will likely increase, given the significant number of non-English-speaking persons who immigrate yearly, and race discrimination cases will focus on both desegregation and efforts to achieve diverse student bodies.

---

[117]U.S. Dep't of Educ., *Dear Colleague Letter* (April 4, 2011), http://www2.ed.gov/about/offices/list/ocr/letters/colleague-201104.html. (This letter is a supplement to the Office for Civil Rights' *Revised Sexual Harassment Guidance* issued in 2001.)

[118]Office for Civil Rights, Dep't of Educ., *Revised Sexual Harassment Guidance: Harassment of Students by School Employees, Other Students, or Third Parties* (Jan. 2001), http://www2.ed.gov/about/offices/list/ocr/docs/shguide.pdf.

[119]*See* Patterson v. Hudson Area Schs., 551 F.3d 438 (6th Cir. 2009) (holding that issues of fact remained regarding whether a school district was deliberately indifferent in responding to harassment of a student who was perceived to be gay); Dawn L. v. Greater Johnstown Sch. Dist., 586 F. Supp. 2d 332 (W.D. Pa. 2008) (finding same-sex sexual harassment had occurred in violation of Title IX); Martin v. Swartz Cmty. Schs., 419 F. Supp. 2d 967 (E.D. Mich. 2006) (denying school district's motion for summary judgment involving a gay student's Title IX claim of peer harassment). *But see* Tyrrell v. Seaford Union Free Sch. Dist., 792 F. Supp. 2d 601 (E.D.N.Y. 2011) (holding that student failed to demonstrate that alleged harassment based on website postings of her engaged in sexual activity with another female student were related to gender).

POINTS TO PONDER

1. A student and coach had a three-month affair that included sexual involvement. The student is eighteen years old and voluntarily participated in all of the activities; the coach was tenured as a social studies teacher. The parents learned of the affair and informed the superintendent and principal. Both the student and coach admitted to their involvement. The coach was fired following an appropriate hearing; the parents nevertheless sued the district claiming a Title IX violation. How will the court respond?

2. An alternative school has been specially designed to address the unique needs of African American males; a comparable program has been developed for African American females. Both are to begin in the fall. Two suits are filed: one alleging a violation of Title IX, the other claiming a Title VI infraction. Who wins each suit, and why?

✳ 3. School officials refused parents' request for a bilingual program for their non-English-speaking children. The parents then retained the services of three nationally known experts on bilingual education; each provided significant data that supported the use of bilingual education in the elimination of language barriers. Nonetheless, the district still refused to provide the requested program and, in the alternative, offered an English as a Second Language program. School officials were unsure which of the two instructional methods was better, but claimed that they were not required to offer the best program. The parents sued the district under Title VI and the Equal Educational Opportunities Act. What will be the outcome of their legal challenge?

4. The local school district has been unitary for ten years. Recently, however, the state implemented (1) a plan allowing students to enroll in private schools, (2) a program in which students are permitted to transfer to any adjacent public school district, and (3) a transfer program in which students may attend any public school in the state if their home school fails to meet state guidelines. Under these provisions, the district once again became racially segregated. A lawsuit was filed under the Fourteenth Amendment and Title VI challenging recent changes that have resulted in resegregation. Will the plaintiffs succeed in this suit?

CHAPTER SEVEN

RIGHTS OF STUDENTS WITH DISABILITIES

Since children with disabilities represent a vulnerable minority group, their treatment has resulted in considerable judicial and legislative concern. Courts have addressed the constitutional rights of such children to attend school and to be classified accurately and instructed appropriately.

LEGAL CONTEXT

Education must be made available to all school-age children. Those with qualifying disabilities have additional rights guaranteeing them a free appropriate public education (FAPE).

Case law supporting the inclusion of children with disabilities, lobbying efforts, and changes in state laws helped to pave the way for the passage of federal laws specially designed to protect and enhance the rights of individuals with disabilities. Section 504 of the Rehabilitation Act, the Americans with Disabilities Act (ADA), and the Individuals with Disabilities Education Act (IDEA) are reviewed briefly below (see Table 7.1).

Section 504 of the Rehabilitation Act

Section 504 of the Rehabilitation Act of 1973 applies to both public and private recipients of federal financial assistance. Section 504 stipulates that otherwise qualified individuals shall not be excluded from participating in, be denied the benefits of, or be subjected to discrimination by recipient programs or activities, if that treatment is due to their disabilities.[1] Under the Rehabilitation Act, an individual with a disability is one who **has a physical or mental impairment**[2] **that substantially limits one or more major life activities, has**

[1] 29 U.S.C. § 794(a) (2012).
[2] 34 C.F.R. § 104.3(j)(2)(i) (2012).

144

TABLE 7.1   Applicability of Selected Federal Laws Affecting Students with Disabilities

FEDERAL LAW	PUBLIC RECIPIENT REQUIRED TO COMPLY	PUBLIC NON-RECIPIENT REQUIRED TO COMPLY	PRIVATE RECIPIENT REQUIRED TO COMPLY	PRIVATE NON-RECIPIENT REQUIRED TO COMPLY
Fourteenth Amendment Equal Protection Clause	Yes	Yes	No	No—except state athletic ass'ns
Fourteenth Amendment Due Process Clause	Yes	Yes	No	No—except state athletic ass'ns
42 USC § 1983	Yes	Yes	No	No—except state athletic ass'ns
Rehabilitation Act § 504	Yes	No	Yes	No
ADA—Title II	Yes	Yes	No	No
ADA—Title III	No	No	Yes	Yes
IDEA	Yes, if recipient of IDEA funds	No	No, service contracts do not qualify	No

a record of impairment, or is regarded as having an impairment.[3] These latter two definitions (i.e., "record of" and "regarded as") apply when a person has been subjected to discrimination, such as a teacher being terminated due to having a record of hospitalization for tuberculosis[4] or excluded from school for being HIV positive.[5] However, only those children who meet the first definition—having an impairment that is substantially limiting—will be eligible for reasonable accommodations and modifications.

In addition, **the disability must *substantially limit a major life activity*.**[6] In making this determination, courts compare the performance difficulties of the student with those of the theoretical "average person" (or in this discussion, "average student") in the general population. **To qualify, the student will have to be either incapable of performing the designated activity or significantly restricted; merely functioning below average will be insufficient.** This assessment requires a case-by-case evaluation, because impairments will vary in severity, affect people differently, and may or may not be restricting given the nature of the life activity.[7] As a result, some students with physical or mental impairments

[3]34 C.F.R. § 104.3(j)(1) (2012).

[4]Sch. Bd. v. Arline, 480 U.S. 273 (1987) (concluding that a teacher suffering from tuberculosis qualified as an individual with a disability because she had a record of physical impairment that limited a major life activity—working).

[5]Ray v. Sch. Dist., 666 F. Supp. 1524 (M.D. Fla. 1987).

[6]Major life activities include caring for oneself, performing manual tasks, walking, seeing, hearing, speaking, breathing, learning, working. *See* 34 C.F.R. § 104.3(j)(2)(ii) (2012).

[7]*See, e.g.,* Smith v. Tingipahoa Parish Sch. Bd., No. 05-6648, 2006 U.S. Dist. LEXIS 85377 (E.D. La. Nov. 22, 2006) (finding student's severe allergy was not an impairment that substantially limited her ability to learn).

Section 504

will be substantially limited and others with the same diagnosis will not, with only the former qualifying as disabled under § 504. Failure to recognize the fact that § 504 provides protection only for persons who are disabled, not for those who are merely impaired, can lead to the overclassification of students. This, then, could result in increased administrative and instructional costs, greater parental expectations for programming, and the increased likelihood of litigation.

When a student's limitation qualifies as a disability, it still is necessary to determine whether he or she is *otherwise qualified*. At the PK–12 level, children qualify if they are of school age or if they are eligible for services for the disabled under either state law or the Individuals with Disabilities Education Act (IDEA).[8] Students who qualify under § 504, but not under IDEA (e.g., general education children who are wheelchair confined) must be provided with accommodation plans that will include individualized aids and services that allow participation in the recipient's program.[9] The programs must be delivered in accessible facilities,[10] and programming must be designed and selected to meet the needs of students with disabilities to the same extent that their nondisabled peers' needs are met. Furthermore, children with disabilities should not be segregated from other children unless in the rare instance that appropriate services cannot otherwise be provided in the general education classroom. Where such segregation exists, programs must be comparable in materials, facilities, teacher quality, length of school term, and daily hours of instruction.

When the recipient and the parents disagree on whether an appropriate education has been provided, the parents have the right to review records, participate in an impartial hearing, and be represented by counsel. Section 504 is not specific as to the procedures that must be followed, but it does acknowledge that providing notice and hearing rights comparable to those mandated under IDEA will suffice. In addition, parents have the right to file a complaint with the Office for Civil Rights within 180 days of the alleged discrimination. Officials are responsible for investigating the claim and reviewing pertinent practices and policies. Where violations exist, federal regulations support the use of informal negotiations and voluntary action on the part of the recipient to become compliant.[11] If the recipient fails to correct its discriminatory practices, federal funds may be terminated.

There is a private right of action (e.g., the right to sue) under § 504, although IDEA exhaustion requirements must be met if the relief sought also is available under IDEA. Moreover, where a suit is filed under both IDEA and § 504, the portion of the § 504 claim dealing with the provision of an appropriate program will be dismissed if the IDEA suit is dismissed.[12] Immunity defenses under the Eleventh Amendment are unlikely to be

---

[8]34 C.F.R. § 104.3(I)(2) (2012).

[9]Furthermore, it is the position of the Office for Civil Rights that a student who qualifies under IDEA is not entitled also to receive a plan formulated consistent with the provisions of § 504. Response to McKethan, 25 INDIVIDUALS WITH DISABILITIES EDUC. L. REP. 295 (OCR 1996).

[10]34 C.F.R. § 104.22 (2012). To comply, a recipient need not make each existing facility or every part of a facility accessible, but must operate its programs so that they are accessible to individuals with disabilities.

[11]34 C.F.R. § 100.7(c), (d) (2012).

[12]*See, e.g.*, N.L. v. Knox Cnty. Schs., 315 F.3d 688 (6th Cir. 2003).

accepted,[13] and attorneys' fees may be awarded to prevailing plaintiffs.[14] In addition, damage awards are available where bad faith or gross misjudgment is supported in cases regarding the failure to provide accommodations and modifications.[15]

Americans with Disabilities Act

In 1990, Congress passed the Americans with Disabilities Act (ADA).[16] Two titles of that Act are of particular importance to students with disabilities: Title II applies to public schools and Title III applies to those that are private. Like § 504, these titles prohibit discrimination against persons (birth to death) who are disabled. Unlike § 504, the ADA requires compliance of schools that do not receive federal aid and were not heretofore federally regulated. Complaints must be filed with the Department of Justice within 180 days of an alleged violation.

Individuals with Disabilities Education Act

Pertaining specifically to education, Part B of the Education of the Handicapped Act was amended by Public Law 94-142 in 1975. This funding law now is known as the Individuals with Disabilities Education Act (IDEA)[17] and is enforced by the Office of Special Education Programs. States, but not local education agencies (e.g., public school districts), have the option of declining IDEA funds, thereby avoiding the myriad compliance requirements. Since states still are required to address the needs of students with disabilities as stipulated in § 504 (and the ADA), all states currently participate in the IDEA financial assistance program. To qualify for services under IDEA, a child must:

- have intellectual disabilities;
- be hard of hearing, deaf, speech or language impaired, visually impaired, blind, or emotionally disturbed;
- be orthopedically impaired;
- be autistic or learning disabled;[18]
- be otherwise health impaired; or
- suffer from traumatic brain injury and, as a result, be in need of special education and related services.[19]

[13]*See, e.g.*, Bowers v. NCAA, 475 F.3d 524 (3d Cir. 2007).

[14]*See, e.g.*, L.T. v. Mansfield Twp. Sch. Dist., No. 04-1381, 2009 U.S. Dist. LEXIS 21737 (D.N.J. Aug. 11, 2009).

[15]*See, e.g.*, B.L. v. Boyertown Area Sch. Dist., 452 F. App'x 172 (E.D. Pa. 2009).

[16]42 U.S.C. §§ 12101–12213 (2012).

[17]20 U.S.C. § 1400 (2012). Revisions of IDEA at times are referred to as Public Law 94-142, IDEA '97, or IDEA '04 (also known as the Individuals with Disabilities Education Improvement Act (IDEIA)). The name of the law, however, has not changed in recent years and will be referred to as the Individuals with Disabilities Education Act.

[18]In determining whether a child has a specific learning disability, the district is not required to consider whether a severe discrepancy exists between achievement and ability. *See* 20 U.S.C. § 1414(b)(6)(A) (2012).

[19]20 U.S.C. § 1401(3)(A) (2012). Not all children with special needs will qualify as disabled. *See, e.g.*, T.B. v. Bryan Indep. Sch. Dist., 628 F.3d 240 (5th Cir. 2010) (finding that a student with attention deficit hyperactivity disorder did not fall within the statutory definition of disabled under IDEA).

Accordingly, it is possible to have a disability but not be in need of special education and, therefore, not qualify for services under the IDEA. Although a child must qualify as "disabled" under one or more of the above categories for the state and district to receive federal funding, it is not necessary to label the child to provide an individualized education program.[20] It is important, however, for the child's needs to be correctly identified and for those needs to be properly addressed. Given that most school controversies involve the IDEA, the next sections focus primarily on various elements of this law.

INDIVIDUALIZED EDUCATION PROGRAMS

Individualized education programs must be designed to provide the child with some educational benefit and be made available in the neighborhood school when appropriate.

The process of preparing and delivering an appropriate program begins when a child with a disability is identified and ends only when the child withdraws or graduates from school, fails to qualify for services, reaches the age of twenty-one, or a parent revokes services. To begin this process, the child is identified and evaluated; then an individualized education program (IEP) is written, and a placement is prepared.

Initial Identification

Under the Individual with Disabilities Education Act's "child find" mandate, states are required to identify, locate, and evaluate all[21] resident children with disabilities (including those who are homeless, limited English proficient, or wards of the state), regardless of the severity of their disability or whether they attend public or private schools.[22] Although federal law requires that children with disabilities be identified, it does not dictate how this is to occur. Nevertheless, courts give deference to districts when their efforts are substantial, in good faith, and ultimately effective.[23] Consequently, state procedures vary widely and include practices such as census taking; community surveys; public awareness activities; referrals by parents, teachers, and medical doctors; and the screening of kindergarten and preschool children.

The screening process may necessitate the use of tests that are administered to all children, not simply those students suspected of having disabilities. Prior to testing, parents

---

[20]20 U.S.C. § 1412 (a)(3)(B) (2012).

[21]No child with a disability is to be denied an appropriate program ("zero reject"). *See* 20 U.S.C. § 1412(a)(2) (2012).

[22]20 U.S.C. § 1412(a)(3)(A) (2012); 20 U.S.C. § 1412(a)(10)(A)(ii) (2012).

[23]*See* P.P. v. West Chester Area Sch. Dist., 585 F.3d 727 (3d Cir. 2009) (finding that the district had complied with "child-find" obligations because their efforts were "comprehensive"—notices in local newspaper and on district's website, information sent to residents in property tax bills, and posters/pamphlets placed in private schools).

must be given notice that identifies the tests to be used and provides a general explanation of their intended purpose. Educators, however, need not acquire consent at this time. When these initial referral and screening efforts have been completed, children potentially in need of special education ideally will be identified and evaluated further.

Evaluation

Next, school districts are responsible for evaluating further those children residing in their respective service areas who may qualify for special education, given referrals or the results of preliminary exams. Although state residency laws vary, generally, children who physically live in the district's service area with a custodial parent, legal guardian, or foster parent; are emancipated minors; or have reached the age of majority and live apart from their parents will qualify as "residents."

Prior to placement of a child with disabilities, IDEA requires the administration of a multifactored evaluation using a variety of valid assessment tools and strategies to gather information related to the child's academic, functional, and developmental abilities. Assessments must be validated for the purposes they are used, administered by qualified personnel, selected and employed in ways that neither racially nor culturally discriminate, given in accordance with instructions, and available in the child's native language or other mode of communication.[24]

Generally, informed parental consent must be acquired prior to personalized testing for either an initial evaluation or reevaluation;[25] but consent is not required for curricular, state, or district-wide assessments.[26] However, **if a parent refuses consent for the initial evaluation or fails to respond to the request to provide consent, the district may undertake due process to authorize an evaluation.**[27] If the hearing officer supports the district's request to perform an assessment, or if reassessment is needed to determine the appropriateness of a contested current placement, the parents are required to make the child available.[28] Evaluations must be completed in a timely manner.[29]

When either parental consent is provided or authorization is acquired from a hearing officer, the IEP team and other qualified professionals are responsible for reviewing

[24]20 U.S.C. § 1414(b)(2), (3) (2012).

[25]20 U.S.C. § 1414(a)(1)(D)(i)(I) (2012). *But see* Shelby S. *ex rel.* Kathleen T. v. Conroe Indep. Sch. Dist., 454 F.3d 450 (5th Cir. 2006) (determining that the district was within its right to reevaluate a child, notwithstanding a lack of parental consent, where such reevaluation was critical to the district preparing an appropriate IEP).

[26]In addition to those assessments used to prepare the IEP, included within the IEP, or required in particular courses, students with disabilities are required to participate in *all* state and district-wide assessments, with accommodations and alternate forms of assessment as appropriate. States may elect to provide students having significant cognitive disabilities with alternate assessments keyed to alternate achievement standards. *See* 20 U.S.C. § 1412(a)(16) (2012).

[27]20 U.S.C. § 1414(a)(1)(D)(ii)(I) (2012).

[28]*See* G.J. v. Muscogee Cnty. Sch. Dist., 668 F.3d 1258 (11th Cir. 2012) (affirming district court's decision that parents' claim of the school's IDEA procedural violation was rendered moot by their refusal to consent to reevaluation of their child).

[29]*See, e.g.*, B.H. v. Joliet Sch. Dist., No. 08-c-4974, 2010 U.S. Dist. LEXIS 28658 (N.D. Ill. Mar. 19, 2010).

existing data on the child, including evaluations and information provided by the parents, current classroom-based assessments, and observations by teachers and related services providers.[30] The IEP team then can identify what additional information, if any, is needed. After all relevant input has been aggregated, the team must ascertain whether the child qualifies as disabled and, if so, whether special education and related services will be required. The team should determine the child's present level of academic achievement and developmental needs and project whether any additions or modifications to the instruction or services are necessary to enable the child to meet measurable annual goals and to participate, as appropriate, in the general education curriculum.[31]

If parents[32] are dissatisfied with the original evaluation or resulting placement decision, they have the right to request an independent second evaluation. The public school pays for the additional evaluation, unless officials contest the need for reassessment through due process or the evaluation already obtained by the parents does not meet district criteria.[33] Where the district elects to challenge payment for a second evaluation, it must be prepared to demonstrate that all procedures and appropriate professional practices were followed. If the impartial hearing officer rules in favor of the district and that decision is not appealed, the parents still may acquire a second, independent evaluation but must pay for it. When additional evaluations are acquired, school personnel are required to consider their results but are not required to follow them.[34]

The 2004 amendments to IDEA were in part designed to reduce the number of evaluations, the frequency of IEP meetings, and the amount of overall paperwork.[35] Generally, placements must be reviewed annually, or more often as appropriate, and a reevaluation must be performed every three years. However, a reevaluation is not required if the IEP team determines that it is unnecessary, in whole or in part, unless requested by the child's parent. Even when parents make routine requests for reevaluation, they need not be performed more than once per year, unless agreed to by the district.[36] Where a reevaluation supports amendment to the IEP, the IDEA permits the district to make the necessary changes, without conducting a full IEP team meeting, if it acquires parental approval.[37]

---

[30]20 U.S.C. § 1414(c)(1)(A) (2012).

[31]20 U.S.C. § 1414(c)(1)(B) (2012).

[32]IDEA defines "parent" broadly as a natural, adoptive, or foster parent; a guardian; an individual acting in place of a natural or adoptive parent (e.g., grandparent, stepparent, or other relative); or a surrogate. *See* 20 U.S.C. § 1401(23) (2012).

[33]34 C.F.R. § 300.502(a)(1), (b) (2012); *see also* Evanston Cmty. Consol. Sch. Dist. No. 65 v. Michael M., 356 F.3d 798 (7th Cir. 2004) (denying reimbursement for a second unnecessary evaluation). Moreover, if a hearing officer requests that an evaluation be conducted, the district bears all costs. *See* 34 C.F.R. § 300.502(d) (2012).

[34]34 C.F.R. § 300.502(c)(1) (2012); *see also* K.E. v. Indep. Sch. Dist. No. 15, 647 F.3d 795 (8th Cir. 2011) (determining that school district personnel had adequately considered results of independent evaluations, even though they did not incorporate all of the recommendations into the student's IEP).

[35]Fifteen states are participating in a pilot program to explore the effectiveness of multiyear IEPs. *See* 20 U.S.C. § 1414(d)(5)(A) (2012).

[36]20 U.S.C. § 1414(a)(2)(B)(i) (2012).

[37]20 U.S.C § 1414(d)(3)(D) (2012).

IEP Team

The school district, through its IEP teams, is responsible for determining whether children qualify under IDEA for services and, if so, for designing appropriate, least restrictive placements. The team includes:

- the parents or a surrogate;
- not less than one general and one special education teacher;
- a representative of the local educational agency who is qualified to provide or supervise specially designed instruction and is knowledgeable about the general education curriculum and available resources;
- an individual who can interpret instructional implications of evaluation results;
- other individuals with special knowledge or expertise; and
- the child, if appropriate.[38]

Some committees consist of ten or more participants, but all need not be present at every meeting. Excusal is permitted when the parents consent and those members not attending have the opportunity to submit their input in writing prior to the meeting.[39] Failure to acquire written consent, particularly for removal from of the general education setting, has been found so significant as to result in an IDEA violation and an inappropriate placement.[40]

IEP Preparation

The parents must agree to the IEP meeting time and location, and the district must ensure that the parents have the opportunity to participate fully, which may require hiring foreign-language translators or sign-language interpreters. Participation may be accomplished through video conferencing and conference calls, where necessary. If no parent is available or willing to attend, school officials should document each effort to encourage parental involvement.

In preparation for the first IEP meeting, the district may elect to prepare a tentative IEP as a basis for discussion. This initial IEP should be presented as a draft and in no way should be represented as final.[41] When agreement is ultimately reached, the IEP should:

- record the child's present level of academic achievement and functional performance;
- state measurable annual goals;
- note how performance will be measured and communicated to parents;

---

[38]20 U.S.C. § 1414(d)(1)(B) (2012).

[39]20 U.S.C. § 1414(d)(1)(C) (2012).

[40]*See, e.g.*, S.B. v. Pomona Unified Sch. Dist., CV 06-4874, 2008 U.S. Dist. LEXIS 31458 (C.D. Cal. Apr. 15, 2008).

[41]*See, e.g.*, H.B. v. Las Virgenes Unified Sch. Dist., 370 F. App'x 843 (9th Cir. 2010) (holding that the school district violated IDEA procedures by predetermining student's public school placement prior to parental input or involvement in IEP meeting).

- identify special education, related services, supplementary aids and services, and transition services (beginning at age sixteen) to be provided;
- explain the extent, if any, to which the child will not be included in general education activities;
- specify any accommodations that will be made in performing state or district assessments (or an explanation of why alternate assessments are necessary);
- describe benchmarks or short-term objectives for children taking alternate assessments;
- identify the date to initiate services;
- project the frequency, location, and duration of services; and
- provide a statement indicating that students have been informed that their IDEA rights transfer (except when the student is found to be incompetent under state law).[42]

Also contributing to the effort to be more cost and time efficient is the provision that requires districts to accept existing IEPs for students who move into the local service area during the school year. The receiving district must provide services comparable to those identified by the former district, whether in state or out of state. This placement should be continued until the district has evaluated the child and developed a new IEP consistent with IDEA procedures.[43]

Free Appropriate Public Education

District personnel must prepare the actual placement and coordinate needed services after agreement is reached on the IEP. Parental consent again is required. Unlike the evaluation phase, however, if the parents refuse the initial placement proposed by the district, educators are not permitted to seek authorization through due process. But if the parents reject a placement, the district is not in violation of IDEA and is not required to convene an IEP meeting or prepare a placement.[44]

Where consent is provided, **all children aged three through twenty-one with qualifying disabilities must be provided a free appropriate public education that is made available in the least restrictive environment.**[45] The placement must address the unique needs of the child and be delivered by "highly qualified" instructors.[46] Moreover, to qualify as appropriate, the placement must:

- be provided at public expense and under public supervision and direction (even if the school district selects a private school placement);
- meet the standards of the state educational agency;

---

[42]20 U.S.C. §§ 1414–1415(m)(1) (2012).

[43]20 U.S.C. § 1414(d)(2)(C)(i) (2012).

[44]20 U.S.C. § 1414(a)(1)(D)(ii)(II), (III) (2012).

[45]This is true unless students aged three to five and eighteen through twenty-one are not served within the state. *See* 20 U.S.C. § 1412(a)(1)(B) (2012).

[46]"Highly qualified" is defined in § 9109 of the Elementary and Secondary Education Act of 1965 (20 U.S.C. § 7801 (2012)); *see also* 20 U.S.C. § 1401(10) (2012). However, there is no private right of action if the child is taught by a teacher who is not highly qualified. *See* 20 U.S.C. § 1401(10)(E) (2012).

- include an appropriate preschool, elementary school, or secondary school education; and
- be delivered in conformity with the IEP.[47]

As needed, students with disabilities also must be provided supplementary aids and services in the general education classroom to enable them to be educated with nondisabled children to the maximum extent appropriate. They must also be provided with transition services to assist in transitioning from school to post-graduation activities such as postsecondary education, vocational training, integrated employment, continuing and adult education, adult services, independent living, or community participation and with assistive technology devices and services to enable the child to increase, maintain, or improve functional capabilities.[48] Moreover, special education and related services should be made available as soon as possible following completion of the IEP, although no specific time line is identified in IDEA.[49] Services must be provided as close to the child's home as possible, and preferably in the school the child would have attended if not disabled. But it is not realistic to assume that all programs can be made available in every neighborhood school.

Even though IEPs must be "appropriate," they need not be "the best" available or represent "optimum" programs that will maximize learning potential.[50] This issue was addressed in 1982 in *Board of Education v. Rowley*,[51] in which parents had requested that the school district provide a sign-language interpreter for their daughter in her academic classes, given her minimal residual hearing. The child's IEP specified a general education first-grade placement with special instruction from a tutor one hour per day and a speech therapist three hours per week, but did not include interpreter services. An interpreter had been provided during a two-week period when she was in kindergarten, but the practice was discontinued based on recommendations by the interpreter and other educators working with the child. Due to this omission, the parents were dissatisfied with the IEP and, after unsuccessful administrative review, filed suit.

On appeal, the Supreme Court rejected the standard proposed by the lower court (i.e., maximization of the potential of children with disabilities commensurate with the opportunity provided to other children[52]) and reasoned that "the intent of the Act was more to open the door of public education to [children with disabilities] on appropriate terms than to guarantee any particular level of education once inside."[53] The IDEA was found to

---

[47]20 U.S.C. § 1401(9) (2012).

[48]20 U.S.C. § 1401(1)–(34) (2012).

[49]*See, e.g.*, D.D. v. N.Y.C. Bd. of Educ., 465 F.3d 503 (2d Cir. 2006).

[50]*See, e.g.*, Lathrop R-II Sch. Dist. v. Gray, 611 F.3d 419 (8th Cir. 2010) (finding that school district's "good faith" efforts to implement strategies outlined in IEP to improve student's behavior provided the student with a Free Appropriate Public Education, even though behavioral progress was not as adequate as the student's parents would have liked), *cert. denied*, 131 S. Ct. 1017 (2011).

[51]458 U.S. 176 (1982).

[52]*Rowley*, 458 U.S. at 200 (finding that the district court [483 F. Supp. 528, 534 (S.D.N.Y. 1980)] and circuit court of appeals [632 F.2d 945 (2d Cir. 1980)] had erred in proposing a standard that was "not the standard that Congress imposed upon States" that receive funding under the IDEA.).

[53]458 U.S. at 192.

guarantee a "basic floor of opportunity,"[54] consisting of access to specialized instruction and related services that are individually designed to provide educational benefit. Applying these principles, the Court held that the student was receiving an appropriate education in that she was incurring educational benefit from individualized instruction and related services, as evidenced by her better-than-average performance in class, promotion from grade to grade, and positive interpersonal relationships with educators and peers.

The Court also made clear that lower courts are not to define an appropriate education. Rather, their review is limited to two questions:

- **Has the state complied with the procedures identified in the IDEA?**
- **Is the IEP developed through these procedures reasonably calculated to enable the child to receive educational benefit?**[55]

Lower courts have interpreted this latter requirement to mandate educational programs that provide more than "trifling goals."[56] But they have also noted that the IDEA does not require a school district to maximize a student's potential or provide the best possible education at public expense.[57] Interestingly, some parents have argued that their child has been denied a FAPE when school officials have not responded appropriately to acts of bullying and harassment. The Third Circuit found in favor of the parents when school officials failed to respond to severe and prolonged verbal and physical harassment that was related to the child's disability.[58]

Courts often defer to state and local educators and administrative review officials regarding the nature of IEPs and matters of pedagogy but still will not uphold proposed placements that are found to be inappropriate and not supported by the data. In such situations, courts have not been reluctant to direct the development of an appropriate public placement or to approve a private one. For example, the Fourth Circuit concluded that a school district failed to provide an appropriate education to a child with autism because its staff was not well trained in a certain type of therapy. Thus, the court found that a home placement was more appropriate in this situation.[59]

Least Restrictive Environment

Children with disabilities are to be educated with children who are not disabled to the maximum extent appropriate. Special classes, separate schooling, or other removal

---

[54]*Id.* at 200.

[55]*Id.* at 207.

[56]*See, e.g.*, C.B. v. Special Sch. Dist. No. 1, 636 F.3d 981 (8th Cir. 2011).

[57]*See, e.g.*, Thompson R2-J Sch. Dist. v. Luke P., 540 F.3d 1143 (10th Cir. 2008).

[58]*See also* Shore Reg'l High Sch. Bd. of Educ. v. P.S., 381 F.3d 194 (3d Cir. 2004); *see also* Long v. Murray Cnty. Sch. Dist., No. 4:10-cv-00015-HLM, 2012 U.S. Dist. LEXIS 86155 (D. Ga. May 21, 2012).

[59]Sumter Cnty. Sch. Dist. 17 v. Heffernan, 642 F.3d 478 (4th Cir. 2011). *But see* M.M. v. Sch. Bd. Miami-Dade Cnty., 437 F.3d 1085 (11th Cir. 2006) (finding that IDEA does not require that the best program be provided and that the methods employed by the district to address plaintiff's severe bilateral sensorial hearing loss provided an appropriate program).

of a child from general education may occur only if the nature or severity of the disability is such that education cannot be achieved satisfactorily in a general education setting.[60] In making least restrictive environment (LRE) decisions, school personnel should determine the types of placements for delivery of the IEP along the continuum of alternative placements and then select the option that is least restrictive. Alternative placements may include:

- a general education classroom with various support services;
- a general education classroom with or without itinerant teachers or resource rooms;
- self-contained special classes;
- special schools or residential instruction;[61] or
- home instruction.

Educational and noneducational benefits for each placement should be assessed, including the effect the child with a disability may have on classmates and staff members.[62]

General education with supplemental aids and services represents the LRE for most children; for a few, however, the LRE will be in a setting that is more restrictive.[63] The IEP team need not select a placement that is entirely in general education or entirely segregated. In some instances, it is appropriate to deliver the child's program within a range of LRE settings (e.g., "pull-out" services for more individualized focus on hearing, speech, and language development, with the majority of instruction through "mainstreaming" in general education classrooms).[64] States are responsible for ensuring that teachers and administrators are fully informed about their LRE responsibilities and for providing them with technical assistance and training.[65] Moreover, children should not be placed experimentally in the general classroom under the guise of full inclusion[66] and then provided appropriate placements only after they fail to meet short-term objectives or acquire educational benefit.

---

[60]20 U.S.C. § 1412 (a)(5)(A) (2012). *See, e.g.*, P. v. Newington Bd. of Educ., 546 F.3d 111 (2d Cir. 2008) (upholding district court's ruling that full-time placement in the general education classroom for the plaintiff would not have been appropriate, and that spending 60 percent to 80 percent of instructional time in general education classroom fulfilled the IDEA's least restrictive environment requirement for this student).

[61]34 C.F.R. § 300.115(b) (2008). If the parents elect not to have their child medicated while at school, the student may not be denied an appropriate placement based on the medication decision. The selection of services and the determination of the least restrictive environment may be affected, however. *See* 20 U.S.C. §1412(a)(25) (2008).

[62]*See, e.g.*, Bd. of Educ. v. Ross, 486 F.3d 267 (7th Cir. 2007) (affirming lower court's decision that school district's determination of LRE for defendant student was influenced by the student's disruptive and sometimes injurious behavior).

[63]*See, e.g.*, D.S. v. Bayonne Bd. of Educ., 602 F.3d 553 (3d Cir. 2010) (supporting placement of student in more restrictive setting—private school for learning disabled students—because student's academic needs were not met in the general education setting of the public school).

[64]*See, e.g.*, J.W. v. Fresno Unified Sch. Dist., 626 F.3d 431 (9th Cir. 2010).

[65]34 C.F.R. § 300.119 (2012); *see also* Houston Indep. Sch. Dist. v. V.P., 582 F.3d 576 (5th Cir. 2009) (affirming district court's decision in favor of student, finding that school district failed to provide a FAPE because staff members were not adequately trained to offer services to provide meaningful educational benefit to student with hearing impairment), *cert. denied*, 130 S. Ct. 1892 (2010).

[66]The term "full inclusion" is used here to refer to placement in general education where the child's educational needs are appropriately addressed through the use of supplemental aids and services.

Private Schools

Many children with disabilities attend private schools. Some are placed in a private program by the public school district, given the lack of an appropriate public school program. Other children attend private schools because of parental preference, given factors such as the nature of the curriculum, program quality, religious orientation, and convenience.

Public Placement of a Child in a Private School.   When a school district cannot effectively address specific individual student needs, where appropriate programs are not available within a child's reasonable commute, or if existing programs are not age appropriate, the IDEA does not necessarily require creation of new programs or schools. In the alternative, placement often may be made in other public schools or in private facilities, including those that are residential. Although the fiscal obligation can be substantial, the school district will be held financially responsible for residential placements that are required to provide an appropriate program. In such instances, the district must cover all nonmedical costs, including room and board. However, if a residential placement is sought by the parents for reasons other than the child's education (e.g., the risk the child poses in the home, the inability to shelter or feed the youth, the student being the target of a parent's abuse), the request may be denied.

When the public school system selects a private placement, a representative of the private school should participate in IEP placement meetings either in person or through a telephone conversation. Subsequent meetings to review and revise the IEP may be initiated and conducted by private school personnel, if approved by district officials. Where this occurs, both the parents and a public school representative must be involved in any decision about the child's IEP, and the district must authorize any change prior to implementation.

It is important to note **that private schools are not required to implement special programs or lower their academic standards to permit placement of children with disabilities.**[67] Applicants who cannot participate effectively in the private school's general education curriculum, assuming the availability of "minor adjustments," may be denied admission.

[handwritten margin note: Private schools May Deny Admission]

Parental Placement of a Child in a Private School.   In some instances, parents elect to place their children in private schools, either initially or when they perceive public programs to be inappropriate. **Parents always have the option of selecting an alternative program, but such placements will be at their expense unless the parents can show that the public placement is inappropriate and that their selected placement is appropriate.**

The Supreme Court addressed this issue in 1985 in *School Committee of Burlington v. Department of Education of Massachusetts.*[68] In that case, a father had disagreed with the school district's proposed educational placement of his child with learning disabilities and, after seeking an independent evaluation from medical experts and initiating the appeals process, enrolled the child in a private school. The Court rejected the school district's argument that a change in placement without district consent waived all rights to

---

[67]St. Johnsbury Acad. v. D.H., 240 F.3d 163 (2d Cir. 2001).

[68]471 U.S. 359 (1985).

reimbursement. In the Court's opinion, denying relief would defeat IDEA's major objective of providing an appropriate program. When the school district's proposed placement is ultimately found to be inappropriate, reimbursement is considered necessary since the review process can be quite lengthy. The Court reasoned that children should not be educationally disadvantaged by an inappropriate placement and that parents should not be economically penalized for removing their children. The Supreme Court, however, issued one caveat: parents who unilaterally seek private placements do so at their own financial risk.[69] Relief can be acquired only if the public placement is inappropriate and the private placement is appropriate.[70]

In a more recent case, the Supreme Court addressed whether the parent of a student, who had never received services at the public school, could be reimbursed for a private placement because the school district could not provide a FAPE. A private specialist diagnosed the student with learning disabilities, and the parents unilaterally removed him from the school and placed him in a private school. After removing their son, the parents requested an administrative hearing on his eligibility for services under the IDEA. The school district found him to be ineligible. The Court disagreed with the school district's findings and held that "[w]hen a public school fails to provide a FAPE and a child's parents place the child in an appropriate private school without the school district's consent, a court may require the district to reimburse the parents for the cost of the private education."[71] The Court further reasoned that the IDEA did not establish a categorical bar to tuition reimbursement for a student who had never received services at the public school. Parental choices are not always found to be either reasonable or appropriate, however. For example, the Eleventh Circuit denied reimbursement because the student had been provided an IEP that was reasonably calculated to confer an appropriate education. The requested residential placement was found to be both unnecessary and not least restrictive. The court also rejected the opinion of an expert hired by the parents who had indicated that the family needed someone to take care of their son in their home because family members had responsibilities other than caretaker and teacher.[72]

In an effort to limit district liability for private placements unilaterally selected by parents, IDEA permits reduction or denial of reimbursement if the parents fail to provide public officials with notification of their intent or if a court finds their conduct unreasonable. Proper notification can be accomplished either by discussing the matter with the IEP team during a formal meeting or by providing the district with written notice, including an explanation of the reasons for the decision, at least ten days prior to the

---

[69]*See* R. H. v. Plano Indep. Sch. Dist., 607 F.3d 1003 (5th Cir. 2010) (finding that the district's placement of the student in a special education preschool setting was proper and that parents were not entitled to reimbursement for enrolling their child in a private preschool), *cert. denied*, 131 S. Ct. 1471 (2011).

[70]*See* Florence Cnty. Sch. Dist. Four v. Carter, 510 U.S. 7 (1993) (ruling that reimbursement was warranted because public program was inappropriate).

[71]Forest Grove Sch. Dist. v. T.A., 557 U.S. 230, 247 (2009).

[72]Devine v. Indian River Cnty. Sch. Bd., 249 F.3d 1289 (11th Cir. 2001); *see also* R.R. v. Manheim Twp. Sch. Dist., 412 F. App'x 544 (3d Cir. 2011) (upholding district court's decision that the IEP was appropriate and denying parents reimbursement for private school); J.E. v. Boyertown Area Sch. Dist., 452 F. App'x 172 (3d Cir. 2011) (finding IEP created at public school to be appropriate and therefore denied parents further reimbursement).

projected removal of the child. At that point, if the district elects to perform additional student evaluations, the parent is required to make the child available. Also, some courts have held that parents must request a due process hearing before transferring their child to another school district.[73]

Services Available in Private Schools.   Students enrolled by their parents in private schools have no individual right to receive special education and related services provided by the school district. Instead, public officials are responsible for meeting with parents and other representatives of the children to decide who is to receive services; what, where, and how services are to be provided; and how services are to be evaluated. In selecting a site for the delivery of services, officials will consider available alternative delivery systems as well as whether provision on campus (e.g., at a religious school) violates state law.[74] If off-campus delivery is selected, eligible children must be transported from the private school to the site and back or to their homes.

IDEA provides funding for private school services at a per-pupil prorated amount equal to the federal funds spent on IEP services provided to children in the public school district.[75] This amount is modest, however, when compared to the dollars contributed by state and local governments. As a result, services that are made available to children enrolled in private schools will tend to be fewer in number or for shorter time periods than those available to children placed or served by the local school district.[76] When parents with children in private schools have challenged this disparity as a violation of the Equal Protection or Free Exercise Clauses, they have generally been unsuccessful.[77]

Change of Placement

Following an appropriate initial placement in a public or private school, adjustments to a child's IEP may be necessary because of the results of an annual review or reevaluation; discontinuation of a school, program, or service; violent or disruptive behavior; or graduation. Before changing a substantive aspect of a student's program, written notice must be given to the parents of their right to review the proposed alteration, and informed consent generally must be provided. However, where the parent does not respond to efforts to communicate, district personnel should document the date and type of each effort and then may proceed to deliver the program as amended.[78] If the parents later contact the district, they may challenge the placement decision through due process.

---

[73]*See* C.N. v. Willmar Pub. Sch., 591 F.3d 624 (8th Cir. 2010).

[74]*See* W.J.M. *ex rel.* K.D.M. v. Reedsport Sch. Dist., 196 F.3d 1046 (9th Cir. 1999) (upholding an Oregon administrative regulation stipulating that if a district decides to provide services to children in private schools, such appropriate special education and services must be provided in a religiously neutral setting).

[75]20 U.S.C. § 1412(a)(10)(A)(i)(I) (2012).

[76]*See, e.g.,* T.F. v. Special Sch. Dist., 449 F.3d 816 (8th Cir. 2006) (concluding that the district had provided the child with a FAPE and need not fund the same services in a private school unilaterally selected by the parents).

[77]*See, e.g.,* Gary S. v. Manchester Sch. Dist., 374 F.3d 15 (1st Cir. 2004).

[78]20 U.S.C. § 1414(c)(3) (2012).

RELATED SERVICES

> When related services are found to be essential elements of a free appropriate public education under the IDEA, they must be provided regardless of cost.

A free appropriate public education may include related services in addition to special education. Related services are defined as transportation and such developmental, corrective, and other supportive services (including speech pathology and audiology, psychological services, physical and occupational therapy, recreation, social work services, early identification and assessment, orientation and mobility services, school health services, counseling services, medical services for diagnostic and evaluation purposes, parent counseling and training, school nurse services, and interpreting services) that are necessary for a child with a disability to benefit from special education.[79] The areas of transportation, psychological services, and health services are reviewed briefly here.

Transportation

Federal regulations require the provision of transportation as a related service for qualified children to and from school, within school buildings, and on school grounds, even if specialized equipment is needed in making programs and activities accessible. A child qualifies for transportation if it is provided for other children or if it is included within an IEP or § 504 plan. Failure to provide the service to qualified students has resulted in courts requiring districts to reimburse parents for transportation costs, time, effort, babysitting services, and interest on their expenses. Nonetheless, courts also have concluded that where alternative transportation was provided, the district was not required to reimburse parents who wanted to transport their own child. Also, a child's hearing impairment did not qualify her for special transportation;[80] and transportation did not have to be provided following involvement in a privately funded after-school program that was unrelated to the IEP.[81]

Psychological Services

Psychological services are explicitly identified in federal law as related services to be included within IEPs where appropriate. Such services include:

- administering and interpreting psychological and educational tests as well as other assessment procedures;
- obtaining, integrating, and interpreting information about the child's behavior and condition;

[79]20 U.S.C. § 1401(a)(26) (2012).

[80]McNair v. Oak Hills Local Sch. Dist., 872 F.2d 153 (6th Cir. 1989).

[81]Roslyn Union Free Sch. Dist. v. Univ. of N.Y., 711 N.Y.S.2d 582 (App. Div. 2000).

- consulting with staff in planning IEPs;
- planning and managing a program of psychological services; and
- assisting in the development of positive behavioral intervention strategies.[82]

When psychological services are needed to help the child to benefit from instruction and are provided by a psychologist or other qualified individual, the services should be included within the IEP. However, if parents request psychiatric and other medical services,[83] or if psychological services are not required to provide a free appropriate public education (FAPE),[84] such requests may be denied.

Health and Nursing Services

Courts have differentiated between medical and health services. As indicated, the IDEA excludes medical services (i.e., those provided by a licensed physician) except for diagnostic and evaluative purposes. Health services (i.e., those provided by a school nurse or other qualified person) such as catheterization often are essential in that they enable the child to attend school and thereby benefit from instruction.[85]

The Supreme Court began its review of school health-care issues in *Irving Independent School District v. Tatro*.[86] In that 1984 case, a child required clean intermittent catheterization every three to four hours. The Court found catheterization to be essential in that it would enable the child to attend school and thereby benefit from instruction, and noted that it could be performed by either a nurse or a trained layperson. Accordingly, the service was not a medical service and could not be excluded from the child's IEP for that reason.

In post-*Tatro* years, the issue of health care has been volatile, given the growing number of medically fragile children now in public schools, the desire of many parents to have their health-impaired child integrated into general education, and the escalating costs of health care. Courts ultimately adopted a bright-line test requiring the provision of all health-care services by anyone other than a physician, if required to enable the child to attend school and benefit from the IEP.

In *Cedar Rapids Community School District v. Garret F.*,[87] a child had a severed spinal column and was paralyzed from the neck down. To remain in school, he required full-time nursing care (e.g., catheterization, suctioning, ambu bagging, ventilator assistance, emergency aid). The school district argued that the services collectively should be viewed as medical, even if individually they qualified as health services, and asserted that it would incur an undue financial burden if required to provide the services. The Supreme Court acknowledged the legitimate financial concerns of the district but noted that the law as currently constructed required the Court to reject the undue burden claim.[88] Moreover, by

---

[82]34 C.F.R. § 300.34(c)(10) (2012).

[83]*See* Richardson Indep. Sch. Dist. v. Michael Z., 580 F.3d 286 (5th Cir. 2009).

[84]*See* Nack v. Orange City Sch. Dist., 454 F.3d 604 (6th Cir. 2006).

[85]Irving Indep. Sch. Dist. v. Tatro, 468 U.S. 883 (1984).

[86]*Id.*

[87]526 U.S. 66 (1999).

[88]Although unavailable under IDEA, the undue burden defense is available under both § 504 and the ADA.

applying the bright-line test, **the Court ruled that any health service a student may need to participate in a school setting**[89] **had to be provided, regardless of cost or resulting financial impact on the district.**

EXTENDED SCHOOL YEAR

Federal statutes require that IEPs be both appropriate and designed to provide educational benefit. In meeting these mandates, it may be necessary for a particular child to receive services beyond the traditional nine-month school year. While school districts can prescribe a fixed number of instructional days for students without disabilities, such a determination must be made on an individual basis for children with disabilities. Nonetheless, where extended school year (ESY) services are found "beneficial" or even "maximizing," but are not "essential" to the provision of an appropriate program, they are not required under IDEA.[90]

Where ESY services are provided, programs will vary widely. Some mandate the extension of the full IEP for one, two, or three additional months; others utilize new or different services; and yet others require all or some of the same services, but in different amounts. Eligibility decisions should be made annually during the IEP review and based on:

- regression-recoupment;[91]
- individual need;
- the nature and severity of the disability;
- self-sufficiency and independence;
- whether educational benefit can be incurred without such services; and
- whether progress is being made toward the accomplishment of goals.

Furthermore, in fairly narrow circumstances, an ESY program may include the delivery of only related services, such as physical therapy during the summer to allow a child to remain sufficiently flexible or mobile to participate within the IEP in the fall. The IEP team is responsible for making individualized decisions regarding eligibility for ESY services and for selecting appropriate services, including their amount and duration.[92]

[89]Note, however, that some health-care services do not have to be provided when the child is homebound.

[90]*See* Bd. of Educ. v. L.M., 478 F.3d 307 (6th Cir. 2007) (holding in favor of the school district because parents did not meet the burden of showing that ESY was necessary to prevent significant academic regression of their child).

[91]"Regression" refers to the loss of knowledge a student may experience during a break in instruction, and "recoupment" refers to the time it takes to regain the knowledge that was lost.

[92]*See* J.H. v. Henrico Cnty. Sch. Bd., 395 F.3d 185 (4th Cir. 2005) (remanding to the lower court with instructions for the hearing officer to determine the amount of ESY services necessary for the plaintiff's speech, language, and occupational skills acquired during kindergarten not to be placed in jeopardy).

■ ■ ■ ■ ■

PARTICIPATION IN SPORTS

Athletic association rules that deny or limit the participation of students with disabilities must qualify as reasonable and reflect the essential elements of the sport.

Children with disabilities often are interested in participating in interscholastic sports. But the requests of these student-athletes to participate have at times been denied because either they failed to meet eligibility requirements or their participation represented too great a risk to themselves or to others. In 2013, the U.S. Department of Education released additional guidance to schools about the participation of students with disabilities in sports.[93] The guidance clarifies existing legal obligations of schools and stresses that students with disabilities who are otherwise qualified should not be excluded from athletics and clubs. Although most disputes are based on either the Rehabilitation Act or the Americans with Disabilities Act (ADA), a few cases have been filed under IDEA.

The IDEA has been at issue in two types of sports-related disability cases: (1) where parents wanted to include sports in the IEP; and (2) where the IEP team included sports in the IEP and the state athletic association penalized the school for allowing an ineligible student to participate. Because sports participation is seldom considered essential for students to incur educational benefit, it typically is not included in IEPs.[94] Furthermore, from the school district's perspective, it generally is not prudent to include sports, or any other extracurricular activity, in IEPs. Such a practice establishes an entitlement to team membership (not to participation per se, however) and enables sports participation to become a right that can be withdrawn only through due process.

Furthermore, if the IEP team were to include sports in the IEP and thereby allow an otherwise ineligible student to participate in an interscholastic contest, school officials may have created a situation that will result in rules violations and penalties. The Montana Supreme Court "strongly encouraged" educators to be prudent in including sports in IEPs and warned that they might be "making a promise [they] simply cannot keep."[95] Given this situation, the district would have to sue the athletic association (presumably under the Fourteenth Amendment[96]) to terminate whatever remedial actions have been taken

---

[93]U.S. Dep't of Educ., *Letter from Seth M. Galanter, Acting Assistant Sec'y for Civil Rights to Dear Colleague: Students with Disabilities in Extracurricular Athletics* (Jan. 25, 2013), http://www2.ed.gov/about/offices/list/ocr/letters/colleague-201301-504.pdf.

[94]*But see* Kling v. Mentor Pub. Sch. Dist., 136 F. Supp. 2d 744 (N.D. Ohio 2001) (granting preliminary injunction to require the participation of an overage athlete who was likely to receive educational benefits only with the inclusion of sports in his IEP).

[95]J.M. v. Mont. High Sch. Ass'n, 875 P.2d 1026, 1032 (Mont. 1994).

[96]Such suits are more likely today given the Supreme Court's ruling in *Brentwood Academy v. Tennessee Secondary School Athletic Association*, 531 U.S. 288 (2001), where the state athletic association was declared a state actor, notwithstanding the fact that it was a private corporation.

against it. Even if the district is to prevail, it will incur substantial expense and have to dedicate considerable personnel time to a problem that could have easily been avoided by not including sports participation in IEPs.

Unlike the IDEA, there are myriad related scenarios and cases regarding athletic participation filed under § 504 and the ADA.[97] Most claims have alleged discrimination due to facially neutral regulations that disproportionately affect students with disabilities, such as age limitations, grade-point average restrictions, one-year residency and transfer requirements, and eight-semester/four-season limitations. Historically, all students were required to meet eligibility criteria and were allowed to play only when they were otherwise qualified to participate *and* if they made the team. The courts permitted and often required the uniform application of such rules, but that trend may be changing. A related issue reviewed by the Supreme Court in a professional sports context has application to interscholastic sports. In *PGA Tour v. Martin* in 2001, the Supreme Court supported a professional golfer's request to ride a cart rather than walk the course, as the event rules required.[98] Walking could lead to hemorrhaging and the development of blood clots or fractures. The Court reasoned that "shot making" was the essence of golf and that walking was neither an essential attribute nor an indispensable feature of the sport. This decision does not require lowering the basket, widening the goal, or bringing in the fences in basketball, soccer, and baseball, respectively, but it does require the evaluation of any rule that disqualifies an otherwise qualified participant with a disability. Review of such rules should reveal whether they are essential features of the sport or are peripheral and therefore subject to alteration or elimination.

DISCIPLINE

Students with disabilities may be expelled only when it can be shown that the behavior on which the disciplinary action is based is not a manifestation of the child's disability.

Students with disabilities are not exempt from reasonable disciplinary measures, although due process exceeding that provided general education students is required at times, and penalties may be limited in type and duration. Sometimes at issue in school discipline cases is the "stay-put provision." This provision requires that a student remain in his or her current educational placement while school officials examine disciplinary proceedings. The only exception available to this rule is if both the parents and school district agree to alter the student's placement. In 1988, the Supreme Court in *Honig v. Doe* held **that an indefinite suspension of two students pending the outcome of**

---

[97]*See* James P. Looby, *Reasonable Accommodations for High School Athletes with Disabilities: Preserving Sports While Providing Access for All*, 19 SPORTS LAW. J. 227–44 (2012) (observing how courts might apply the ADA for student athletes with regard to age limitations and eligibility requirements).

[98]532 U.S. 661 (2001).

expulsion proceedings was a prohibited change in placement and violated the stay-put provision of IDEA.[99] The state superintendent of public instruction had urged the Supreme Court to recognize a "dangerousness" exception to the stay-put requirement. Notwithstanding, the Court stated that Congress deliberately stripped schools of the unilateral authority to exclude students with disabilities. The history of exclusion of such students prior to passage of IDEA and the early litigation that guided the development of the law convinced the Court that the conspicuous absence of an emergency exception was intentional.

The Supreme Court, however, emphasized that school officials are not without options when confronted with a dangerous student. They may use a range of normal procedures (e.g., suspension of up to ten days, detention, time-out[100]). In addition, the Court indicated that if other forms of discipline are not successful, and the student already has been suspended for the maximum ten-day period but continues to pose a threat, school officials may seek injunctive relief if the parents refuse to agree to a change in placement. It is important to note that after *Honig*, Congress created a *dangerousness* exception when it granted school personnel the ability to remove a student for up to forty-five days to an interim alternative educational setting if the student brought drugs, a gun, or any other weapon to school.[101]

Among the disciplinary options available to school officials, suspension and expulsion have resulted in considerable judicial action. Each is reviewed here in greater detail.

Suspension

The IDEA allows school officials to consider unique circumstances on a case-by-case basis if there has been a violation of the student conduct code. When officials determine that a *suspension* (i.e., removal of a student from the educational setting for ten or fewer days) is justified, no procedures beyond those that apply to general education students are required. The resulting suspension may be either an in-school assignment to a suspension room or out-of-school, requiring complete removal from the school setting. **Students with disabilities may not generally be suspended for more than ten consecutive days or receive repetitive brief suspensions that aggregate to more than ten days during the school year.** If a student is suspended for more than ten days, a manifestation determination review will be held to determine if there is a direct and substantial relationship between the student's conduct and the disability. If there is no relationship, the student can be suspended beyond ten days. In the comparatively exceptional circumstance where removal

---

[99]484 U.S. 305 (1988).

[100]Not all assignment to time-out will be found legal, however. *See, e.g.*, Covington v. Knox Cnty. Sch. Sys., 205 F.3d 912 (6th Cir. 2000) (finding inappropriate that plaintiff had been routinely locked in a small time-out room for up to several hours at a time); *see* U.S. Dep't of Educ., *Restraint and Seclusion: Resource Document* (2012), http://www2.ed.gov/policy/seclusion/restraints-and-seclusion-resources.pdf, for further discussion on restraints, seclusion, and time-out rooms.

[101]20 U.S.C. § 1415(k)(1)(A)(ii) (2013).

justifiably exceeds the ten-day limit, services consistent with the IEP must be provided beginning the eleventh day.[102]

Whether the child has been removed from the IEP—not whether the child has received an in-school or out-of-school suspension—determines that a suspension day applies toward the total. If a student is assigned to a time-out room rather than an in-school suspension room, and instruction and services identified within the IEP continue to be delivered by properly credentialed individuals, it is unlikely that the time removed from the general education classroom will contribute to the ten-day limit. To reduce the likelihood of litigation, however, it is recommended that assignment to time-out be included within the IEPs of students who are likely to require such assignments as a form of behavior modification or intervention. Once the parent has agreed to such a provision, assignment to time-out will be consistent with rather than removal from the IEP.

Expulsion

When violations of the conduct code are excessive or severe, school officials have the authority to approve expulsions. *Expulsion* is the removal of a student for more than ten consecutive days. Expulsion of students with disabilities results in a change of placement, and procedures that exceed those required for general education students are required. In such instances, an expulsion will be justified only if the district has properly implemented the student's IEP and the contested conduct does not have a direct and substantial relationship to the student's disability.[103] **A manifestation determination review will be held to determine if this direct and substantial relationship to the student's disability exists.**

Assuming expulsion is supported, the student may be assigned either to a home placement or to an interim alternative educational setting. The student's record may include reference to the student being expelled and the basis for the expulsion. Notwithstanding the above, if the student is to be removed from his or her current placement for more than ten days, services consistent with the IEP must be delivered in the new environment that will enable the student to make progress toward achieving identified goals and objectives. These services are required regardless of whether the behavior was disability related.[104] In short, **educational services cannot be terminated for children with disabilities for longer than ten days.**

Where there is a determination that the behavior is a manifestation of the student's disability, the IEP team is responsible for conducting a functional behavioral assessment and implementing a behavioral intervention plan.[105] Interventions should address the conduct

---

[102]34 C.F.R. §§ 300.530(b), 300.536 (2012).

[103]20 U.S.C. § 1415(k)(1)(E)(i) (2012).

[104]20 U.S.C. § 1415(k)(1)(D) (2012).

[105]20 U.S.C. § 1415(k)(1)(F)(i) (2012). Failure to provide such a plan can result in the denial of a FAPE and an IDEA violation. *See* Metro. Bd. of Pub. Educ. v. Bellamy, 116 F. App'x 570 (6th Cir. 2004). Also, it is only when behavior impedes learning that the IEP team must consider the use of behavioral interventions. *See* Park Hill Sch. Dist. v. Dass, 655 F.3d 762 (8th Cir. 2011).

that resulted in the disciplinary action and should be modified when needed. Also, assignment to an alternative setting for up to forty-five days is permissible under the IDEA, even when the student's behavior is disability related. This may occur only where the student has committed one of the following violations on school grounds or at a school function:

- carries a weapon;
- knowingly possesses, uses, sells, or solicits illegal drugs; or
- inflicts serious bodily injury upon another.[106]

If the parents disagree with a decision to remove their child from school, they may appeal that decision to a hearing officer. Similarly, school officials may appeal when they are concerned that a student's continued presence within the school setting is substantially likely to result in injury to the student or others. The hearing officer has the authority to either return the student to the placement from which he or she was removed or order placement in an interim alternative educational setting. The hearing should occur within twenty school days of the date of the request, and a decision must be provided within ten school days after the hearing. During this period, the student remains in the current placement (i.e., the interim alternative setting), unless the removal period has expired or the parent and district agree otherwise.[107]

Interestingly, even students who are not yet identified as disabled may be protected at times by IDEA, but only if school officials had "knowledge" that they may be disabled. Knowledge exists where parents request an evaluation or express in writing to administrative or supervisory personnel their concern that their child may be in need of special education and related services. Knowledge also may be established where an educator expresses concern about a student's behavior directly to supervisory personnel. Note, however, that the student is not entitled to IDEA protection in a given disciplinary hearing if:

- notification of a possible disability occurred following the inappropriate conduct;
- the child was found not to qualify as disabled given the results of an expedited evaluation;
- the parents did not allow the district to conduct the evaluation; or
- the parents previously refused IDEA services.[108]

Where an evaluation is conducted and the student does not qualify as both disabled and in need of special education and related services, instruction during the removal period need not be provided unless available to other general education students who have been removed from school. In contrast, if the student does qualify as disabled, special education and related services consistent with the newly developed IEP need to be provided no later than practical and feasible, and preferably no later than the tenth day of removal.[109]

---

[106]20 U.S.C. § 1415(k)(1)(G) (2012).

[107]20 U.S.C. § 1415(k)(3)(B), (4) (2012).

[108]20 U.S.C. § 1415(k)(5) (2012).

[109]20 U.S.C. § 1415(k)(5)(D)(ii) (2012).

The IDEA does not prohibit personnel from reporting to law enforcement any crime a student may have committed.[110] Law enforcement officials are not bound by IDEA and may require an unruly or delinquent student to submit to treatment, home detention, or incarceration, in addition to any penalty the district may provide.

PROCEDURAL SAFEGUARDS

Whenever parents disagree with the placement committee or an action taken by the district, they are entitled to procedural due process.

School officials generally make good faith efforts to meet the needs of children with disabilities, yet there will be times when the parents disagree with evaluation, program, or placement decisions. Understandably, many parents seek the best possible education for their children. Alternatively, school districts may offer what parents perceive as only a minimally appropriate program, or even less. Where disagreement persists, the IDEA has provided a variety of means by which parents or districts may seek third-party review.

Figure 7.1 provides a chart of the complaint procedures. Parents are entitled to receive a copy of the IDEA procedural safeguards at least one time per year in addition to the initial referral or request for evaluation, upon filing of a complaint, or upon request. Moreover, during IDEA administrative appeals, the student must be assigned to the then current educational placement, an interim alternative educational setting (if placed following an appropriate disciplinary hearing), or another placement agreed to by the parents and school officials.[111]

Both informal meetings and mediation must be offered to the parents in an effort to resolve disputes quickly and in a less adversarial manner. Participation is voluntary and at times is not selected. When a hearing is conducted, parties must disclose any evaluations, recommendations, and evidence that they intend to use. The burden of persuasion is on the party seeking relief in an administrative hearing,[112] while the hearing officer's opinion must be based only on evidence presented by the parties.

If the impartial hearing is conducted at the local level, either party aggrieved by the findings and decision may appeal to the state. At the state level, the review official is responsible for ensuring that the hearing officer followed appropriate procedures, impartially reviewed the record in its entirety, and sought additional evidence if necessary. After completion of these procedures, the reviewer must make an independent decision and provide the parties with written findings. Prior to filing an IDEA suit, parents are required to exhaust administrative remedies (i.e., all internal protocols and procedures to address grievances must be adhered to prior to filing a lawsuit under IDEA).

[110]20 U.S.C. §1415(k)(6) (2012).

[111]20 U.S.C. § 1415(j) (2012); 20 U.S.C. § 1415(k)(4)(A) (2012).

[112]*See* Schaffer v. Weast, 546 U.S. 49 (2005).

FIGURE 7.1   IDEA Complaint Procedure

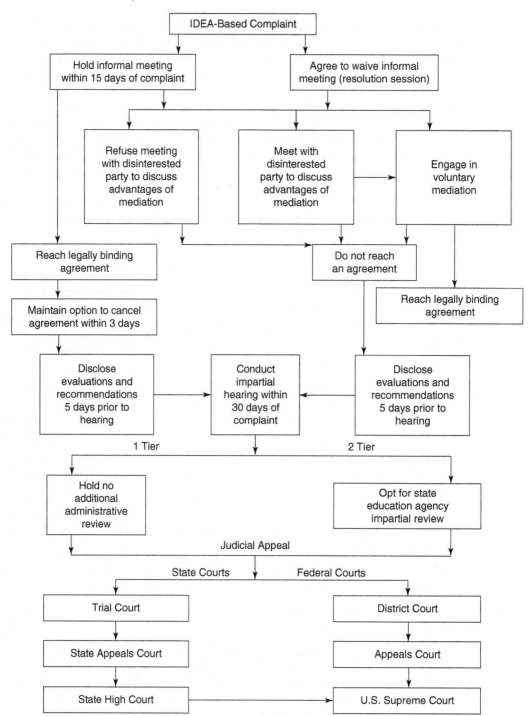

CONCLUSION

The rights of students with disabilities have expanded significantly since 1975 and include rights to accessible facilities, appropriate programs, and least restrictive placements. Also, students must be given the equal opportunity to participate in extracurricular activities, including sports, assuming that their participation does not represent a danger to themselves or others.

School districts are responsible for identifying, assessing, and placing all qualified students with disabilities. All placements must be both appropriate and least restrictive; most will require a public placement, although some placements will be in private schools. Also, students with disabilities may be disciplined in the same manner as other students, although there may be additional procedural requirements to meet. Moreover, when expulsion is merited, services consistent with the IEP must continue to be delivered. Understanding what federal laws both allow and require should help educators prepare legal and effective placements for children with disabilities.

POINTS TO PONDER

1. The state provides limited support to children with special needs above that provided for all children ($7,000 per pupil). A family moves into a small, poor, rural community and requests appropriate programs for two children, ages five and six, with severe physical and mental disabilities. The cost per child will be over $100,000, primarily for health care. Following unsuccessful administrative review, the parents sued the district under the IDEA seeking a FAPE for their children. Are the parents likely to win the suit? Why or why not?

2. The school district considers itself to be a "full-inclusion" district. All children are initially placed in general education with supplemental aids and services, as directed by the school administration. The parents contend that general education is clearly not the appropriate placement for their child with severe disabilities and have significant documentation supporting their position. They request a more segregated placement, which is denied by school authorities based on procedures mandating full inclusion. Following unsuccessful administrative appeals, the parents sued under the IDEA. Which party is likely to prevail? Why?

3. A child in your homeroom has a mild learning disability. He lives one-half mile from school. His parents requested that transportation services be provided, but the request was denied. The district noted that the family lives less than a mile from the school and that the nature of the student's disability does not necessitate the provision of transportation. The parents point out that the bus travels in front of their home each day and would merely need to stop to allow their son to board. The district would incur no additional cost. The parents sued under the IDEA and § 504. Are they likely to win? Why or why not?

4. A student receiving services under IDEA was subjected to severe harassment and bullying in school. His classmates regularly called him "faggot," "queer," and "loser." By eighth grade, the harassment became so severe that the student attempted suicide. His parents had contacted school officials on numerous occassions throughout his eighth-grade year, arguing that their son was being denied a FAPE because school officials failed to stop the harassment against their child. Could the parents bring an action under IDEA alleging a violation of FAPE? Would they be successful in this case? Could they file a lawsuit under § 504 or the ADA for discrimination based on disability?

CHAPTER EIGHT

STUDENT DISCIPLINE

Student misconduct continues to be one of the most persistent and troublesome problems confronting educators. Public concern has focused on school disciplinary problems, particularly for student behavior involving use of illicit drugs, alcohol abuse, and violence. In response, schools have directed more efforts toward violence-prevention strategies, including not only stringent security measures but also modification of the curricula to strengthen students' social skills and the training of teachers and administrators to monitor the school climate. Some states and local school districts also have enacted restrictive laws or policies that call for zero tolerance of weapons, drugs, and violence on campus. The efficacy of legislating tougher approaches to create safe schools has evoked volatile debates.[1] This chapter does not address the merits of these measures; rather, it examines the range of strategies employed by educators to maintain a safe and secure learning environment from a legal perspective. The analyses focus on the development of conduct regulations, the imposition of sanctions for noncompliance, and the procedures required in the administration of student punishments.

In the late 1960s and early 1970s, courts moved from exercising limited review of discipline policies and practices to the active protection of students' rights. These judicial developments, however, have not eroded educators' rights or their responsibilities. **The United States Supreme Court "has repeatedly emphasized the need for affirming the comprehensive authority of the states and of school officials, consistent with fundamental constitutional safeguards, to prescribe and control conduct in the schools."**[2] Reasonable disciplinary regulations, even those impairing students' protected liberties, have been upheld if justified by a legitimate educational interest. After an overview of conduct regulations, subsequent sections of this chapter address legal issues related to expulsions and suspensions, corporal punishment, academic sanctions, search and seizure, and remedies for unlawful disciplinary actions.

---

[1]Daniel Losen, *Discipline Policies, Successful Schools, and Racial Justice* (Boulder: National Education Policy Center, Oct. 5, 2011), http://nepc.colorado.edu/publication/discipline-policies; Catherine Kim, Daniel Losen & Daniel Hewitt, The School-to-Prison Pipeline (New York: NYU Press, 2010).

[2]Tinker v. Des Moines Indep. Cmty. Sch. Dist., 393 U.S. 503, 507 (1969).

CONDUCT REGULATIONS

School boards are granted considerable latitude in establishing and interpreting their own disciplinary rules and regulations.

The Supreme Court has held that the interpretation of a school regulation resides with the body that adopted it and is charged with its enforcement.[3] Disciplinary policies, however, have been struck down if unconstitutionally vague. Policies prohibiting "improper conduct" and behavior "inimical to the best interests of the school" have been invalidated because they have not specified the precise nature of the impermissible conduct.[4] Although policies should be precise, courts have recognized that disciplinary regulations do not have to satisfy the stringent criteria or level of specificity required in criminal statutes. The Eighth Circuit noted that the determining factor is whether a regulation's wording is precise enough to notify an individual that specific behavior is clearly unacceptable.[5]

In addition to reviewing the validity of the conduct regulation on which a specific punishment is based, courts evaluate the nature and extent of the penalty imposed in relation to the gravity of the offense. Courts consider the age, sex, mental condition, and past behavior of the student in deciding whether a given punishment is appropriate. The judiciary has sanctioned punishments such as suspension, expulsion, corporal punishment, denial of privileges, and detention after school. Any of these punishments, however, could be considered unreasonable under a specific set of circumstances. Consequently, courts examine each unique factual situation; they do not evaluate the validity of student punishments in the abstract.

Litigation challenging disciplinary practices often has focused on the procedures followed in administering punishment rather than on the substance of disciplinary rules or the nature of the sanctions imposed. Implicit in all judicial declarations regarding school discipline is the notion that severe penalties require more formal procedures whereas minor punishments necessitate only minimal due process (e.g., notice of the charges and an opportunity to refute them). Nonetheless, **any disciplinary action should be accompanied by some procedure to ensure the rudiments of fundamental fairness and to prevent mistakes in the disciplinary process.** Courts have emphasized that required procedures vary depending on the seriousness of the punishment to be imposed.

The judiciary has recognized that punishment for student conduct off school grounds must be supported by evidence that the behavior has a detrimental impact on other pupils,

[3]Bd. of Educ. v. McCluskey, 458 U.S. 966 (1982); Wood v. Strickland, 420 U.S. 308 (1975); *see also* Price v. N.Y.C. Bd. of Educ., 837 N.Y.S.2d 507 (App. Div. 2008) (holding that a board's ban on possession of cell phones had a rational basis).

[4]*See* Monroe Cnty. Bd. of Educ. v. K.B., 62 So. 3d 513 (Ala. Civ. App. 2010) (concluding that a school's policy prohibiting use of alcohol at school or a school function did not encompass consumption *prior to* a school function; policy was found to be unconstitutionally vague). *But see* Esfeller v. O'Keefe, 391 F. App'x 337, 340 (5th Cir. 2010) (ruling that student code prohibiting "extreme, outrageous or persistent acts, or communications that are intended or reasonably likely to harass, intimidate, harm, or humiliate another" was not facially overbroad).

[5]Woodis v. Westark Cmty. Coll., 160 F.3d 435 (8th Cir. 1998).

FIGURE 8.1   Guidelines for the Development of a Student Conduct Code

- Rules must have an explicit purpose and be clearly written to accomplish that purpose.
- Any conduct regulation adopted should be necessary in order to carry out the school's educational mission; rules should not be designed merely to satisfy the preferences of school board members, administrators, or teachers.
- Rules should be publicized to students and their parents.
- Rules should be specific and clearly stated so students know what behaviors are expected and what behaviors are prohibited.
- Student handbooks that incorporate references to specific state laws should also include the law or paraphrase the statutory language.
- Regulations should not impair constitutionally protected rights unless there is an overriding public interest, such as a threat to the safety of others.
- A rule should not be *ex post facto*; it should not be adopted to prevent a specific activity that school officials know is being planned or has already occurred.
- Punishments should be appropriate to the offense, taking into consideration the child's age, gender, disability (if any), and past behavior.
- Some procedural safeguards should accompany the administration of all punishments; the formality of the procedures should be in accord with the severity of the punishment.
- Periodic review to revise and refine the student handbook should involve students and school staff members.

teachers, or school activities. This has become a much more contentious area with students' increased use of the Internet at home. Personal websites and use of social networks such as Myspace and Facebook raise difficult First Amendment issues for school officials attempting to discipline students for off-campus conduct.[6]

School personnel should avoid placing unnecessary constraints on student behavior. In developing disciplinary policies, all possible means of achieving the desired outcomes should be explored, and means that are least restrictive of students' personal freedoms should be selected (see Figure 8.1 for general guidelines).[7] Once it is determined that a specific conduct regulation is necessary, the rule should be clearly written so that it is not open to multiple interpretations. Each regulation should include the rationale for enacting the rule as well as the penalties for infractions. Considerable discretion exists in determining that certain actions deserve harsher penalties (i.e., imposing a more severe punishment for the sale of drugs as opposed to the possession or use of drugs). **To ensure that students are knowledgeable of the conduct rules, it is advisable to require them to sign a form indicating that they have read the conduct regulations.**

In designing and enforcing student conduct codes, it is important for school personnel to bear in mind the distinction between students' substantive and procedural rights. If a disciplinary regulation or the administration of punishment violates substantive rights (e.g., restricts protected speech), the regulation cannot be enforced nor the punishment imposed. When only procedural rights are impaired, however, the punishment generally can be administered if it is determined at an appropriate hearing that the punishment is warranted.

---

[6]See Chapter 5 for an extensive discussion of students' Internet activity initiated off school campuses.

[7]See Thomas Baker, *Construing the Scope of Student Conduct Codes*, 174 Educ. L. Rep. 555–88 (2003), for an extensive discussion of the development of conduct codes.

EXPULSIONS AND SUSPENSIONS

Some type of procedural due process should be afforded to students prior to the imposition of expulsions or suspensions.

Expulsions and suspensions are among the most widely used disciplinary measures. Courts uniformly have upheld educators' authority to use such measures as punishments, but the procedural requirements (i.e., notice, hearing, etc.) discussed in this section must be provided to ensure that students are afforded fair and impartial treatment. States have recognized that students have a property right to an education, but students may be deprived of this right if they violate school rules.

Expulsions

State laws and school board regulations are usually quite specific regarding the grounds for *expulsions*—that is, the removal of students from school for a lengthy period of time (in excess of ten days). Such grounds are not limited to occurrences during school hours and can include infractions on school property immediately before or after school, at school-sponsored activities on or off school grounds, or en route to or from school. Despite the fact that specific grounds vary from state to state, infractions typically considered legitimate grounds for expulsion include:

- engaging in violence;
- stealing or vandalizing school or private property;
- causing or attempting to cause physical injury to others;
- possessing a weapon;
- possessing or using drugs or alcohol; and
- engaging in criminal activity or other behavior forbidden by state laws.

Procedural Requirements. State statutes specify procedures for expulsion and the limitations on their length. Except for the possession of weapons, a student generally cannot be expelled beyond the end of the current academic year unless the expulsion takes place near the close of the term. A teacher or administrator may initiate expulsion proceedings, but usually only the school board can expel a student. **Prior to expulsion, students must be provided procedural protections guaranteed by the U.S. Constitution; however, school officials can remove students immediately if they pose a danger or threat to themselves or others.** No duty exists to provide an educational alternative for a properly expelled student unless the school board policies or state mandates specify that alternative programs must be provided or the student is receiving special education services.[8]

[8]See text accompanying note 103, Chapter 7 for a discussion of the expulsion of children with disabilities.

FIGURE 8.2   Procedural Due Process for Student Expulsions

- Written notice of the charges; the intention to expel; the place, time, and circumstances of the hearing; and sufficient time for a defense to be prepared
- A full and fair hearing before an impartial adjudicator
- The right to legal counsel or some other adult representation
- The right to be fully apprised of the proof or evidence
- The opportunity to present witnesses or evidence
- The opportunity to cross-examine opposing witnesses
- Some type of written record demonstrating that the decision was based on the evidence presented at the hearing

Even though the details of required procedures must be gleaned from state statutes and school board regulations, courts have held that students facing expulsion from public school are guaranteed at least minimum due process under the Fourteenth Amendment (see Figure 8.2 for procedural elements). The procedural safeguards required may vary, depending on the circumstances of a particular situation. In a Mississippi case, a student and his parents claimed that prior to an expulsion hearing, they should have been given a list of the witnesses and a summary of their testimony.[9] Recognizing that such procedural protections generally should be afforded prior to a long-term expulsion, the Fifth Circuit nonetheless held that they were not requisite in this case. The parents had been fully apprised of the charges, the facts supporting the charges, and the nature of the hearing. In a later case involving expulsion for possession of drugs, the same court found no impairment of a student's rights when he was denied an opportunity to confront and rebut witnesses who accused him of selling drugs.[10] The names of student witnesses had been withheld to prevent retaliation against them. Similarly, the Sixth Circuit noted that it is critical to protect the anonymity of students who blow the whistle on classmates involved in serious offenses, such as drug dealing.[11]

State laws and school board policies often provide students facing expulsion with more elaborate procedural safeguards than the constitutional protections noted. Once such expulsion procedures are established, courts will require that they be followed.

 Zero-Tolerance Policies.   Concerns about school safety led to specific federal and state laws directed at the discipline of students who bring weapons onto school campuses. Under the Gun-Free Schools Act of 1994, all states enacted legislation requiring at least a one-year expulsion for students who bring firearms to school.[12] In expanding the scope of the federal law beyond guns, state laws have included weapons such as knives, explosive devices, hand chains, and other offensive weapons, as well as drugs and violent

[9]Keough v. Tate Cnty. Bd. of Educ., 748 F.2d 1077 (5th Cir. 1984).

[10]Brewer v. Austin Indep. Sch. Dist., 779 F.2d 260 (5th Cir. 1985).

[11]Newsome v. Batavia Local Sch. Dist., 842 F.2d 920 (6th Cir. 1988); *see also* Scanlon v. Las Cruces Pub. Schs., 172 P.3d 185 (N.M. Ct. App. 2007) (ruling that a student's procedural due process rights were not violated when school officials did not disclose the names of student informants).

[12]20 U.S.C. § 7151 (2012). Additionally, most states have enacted gun-free or weapons-free school zone laws restricting possession of firearms in or near schools.

acts.[13] The federal law also requires states to permit the local school superintendent to modify the expulsion requirement on a case-by-case basis and allows officials to assign students to alternative instructional programs.

Severe criticism has been directed at zero-tolerance policies when school officials fail to exercise discretion and flexibility. The American Bar Association and others have called for an end to such policies that require automatic penalties without assessing the circumstances.[14] A Virginia case underscores the harsh consequences when students encounter inflexible policies. In that case, a thirteen-year-old student, attempting to save a suicidal friend's life, took the friend's binder containing a knife and placed it in his own locker. Despite the fact that the assistant principal believed the student was attempting to save his friend's life and at no time posed a threat to anyone, he was expelled from school for four months. The Fourth Circuit, in upholding the expulsion, noted its harshness but found no violation of the student's due process rights.[15] Such harshness, however, has led policy makers and educators to rethink zero-tolerance discipline measures, particularly for behavior unrelated to the possession of weapons.[16] Among the states debating new laws or policies to lessen the impact of zero tolerance are California, Colorado, Georgia, Maryland, Michigan, North Carolina, and Virginia.

Invoking mandatory expulsion policies may implicate constitutional rights if administrators fail to take into consideration the individual student's history and the circumstances surrounding the conduct. For example, the Sixth Circuit noted that expelling a student for weapons possession when the student did not know the weapon was in his car could not survive a due process challenge.[17] Most courts, however, have been reluctant to impose the *knowing possession* standard that would require the determination of a student's intent.[18]

---

[13]*See* R.H. v. State, 56 So. 3d 156 (Fla. Dist. Ct. App. 2011) (holding that a student who brought a common pocketknife to school could not be charged with a crime because Florida law, unlike many other state laws, specifically exempts pocketknives from its ban on weapons); *see also* F.R. v. State, 81 So. 3d 572 (Fla. Dist. Ct. App. 2012) (determining that a folding knife with a notch grip, a locking blade mechanism, and a hilt guard was not a pocket-knife exempt under Florida law).

[14]Am. Psychol. Ass'n Zero Tolerance Task Force, *Are Zero Tolerance Policies Effective in the Schools*, 63 AM. PSYCHOLOGIST 852 (2008) (finding zero tolerance has not been an effective means of improving school safety or climate); ABA Report to the ABA House of Delegates, Chicago, IL (Feb. 19, 2001); *see also* Peter Follenweider, *Zero Tolerance: A Proper Definition*, 44 J. MARSHALL L. REV. 1107 (2011).

[15]Ratner v. Loudoun Cnty. Pub. Schs., 16 F. App'x 140, 143 (4th Cir. 2001). *See also Virginia Student's Expulsion Renews Debate Over Zero Tolerance Policies*, LEGAL CLIPS, (Feb. 3, 2011), http://legalclips.nsba.org/?p=4572 (reporting a school board's expulsion of a student under its rule against violent criminal conduct when the student used a plastic pipe to blow plastic pellets at other students during lunch). Under the zero-tolerance discipline policy, the Virginia student was expelled for the possession and use of a weapon. A state court judge and the state supreme court upheld the school board's decision, and the U.S. Supreme Court denied review. Mikel v. Sch. Bd. of Spotsylvania Cnty., 133 S. Ct. 34 (2012).

[16]Donna St. George, *More Schools Rethinking Zero-Tolerance Discipline Stand,* WASH. POST, (June 1, 2011), http://www.washingtonpost.com/local/education/more-schools-are-rethinking-zero-tolerance/2011/05/26/AGSIKmGH_story.html.

[17]Seal v. Morgan, 229 F.3d 567 (6th Cir. 2000).

[18]*See, e.g.*, Bundick v. Bay City Indep. Sch. Dist., 140 F. Supp. 2d 735, 740 (S.D. Tex. 2001); *In re* B.N.S., 641 S.E.2d 411 (N.C. Ct. App. 2007).

FIGURE 8.3 Procedural Due Process for Student Suspensions

- Oral or written notification of the nature of the violation and the intended punishment
- An opportunity to refute the charges before an objective decision maker (such a discussion may immediately follow the alleged rule infraction)
- An explanation of the evidence on which the disciplinarian is relying

Suspensions

Suspensions are frequently used to punish students for violating school rules and standards of behavior when the infractions are not of sufficient magnitude to warrant expulsion. Suspensions include short-term removals (ten days or less) from school as well as the denial of participation in regular courses and activities (in-school suspension). Most legal controversies have focused on out-of-school suspensions, but it is advisable to apply the same legal principles to any disciplinary action that separates the student from the regular instructional program, even for a short period of time.

Procedural Requirements.   In 1975, the Supreme Court provided substantial clarification regarding the constitutional rights of students faced with short-term suspensions. In *Goss v. Lopez,* the Court held that minimum due process must be provided before a student is suspended for even a brief period of time.[19] **Recognizing that a student's state-created property right to an education is protected by the Fourteenth Amendment, the Court ruled that such a right cannot be impaired unless the student is afforded notice of the charges and an opportunity to refute them before an impartial decision maker** (see Figure 8.3). The Supreme Court also emphasized that suspensions implicate students' constitutionally protected liberty interests because of the potentially damaging effects that the disciplinary process can have on a student's reputation and permanent record.

Even though the Supreme Court's *Goss* decision established the rudimentary procedural requirements for short-term suspensions, students continue to seek expansion of their procedural rights. The Court specifically noted that such formal procedures as the right to secure counsel, to confront and cross-examine witnesses, and to call witnesses are not constitutionally required. The Court reiterated this stance in a later case by noting that a two-day suspension "does not rise to the level of a penal sanction calling for the full panoply of procedural due process protections applicable to a criminal prosecution."[20]

Decisions by lower state and federal courts indicate a reluctance to impose additional requirements unless mandated by state law. The *right to remain silent* has been advanced, with students arguing that school disciplinary proceedings should be governed by the Supreme Court's ruling in *Miranda v. Arizona* (that persons subjected to custodial interrogation must be advised of their right to remain silent, that any statement made may be used against them, and that they have the right to legal counsel).[21] Courts have readily dismissed these claims, finding that discussions with school administrators are noncustodial. In the

Goss v. Lopez Case

[19]419 U.S. 565 (1975). Individuals posing a danger or threat may be removed immediately, with notice and a hearing following as soon as possible.

[20]Bethel Sch. Dist. No. 403 v. Fraser, 478 U.S. 675, 686 (1986).

[21]384 U.S. 436 (1966).

Miranda decision, the Supreme Court was interpreting an individual's Fifth Amendment right against self-incrimination when first subjected to police questioning in connection with criminal charges.[22] A Maine student claimed a violation of procedural due process because the school administrator denied him permission to leave during questioning and failed to advise him of his right to remain silent or to have his parents present during the interrogation. The court rejected all claims, noting that there was no legal authority to substantiate any of the asserted rights.[23] The court reasoned that to rule otherwise would, in fact, contradict the informal procedures outlined in *Goss* allowing for immediate questioning and disciplinary action.

The Supreme Court in *Goss* recognized the possibility of "unusual situations" that would require more formal procedures than those outlined, but little guidance was given about what these circumstances might be. The only suggestion offered in *Goss* was that a disciplinarian should adopt more extensive procedures in instances involving factual disputes "and arguments about cause and effect."[24] Courts have declined to expand on this brief listing. The Sixth Circuit rejected a student's contention that drug charges constituted such an "unusual situation" because of the stigmatizing effect on his reputation. The court did not believe that an eighth-grade student suspended for ten days for possessing a substance that resembled an illegal drug was "forever faced with a tarnished reputation and restricted employment opportunities."[25] More extensive procedures also have been found unnecessary when students are barred from interscholastic athletics and other activities.[26]

Students have asserted that suspensions involving loss of course credit or occurring during exam periods require greater due process than outlined in *Goss*. The Fifth Circuit, however, did not find that the loss incurred for a ten-day suspension during final examinations required more than a mere give-and-take discussion between the principal and the student. In refusing to require more formal proceedings, the court noted that *Goss* makes no distinction as to when a short-term suspension occurs, and a contrary ruling would "significantly undermine, if not nullify, its definitive holding."[27]

In-School Suspensions. In-school suspensions or isolation may entitle students to minimal due process procedures if they are deprived of instruction or the opportunity to learn. A Tennessee federal district court found that a student's placement in a classroom "time-out box" did not require due process because he continued to work on class assignments

---

[22]*See infra* text accompanying note 129.

[23]Boynton v. Casey, 543 F. Supp. 995 (D. Me. 1982). *But see In re* T.A.G., 663 S.E.2d 392 (Ga. 2008) (affirming trial court's suppression of a student's statements when he was interviewed by an assistant principal and an armed *police officer*); *In re* R.H., 791 A.2d 331 (Pa. 2002) (holding that *school police officers* were required to give a student *Miranda* warnings prior to interrogation since they exercised the same powers as municipal police and the interrogation led to charges by the police, not punishment by school officials); *infra* text accompanying note 129.

[24]Goss v. Lopez, 419 U.S. 565, 583–84 (1975).

[25]Paredes v. Curtis, 864 F.2d 426, 429 (6th Cir. 1988).

[26]*See, e.g.,* Donovan v. Ritchie, 68 F.3d 14 (1st Cir. 1995); *see also* Mather v. Loveland City Sch. Dist., 908 N.E.2d 1039 (Ohio Ct. App. 2009) (interpreting OHIO REV. CODE § 3313.66(E) as providing a student the right to appeal an expulsion or suspension from curricular activities but not extracurricular ones).

[27]Keough v. Tate Cnty. Bd. of Educ., 748 F.2d 1077, 1081 (5th Cir. 1984).

and could hear and see the teacher from the confined area.[28] The court emphasized that teachers must be free to administer minor forms of classroom discipline such as time-out, denial of privileges, and special assignments. Similarly, the Sixth Circuit held that a one-day in-school suspension in which a student completed school work and was considered in attendance did not implicate a property interest in educational benefits or a liberty interest in reputation; it was simply too *de minimis*.[29]

Disciplinary Transfers to Alternative Educational Placements.   Closely related to suspensions are *involuntary transfers* of students to alternative educational placements for disciplinary reasons. Such transfers generally do not involve denial of public education, but they may implicate protected liberty or property interests. In an illustrative case, the Fifth Circuit declined to find a federally protected property or liberty interest when a student arrested for aggravated assault was reassigned to an alternative education program under a Texas statute. According to the court, the student was not even temporarily denied a public education. In dismissing the case, the court did note that to ensure fairness, the state and local school districts should provide students and parents an opportunity to explain why a disciplinary transfer may not be warranted; however, failure to do so does not infringe constitutional rights.[30]

Legal challenges to the use of disciplinary transfers have addressed primarily the adequacy of the procedures followed. Recognizing that students do not have an inherent right to attend a given school, some courts nonetheless have held that pupils facing involuntary reassignment are entitled to minimal due process if such transfers are the result of misbehavior[31] or if required by school board policy.[32]

Anti-Bullying Laws.   Numerous studies document the pervasiveness of bullying behavior and its detrimental impact on students' learning and mental health. School personnel have always had the authority to discipline students for such behavior. New state laws, however, formalize the responsibility for disrupting and deterring bullying behavior. In developing and administering anti-bullying policies, school officials must take into consideration students' procedural due process rights. Policies imposing short-term suspensions must comply at least with the minimum requirements of *Goss*;[33] more extensive disciplinary measures for bullying behavior will necessitate formal hearings.

---

[28]Dickens v. Johnson Cnty. Bd. of Educ., 661 F. Supp. 155 (E.D. Tenn. 1987); *see also* Rasmus v. Arizona, 939 F. Supp. 709 (D. Ariz. 1996) (holding that denying a student the ability to work on class assignments during a ten-minute time-out was *de minimis* and did not violate a property right).

[29]Laney v. Farley, 501 F.3d 577 (6th Cir. 2007).

[30]Nevares v. San Marcos Consol. Indep. Sch. Dist., No. 96-50420, 1997 U.S. App. LEXIS 14955 (5th Cir. Apr. 11, 1997); *see also* Harris v. Pontotoc Cnty. Sch. Dist., 635 F.3d 685 (5th Cir. 2011) (concluding that an assignment to an alternative school does not involve a denial of education requiring procedural protection); Anderson v. Hillsborough Cnty. Sch. Bd., 390 F. App'x 902 (11th Cir. 2010) (finding that the minimum due process provided was sufficient for an alternative placement).

[31]*See, e.g.*, McCall v. Bossier Parish Sch. Bd., 785 So. 2d 57 (La. Ct. App. 2001).

[32]*See, e.g.*, Rone v. Winston-Salem/Forsyth Cnty. Bd. of Educ., 701 S.E.2d 284 (N.C. Ct. App. 2010).

[33]*See supra* text accompanying note 19.

All states except Montana have enacted anti-bullying legislation because of concerns about connections between school violence and bullying. Like the mandate under the zero-tolerance laws, these state laws, which may reside in the education, criminal, and/or juvenile justice codes, require local school districts to include an anti-bullying policy in their discipline codes.[34] Most state laws provide a broad definition of what constitutes bullying behavior. The laws refer to intentional, aggressive behavior, repeated over time, that imposes harm on others. Typically, proscribed behavior includes name-calling, teasing, intimidation, ridicule, humiliation, physical acts, and taunts.[35] The scope of the laws specifies behavior occurring not only on school property but also at school-sponsored events and on school buses and at bus stops, as well as off-campus conduct. For example, Massachusetts's law prohibits bullying at any location unrelated to the school "if the bullying creates a hostile environment at school for the victim, infringes on the rights of the victim at school, or materially and substantially disrupts the education process or the orderly operation of a school."[36] Most states specifically include electronic bullying that inflicts fear and harm.

Although a few state laws identify the specific penalties for bullying behavior, most states mandate that school districts develop a bullying policy that delineates the penalties and the measures that will be taken to prevent bullying. Oregon law is typical, requiring that policies include consequences for bullying behavior, but it also goes further by specifying that remedial measures should be taken with the students who bully.[37] Georgia law does not address initial consequences but specifies student assignment to an alternative school after three bullying offenses.[38]

In conclusion, **fundamental fairness requires at least minimal due process procedures when students are denied school attendance or removed from the regular instructional program.** Severity of the separation dictates the amount of process due under the United States Constitution and state laws. Permanent expulsion from school triggers the most extensive process, whereas minor infractions may involve a brief give-and-take between school officials and students. Simply providing students the opportunity to be heard not only reduces mistakes but also preserves trust in the school system.

CORPORAL PUNISHMENT

If not prohibited by law or school board policy, reasonable corporal punishment can be used as a disciplinary measure.

Many states have banned educators' use of corporal punishment either by law or state regulation. In 1971, only one state prohibited corporal punishment; today, more than half

[34]For an analysis of state bullying laws adopted through January 2013, see Cyberbullying Research Ctr., (Feb. 2013) http://www.cyberbullying.us/Bullying_and_Cyberbullying_Laws.pdf; *see also* text accompanying note 46, Chapter 5.

[35]*See, e.g.*, IND. CODE ANN. § 20-33-8-0.2 (2012).

[36]71 MASS. GEN. LAWS § 370 (2012).

[37]OR. REV. STAT. §339.356(1) (2012).

[38]GA. CODE ANN. § 20-2-751.4(b)(2) (2012).

proscribe its use.[39] Generally, when state law and school board policy permit corporal punishment, courts have upheld its reasonable administration and have placed the burden on the aggrieved students to prove otherwise. **In evaluating the reasonableness of a teacher's actions in administering corporal punishment, courts have assessed the child's age, maturity, and past behavior; the nature of the offense; the instrument used; any evidence of lasting harm to the child; and the motivation of the person inflicting the punishment.** This section provides an overview of the constitutional and state law issues raised in the administration of corporal punishment.

Constitutional Issues

The Supreme Court held in *Ingraham v. Wright* that **the use of corporal punishment in public schools does not violate either the Eighth Amendment's prohibition against the government's infliction of cruel and unusual punishment or the Fourteenth Amendment's procedural due process guarantees.**[40] While recognizing that corporal punishment implicates students' constitutionally protected liberty interests, the Court emphasized that state remedies are available, such as assault and battery suits, if students are excessively or arbitrarily punished by school personnel. In essence, the Court majority concluded that state courts, under provisions of state laws, should handle cases dealing with corporal punishment. The majority distinguished corporal punishment from a suspension from school by noting that the denial of school attendance is a more severe penalty, depriving students of a property right and thus necessitating procedural safeguards.

The Supreme Court's ruling in *Ingraham*, however, does not foreclose a successful constitutional challenge to the use of *unreasonable* corporal punishment. Most federal appellate courts have held that students' substantive due process right to be free of brutal and egregious threats to bodily security might be impaired by the use of shockingly excessive corporal punishment.[41] For example, the Fourth Circuit concluded that although *Ingraham* bars federal litigation on procedural due process issues, excessive or cruel corporal punishment may violate students' substantive due process rights, which protect individuals from arbitrary and unreasonable governmental action. According to the appellate court, the standard for determining if such a violation has occurred is "whether the force applied caused injury so severe, was so disproportionate to the need presented, and was so inspired by malice or sadism rather than a merely careless or unwise excess of zeal that it amounted to a brutal and inhumane abuse of official power literally shocking to the conscience."[42]

---

[39]Most recently, New Mexico (2011) and Ohio (2009) enacted laws to abolish corporal punishment. See GLOBAL INITIATIVE TO END ALL CORPORAL PUNISHMENT OF CHILDREN, http://www.endcorporalpunishment.org/pages/frame.html, for the status of corporal punishment laws in each state and country in the world. The American Academy of Pediatrics has recommended that corporal punishment be abolished in all states because of its detrimental effect on students' self-image and achievement as well as possible contribution to disruptive and violent behavior. Am. Acad. of Pediatrics, *Corporal Punishment in Schools*, 106 PEDIATRICS 343 (Aug. 2000); reaffirming 2000 statement, 118 PEDIATRICS 1266 (Sept. 2006).

[40]430 U.S. 651 (1977).

[41]*See, e.g.*, Johnson v. Newburgh Enlarged Sch. Dist., 239 F.3d 246 (2d Cir. 2001); Neal v. Fulton Cnty. Bd. of Educ., 229 F.2d 1069 (11th Cir. 2000).

[42]Hall v. Tawney, 621 F.2d 607, 613 (4th Cir. 1980).

Clearly, student challenges to the reasonable use of ordinary corporal punishment are precluded by this standard. Disciplinary actions that have *not risen* to this level include requiring a ten-year-old boy to clean out a stopped-up toilet with his bare hands,[43] physically and forcefully restraining a student in multiple incidents,[44] and shoving a student's head into a trash can.[45] In contrast, substantive due process rights were implicated when conscience-shocking behavior involved a coach knocking a student's eye out of the socket with a metal weight lock;[46] a substitute teacher slamming an elementary student's head into a chalkboard, throwing her to the floor, and choking her;[47] and a teacher and a teaching assistant maliciously restraining a severely disabled child in her wheelchair for hours at a time.[48]

State Law

The Supreme Court has ruled that the U.S. Constitution does not prohibit corporal punishment in public schools but notes that its use may conflict with state law provisions or local administrative regulations. As noted, most states now prohibit corporal punishment, and others have established procedures or conditions for its use. Teachers can be disciplined or discharged for violating these state and local provisions regulating corporal punishment. Courts have upheld dismissals based on insubordination for failure to comply with reasonable school board requirements in administering corporal punishment. For example, a Michigan teacher was dismissed because he violated board policy by using corporal punishment after having been warned repeatedly to cease.[49] Teachers also have been dismissed under the statutory grounds of "cruelty" for improper use of physical force with students. In Illinois, a tenured teacher was dismissed on this ground for using a cattle prod in punishing students.[50] Other disciplinary measures also may be taken against teachers. A Nebraska teacher who "tapped" a student on the head was suspended without pay for thirty days under a state law that prohibits the use of corporal punishment.[51]

Beyond statutory or board restrictions, other legal means exist to challenge the use of unreasonable corporal punishment in public schools. Teachers can be charged with criminal

---

[43]Harris v. Robinson, 273 F.3d 927 (10th Cir. 2001).

[44]T.W. v. Sch. Bd. of Seminole Cnty., 610 F.3d 588 (11th Cir. 2010); *see also* Davis v. Carter, 555 F.3d 979 (11th Cir. 2009) (finding that a coach's deliberate indifference to a football player who suffered from dehydration and exhaustion was insufficient to establish a constitutional violation; the coach's actions did not involve corporal punishment, nor did the coach act in a malicious way with the intent to injure the student).

[45]Monroe v. Ben Hill Cnty. Sch. System, 377 F. App'x 913 (11th Cir. 2010).

[46]Neal v. Fulton Cnty. Bd. of Educ., 229 F.3d 1069 (11th Cir. 2000).

[47]Ellis *ex rel.* Pendergrass v. Cleveland Mun. Sch. Dist., 455 F.3d 690 (6th Cir. 2006).

[48]H.H. v. Moffett, 335 F. App'x 306, 314 (4th Cir. 2009).

[49]Tomczik v. State Tenure Comm'n, 438 N.W.2d 642 (Mich. Ct. App. 1989).

[50]Rolando v. Sch. Dirs. of Dist. No. 125, 358 N.E.2d 945 (Ill. App. Ct. 1976).

[51]Daily v. Bd. of Educ., 588 N.W.2d 813 (Neb. 1999).

assault and battery, which might result in fines and/or imprisonment. Civil assault and battery suits for monetary damages also can be initiated against school personnel.[52]

Teachers should become familiar with relevant state laws and school board policies before attempting to use corporal punishment in their classrooms. If teachers administer corporal punishment, they would be wise to keep a record of incidents and adhere to minimum procedural safeguards, such as notifying students of behavior that will result in a paddling, asking another staff member to witness the act, and providing parents on request written the reasons for the punishment.

ACADEMIC SANCTIONS

Academic sanctions for nonacademic reasons should be reasonable; related to performance, absences, or other academic concerns; and serve a legitimate school purpose.

It is indisputable that school authorities have the right to use academic sanctions for poor academic performance. Consistently, courts have been reluctant to substitute their own judgment for that of educators in assessing students' academic accomplishments. Failing grades, denial of credit, academic probation, grade retention, and expulsion from particular programs have been upheld as legitimate means of dealing with poor academic performance.

Courts have granted broad discretionary powers to school personnel in establishing academic standards, but less agreement exists regarding the use of grade reductions or academic sanctions as punishments for student absences and misbehavior. More complex legal issues are raised when academic penalties are imposed for nonacademic reasons. These issues are explored next in connection with grade reductions for absences and misconduct.

Absences

Excessive student absenteeism continues to be a concern and has led many school boards to impose academic sanctions for absences. These practices have generated legal challenges related to students' substantive due process rights. To meet the due process requirements, the sanction must be reasonable—that is, rationally related to a valid educational purpose. Since students must attend class to benefit from the educational program, most courts have found that academic penalties for absenteeism serve a valid educational goal.

In an illustrative case, the Supreme Court of Connecticut drew a sharp distinction between academic and disciplinary sanctions, noting that the school board's policy of reducing grades for unapproved absences was academic, rather than disciplinary, in intent and effect. Specifically, the court found that a board's determination that grades should

---

[52]*Ex parte* Monroe Cnty. Bd. of Educ. v. Monroe Cnty. Bd. of Educ., 48 So. 3d 621 (Ala. 2010) (ruling that a teacher was not entitled to state-agent immunity in a tort suit when she did not follow the school board's policy for administering corporal punishment); *see also* text accompanying note 48, Chapter 2.

reflect more than examinations and papers "constitutes an academic judgment about academic requirements."[53]

Some courts have upheld the imposition of academic penalties even though policies do not differentiate between excused and unexcused absences. For example, the Supreme Court of Arkansas upheld a board policy that disallowed course credit and permitted expulsion of students who accumulated more than twelve absences per semester.[54] The court, in refusing to substitute its judgment for the school board's, concluded that this action was legal under state law and that it was within the board's power to make reasonable rules and regulations. Similarly, a New York appellate court found that a policy denying course credit for absences in excess of nine classes for semester courses and eighteen absences for full-year courses was rational; students were permitted and encouraged to make up the classes before they exceeded the limit.[55]

Given the serious truancy problem confronting many school districts, it seems likely that school boards will continue to consider the imposition of academic sanctions. The legality of such policies will depend primarily on judicial interpretation of applicable state law.

Misconduct

Academic sanctions imposed for student misconduct also have been challenged. It is generally accepted that students can be denied credit for work missed while suspended from school. More controversy has surrounded policies that impose an additional grade reduction for suspension days, and courts have not agreed regarding the legality of this practice.

For example, a Pennsylvania court found grade reductions for suspensions to be beyond a school board's authority.[56] In the court's opinion, it was a clear misrepresentation of students' scholastic achievement; the penalty went beyond the five-day suspension and downgraded achievement for a full grading period. The Mississippi Supreme Court, relying on a state law mandating the maintenance of alternative schools for suspended students, concluded that students attending these schools are not absent from school.[57] Under this law, a school board cannot count suspension days as unexcused for grading purposes unless the student fails to attend the alternative school. In contrast, the Supreme Court of Indiana upheld the denial of course credit for a high school junior expelled three days before the end of a semester. The court noted that state law did not mandate loss of credit, but the board could impose such a penalty.[58]

Generally, courts have ruled that academic course credit or high school diplomas cannot be withheld solely for disciplinary reasons. For example, a Pennsylvania court held that a student who completed all coursework and final exams while expulsion proceedings were pending could not be denied a diploma, because state law specifies that a diploma

[53]Campbell v. Bd. of Educ., 475 A.2d 289, 294 (Conn. 1984).

[54]Williams v. Bd. of Educ., 626 S.W.2d 361 (Ark. 1982).

[55]Bitting v. Lee, 564 N.Y.S.2d 791 (App. Div. 1990).

[56]Katzman v. Cumberland Valley Sch. Dist., 479 A.2d 671 (Pa. Commw. Ct. 1984).

[57]Bd. of Trs. v. T.H., 681 So. 2d 110 (Miss. 1996).

[58]S. Gibson Sch. Bd. v. Sollman, 768 N.E.2d 437 (Ind. 2002).

must be issued once all requirements are met.[59] However, a student suspended at the end of the semester may be denied *participation* in the graduation ceremony.[60]

Even though the use of academic sanctions for student misconduct and truancy is prevalent, students will likely continue to challenge such practices. To ensure fairness, any regulation stipulating that grades will be lowered should be reasonable, related to absences from class, and serve a legitimate educational purpose. Furthermore, students must be informed of these rules through the school's official student handbook or similar means.

SEARCH AND SEIZURE

School personnel can search students' lockers or personal effects based on reasonable suspicion that the students possess contraband that is either illegal or in violation of school policy.

The majority of search and seizure cases in public schools involve the confiscation of either illegal drugs or weapons. Students have asserted that warrantless searches conducted by school officials impair their rights under the Fourth Amendment of the U.S. Constitution. Through an extensive line of decisions, the Supreme Court has affirmed that the basic purpose of the Fourth Amendment is to "safeguard the privacy and security of individuals against arbitrary invasions by governmental officials."[61] This amendment protects individuals against unreasonable searches by requiring state agents to obtain a warrant based on probable cause prior to conducting a search. Under the *probable cause standard*, a governmental official must have reasonable grounds of suspicion, supported by sufficient evidence, to cause a cautious person to believe that the suspected individual is guilty of the alleged offense and that the search will produce evidence of the crime committed (see Figure 8.4). Governmental officials violating Fourth Amendment rights may be subject to criminal or civil liability, but the most important remedy for the aggrieved individual is the exclusionary rule, which renders evidence of an illegal search inadmissible in criminal prosecutions.

Application of the Fourth Amendment to Students

Since Fourth Amendment protections apply only to searches conducted by agents of the state, a fundamental issue in education cases is whether school authorities function as private individuals or as state agents. In 1985, the Supreme Court ruled in *New Jersey v. T.L.O.* that **school officials are state agents, and all governmental actions—not**

---

[59]Ream v. Centennial Sch. Dist., 765 A.2d 1195 (Pa. Commw. Ct. 2001).

[60]Walters v. Dobbins, 2010 Ark. 260 (Ark. 2010)*; see also* Khan v. Fort Bend Indep. Sch. Dist., 561 F. Supp. 2d 760 (S.D. Tex. 2008) (finding that suspended student had no property right to attend the graduation ceremony or to deliver the valedictorian address).

[61]Camara v. Mun. Court, 387 U.S. 523, 528 (1967).

FIGURE 8.4   **Standards for Searches**

Probable Cause Standard

- Police officers must secure a warrant prior to conducting a search.
- Facts or evidence must indicate that a person has committed, is committing, or will be committing a crime. Evidence may include witnesses, credible informants, victims of a crime, police officer observations, etc.
- A judge issues a warrant describing the place to be searched and the individual or items to be seized.

Reasonable Suspicion Standard

- School officials are not required to obtain a warrant to search students.
- The legality of a search of a student depends "simply on the reasonableness, under all the circumstances, of the search."*
- Two tests are used to determine reasonableness.
  - Is the search justified at its inception?
    Reasonable suspicion exists that the student has violated, is violating, or will be violating the law or the school discipline code.
  - Is the scope of the search reasonable?
    The type of search (lockers, personal possessions, cars, etc.) is reasonably related to the reason for the search and not overly intrusive for the nature of the suspected infraction and the age and sex of the student.

---

*New Jersy v. T.L.O., 469 U.S. 325, 341 (1985).

merely those of law enforcement officers—come within the constraints of the Fourth Amendment.[62]

Even though the Fourth Amendment is applicable, the Court in *T.L.O.* concluded that educators' substantial interest in maintaining discipline required "easing" the warrant and probable cause requirements imposed on police officers. The Court reasoned that requiring educators to obtain a warrant before searching students suspected of violating school rules or criminal laws would interfere with the administration of prompt and informal disciplinary procedures needed to maintain order. In modifying the level of suspicion required to conduct a search, the Court found the public interest was best served in the school setting with a standard less than probable cause. Accordingly, **the Court held that the legality of a search should depend "simply on the reasonableness, under all the circumstances, of the search."**[63]

As shown in Figure 8.4, the Court in *T.L.O.* advanced two tests for determining reasonableness. First, is the search justified at its inception? That is, reasonable grounds exist to suspect the search will yield evidence that the student has violated a school rule or the law.[64] Second, is the scope of the search reasonable? This means the type of search is related to the objective of the search and not excessively intrusive.[65]

---

[62]469 U.S. 325 (1985).

[63]*Id.* at 341; *see also In re* M.A.D., 233 P.3d 437 (Or. 2010) (holding that under the state constitution, probable cause was not required to search when a school official had credible information that a student possessed drugs and attempted to sell them earlier in the day).

[64]*T.L.O.*, 469 U.S. at 342.

[65]*Id.*

The "reasonableness" standard allows courts substantial latitude in interpreting Fourth Amendment rights. Among factors courts have considered in assessing reasonable grounds for a search are the child's age, history, and record in the school; prevalence and seriousness of the problem in the school to which the search is directed; exigency to make the search without delay and further investigation; probative value and reliability of the information used as a justification for the search; the school officials' experience with the student and with the type of problem to which the search is directed; and the type of search. Clearly, reasonable suspicion requires more than a hunch, good intentions, or good faith. The Supreme Court, in upholding an exception to the warrant requirement for a "stop and frisk" search for weapons by police officers, concluded that to justify the intrusion the police officer must be able to point to "specific and articulable facts."[66] In recognizing an exception for school searches, it appears that, at a minimum, the judiciary will require searches of students to be supported by objective facts.

Informants often play an important role in establishing the "specific and articulable facts" necessary to justify a search. Reliability of informants can be assumed unless school officials have reason to doubt the motives of the reporting student, teacher, parent, citizen, or anonymous caller. The amount of detail given by an informant adds to the veracity of the report—that is, identifying a specific student by name, what the student is wearing, and the specific contraband and where it is located will support a decision to search.[67] Additionally, even with limited information, the level of danger presented by an informant's tip may require an immediate response.

Another aspect of reasonableness is individualized suspicion. The Supreme Court in *T.L.O.* did not address individualized suspicion, but the Court did state that "exceptions to the requirement of individualized suspicion are generally appropriate only where the privacy interests implicated by a search are minimal and where 'other safeguards' are available 'to assure that the individual's reasonable expectation of privacy is not subject to the discretion of the official in the field.'"[68] **Courts have been reluctant to support personal searches lacking individualized suspicion unless the safety of the students necessitates an immediate search.**

In assessing the constitutionality of searches in the public schools, two questions are central: (1) What constitutes a search? (2) What types of searches are reasonable? According to the Supreme Court's rulings, essential considerations in determining whether an action is a search are an individual's reasonable expectation of privacy (reasonable in the sense that society is prepared to recognize the privacy)[69] and the extent of governmental intrusion.[70] The reasonableness of a specific type of search must be evaluated in terms of all of the circumstances surrounding the search. This would include variables such as who initiated the search, who conducted the search, the need for the search, the purpose of the search, information or factors

---

[66]Terry v. Ohio, 392 U.S. 1, 21 (1968).

[67]*See* People v. Perreault, 781 N.W.2d 796 (Mich. 2010) (holding that an anonymous tip providing names of students, grade levels, vehicle types, and drugs being sold established reasonable suspicion to search a student's vehicle).

[68]New Jersey v. T.L.O., 469 U.S. 325, 342 n.8 (1985) (citing Delaware v. Prouse, 440 U.S. 648, 654–55 (1976)).

[69]*T.L.O.*, 469 U.S. at 361 (Harlan, J., concurring).

[70]United States v. Chadwick, 433 U.S. 1, 7 (1977).

prompting the search, what or who was searched, and use of the evidence. In the next sections, various types of school searches are examined within this context.

Lockers

Courts have singled out school lockers as generating a *lower* expectation of privacy, frequently distinguishing locker searches on the basis that a locker is school property, and students do not retain exclusive possession. This is particularly likely when they have signed a form acknowledging that the locker is school property and subject to inspection. **Under the view of joint control, school officials have been allowed to inspect lockers or even to consent to locker searches by law enforcement officers.**[71]

Most student conduct codes and some state laws specify guidelines for locker searches. These codes or laws may establish that reasonable suspicion is required prior to conducting a search. In a Pennsylvania case, the state supreme court relied on the *T.L.O.* decision and the student code in establishing a legitimate expectation of privacy in lockers. The code specified: "Prior to a locker search a student shall be notified and given an opportunity to be present. However, where school authorities have a *reasonable suspicion* that the locker contains materials which pose a threat to the health, welfare, and safety of students in the school, students' lockers may be searched without prior warning" (emphasis added).[72] The court held that students possessed a reasonable expectation of privacy in their lockers; yet, in balancing students' privacy interests and school officials' concerns, the court found a school-wide blanket search reasonable based on the heightened awareness of drug activity that permeated the entire school and the compelling concern about drug use.

Because of incidents of school violence in recent years, some states have enacted broad laws eliminating any presumption of privacy in school lockers. For example, a Michigan law states: "A pupil who uses a locker that is the property of a school district . . . is presumed to have no expectation of privacy in that locker or that locker's content."[73] Furthermore, Michigan school officials can search the lockers at any time and can request the assistance of the local law enforcement agency. It is likely that statutes such as these will be challenged regarding students' expectation of privacy in the contents of their lockers as well as the use of law enforcement personnel.

Search of Personal Possessions: Purses, Book Bags, and Other Property

Students have a greater expectation of privacy in their personal property or effects than in their school lockers. In the *T.L.O.* case, a teacher had reported a student for smoking in the restroom.[74] Upon questioning by the assistant principal, the student denied smoking and,

---

[71]But see *infra* text accompanying note 124 for cases addressing the involvement of law enforcement personnel.

[72]Commonwealth v. Cass, 709 A.2d 350, 353 (Pa. 1998); *see also In re* S.M.C., 338 S.W.3d 161 (Tex. App. 2011) (concluding that a student informant's tip indicating another student was "high" on drugs justified the search of a student and his locker).

[73]MICH. COMP. LAWS ANN. § 380.1306 (2012).

[74]New Jersey v. T.L.O., 469 U.S. 325 (1985).

in fact, denied that she even smoked. The assistant principal, opening the student's purse seeking evidence to substantiate that she did smoke, found marijuana as well as other evidence implicating her in drug dealing. Using the "reasonable suspicion" test, the Supreme Court held that the search in *T.L.O.* was reasonable. The school official had a basis for suspecting that the student had cigarettes in her purse. Although possession was not a violation of a school rule, it was not irrelevant; discovery of cigarettes provided evidence to corroborate that she had been smoking and challenged her credibility. Characterizing this as a "common sense" conclusion, the Court noted that "the requirement of reasonable suspicion is not a requirement of absolute certainty: 'sufficient probability, not certainty, is the touchstone of reasonableness under the Fourth Amendment.'"[75]

Most courts have noted that searches of students' personal possessions—such as wallets, purses, and book bags—violate students' subjective expectations of privacy and, as such, require individualized suspicion that a violation of a law or school rule has occurred. The Eighth Circuit found that a Little Rock school district policy permitting school officials to conduct full-scale, random, periodic inspections of students' book bags and other personal possessions without any individualized suspicion constituted a major invasion of students' expectation of privacy.[76] The court held that school officials could not argue, because of the policy, that students waived their privacy rights when they brought their possessions onto school property. However, in a more recent Eighth Circuit case upholding a drug dog sniffing backpacks in an empty classroom, the court found the five-minute sniffing differed from inspecting personal possessions because it was minimally intrusive.[77] In a Louisiana case, a high school student was searched after being caught smoking cigarettes in the restroom. As part of the search, the student was required to remove his shoes, whereby narcotics were found. A state appellate court affirmed a lower court's ruling suppressing the evidence because the search of the shoes was "excessive and unwarranted."[78] While reasonable grounds existed to search the student, no reasonable grounds existed to search the shoes since it would not be possible to conceal cigarettes in shoes and still smoke them.

Conversely, the New York high court concluded that a security officer's investigation of a student's book bag was reasonable based on hearing an "unusual metallic thud" when the student tossed the bag on a metal shelf. Following the sound, the security officer ran his fingers over the outside of the book bag and detected the outline of a gun. The court noted that the sound alone was insufficient to justify searching the bag, but the discovery of the presence of a gun-like shape established reasonable suspicion for him to open the bag.[79] In a California case, the court found the search of a student's pockets and backpack reasonable under the school district's established policy that all students who leave campus during the

---

[75]*Id.* at 346 (quoting Hill v. California, 401 U.S. 797, 804 (1971)).

[76]Doe v. Little Rock Sch. Dist., 380 F.3d 349 (8th Cir. 2004). *But see* H.Y. *ex rel.* K.Y. v. Russell Cnty. Bd. of Educ., 490 F. Supp. 2d 1174 (M.D. Ala. 2007) (holding that the classroom search of students' book bags and personal possessions for missing money was justified to promote order and discipline even though individualized suspicion did not exist).

[77]Burlison v. Springfield Pub. Schs., 708 F.3d 1034 (8th Cir. 2013).

[78]State v. Taylor, 50 So. 3d 922, 924 (La. Ct. App. 2010), *review denied*, 57 So. 3d 333 (La. 2011).

[79]*In re* Gregory M., 627 N.E.2d 500 (N.Y. 1993).

school day and return are subjected to a search.[80] Students and parents were informed of the policy, and it was deemed necessary to maintain a safe school environment.

With the prevalent use of cell phones by students, the phones have become ubiquitous in schools and thus subject to search when school officials suspect wrongdoing. Like other personal items, reasonable suspicion is needed to search a cell phone. In a Pennsylvania case, school officials seized Christopher Klump's cell phone when it fell from his pocket; his action violated the school policy against displaying or using a cell phone during the school day.[81] School officials, attempting to determine if other students were violating the policy, used Christopher's phone to call students in the phone's directory, check the messages, and hold an instant messaging conversation without identifying themselves. The court found school officials justified in taking the cell phone; however, the scope of the search was unreasonable. According to the court, the officials "had no reason to suspect at the outset that such a search would reveal that Christopher Klump himself was violating another school policy; rather, they hoped to utilize his phone as a tool to catch other students' violations."[82] A Mississippi federal district court, however, held that school officials did not violate a middle school student's rights when they opened his phone and saw personal photographs of the student. Unlike the Pennsylvania case, the court noted that the cell phone was contraband with the student having diminished expectations of privacy since he could not possess or use a cell phone at school.[83]

A student's car, like other personal possessions, may be searched if reasonable suspicion can be established. The Supreme Court of New Jersey rejected a student's claim that a greater expectation of privacy existed for his automobile parked on school grounds, necessitating probable cause to conduct a search.[84] Noting school officials' responsibilities to maintain safety and order, the state high court held that only reasonable suspicion was required. A report from a student who appeared to be intoxicated from a pill purchased from the student, as well as items found in his locker, established the necessary reasonable suspicion. Similarly, reasonable suspicion was found in an Idaho case when a school official searched a student's car because he smelled tobacco smoke on him.[85] A school policy banned the possession of tobacco products on campus; individualized suspicion existed that the student was in violation of this school rule.

---

[80]*In re* Sean, 120 Cal. Rptr. 3d 72 (Ct. App. 2010).

[81]Klump v. Nazareth Area Sch. Dist., 425 F. Supp. 2d 622 (E.D. Pa. 2006); *see also* G.C. v Owensboro Pub. Schs., 711 F.3d 623 (6th Cir. 2013) (ruling that school officials' search of a student's text messages was unjustified; texting in class violated a school rule but did not establish reasonable grounds to suspect that the student was involved in any improper activity).

[82]*Klump*, 425 F. Supp. 2d at 640.

[83]J.W. v. Desoto Cnty. Sch. Dist., No. 2:09-cv-00155-MPM-DAS, 2010 U.S. Dist. LEXIS 116328 (N.D. Miss. Nov. 1, 2010); *see also* Koch v. Adams, 361 S.W.3d 817 (Ark. 2010) (rejecting student's claim that state law did not permit school authorities to seize his cell phone; the state law specified types of penalties for violating school discipline codes but did not limit school authorities in using others, such as seizure of a cell phone).

[84]State v. Best, 987 A.2d 605 (N.J. 2010); *see also* State v. Schloegel, 769 N.W.2d 130 (Wis. Ct. App. 2009) (finding search of a vehicle reasonable when school officials were alerted that a student was in possession of drugs).

[85]State v. Voss, 267 P.3d 735 (Idaho Ct. App. 2011), *review denied*, No. 38366-2010, 2012 Idaho LEXIS 41 (Idaho Jan. 27, 2012); *see also* People v. Perreault, 781 N.W.2d 796 (Mich. 2010) (ruling that an anonymous tip established reasonable suspicion to search a student's truck when based on the totality of the circumstances).

Personal Search of Students

Warrantless searches of a student's person raise significant legal questions. Unlike locker searches, it cannot be asserted that there is a lower expectation of privacy. **Students have a legitimate expectation of privacy in the contents of their pockets and their person.** The Fifth Circuit noted: "The Fourth Amendment applies with its fullest vigor against any intrusion on the human body."[86] In personal searches, not only is it necessary to have reasonable cause to search, but also the search itself must be reasonable. Reasonableness is assessed in terms of the specific facts and circumstances of a case.

Search of Students' Clothing.   In applying the *T.L.O.* standard, a New Mexico appellate court found the search of a student's pockets reasonable.[87] In this case, an assistant principal and a police officer assigned full time to the school asked a student to empty his pockets based on his evasive behavior, the smell of burnt marijuana, and a large bulge in his right pocket. When the student refused to remove his hand from his pocket, the school official asked the resource officer to search the student. The officer removed the student's hand from his right pocket and reached in and pulled out a .38 caliber handgun. The court held that the search was justified on the basis of suspicious behavior and that the scope of the search was not excessive or intrusive. However, the Washington appellate court declined to support the search of a student's pockets because he was in the school parking lot during the school day—a violation of the closed campus policy. The court emphasized that "there must be a nexus between the item sought and the infraction under investigation."[88] In the absence of other suspicious factors about the student, violation of the school's closed campus rule did not justify the automatic search that led to the discovery of marijuana.

The Minnesota federal district court concluded that school officials violated the Fourth Amendment rights of special education students when the students were subjected each day to searches of their backpacks and purses, as well as being asked to "remove their shoes and socks, turn down the waistband of their pants, empty their pockets, and (at least sometimes) to submit to a patdown."[89] In issuing a temporary restraining order, the New Mexico federal district court noted a substantial likelihood that students attending the high school prom would be successful in showing an intrusive pat-down search of all students violated the Fourth Amendment.[90] The court, however, concluded that a search of possessions, which is less intrusive, would not be unconstitutional since it served a valid purpose in ensuring a safe environment.

---

[86]Horton v. Goose Creek Indep. Sch. Dist., 690 F.2d 470, 478 (5th Cir. 1982).

[87]*In re* Josue T., 989 P.2d 431 (N.M. Ct. App. 1999); *see also In re* B.A.H., 263 P.3d 1046 (Or. Ct. App. 2011) (ruling under the Oregon Constitution that the search of a student's clothing was reasonable based on reliable information that he possessed illegal drugs).

[88]State v. B.A.S., 13 P.3d 244, 246 (Wash. Ct. App. 2000); *see also* Commonwealth v. Damian D., 752 N.E.2d 679 (Mass. 2001) (finding that a student's truancy did not establish reasonable suspicion to support school officials' search).

[89]Hough v. Shakopee Pub. Schs., 608 F. Supp. 2d 1087, 1105 (D. Minn. 2009) (finding the searches to be extraordinarily intrusive).

[90]Herrera v. Santa Fe Pub. Sch. Dist., 792 F. Supp. 2d 1174 (D.N.M. 2011).

Strip Searches.   Early court decisions proclaimed the seriousness of school officials conducting strip searches of students. The Second Circuit noted that "as the intrusiveness of the search intensifies, the standard of Fourth Amendment 'reasonableness' approaches probable cause, even in the school context."[91] The Seventh Circuit, in a strongly worded statement, proclaimed in an Indiana case: "It does not require a constitutional scholar to conclude that a nude search of a thirteen-year-old child is an invasion of constitutional rights of some magnitude. More than that: it is a violation of any known principle of human decency."[92]

The U.S. Supreme Court in *Safford Unified School District v. Redding* provided guidance regarding students' constitutional rights related to strip searches.[93] In this 2009 case, the assistant principal took Savanna Redding to his office based on another student's report that Savanna had given her prescription-strength and over-the-counter pain medication. After searching her backpack and finding no pills, a female assistant and the school nurse then searched Savanna's jacket, socks, and shoes and told her to remove her pants and T-shirt. Savanna also was told to pull her bra away from her body and shake it as well as to pull out the elastic of her underpants. No contraband was found.

The Supreme Court applied the reasonableness standard articulated in *T.L.O.*, quoting its earlier statement that a school search "will be permissible in its scope when the measures adopted are reasonably related to the objectives of the search and not excessively intrusive in light of the age and sex of the student and the nature of the infraction."[94] The Court found that sufficient evidence existed related to pill distribution to justify searching Savanna's backpack and outer clothing. The further strip search, however, was found to be unreasonable. The Court noted that requiring Savanna to expose her breasts and pelvic area violated "societal expectations of personal privacy," thereby "requiring distinct elements of justification on the part of school authorities for going beyond a search of outer clothing and belongings."[95] In this case, the level of suspicion fell far short for the degree of intrusion. The painkillers, which violated school rules, posed only a limited threat to the school, and, furthermore, no evidence pointed to Savanna hiding the pills in her underwear. Thus, the Court stated that there must be a reasonable suspicion of danger or that the search of underwear will produce evidence of wrongdoing before the "quantum leap from outer clothes and backpacks to exposure of intimate parts."[96]

In *Redding*, the Supreme Court concluded that school officials could not be held liable for the unreasonable search since the law was not well established regarding strip searches. Following *Redding*, however, several courts have denied school officials qualified immunity for similar actions that occurred prior to the Supreme Court's ruling, noting that the law in their circuits was already "clearly established." For example, the Sixth Circuit, in a case on remand, ruled that school officials were not entitled to qualified immunity

---

[91]M.M. v. Anker, 607 F.2d 588, 589 (2d Cir. 1979).

[92]Doe v. Renfrow, 631 F.2d 91, 92–93 (7th Cir. 1980).

[93]557 U.S. 364 (2009).

[94]*Id.* at 370.

[95]*Id.* at 374.

[96]*Id.* at 377.

when they subjected about fifteen nursing students in a vocational school to a highly intrusive search for a missing credit card and some cash.[97] The students in this instance were required to unhook and shake their bras under their tops and to lower their pants halfway down their thighs. Because the Sixth Circuit had established in an earlier case that strip searches such as this one were unconstitutional, the court considered the law in its circuit to be clearly settled and thus denied the school officials qualified immunity.[98]

The Supreme Court did not prohibit strip searches of students, but enough caveats exist to alert school officials of the inherent risks of such intrusive personal searches. Before conducting such a search, school officials must have individualized suspicion that a student is involved in wrongdoing that poses a threat to the health and safety of the school. Furthermore, the scope must not be more intrusive than demanded in the circumstances; a more dangerous item would justify a more intrusive search.

Seizure of Students.   Courts have examined claims that detentions of students by school officials constitute an unlawful seizure. A seizure occurs when individuals feel they are not free to leave, such as when students are detained by school administrators for questioning. The Tenth Circuit, however, noted: "To qualify as a seizure in the school context, the limitation on the student's freedom of movement must significantly exceed that inherent in every-day, compulsory attendance."[99]

As in the cases involving searches, courts examine school officials' actions to determine if a seizure or detainment of a student is reasonable—that is, justified at its inception and not excessively intrusive in light of the student's age and sex and the specific infraction. The Third Circuit found the "seizure" of a student for approximately four hours while school officials investigated a claim of sexual harassment to be reasonable in light of the serious nature of the accusation against the student.[100] Also, a California district court concluded that the detention of an eighth-grade student in the principal's office for three hours was justified to prevent classroom disruptions, to discipline the student, and to prevent her from using drugs or giving them to others.[101]

---

[97]Knisley v. Pike Cnty. Joint Vocational Sch. Dist., 604 F.3d 977 (6th Cir. 2010). *But see* Hearring v. Sliwowski, 712 F.3d 275 (6th Cir. 2013) (finding that a nurse was entitled to qualified immunity when she checked a six-year-old girl's vaginal area for a possible urinary infection without parental consent or a medical emergency; the nurse was not searching for contraband but attempting to check the student's medical condition).

[98]*See* Beard v. Whitmore Lake Sch. Dist., 402 F.3d 598 (6th Cir. 2005); *see also* Brannum v. Overton Cnty. Sch. Bd., 516 F.3d 489, 499 (6th Cir. 2008) (denying qualified immunity to school officials who installed security cameras in girls' and boys' locker rooms; the right to personal privacy was "clearly established").

[99]Couture v. Bd. of Educ., 535 F.3d 1243, 1251 (10th Cir. 2008) (holding that repeated and lengthy time-outs were not unreasonable when related to the school's efforts to modify the student's behavior problems).

[100]Shuman v. Penn Manor Sch. Dist., 422 F.3d 141 (3d Cir. 2005). *But see* Jones v. Hunt, 410 F.3d 1221 (10th Cir. 2005) (finding that a social worker's and police officer's three- to four-hour encounter with a student in the high school constituted a seizure and was not justified at its inception); Wofford v. Evans, 390 F.3d 318 (4th Cir. 2004) (finding that school officials seized a student but did not have to notify parents prior to detaining the student for questioning); Pacheco v. Hopmeier, 770 F. Supp. 2d 1174 (D.N.M. 2011) (holding that an unreasonable seizure occurred when a school principal permitted police officers to take a student, who was a potential witness to a crime, to the police station against his will).

[101]Bravo *ex rel.* Ramirez v. Hsu, 404 F. Supp. 2d 1195 (C.D. Cal. 2005).

Emphasizing that students cannot leave the school premises during the school day, the Ninth Circuit held that detaining a classroom of students for five to ten minutes in a snack bar area while school officials conducted an "unquestionably legitimate dog sniff" was not an impermissible seizure under the Fourth Amendment.[102] Similarly, a federal district court found that a New Hampshire school district's removal of students from their classrooms to the football field for ninety minutes while multiple police dogs sniffed the classrooms did not constitute a seizure.[103]

A teacher's momentary physical restraint of students has typically not been considered a "seizure" under the Fourth Amendment. Citing the special nature of the school environment, courts have ruled that physical restraint in disciplinary situations in the school environment does not involve the deprivation of liberty the Fourth Amendment prohibits. Thus, a teacher who physically grabs a student by the shoulders and escorts him out of the classroom would not violate the student's Fourth Amendment right to be free from an unreasonable seizure.

Metal Detectors

With the concern about the high rate of violence in schools, metal detectors have become more commonplace as school officials seek to maintain a safe educational environment. Moreover, the use of metal detectors is no longer limited to secondary schools. In 2000, the Chicago chief education officer approved metal detectors for all of the district's 489 elementary schools.[104] Metal detectors are used in airports and many public buildings, but their use does constitute a search for Fourth Amendment purposes. Such public searches have been found to be reasonable in balancing the threat of violence against the minimally intrusive nature of the search. As challenges have been raised about the use of metal detectors in schools, similar reasoning has been applied. **General scanning of students with metal detectors is only minimally intrusive on students' Fourth Amendment rights when weighed against school officials' interest in providing a safe school environment.**

The Pennsylvania high court upheld a general, uniform search of all students for weapons as they entered the high school building; each student's personal belongings were searched, and then a security officer scanned each student with a metal detector.[105] Individualized suspicion was not required in light of the high rate of violence in the school district. The court concluded that the search involved a greater intrusion on students' privacy interests than the search of a locker, but with the nonintrusive nature of the search, it remained a minimal intrusion. Similarly, the Eighth Circuit found a search of all male students from grades six to twelve for dangerous weapons to be minimally intrusive based on reasonable suspicion that weapons had been brought to school that day.[106] Students were scanned with a metal detector after they removed their shoes and the contents of their pockets. If the metal detector sounded, a subsequent "pat-down" search was conducted.

[102]B.C. v. Plumas Unified Sch. Dist., 192 F.3d 1260, 1269 (9th Cir. 1999).

[103]Doran v. Contoocook Valley Sch. Dist., 616 F. Supp. 2d 184 (D.N.H. 2009).

[104]Jessica Portner, *Girl's Slaying Elicits Calls for Metal Detectors*, EDUC. WK., Mar. 15, 2000, at 3.

[105]*In re* F.B., 726 A.2d 361 (Pa. 1999).

[106]Thompson v. Carthage Sch. Dist., 87 F.3d 979 (8th Cir. 1996).

An Illinois appellate court assessed the reasonableness of the use of metal detectors from the perspective of schools' "special needs."[107] In the first year of using the detectors, Chicago school officials confiscated over 300 weapons (including fifteen guns) from the high schools. With continued use of these devices, they showed a reduction of about 85 percent in weapons confiscated. The court, in concluding that individualized suspicion was not required to use metal detectors, noted that the purpose of the screening was to ensure a safe school environment for all students, not to secure evidence of a crime.

In each of the cases litigated, courts pointed to the violent context that led school officials to use metal detectors and the minimally intrusive nature of these devices. With increasing use, it can be expected that courts will continue to review the constitutional issues raised by metal detectors in school searches.

Drug-Detecting Canines

The use of drug-detecting dogs in searches raises several controversial questions regarding Fourth Amendment rights. Does the presence of a dog sniffing students constitute a search? Must reasonable suspicion exist to justify the use of dogs? Does the alert of a dog establish reasonable suspicion? A few courts have addressed these issues.

The Fifth Circuit confronted the question of whether sniffing by a dog is a search in terms of an individual's reasonable expectation of privacy.[108] The appellate court noted that most courts, including the U.S. Supreme Court, have held that law enforcement use of canines for sniffing objects does not constitute a search. Specifically, the appellate court referenced cases involving checked luggage, shipped packages, public lockers, and cars on public streets.[109] According to the court, a reasonable expectation of privacy does not extend to the airspace surrounding these objects. The court maintained that what has evolved is a doctrine of "public smell," equivalent to the "plain view" theory (that is, an object in plain view can be seized under certain circumstances).

From this line of reasoning, the Fifth Circuit noted that the use of canines has been seen as merely enhancing the ability to detect an odor, as the use of a flashlight improves vision. Accordingly, the court concluded that sniffing of student lockers and cars in public view was not a search, and therefore the Fourth Amendment did not apply. Even though permitting the use of dogs to detect drugs, the court held that reasonable suspicion is required for a further search by school officials of a locker or car. The court additionally noted that reasonable suspicion could be established only on a showing that a dog is reasonably reliable in detecting the actual presence of contraband. However, the Supreme Court in 2013 ruled that police officers were not required to produce evidence of a dog's reliable performance to substantiate probable cause to search a vehicle.[110] The Court emphasized that the

---

[107]People v. Pruitt, 662 N.E.2d 540 (Ill. App. Ct. 1996).

[108]Horton v. Goose Creek Indep. Sch. Dist., 690 F.2d 470 (5th Cir. 1982); *see also* Sims v. Bracken Cnty. Sch. Dist., No. 10-33DLB, 2010 U.S. Dist. LEXIS 110822 (E.D. Ky. Oct. 10, 2010) (noting in a motion to dismiss that an alert from a drug-sniffing dog establishes reasonable suspicion to search a student's car).

[109]More recently, the Supreme Court found a police officer's use of a drug-sniffing dog constituted a search when the dog was brought to the front porch of an individual's home. Individuals have a reasonable expectation of privacy in their home and the immediate surrounding area that is not recognized in public places. Florida v. Jardines, 133 S. Ct. 1409 (2013).

[110]Florida v. Harris, 133 S. Ct. 1050 (2013).

legality of a search must be assessed by whether all of the facts surrounding the dog's alert would lead a reasonable person to suspect that a search would turn up illegal drugs.

In most instances, judicial support for the use of dogs has been limited to the sniffing of objects. The Seventh Circuit, however, concluded that the presence of dogs in a classroom was not a search.[111] In this Indiana case, school officials with the assistance of police officers conducted a school-wide inspection for drugs in which trained dogs were brought into each classroom for approximately five minutes. When a dog alerted beside a student, school officials requested that the student remove the contents of his or her pockets or purse. A continued alert by the dog resulted in a strip search. The appellate court, in weighing the minimal intrusion of the dogs against the school's desire to eliminate a significant drug problem, concluded that sniffing of the students by the dogs did not constitute a search invoking Fourth Amendment protections. The search of pockets and purses did involve an invasion of privacy but was justified because the dog's alert constituted reasonable cause to believe that the student possessed drugs. However, as noted previously, the court drew the line at conducting a strip search based on a dog's alert.

In contrast to the reasoning of the Seventh Circuit, the Fifth Circuit held that sniffing of students by dogs significantly intrudes on an individual's privacy, thereby constituting a search.[112] Although recognizing that the sniffing of a person is a search, the court did not prohibit such searches but held that their intrusiveness must be weighed against the school's need to conduct the search. The court concluded that even with a significant need to search, individualized suspicion is required prior to the use of dogs because of the degree of intrusion on personal dignity and security. The Ninth Circuit concurred, noting that the significant intrusion on a student's expectation of privacy posed by dogs requires individualized suspicion.[113]

Given the concern about drugs in schools, it seems likely that school districts will continue to consider the use of drug-detecting canine units. Use of these canine units is unlikely to violate students' constitutional privacy rights so long as school officials focus on property or objects and do not have dogs sniff students.[114]

Drug Testing

In an effort to control drug use among students,[115] some districts have considered school-wide drug-testing programs. Such programs raise serious questions about students' privacy rights. In 1989, the Supreme Court held that urinalysis, the most frequently used means

[111]Doe v. Renfrow, 631 F.2d 91 (7th Cir. 1980).

[112]*Horton*, 690 F.2d 470.

[113]B.C. v. Plumas Unified Sch. Dist., 192 F.3d 1260 (9th Cir. 1999).

[114]*See* Todd A. DeMitchell, *Canine Drug Searches: A Law and Policy Discussion*, 269 EDUC. LAW REP. 435 (2011).

[115]In 2012, the National Center on Addiction and Substance Abuse in its annual back-to-school survey of twelve- to seventeen-year-olds reported that more than 60 percent of teens continue to attend a high school that is drug-infested. The data also showed that teens who spend time on social networking sites are more likely to smoke and to use alcohol and marijuana than teens who do not spend any time on the sites. Nat'l Ctr. on Addiction & Substance Abuse, *National Survey of American Attitudes on Substance Abuse XVII: Teens and Parents* (NY: Columbia Univ., Aug. 2012), http://casacolumbia.org (follow Publications & Research; then Reports; then search Reports for Surveys).

for drug testing, is a search under the Fourth Amendment.[116] The Court upheld the testing of government employees for drug use in two decisions, but the holdings were narrowly drawn and based on compelling governmental interests in ensuring public safety and national security. Individualized suspicion was not a precondition for conducting the urinalysis in these cases; however, the narrow circumstances justifying the testing programs minimized the discretion of supervisors and the potential for arbitrariness.

The Supreme Court has rendered two decisions regarding the drug testing of students. **In 1995, the Court in *Vernonia School District 47J v. Acton* upheld a school district's drug policy authorizing random urinalysis drug testing of students participating in athletic programs.**[117] Emphasizing the district's "custodial and tutelary" responsibility for children, the Court recognized that school personnel could exercise a degree of supervision and control over children that would not be permitted over adults. This relationship was held to be pivotal in assessing the reasonableness of the district's drug policy.[118] Addressing students' legitimate privacy expectations, the court noted that the lower privacy expectations within the school environment are reduced even further when a student elects to participate in sports.

In 2002, the Supreme Court in *Board of Education v. Earls* again reviewed a drug-testing policy, but one that applied to students in all extracurricular activities, including athletics.[119] The policy required students to take a drug test prior to participation, to submit to random drug testing while involved in the activity, and to agree to be tested at any time when reasonable suspicion existed. In sustaining the drug-testing policy in *Earls*, the Court reasoned that the collection procedures were minimally intrusive, information was kept in confidential files with limited access, and test results were not given to law enforcement authorities. Based on these factors, the Court concluded that the drug-testing policy was not a significant invasion of students' privacy rights.

It is clear that specific subgroups of students, such as athletes and participants in extracurricular activities, can be subjected to drug testing; however, courts have not permitted blanket testing of *all* students. A Texas federal district court did not find exigent circumstances or other demonstrated compelling interests to justify a mandatory testing program of *all* students in grades six through twelve.[120] Accordingly, the federal court held the program unreasonable and unconstitutional under the Fourth Amendment. The Seventh Circuit rejected a school district's policy requiring drug and alcohol testing of all students suspended for three or more days for violating any school rule.[121] In this case, the student was suspended for fighting, and upon his return to school was informed that he was required to submit to a test for drug and alcohol use. When he refused, school officials suspended him again; refusal to take the test was treated as admission of unlawful drug use.

---

[116]Skinner v. Ry. Labor Executives' Ass'n, 489 U.S. 602 (1989); Nat'l Treasury Emps. Union v. Von Raab, 489 U.S. 656 (1989).

[117]515 U.S. 646 (1995).

[118]*Id.* at 665.

[119]536 U.S. 822 (2002).

[120]Tannahill *ex rel.* Tannahill v. Lockney Indep. Sch. Dist., 133 F. Supp. 2d 919 (N.D. Tex. 2001).

[121]Willis v. Anderson Cmty. Sch., 158 F.3d 415 (7th Cir. 1998).

In ruling that the policy violated the Fourth Amendment, the court did not find a connection between fighting and the use of drugs. Furthermore, the suspension procedures in Indiana require school officials to meet with students prior to suspension. At that point, it is possible to determine if individualized suspicion exists to support testing a particular student for drugs or alcohol.

Despite the fact that blanket or random drug testing of *all* students is not likely to withstand judicial challenge, **many schools subject students to urinalysis based on individualized suspicion, and such practices have been upheld by courts.** Any drug-testing program, however, must be carefully constructed to avoid impairing students' Fourth Amendment privacy rights.[122] The policy must be clearly developed, specifically identifying reasons for testing. Data collection procedures must be precise and well defined.[123] Students and parents should be informed of the policy, and it is advisable to request students' consent prior to testing. If the test indicates drug use, the student must be given an opportunity to explain the results. Providing for the rehabilitation of the student rather than punishment strengthens the policy.

Police Involvement

A "reasonable suspicion" or a "reasonable cause to believe" standard is invoked in assessing the legality of school searches, but a higher standard generally is required when police officers are involved. The nature and extent of such involvement are important considerations in determining whether a search is reasonable. **If the police role is one of finding evidence of a crime, a warrant based on probable cause would be required.** Whereas early decisions generally supported police participation in searches initiated and conducted by school officials, more recently, courts have tended to draw a distinction between searches with and without police assistance.[124]

The more stringent judicial posture is represented in an illustrative Illinois case in which a school principal received a call that led him to suspect that three girls possessed illegal drugs.[125] On advice from the superintendent, the principal called the police to assist in the investigation. After the police arrived, the school nurse and the school psychologist searched each girl; however, no drugs were discovered. The court found that the police were not called merely to assist in maintaining school discipline but to search

---

[122]*See* Gruenke v. Seip, 225 F.3d 290 (3d Cir. 2000) (concluding under the *Vernonia* standard that compelling a student athlete to submit to a pregnancy test, absent a legitimate health concern, was an unreasonable search).

[123]An Indiana student, suspected of drug use, claimed that the manner in which the urinalysis test was administered violated his Fourth Amendment rights. The student was required to give the sample as he faced two male school administrators. The federal district court denied summary judgment to the school district but granted the administrators qualified immunity because the law was not clearly established. Long v. Turner, 664 F. Supp. 2d 930 (S.D. Ind. 2009).

[124]However, searches by trained police officers employed by or assigned to a school district generally are governed by the *T.L.O.* reasonable suspicion standard rather than the probable cause standard. *See, e.g.*, State v. Alaniz, 815 N.W. 2d 234 (N.D. 2012); State v. J.M., 255 P.3d 828 (Wash. Ct. App. 2011). *But see* State v. Meneese, 282 P.3d 83 (Wash. 2012) (finding that a school resource officer's (SRO) search of a student's backpack required a warrant because the SRO was seeking evidence of a crime, not enforcing school discipline).

[125]Picha v. Wielgos, 410 F. Supp. 1214 (N.D. Ill. 1976).

for evidence of a crime. Under the circumstances, the court concluded that the students had a constitutional right not to be searched unless the police had a warrant based on probable cause.

In contrast, the same Illinois court held that a police officer's involvement in persuading a student to relinquish the contents of his pockets did not violate Fourth Amendment rights under the *T.L.O.* standard.[126] The police officer's role was quite limited in this case. He was in the school building on another matter, and his role in the search was restricted simply to asking the student to empty his pockets. There was no police involvement in the investigation that led to detaining the student, nor was the evidence used for criminal prosecution. Similarly, the Eighth Circuit held that the assistance of a police officer assigned as a liaison officer in a high school did not subject a search for stolen property to the Fourth Amendment's probable cause standard.[127]

Courts have recognized the special role of school liaison or resource officers when they are working with school officials to maintain a safe school environment.[128] With the growing presence and involvement of school resource officers (SROs), however, students' right to be free from custodial police interrogation arises. Depending on a child's age and the nature of the questioning, the U.S. Supreme Court has held SROs or other police officers involved in *custodial interrogations* must provide *Miranda* warnings—informing the student of the right to remain silent, that any statements may be used as evidence, and that he or she has the right to an attorney.[129] The Court specifically noted that determining whether an officer's conversation with a student is a custodial interrogation would be "nonsensical absent some consideration of the suspect's age."[130] Recognizing the absurdity of evaluating the situation from the perspective of a reasonable person of average years rather than the child's age, the Court elaborated: "In other words, how would a reasonable adult understand his situation, after being removed from a seventh-grade social studies class by a uniformed school resource officer; being encouraged by his assistant principal to 'do the right thing'; and being warned by a police investigator of the prospect of juvenile detention and separation from his guardian and primary caretaker?"[131] According to the Court, the critical question is whether a reasonable juvenile of the child's age under the circumstances understood that he or she did not have to answer the police officer's questions and was free to leave at any time. Custodial interrogation is an issue only when police officers are involved in the questioning of students; school officials remain free to meet with students and inquire into their actions.

Students possess Fourth Amendment rights against unreasonable searches, but educators can search when suspicion exists that a student is violating a school rule or the law. Searches that are highly intrusive, however, must be supported by a greater degree

---

[126]Martens v. Dist. No. 220, 620 F. Supp. 29 (N.D. Ill. 1985).

[127]Cason v. Cook, 810 F.2d 188 (8th Cir. 1987).

[128]*See, e.g.*, Wilson *ex rel.* Adams v. Cahokia Sch. Dist., 470 F. Supp. 2d 897 (S.D. Ill. 2007); Ortiz v. State, 703 S.E.2d 59 (Ga. Ct. App. 2010).

[129]J.D.B. v. North Carolina, 131 S. Ct. 2394 (2011).

[130]*Id.* at 2405.

[131]*Id.*

FIGURE 8.5 Degree of Suspicion Required to Conduct Student Searches

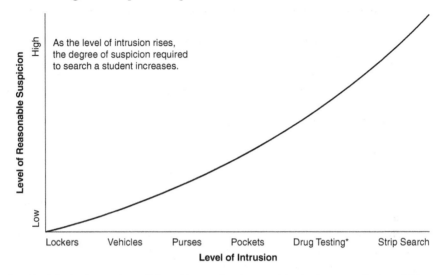

*Under school district drug-testing policies, athletes and students participating in extracurricular activities can be subjected to drug tests without individualized suspicion.

of suspicion (see Figure 8.5). Additionally, school personnel can protect themselves by adhering to a few basic guidelines:

- Students and parents should be informed at the beginning of the school term of the procedures for conducting locker and personal searches.
- Any personal search conducted should be based on "reasonable suspicion" that the student possesses contraband that may be disruptive to the educational process.
- The authorized person conducting a search should have another staff member present who can verify the procedures used in the search.
- School personnel should refrain from using strip searches or mass searches of groups of students.
- If police officials conduct a search in the school, either with or without the school's involvement, it is advisable to ensure that they first obtain a search warrant.

REMEDIES FOR UNLAWFUL DISCIPLINARY ACTIONS

If students are unlawfully punished, they are entitled to be restored (without penalty) to their status prior to the imposition of the punishment and to have their records expunged of any reference to the illegal punishment.

Several remedies are available to students who are unlawfully disciplined by school authorities. When physical punishment is involved, students can seek damages through assault and battery suits against those who inflicted the harm. For unwarranted suspensions or expulsions, students are entitled to reinstatement without penalty to grades and to have their school records expunged of any reference to the illegal disciplinary action. Remedies for violation of procedural due process rights may include reversal of a school board's decision rather than remand for further proceedings. If academic penalties are unlawfully imposed, grades must be restored and transcripts altered accordingly. For unconstitutional searches, illegally seized evidence may be suppressed, school records may be expunged, and damages may be awarded if the unlawful search results in substantial injury to the student. Courts also may award court costs when students successfully challenge disciplinary actions.[132]

The Supreme Court has held that school officials can be sued for monetary damages in state courts as well as in federal courts under 42 U.S.C. § 1983 if they arbitrarily violate students' federally protected rights in disciplinary proceedings.[133] In *Wood v. Strickland*, the Court declared that ignorance of the law is not a valid defense to shield school officials from liability if they should have known that their actions would impair students' clearly established federal rights.[134] The Court recognized in *Wood* that educators are not charged with predicting the future direction of constitutional law. Other courts have reiterated school officials' potential liability in connection with student disciplinary proceedings, but to date, students have not been as successful as teachers in obtaining monetary awards for constitutional violations.

In 1978, the Supreme Court placed restrictions on the amount of damages that could be awarded to students in instances involving the impairment of procedural due process rights. In *Carey v. Piphus*, **the Court declared that students who were suspended without a hearing, but were not otherwise injured, could recover only nominal damages (not to exceed one dollar).**[135] This decision may appear to have strengthened the position of school boards in exercising discretion in disciplinary proceedings, but the Supreme Court indicated that students might be entitled to substantial damages if suspensions are proven to be unwarranted.[136] In addition to damages, students also may be awarded attorneys' fees. However, a student who continues to pursue litigation when a claim is meritless may be responsible for the school district's attorneys' fees.[137]

Educators should take every precaution to afford fair and impartial treatment to students. School personnel would be wise to provide at least an informal hearing if in doubt as to whether a particular situation necessitates due process. Liability never results from the provision of too much due process, but damages can be assessed if violations of procedural rights result in unjustified suspensions, expulsions, or other disciplinary actions. Although

---

[132]Also, under state law, school districts may be awarded restitution if a student's action resulted in costs. The Wisconsin appellate court awarded restitution of $18,026.01 to a school district for losses incurred when a student made a bomb threat. This included costs for salaries and benefits of employees during the evacuation. State v. Vanbeek, 765 N.W.2d 834 (Wis. Ct. App. 2009).

[133]Howlett v. Rose, 496 U.S. 356 (1990).

[134]420 U.S. 308 (1975).

[135]435 U.S. 247 (1978).

[136]*See* Kennedy v. Dexter Consol. Schs., 10 P.3d 115 (N.M. 2000) (affirming award of substantial compensatory and punitive damages to two high school students subjected to an unconstitutional strip search).

[137]Workman v. Dist. 13 Tanque Verde Unified Sch. Dist., 402 F. App'x 292 (9th Cir. 2010).

constitutional and statutory due process requirements do not mandate that a specific procedure be followed in every situation, courts will carefully study the record to ensure that any
procedural deficiencies do not impede the student's efforts to present a full defense.

CONCLUSION

In 1969, Justice Black noted: "School discipline, like parental discipline, is an integral
and important part of training our children to be good citizens—to be better citizens."[138]
Accordingly, school personnel have been empowered with the authority and duty to regulate pupil behavior in order to protect the interests of the student body and the school.
Reasonable sanctions can be imposed if students do not adhere to legitimate conduct regulations. Courts, however, will intervene if disciplinary procedures are arbitrary or impair
students' protected rights.

Some type of procedural due process should be afforded to students prior to the
imposition of punishments. For minor penalties, an informal hearing suffices; for serious
punishments, more formal procedures are required (e.g., notification of parents, representation by counsel, opportunity to cross-examine witnesses). Legitimate punishments
include suspensions, expulsions, academic sanctions, and transfer to other programs or
schools. If state law or school board policy does not prohibit, reasonable corporal punishment also can be used as a disciplinary technique. Additionally, school personnel can
search students if reasonable suspicion exists that the students possess contraband that
will disrupt the school.

School authorities should ensure that constraints placed on student conduct are necessary for the proper functioning of the school. If students are unlawfully punished, school
officials can be held liable for damage. Educators, however, have considerable latitude
in controlling student behavior to maintain an appropriate educational environment and
should not feel that the judiciary has curtailed their authority to discipline students.

POINTS TO PONDER

1. Under a school district's zero-tolerance discipline policy, a middle school student was
   expelled for one year for the possession of a knife on school property. A teacher discovered
   the knife when the student dropped his unzipped backpack and several items fell out, including a small Boy Scout pocketknife. The student claimed he had used the backpack for a
   camping trip the prior weekend and had forgotten to remove the knife. The parents filed suit,
   arguing that the automatic one-year expulsion was arbitrary and violated their son's due process rights. What issues will the court consider? What is the likely outcome of the case?

2. A high school honor student was suspended for five days at the end of the fall semester. The
   suspension period included two days of the final exam period, and his request to make up
   three exams was denied. He asserted that the detrimental impact on his overall grade point
   average demanded greater due process than an informal conversation with the principal.
   What procedural protections are due in this suspension?

---

[138]Tinker v. Des Moines Indep. Cmty. Sch. Dist., 393 U.S. 503, 524 (1969) (Black, J., dissenting).

3. A thirteen-year-old student, who was in the hallway without a pass, belligerently responded when a teacher ordered him to return to his classroom. The teacher reacted by grabbing the student and throwing him against a locker. The boy suffered a cut to the forehead requiring stitches. He filed suit, claiming that the teacher's action impaired his substantive due process right to be free from unreasonable physical punishment. What issues are involved in this claim? Will the student succeed in his challenge?

4. A high school student discovered that his small digital recorder was missing from his backpack. He had left the backpack open at his desk while he worked in a small group across the room. The teacher asked everyone to look around the classroom for the recorder. When it was not found, the teacher requested that the students bring their backpacks and jackets to the front of the room to be searched. All students' possessions were searched, but the recorder was not found. The next day, one student's parents filed a complaint with the school principal, protesting the search of their son's possessions. Was this search reasonable under the circumstances? Explain.

CHAPTER NINE

TERMS AND CONDITIONS
OF EMPLOYMENT

Maintenance of a uniform system of public schools is one of the preeminent functions of the state legislature. The judiciary has clearly recognized the plenary power of the state in establishing, conducting, and regulating all public education functions. The legislature, through statutory law, establishes the boundaries within which educational systems operate; however, the actual administration of school systems is delegated to state boards of education, state departments of education, and local boards of education. These agencies enact rules and regulations pursuant to legislative policy for the operation of public schools.

State statutes and regulations play a prominent role in defining school personnel's employment rights, but they cannot be viewed independently of state and federal constitutional provisions, civil rights laws, and negotiated agreements between school boards and teachers' unions. These provisions may restrict or modify options available under the state school code. For example, the authority to transfer teachers may be vested in the school board, yet the board cannot use this power to discipline a teacher for exercising protected constitutional rights. The board's discretion may be further limited if it has agreed in the master contract with the teachers' union (known as a collective bargaining agreement) to follow certain procedures prior to transferring an employee.

Among the areas affected by state statutory and regulatory provisions are the terms and conditions of educators' employment. With the intense public pressure to improve students' academic performance to meet annual yearly progress (AYP) under the No Child Left Behind (NCLB) Act,[1] most states have enacted education reform legislation demanding greater accountability from public schools. Likewise, as discussed in Chapter 4, most states have adopted the Common Core Standards.[2] These efforts have had an impact not only on the curriculum and operation of schools but also on expectations for educators. NCLB demands that students be taught only by highly qualified educators in core subjects in each elementary and secondary school in all districts. At a minimum, highly qualified

---

[1]20 U.S.C. § 6301 (2012).

[2]Nat'l Governor's Ass'n, *Common Core Standards* (2012), http://www.corestandards.org/the-Standards. *See* text accompanying note 2, Chapter 4.

teachers hold a bachelor's degree, possess full state certification or licensure, and have demonstrated competence in their subject areas. Local school boards must ensure that these new demands are met, and courts have recognized the boards' expansive authority to fulfill these responsibilities. This chapter presents an overview of state requirements pertaining to licensure, employment, contracts, tenure, collective bargaining, and other related aspects of employment. Specific job requirements that implicate constitutional rights or anti-discrimination mandates are addressed in subsequent chapters.

LICENSURE

The state establishes minimum qualifications for licensure, which may include professional preparation as well as other prerequisites.

To qualify for a teaching position in public schools, **prospective teachers must acquire a valid license or certificate[3] from their state.** Licenses are issued according to each state's statutory provisions.[4] States have not only the right but also the duty to establish minimum qualifications and to ensure that teachers meet these standards. Although the responsibility for licensing resides with state legislatures, administration of the process has been delegated to state boards of education and departments of education. In addition to state licensure, many teachers seek National Board Certification, involving an intensive assessment of teaching knowledge and skills by the National Board for Professional Teaching Standards. States and local school districts often provide financial support for teachers seeking this designation and also may provide annual stipends for National Board Certified Teachers.[5]

Licenses are granted primarily on the basis of professional preparation. In most states, educational requirements include a college degree, with minimum credit hours or courses in various curricular areas. Other prerequisites to licensure may include a minimum age, U.S. citizenship, signing of a loyalty oath, and passage of an academic examination. In addition, an applicant for certification may be required to have "good moral character." The definition of what constitutes good character often is elusive, with several factors entering into the determination.[6] Courts generally will not rule on the wisdom of a

---

[3]The words *licensure* and *certification* are used interchangeably in this chapter.

[4]Courts have upheld legislative efforts to alter licensure standards by imposing new or additional requirements as prerequisites to renew a license. *See, e.g.,* State v. Project Principle, 724 S.W.2d 387 (Tex. 1987).

[5]See National Board for Professional Teaching Standards, http://http://www.nbpts.org/state-local-information, for information regarding each state.

[6]*See* Landers v. Ark. Dep't of Educ., 374 S.W.3d 795 (Ark. 2010) (upholding the denial of an applicant's teaching license because of her single felony theft conviction that had been expunged from her record); Wright v. Kan. State Bd. of Educ., 268 P.3d 1231 (Kan. Ct. App. 2012) (upholding the state board's denial of a disbarred attorney's application for a teaching license because of his prior conviction involving theft).

certifying agency's assessment of character; they will intervene only if statutory or constitutional rights are abridged.

Licensure of teachers by examination was common prior to the expansion of teacher education programs in colleges and universities. With the emphasis on improving the quality of teachers and the strong movement toward standards-based licensure, most states now require some type of standardized test or performance-based assessment for teacher education programs, initial license, and/or license renewal.[7] **If a state establishes a test or assessment process as an essential eligibility requirement, it can deny a license to individuals who do not pass.** The United States Supreme Court has upheld the use of tests even though some have been shown to disproportionately disqualify minority applicants.[8]

Signing a loyalty oath may be a condition of obtaining a teaching license, but such oaths cannot be used to restrict association rights guaranteed under the United States Constitution. The Supreme Court has invalidated oaths that require teacher applicants to swear that they are not members of subversive organizations;[9] however, teachers can be required to sign an oath pledging faithful performance of duties and support for the U.S. Constitution and their state's constitution.[10] According to the Supreme Court, these oaths must be narrowly limited to affirmation of support for the government and a pledge not to act forcibly to overthrow the government.[11] Following the September 11, 2001, terrorist attacks, many states began enforcing the signing of existing loyalty oaths for public employment or enacted new laws. For example, Ohio's PATRIOT (Providing Appropriate Tools Required to Intercept and Obstruct Terrorism) Act requires applicants for public employment to swear they are not terrorists and have no involvement with terrorist groups; refusal to sign the oath can result in exclusion from employment consideration.[12] Several of these new loyalty oaths potentially could be challenged as too broad under the Supreme Court's earlier rulings.

Licenses are issued for designated periods of time under various classifications such as emergency, temporary, provisional, professional, and permanent. Renewing or upgrading a license may require additional university coursework, other continuing education activities, or passage of an examination. Licenses also specify professional position (e.g., teacher, administrator, librarian), subject areas (e.g., history, English, math), and grade levels (e.g., elementary, high school). Where licensure subject areas have been established, a teacher must possess a valid license to teach a specific subject. A school district's failure to employ licensed teachers may result in the loss of state accreditation and financial support.

---

[7]Almost half the states have set up professional standards boards to govern and regulate standards-based criteria and assessment for licenses. The primary purpose of these boards, whose membership is composed mostly of teachers, is to address issues of educator preparation, licensure, and relicensure.

[8]United States v. South Carolina, 445 F. Supp. 1094 (D.S.C. 1977), *aff'd sub nom.* Nat'l Educ. Ass'n v. South Carolina, 434 U.S. 1026 (1978).

[9]Keyishian v. Bd. of Regents, 385 U.S. 589 (1967).

[10]Ohlson v. Phillips, 397 U.S. 317 (1970).

[11]Cole v. Richardson, 405 U.S. 676 (1972); Connell v. Higginbotham, 403 U.S. 207 (1971).

[12]Ohio Rev. Code § 2909.34 (2012).

A license indicates only that a teacher has satisfied minimum state requirements; no absolute right exists to acquire a position. It does not entitle an individual to employment in a particular district or guarantee employment in the state, nor does it prevent a local school board from attaching additional prerequisites to employment. For example, a California appellate court ruled that it was within a school board's authority to terminate a teacher who refused to obtain a certificate to teach English language learners.[13] If a local board imposes additional standards, however, the requirements must be uniformly applied.

Teaching credentials must be in proper order to ensure full employment rights. Under most state laws, teachers must file their licenses with the district where they are employed. Failure to renew a license prior to expiration or to meet educational requirements necessary to maintain or acquire a higher-grade license can result in loss of employment. Without proper licensure, a teaching contract is unenforceable.

The state is empowered not only to license teachers but also to suspend or revoke licensure. Although a local board may initiate charges against a teacher, only the state can alter the status of a teacher's license. Revocation is a harsh penalty, generally foreclosing future employment as a teacher. As such, it must be based on statutory causes with full procedural rights provided to the teacher.[14] The most frequently cited grounds for revoking licenses are immorality, incompetency, contract violation, and neglect of duty. Examples of actions justifying revocation include misrepresenting experience and credentials in a job application and altering the license to misrepresent areas of licensure (immorality);[15] theft of drugs and money (conduct unbecoming a teacher);[16] abusive comments to students and threats made in a letter of resignation (unprofessional conduct);[17] and assault on a minor female (lack of good moral character).[18]

When revocation or suspension of a license is being considered, assessment of a teacher's competency encompasses not only classroom performance but also actions outside the school setting that may impair his or her effectiveness. A California appellate court upheld the State Commission on Teacher Credentialing's decision to suspend a teacher's license because she had three drunken driving convictions.[19] In a Texas case, an appellate court upheld the license revocation of a teacher who had exposed his penis in public and engaged in other indecent exposure inciXdents, finding the conduct rendered him unworthy to instruct.[20] Courts will not overturn the judgment of a state board regarding an educator's fitness to teach unless evidence clearly establishes that the decision is unreasonable or unlawful.

---

[13]Governing Bd. v. Comm'n on Prof'l Conduct, 99 Cal. Rptr. 3d 903 (Ct. App. 2009).

[14]*See also* text accompanying notes 22–24, Chapter 12, for details of procedural due process.

[15]Nanko v. Dep't of Educ., 663 A.2d 312 (Pa. Commw. Ct. 1995).

[16]Crumpler v. State Bd. of Educ., 594 N.E.2d 1071 (Ohio Ct. App. 1991).

[17]Knight v. Winn, 910 So. 2d 310 (Fla. Dist. Ct. App. 2005).

[18]*In re* Morrill, 765 A.2d 699 (N.H. 2001).

[19]Broney v. Cal. Comm'n on Teacher Credentialing, 184 Cal. App. 4th 462 (App. Ct. 2010).

[20]Gomez v. Tex. Educ. Agency, 354 S.W.3d 905 (Tex. App. 2011), *review denied*, No. 12-0014, 2012 Tex. LEXIS 303 (Tex. Mar. 30, 2012).

EMPLOYMENT BY LOCAL SCHOOL BOARDS

School boards are vested with the power to appoint teachers and to establish professional and academic employment standards above the state minimums.

As noted, a license does not guarantee employment in a state; it attests only that educators have met minimum state requirements. The decision to employ a licensed teacher or administrator is among the discretionary powers of local school boards. Although such powers are broad, school board actions may not be arbitrary, capricious, or violate an individual's statutory or constitutional rights.[21] Furthermore, boards must comply with mandated statutory procedures as well as locally adopted procedures. Employment decisions also must be neutral as to race, religion, national origin, and sex.[22] Unless protected individual rights are abridged, courts will not review the wisdom of a local school board's judgment in employment decisions made in good faith.

The responsibility for hiring teachers and administrators is vested in the school board as a collective body and cannot be delegated to the superintendent or board members individually. In most states, binding employment agreements between a teacher or an administrator and the school board must be approved at legally scheduled board meetings. Most state laws specify that the superintendent must make employment recommendations to the board; however, the board is not compelled to follow these recommendations unless mandated to do so by law.

School boards possess extensive authority in establishing job requirements and conditions of employment for school personnel. The following sections examine the school board's power to impose specific conditions on employment and to assign personnel.

Employment Requirements

The state's establishment of minimum licensure standards for educators does not preclude the local school board from requiring higher professional or academic standards so long as they are applied in a uniform and nondiscriminatory manner. For example, school boards often establish continuing education requirements for teachers, and a board's right to dismiss teachers for failing to satisfy such requirements has been upheld by the Supreme Court.[23] The Court concluded that school officials merely had to establish that the requirement was rationally related to a legitimate state objective, which in this case was to provide competent, well-trained teachers.

School boards can adopt reasonable health and physical requirements for school personnel. Courts have recognized that such standards are necessary to safeguard the health

---

[21]See generally Chapter 10 for a discussion of teachers' constitutional rights.

[22]See generally Chapter 11 for a discussion of discriminatory employment practices. Under limited circumstances, sex may be a bona fide occupational qualification (e.g., supervision of the girls' locker room).

[23]Harrah Indep. Sch. Dist. v. Martin, 440 U.S. 194 (1979) (upholding a policy requiring teachers to earn an additional five semester hours of college credit every three years while employed).

and welfare of students and other employees. For example, the First Circuit held that a school board could compel an administrator to submit to a psychiatric examination as a condition of continued employment because a reasonable basis existed for the board members to believe that the administrator might jeopardize the safety of students.[24] Similarly, the Sixth Circuit ruled that a school board could justifiably order a teacher to submit to mental and physical examinations when his aberrant behavior affected job performance.[25] Standards for physical fitness must be rationally related to the ability to perform teaching duties, and regulations must not contravene various state and federal laws designed to protect the rights of persons with disabilities.[26]

Under state laws, most school boards are required to conduct a criminal records check of all employees prior to employment. The screening process may require individuals to consent to fingerprinting. Concern for students' safety also has led some school districts to require teacher applicants to submit to drug testing. To date, the Sixth Circuit is the only federal appellate court that has upheld such testing, noting that teachers occupy safety-sensitive positions in a highly regulated environment with diminished privacy expectations.[27]

Unless prohibited by law, school boards may require school personnel to live within the school district as a condition of employment. Typically, residency requirements have been imposed in urban communities and encompass all city employees, including educators. The Supreme Court upheld a municipal regulation requiring all employees hired after a specified date in Philadelphia to be residents of the city, finding no impairment of Fourteenth Amendment equal protection rights or interference with interstate and intrastate travel.[28] Those already employed were not required to alter their residence. In upholding the regulation, the Court distinguished a requirement of residency of a given duration prior to employment (which violates the right to interstate travel) from a continuing residency requirement applied after employment. Lower courts have applied similar reasoning in upholding residency requirements for public educators.[29] Although residency requirements after employment do not violate the Constitution, they may be impermissible under state law.[30]

Unlike residency requirements, school board policies requiring employees to send their children to public schools have been declared unconstitutional. Parents have a constitutionally protected right to direct the upbringing of their children that cannot be restricted without a compelling state interest. The Eleventh Circuit held that a school board policy requiring employees to enroll their children in public schools could not be justified to

---

[24]Daury v. Smith, 842 F.2d 9 (1st Cir. 1988).

[25]Sullivan v. River Valley Sch. Dist., 197 F.3d 804 (6th Cir. 1999); *see also* Gardner v. Niskayuna Cent. Sch. Dist., 839 N.Y.S.2d 317 (App. Div. 2007) (finding that a school board is charged with determining that teachers are fit to teach; thereby, teachers may be required to submit to physical or mental exams).

[26]See Chapter 11 for a discussion of discrimination based on disabilities.

[27]Knox Cnty. Educ. Ass'n v. Knox Cnty. Bd. of Educ., 158 F.3d 361 (6th Cir. 1998). For further discussion of Fourth Amendment rights of employees, see text accompanying note 87, Chapter 10.

[28]McCarthy v. Phila. Civil Serv. Comm'n, 424 U.S. 645 (1976).

[29]*See, e.g.,* Wardwell v. Bd. of Educ., 529 F.2d 625 (6th Cir. 1976); Providence Teachers' Union Local 958 v. City Council, 888 A.2d 948 (R.I. 2005).

[30]*See, e.g.,* IND. CODE ANN. § 20-28-10-13 (2012); 71 MASS. GEN. LAWS § 38 (2012).

promote an integrated public school system and good relationships among teachers when weighed against the right of parents to direct the education of their children.[31]

Assignment of Personnel and Duties

The authority to assign teachers to schools within a district resides with the board of education. As with employment in general, these decisions must not be arbitrary or made in bad faith or in retaliation for the exercise of protected rights. Within the limits of a license, a teacher can be assigned to teach in any school at any grade level. Assignments designated in the teacher's contract, however, cannot be changed during a contractual period without the teacher's consent. That is, a board cannot reassign a teacher to a first-grade class if the contract specifies a fifth-grade assignment. If the contract designates only a teaching assignment within the district, the assignment still must be in the teacher's licensure area. Also, objective, nondiscriminatory standards must be used in any employment or assignment decision. Assignments to achieve racial balance may be permitted in school districts that have not eliminated the effects of school segregation. Any racial classification, however, must be temporary and necessary to eradicate the effects of prior discrimination.

School boards retain the authority to assign or transfer teachers, but such decisions often are challenged as demotions requiring procedural due process. Depending on statutory law, factors considered in determining whether a reassignment is a demotion may include reduction in salary, responsibility, and stature of position. A transfer from one grade level to another is not usually considered a demotion. Courts recognize the pervasive authority of the superintendent and board to make teaching assignments, so long as the assignments do not conflict with state law, federal rights, or the collective bargaining contract.[32]

Administrative reassignments frequently are challenged as demotions because of reductions in salary, responsibility, and status of the position. Again, as in the assignment of teachers, statutory law defines an individual employee's rights. The appellate court concluded that the reassignment of an assistant superintendent to a principal position was within the school board's discretion when it did not involve a reduction in salary or violate the district's regulations.[33] Similarly, the Seventh Circuit found that the reassignment of a principal to a central office position did not involve an economic loss requiring an opportunity for a hearing.[34] Moreover, reassignment from an administrative to a teaching position because of financial constraints or good faith reorganization is not a demotion requiring due process unless procedural protections are specified in state law.

The assignment of noninstructional duties often is defined in a teacher's contract or the master contract negotiated between the school board and the teachers' union. In the absence of such specification, school officials can make reasonable and appropriate

---

[31]Stough v. Crenshaw Cnty. Bd. of Educ., 744 F.2d 1479 (11th Cir. 1984).

[32]*See, e.g.,* Kodl v. Bd. of Educ., 490 F.3d 558 (7th Cir. 2007) (finding that a middle school teacher's transfer to an elementary school did not violate any federal rights).

[33]Barr v. Bd. of Trs., 462 S.E.2d 316 (S.C. Ct. App. 1995).

[34]Bordelon v. Chi. Sch. Reform Bd. of Trs., 233 F.3d 524 (7th Cir. 2000).

assignments, such as activities that are an integral part of the school program and related to the employee's teaching responsibilities. Reasonableness of an assignment is typically evaluated in terms of time involvement, teachers' interests and abilities, benefits to students, and the professional nature of the duty. Refusal to accept reasonable assigned duties can result in dismissal.

CONTRACTS

Teacher contracts must satisfy the general principles of contract law as well as conform to any additional specifications contained in state law or the collective bargaining agreement.

The employment contract defines the rights and responsibilities of the teacher and the school board in the employment relationship. The general principles of contract law apply to this contractual relationship. Like all other legal contracts, it must contain the basic elements of (1) offer and acceptance, (2) competent parties, (3) consideration, (4) legal subject matter, and (5) proper form.[35] Beyond these basic elements, it also must meet the requirements specified in state law and administrative regulations.

The authority to contract with teachers is an exclusive right of the board. The school board's offer of a position to a teacher—including (1) designated salary, (2) specified period of time, and (3) identified duties and responsibilities—creates a binding contract when accepted by the teacher. In most states, only the board can make an offer, and this action must be approved by a majority of the board members in a properly called meeting. In a Washington case, the coordinator of special services extended a teacher an offer of employment at the beginning of the school year, pending a check of references from past employers. The recommendations were negative, and the teacher was not recommended to the board, even though she had been teaching for several weeks. The state appellate court held that no enforceable contract existed; under state law, hiring authority resides with the board.[36]

Contracts also can be invalidated because of lack of competent parties. To form a valid, binding contract, both parties must have the legal capacity to enter into an agreement. The school board has been recognized as a legally competent party with the capacity to contract. A teacher who lacks a license or is under the statutorily required age for licensure is not considered a competent party for contractual purposes. Consequently, a contract made with such an individual is not enforceable.

Consideration is another essential element of a valid contract. Consideration is something of value that one party pays in return for the other party's performance. Teachers'

---

[35]For a discussion of contract elements, see Kern Alexander & M. David Alexander, American Public School Law (Belmont, CA: West/Thomson Learning, 8th ed. 2012).

[36]McCormick v. Lake Wash. Sch. Dist., 992 P.2d 511 (Wash. Ct. App. 2000). *But see* Trahan v. Lafayette Parish Sch. Bd., 978 So. 2d 1105 (La. Ct. App. 2008) (upholding employment contract executed by superintendent on behalf of board); Ky. Rev. Stat. Ann. § 160.370 (2012) (stating that superintendent has the power regarding employment contract decisions).

monetary compensation and benefits are established in the salary schedule adopted by the school board or negotiated between the school board and the teachers' association.[37] The contract also must involve a legal subject matter and follow the proper form required by law. Most states require a teacher's contract to be in writing to be enforceable,[38] but if there is no statutory specification, an oral agreement is legally binding on both parties.

In addition to employment rights derived from the teaching contract, provisions of any collective bargaining agreement (master contract) are part of the employment contract. Statutory provisions and school board rules and regulations also may be considered part of the terms and conditions of the contract. If not included directly, the provisions existing at the time of the contract may be implied. Moreover, the contract cannot be used as a means of waiving teachers' statutory or constitutional rights.[39]

Term and Tenure Contracts

Two basic types of employment contracts are issued to teachers: term contracts and tenure contracts. *Term contracts* are valid for a fixed period of time (e.g., one or two years). At the end of the contract period, renewal is at the discretion of the school board; nonrenewal requires no explanation unless mandated by statute. Generally, a school board is required only to provide notice prior to the expiration of the contract that employment will not be renewed. *Tenure contracts*, created through state legislative action, ensure teachers that employment will be terminated only for adequate cause and that procedural due process will be provided. **After the award of tenure or *within* a term contract, school boards cannot unilaterally abrogate teachers' contracts. At a minimum, the teacher must be provided procedural protections consisting of notice of the dismissal charges and a hearing.**[40]

Since tenure contracts involve statutory rights, specific procedures and protections vary among the states. Consequently, judicial interpretations in one state provide little guidance in understanding another state's law. Most tenure statutes specify requirements and procedures for obtaining tenure and identify causes and procedures for dismissing a tenured teacher. In interpreting tenure laws, courts have attempted to protect teachers' rights while simultaneously preserving school officials' flexibility in personnel management.

Prior to a school board awarding a tenure contract to a teacher, most states require a probationary period of approximately three years to assess a teacher's ability and competence. During this probationary period, teachers receive term contracts, and there is no guarantee of employment beyond each contract. Tenure statutes generally require regular and continuous service to complete the probationary period.

---

[37]*See* Davis v. Greenwood Sch. Dist., 620 S.E.2d 65 (S.C. 2005) (holding that the reduction of a 10 percent annual incentive payment to teachers for acquiring national board certification to a $3,000 flat rate per year did not violate the teachers' contracts and was within the board's discretion to manage the district's finances).

[38]*See* Sexton v. KIPP Reach Acad. Charter Sch., 260 P.3d 435 (Okla. Civ. App. 2011) (finding an implied contract may have been created when a teacher was given a faculty-only cell phone, provided a letter of intent, and enrolled in a teacher's conference).

[39]*See* Denuis v. Dunlap, 209 F.3d 944 (7th Cir. 2000) (holding that a teacher was not required to relinquish constitutional privacy rights regarding medical or financial records for an employment background check).

[40]See text accompanying notes 22–24, Chapter 12, for discussion of procedural due process requirements.

The authority to grant a tenure contract is a discretionary power of the local school board that cannot be delegated. Although the school board confers tenure, it cannot alter the tenure terms established by the legislature; the legislature determines the basis for tenure, eligibility requirements, and the procedures for acquiring tenure status. Thus, if a statute requires a probationary period, this term of service must be completed prior to the school board's awarding tenure. A board may be compelled to award tenure if a teacher completes the statutory requirements and the school board does not take action to grant or deny tenure. Unless specified in statute, however, tenure is not transferable from one school district to another. This ensures that school officials are provided an opportunity to evaluate teachers before granting tenure.

States often limit the award of tenure to teaching positions, thereby excluding administrative, supervisory, and staff positions. Where tenure is available for administrative positions, probationary service and other specified statutory terms must be met. Tenure as a teacher usually does not imply tenure as an administrator, yet most courts have concluded that continued service as a certified professional employee, albeit as an administrator, does not alter tenure rights acquired as a teacher.

Supplemental Contracts

School boards can enter into supplement contracts with teachers for duties beyond the regular teaching assignments. As with teaching contracts, authority to employ resides with the school board. Generally, these are limited contracts specifying the additional duties, compensation, and time period. Extra duties often relate to coaching, chairing a department, supervising student activities or clubs, and other special assignments.

Supplemental service contracts are usually considered outside the scope of tenure protections. Coaches, in particular, have asserted that supplemental contracts are an integral part of the teaching position and thereby must be afforded the procedural and substantive protections of state tenure laws. Generally, tenure rights apply only to employment in licensure areas, and the lack of licensure requirements for coaches in a state often negates tenure claims for such positions.

Some courts also have distinguished coaching and various extra duties from teaching responsibilities based on the extracurricular nature of the assignment and supplemental compensation. In denying the claim of a ten-year veteran baseball coach who was fired from his coaching position but not from teaching, the Ninth Circuit held that the coach did not have a protected interest in his coaching position, since California law specified that extra-duty assignments could be terminated by the school board at any time.[41] When both classroom teaching and extra-duty assignments are covered in the same contract, however, protected property interests may be created. Accordingly, the teacher would be entitled to due process prior to the termination of the extra-duty assignment.

Because coaching assignments typically require execution of a supplemental contract, a teacher can resign from a coaching position and maintain the primary teaching position. School boards having difficulty in filling coaching positions, however, may tender

---

[41]Lagos v. Modesto City Schs. Dist., 843 F.2d 347 (9th Cir. 1988); *see also* Bd. of Educ. v. Code, 57 S.W.3d 820 (Ky. 2001) (ruling that the basketball coach was not entitled to a formal evaluation prior to nonrenewal of his contract).

an offer to teach on the condition that an individual assume certain coaching responsibilities. If a single teaching and coaching contract is found to be indivisible, a teacher cannot unilaterally resign the coaching duties without relinquishing the teaching position.[42] Individual state laws must be consulted to determine the status of such contracts.

When teaching and coaching positions are combined, a qualified teaching applicant who cannot assume the coaching duties may be rejected. This practice, however, may be vulnerable to legal challenge if certain classes of applicants, such as women, are excluded from consideration. In an Arizona case, female plaintiffs successfully established that a school district was liable for sex discrimination by coupling a high school biology teaching position with a football coaching position. The school board was unable to demonstrate a business necessity for the practice that resulted in female applicants for the teaching position being eliminated from consideration.[43]

Domestic Partner Benefits

Increasingly, legal challenges are being brought to secure health, retirement, and other benefits for domestic partners of lesbian, gay, bisexual, and transgendered (LGBT) employees. Same-sex marriage has not yet been recognized by the federal government, but rights for LGBT employees may exist under state constitutional and statutory provisions or institutional policies. Vermont, Washington, Iowa, Massachusetts, New Hampshire, New York, Maryland, Connecticut, and the District of Columbia allow same-sex marriage. States that allow civil unions or domestic partnerships include Oregon, California, Nevada, Colorado, Illinois, Wisconsin, Hawaii, New Jersey, Rhode Island, Maine, and Delaware.[44] In reviewing claims for benefits, some courts have held that the denial of benefits discriminates on the basis of marital status and is unrelated to any legitimate governmental interest.[45]

Yet other courts have firmly upheld the denial of benefits, finding no discrimination.[46] With the federal Defense of Marriage Act (DOMA) and subsequent adoption of mini-DOMAs in over forty states, employees will continue to face significant challenges in achieving equality of benefits for their domestic partners.[47] For example, in 2007, the

---

[42]*See, e.g.*, Smith v. Petal Sch. Dist., 956 So. 2d 273 (Miss. Ct. App. 2006).

[43]Civil Rights Div. of Ariz. Dep't of Law v. Amphitheater Unified Sch. Dist. No. 10, 706 P.2d 745 (Ariz. Ct. App. 1985).

[44]Lindsay Powers & Jerry Mosemak, *Where States Stand on Same-Sex Marriage*, USA TODAY (May 1, 2012), http://www.usatoday.com/news/nation/story/2012-03-01/maryland-gay-marriage-law/53319758/1.

[45]*See, e.g.*, Snetsinger v. Mont. Univ. Sys., 104 P.3d 445 (Mont. 2004); Tanner v. Or. Health Scis. Univ., 971 P.2d 435 (Or. Ct. App. 1998); Baker v. State, 744 A.2d 864 (Vt. 1999).

[46]*See* Donna Euben, Am. Ass'n of Univ. Professors, *Domestic Partner Benefits on Campus: A Litigation Update* (Aug. 2005), http://www.aaup.org/AAUP/issues/WF/partners.htm.

[47]*See* Defense of Marriage Act, 1 U.S.C. § 7 (2012); 28 U.S.C. § 1738C (2012). Congress passed the DOMA in reaction to growing concern about states recognizing same-sex marriages. Under the federal law, marriage is defined as a union between a man and a woman. Furthermore, the Act states that individual states are not required to recognize same-sex marriages sanctioned by other states. However, in 2011, the Obama Administration stated it would no longer defend the constitutionality of § 3 of the DOMA in court. *See* Press Release, Dep't of Justice, Statement of the Attorney General on Litigation Involving the Defense of Marriage Act (Feb. 23, 2011), http://www.justice.gov/opa/pr/2011/February/11-ag-222.html.

Michigan Court of Appeals interpreted the state's constitutional marriage amendment as precluding employers from providing same-sex domestic partner benefits. The court ruled that the law, which provides that "the union of one man and one woman in marriage shall be the only agreement recognized as a marriage or similar union for any purpose," blocks the recognition of domestic partnership agreements because it is a status *similar* to marriage.[48] Contrarily, both the First and Second Circuits struck down portions of DOMA.[49] With the Second Circuit case under review by the Supreme Court, it is likely that many of the current issues surrounding DOMA will be clarified in 2013.

Leaves of Absence

Contracts may specify various types of leaves of absence. Within the parameters of state law, school boards have discretion in establishing requirements for these leaves. A school board may place restrictions on when teachers can take personal leave—for example, no leaves on the day before or after a holiday, or no more than two consecutive days of personal leave.[50] This topic often is the subject of collective bargaining, with leave provisions specified in bargained agreements. School boards, however, cannot negotiate leave policies that impair rights guaranteed by the United States Constitution and various federal and state anti-discrimination laws.[51] Likewise, where state law confers specific rights, local boards do not have the discretion to deny or alter these rights. Generally, statutes identify employees' rights related to various kinds of leave, such as sick leave, personal leave, pregnancy or child-care leave, sabbatical leave, disability leave, family leave, and military leave. State laws pertaining to leaves of absence usually specify eligibility for benefits, minimum days that must be provided, whether leave must be granted with or without pay, and restrictions that may be imposed by local school boards. If a teacher meets all statutory and procedural requirements for a specific leave, a school board cannot deny the request.

PERSONNEL EVALUATIONS

A school board's extensive authority to determine teacher performance standards may be restricted by state-imposed evaluation requirements.

As a result of the federal "Race to the Top" competition, more states are requiring annual teacher evaluations, and many are using evidence of student learning in these

---

[48]Nat'l Pride at Work v. Governor of Mich., 732 N.W.2d 139, 143 (Mich. Ct. App. 2007), *aff'd*, 748 N.W.2d 524 (Mich. 2008).

[49]Massachusetts v. U.S. Dep't of Health & Human Servs., 682 F.3d 1 (1st Cir. 2012); Windsor v. United States, 699 F.3d 169 (2d Cir. 2012), *cert. granted*, 133 S. Ct. 1521 (2013); *see* text accompanying note 49, Chapter 11.

[50]*See, e.g.*, Amaral-Whittenberg v. Alanis, 123 S.W.3d 714 (Tex. App. 2003).

[51]Charges of discrimination in connection with leave policies pertaining to pregnancy-related absences and the observance of religious holidays are discussed in Chapter 11.

evaluations.[52] To be eligible for funding from the Race to the Top program, states must consider student test scores in teacher evaluation and allow charter schools to play a bigger role in turning around lower-performing schools. Some states are considering paying teachers for performance as well.[53] Beyond the purposes of faculty improvement and remediation, results of evaluations may be used in a variety of employment decisions, including retention, tenure, dismissal, promotion, salary, reassignment, and reduction-in-force. When adverse personnel decisions are based on evaluations, legal concerns of procedural fairness arise. Were established state and local procedures followed? Did school officials employ equitable standards? Was sufficient evidence collected to support the staffing decision? Were evaluations conducted in a uniform and consistent manner?

Historically, school systems have had broad discretionary powers to establish teacher performance criteria, but more state statutes are beginning to impose specific evaluation requirements. Between 2009 and 2011, thirty-three states made changes to their teacher evaluation policies.[54] Content and requirements vary substantially across states, with some states merely mandating the establishment of an appraisal system and others specifying procedures and criteria to be employed. For example, Indiana requires that the objective measure of student achievement inform the evaluation.[55] Maine enacted legislation that permits school districts to use student assessments as part of the teaching evaluation.[56] The proposed changes to the evaluation of teachers have led to litigation.[57]

Courts generally require strict compliance with evaluation requirements and procedures identified in statutes, board policies, or employment contracts. Where school boards have been attentive to these requirements, courts have upheld challenged employment decisions. Courts are reluctant to interject their judgment into the teacher evaluation process. Judicial review generally is limited to the procedural issues of fairness and reasonableness. Several principles emerge from case law to guide educators in developing equitable systems: standards for assessing teaching adequacy must be defined and communicated to teachers; criteria must be applied uniformly and consistently; an opportunity and direction for improvement must be provided; and procedures specified in state laws and school board policies must be followed.

---

[52]Race to the Top (RTTT), a federal funding program initiated under President Obama's stimulus plan, has directed billions of dollars to states to adopt transformational school models for schools performing in the bottom 5 percent. In the 2010 RTTT competition, each of the thirty-six states that applied for funding included pay for performance in their proposals. *See* Jennifer Dounay Zinth, Educ. Comm'n of the States, *Teacher Evaluation: New Approaches for a New Decade* (June 2012), http://www.ecs.org/clearinghouse/86/21/8621.pdf.

[53]Stephanie Rose, Educ. Comm'n of the States, *Pay for Performance*, (July 20, 2010), http://www.ecs.org/clearinghouse/87/06/8706.pdf.

[54]Emily Douglas, *The State of Teacher Evaluation: Part I*, EDUC. WK. BLOG (Jan. 26, 2012), http://blogs.edweek.org/topschooljobs/k-12_talent_manager/2012/01/the_state_of_teacher_evaluation_part_1.html/.

[55]IND. CODE ANN., § 20-28-11.5-4(c)(2) (2012).

[56]Me. Pub. L. ch. 646, SP704 (LD 1799) (2012) (to be codified at ME. REV. STAT. tit. 20A).

[57]*See* Stephen Frank, *Lawsuit Against LAUSD Could Shake Up How California Evaluates Teachers*, CAL. POLITICAL NEWS & VIEWS (Jan. 20, 2012), http://capoliticalnews.com/2012/01/20/lawsuit-against-lausd-could-shake-up-how-ca-evaluates-teachers/

PERSONNEL RECORDS

Maintenance, access, and dissemination of personnel information must conform to federal and state laws and contractual agreements.

Because multiple statutes in each state as well as employment contracts govern school records, it is difficult to generalize about the specific nature of teachers' privacy rights regarding personnel files. State privacy laws that place restrictions on maintenance and access to the school records typically protect personnel information. Among other provisions, these laws usually require school boards to:

- maintain only necessary and relevant information;
- provide individual employees access to their files;
- inform employees of the various uses of the files; and
- establish a procedure for challenging the accuracy of information.

Collective bargaining contracts may impose additional and more stringent requirements regarding access and dissemination of personnel information.

A central issue in the confidentiality of personnel files is whether the information constitutes a public record that must be reasonably accessible to the general public. Public record, freedom of information, or right-to-know laws that grant broad access to school records may directly conflict with privacy laws, requiring courts to balance the interests of the teacher, the school officials, and the public. The specific provisions of state laws determine the level of confidentiality granted to personnel records.[58] The federal Freedom of Information Act (FOIA),[59] which serves as a model for many state FOIAs, often is used by courts in interpreting state provisions. Unlike the federal law, however, many states do not exempt personnel records.

In the absence of a specific exemption, most courts have concluded that **any doubt concerning the appropriateness of disclosure should be decided in favor of public disclosure.** The Supreme Court of Michigan held that teachers' personnel files are open to the public because they are not specifically exempt by law.[60] The Supreme Court of Washington noted that the Public Records Act mandated disclosure of information that is of legitimate public concern.[61] As such, the state superintendent of public instruction was required

---

[58]*See* Wakefield Teachers Ass'n v. Sch. Comm., 731 N.E.2d 63 (Mass. 2000) (concluding that a disciplinary report is personnel information that is exempt under the state's public records law); Bangor Area Educ. Ass'n v. Angle, 720 A.2d 198 (Pa. Commw. Ct. 1998) (confirming that teachers' personnel files are not public records); Abbott v. N.E. Indep. Sch. Dist., 212 S.W.3d 364, 367 (Tex. App. 2006) (concluding that a principal's memorandum to a teacher about complaints and providing her directions for improvement was "a document evaluating the performance of a teacher" and thus exempt from release under the state's public information Act).

[59]5 U.S.C. § 552 (2012).

[60]Bradley v. Bd. of Educ., 565 N.W.2d 650 (Mich. 1997).

[61]Brouillet v. Cowles Pub. Co., 791 P.2d 526 (Wash. 1990).

to provide a newspaper publisher records specifying the reasons for teacher certificate revocations. The Supreme Court of Connecticut interpreted the state FOIA exemption, prohibiting the release of information that would constitute an invasion of personal privacy, to include employees' evaluations[62] but not their sick-leave records.[63] In the termination of a teacher for conducting pornographic Internet searches on his work computer, the Supreme Court of Wisconsin held that a memorandum and CD created from a forensic analysis of the teacher's computer were "records" subject to release under the state's Open Records Law after the school district completed its investigation.[64] **In general, information that must be maintained by law is a public record (e.g., personal directory information, salary information, employment contracts, leave records, and teaching license) and must be released.**

Educators have not been successful in asserting that privacy interests in personnel records are protected under either the Family Educational Rights and Privacy Act (FERPA) or the United States Constitution. FERPA applies only to students and their educational records, not to employees' personnel records. Similarly, employees' claims that their constitutional privacy rights bar disclosure of their personnel records have been unsuccessful. In a case in which a teacher's college transcript was sought by a third party under the Texas Open Records Act, the Fifth Circuit ruled that even if a teacher had a recognizable privacy interest in her transcript, that interest "is significantly outweighed by the public's interest in evaluating the competence of its school teachers."[65]

Access to personnel files also has been controversial in situations involving allegations of employment discrimination.[66] Personnel files must be relinquished if subpoenaed by a court. The Equal Employment Opportunity Commission (EEOC) also is authorized to subpoena relevant personnel files to investigate thoroughly allegations that a particular individual has been the victim of discriminatory treatment. The Supreme Court held that confidential peer review materials used in university promotion and tenure decisions were not protected from disclosure to the EEOC. The Court ruled that under Title VII of the Civil Rights Act of 1964, the EEOC must only show relevance, not special reasons or justifications, in demanding specific records. Regarding access to peer review materials, the Court noted that "if there is a 'smoking gun' to be found that demonstrates discrimination in tenure decisions, it is likely to be tucked away in peer review files."[67]

---

[62]Chairman v. Freedom of Info. Comm'n, 585 A.2d 96 (Conn. 1991).

[63]Perkins v. Freedom of Info. Comm'n, 635 A.2d 783 (Conn. 1993).

[64]Zellner v. Cedarburg Sch. Dist., 731 N.W.2d 240 (Wis. 2007); *see also* Navarre v. S. Wash. Cnty. Schs., 652 N.W.29 (Minn. 2002) (finding that the release of information about a disciplinary matter before *final* disposition violated the counselor's rights under state law protecting private personnel data).

[65]Klein Indep. Sch. Dist. v. Mattox, 830 F.2d 576, 580 (5th Cir. 1987).

[66]The Federal Procedural Rules, approved by the Supreme Court in April 2006 and effective December 1, 2006, require employers to be more aware about the storage of electronic information. When school officials are involved in the discovery phase of litigation, they must be able to produce e-mails, instant messages, and other digital communications created in their system. The rules send a clear message that digital and electronic communications must be preserved as other documents are preserved.

[67]Univ. of Pa. v. EEOC, 493 U.S. 182, 193 (1990).

With respect to the maintenance of records, information clearly cannot be placed in personnel files in retaliation for the exercise of constitutional rights. Courts have ordered letters of reprimand expunged from files when they have been predicated on protected speech and association activities.[68] Reprimands, although not a direct prohibition on protected activities, may present a constitutional violation because of their potentially chilling effect on the exercise of constitutional rights.

REPORTING SUSPECTED CHILD ABUSE

All states require teachers to report suspected child abuse and grant them immunity from liability if reports are made in good faith.

Child abuse and neglect are recognized as national problems, with reported cases remaining at a high level.[69] Because the majority of these children are school age, educators are in a unique role to detect signs of potential abuse. States, recognizing the daily contact teachers have with students, have imposed certain *duties* for reporting suspected abuse.

All states have enacted laws identifying teachers among the professionals required to report signs of child abuse. Most state laws impose criminal liability for failure to report suspected abuse. Penalties may include fines ranging from $500 to $5,000, prison terms up to one year, and/or public service. Civil suits also may be initiated against teachers for negligence in failing to make such reports.[70] In addition, school systems may impose disciplinary measures against a teacher who does not follow the mandates of the law. The Seventh Circuit upheld the suspension and demotion of a teacher-psychologist for not promptly reporting suspected abuse.[71] The court rejected the teacher's claim to a federal right of confidentiality, noting the state's compelling interest to protect children from mistreatment.

Although specific aspects of the laws may vary from one state to another, definitions of abuse and neglect often are based on the federal Child Abuse Prevention and Treatment

---

[68]*See* Aebisher v. Ryan, 622 F.2d 651 (2d Cir. 1980) (concluding that a letter of reprimand for speaking to the press about violence in the school implicated protected speech); Columbus Educ. Ass'n v. Columbus City Sch. Dist., 623 F.2d 1155 (6th Cir. 1980) (holding that a letter of reprimand issued to a teacher who was also a union representative for zealous advocacy of a fellow teacher violated the First Amendment).

[69]In 2009, 3.3 million referrals (involving approximately 6 million children) were made to child protection agencies. U.S. Dep't of Health and Human Servs., Admin. for Children & Families, *Child Maltreatment 2009* (Washington, D.C.: U.S. Government Printing Office, 2009). Public concern regarding violent sexual offenders led to the enactment of a federal law requiring states to develop procedures for notifying the public when a sex offender is released into the their community. Adam Walsh Child Protection and Safety Act of 2006, 42 U.S.C. § 16901(1) (2012).

[70]See Chapter 2 for a discussion of the elements of negligence.

[71]Pesce v. J. Sterling Morton High Sch. Dist. 201, 830 F.2d 789 (7th Cir. 1987).

Act (CAPTA), which provides funds to identify, treat, and prevent abuse. The CAPTA identifies *child abuse* and *neglect* as:

> the physical or mental injury, sexual abuse or exploitation, negligent treatment, or maltreatment of a child under the age of eighteen, or the age specified by the child protection law of the state in question, by a person who is responsible for the child's welfare under the circumstances which indicate that the child's health or welfare is harmed or threatened thereby.[72]

Several common elements are found in state child abuse statutes. The laws mandate that certain professionals such as doctors, nurses, and educators report suspected abuse. Statutes do not require that reporters have absolute knowledge, but rather "reasonable cause to believe" or "reason to believe" that a child has been abused or neglected. Once abuse is suspected, the report must be made immediately to the designated child protection agency, department of welfare, or law enforcement unit as specified in state law. All states grant immunity from civil and criminal liability to individuals if reports are made in good faith.

School districts often establish reporting procedures that require teachers to report suspected abuse to their principal or school social worker. However, if statutory provisions specify that teachers must promptly report suspected abuse to another agency or to law enforcement, teachers are not relieved of their individual obligation to report to state authorities. Some state laws, however, do relieve teachers of the obligation to report if someone else has already reported or will be reporting the incident. But teachers should always follow up to be sure the report was made to the appropriate agency.

State laws are explicit on reporting requirements for suspected child abuse, but it is difficult to prove that a teacher had sufficient knowledge of abuse to trigger legal liability for failure to report. Therefore, it is desirable for school officials to establish policies and procedures to encourage effective reporting. The pervasiveness of the problem and concern about the lack of reporting by teachers also indicate a need for in-service programs to assist teachers in recognizing signs of abused and neglected children.

COLLECTIVE BARGAINING

Teachers have a constitutionally protected right to form and join a union; specific bargaining rights are conferred through state statutes or judicial interpretations of state constitutions, thus creating wide divergence in teachers' bargaining rights across states.

Although basic differences in employment exist between the public and private sectors, collective bargaining laws (specifically, the National Labor Relations Act[73] and the Taft-Hartley Act[74]) that apply only to the private sector have been significant in shaping statutory and

---

[72]42 U.S.C. § 5101 (2012).

[73]The Act states that "employees shall have the right to self-organization, to form, join or assist labor organizations, to bargain collectively through representatives of their own choosing, and to engage in concerted activities, for the purpose of collective bargaining or other mutual aid or protection." 29 U.S.C. § 157 (2012).

[74]29 U.S.C. § 141 (2012).

judicial regulation of public negotiations. Similarities between the two sectors can be noted in many areas, such as unfair labor practices, union representation, and impasse procedures. However, several basic differences distinguish bargaining in the public and private sectors. First, the removal of decision-making authority from public officials through bargaining has been viewed as an infringement on the government's sovereign power, which has resulted in the enactment of state labor laws strongly favoring public employers. Public employees' rights have been further weakened by prohibitions of work stoppages. Whereas employees' ability to strike is considered *essential* to the effective operation of collective decision making in the private sector, this view has been rejected in the public sector because of the nature and structure of governmental services.

Context of Bargaining Rights

Bargaining rights developed slowly for public employees who historically had been deprived of the right to organize and bargain collectively. It was not until the late 1960s that public employees' constitutional right to join a union was firmly established. A large number of public employees actively participated in collective bargaining, but statutes and regulations in some states prohibited union membership. These restrictions against union membership were challenged as impairing association freedoms protected by the First Amendment. Although not addressing union membership, **the Supreme Court held in 1967 that public employment cannot be conditioned on the relinquishment of free association rights.**[75] In a later decision, the Seventh Circuit clearly announced that "an individual's right to form and join a union is protected by the First Amendment."[76] Other courts followed this precedent by invalidating state statutory provisions that blocked union membership. School officials have been prohibited from retaliating against teachers, imposing sanctions, or denying benefits to discourage protected association rights.

The United States Constitution has been interpreted as protecting public employees' rights to organize, but the right to form and join a union does not ensure the right to bargain collectively with a public employer; individual state statutes and constitutions govern such bargaining rights. Whether identified as professional negotiations, collective negotiations, or collective bargaining, **the process entails bilateral decision making in which the teachers' representative and the school board attempt to reach mutual agreement on matters affecting teacher employment.** The judiciary has been reluctant to interfere with legislative authority to define the collective bargaining relationship between public employers and employees unless protected rights have been compromised.

Most recently, we have seen unprecedented attacks on public employees' bargaining rights, resulting in radical changes to the public employee bargaining laws in some states. Governors across these states have used their financial crises to argue that public employers must have greater flexibility in controlling their budgets. The most publicized of the state changes occurred in Wisconsin, which in 1959 was the first state to recognize public employees' right to bargain. Under the 2011 Wisconsin law for general public employees (not safety employees), the scope of bargaining is restricted as follows: base pay rates cannot exceed the rate of inflation unless submitted to a referendum for approval;

[75]Keyishian v. Bd. of Regents, 385 U.S. 589 (1967).

[76]McLaughlin v. Tilendis, 398 F.2d 287, 289 (7th Cir. 1968).

dues checkoff enabling union dues to be paid through payroll deduction is prohibited; and fair share agreements where nonmembers pay a fee are impermissible. In addition, unions must be certified each year by a majority of the union members (not a majority of members voting).[77] A Wisconsin federal district court issued an injunction in March 2012 requiring school districts to continue to deduct dues and enjoining the recertification of unions based on the more favorable treatment of safety employees in the new Wisconsin law.[78] However, the Seventh Circuit reversed the lower court's decision, finding that the state had a rational basis for distinguishing between general safety employees and general public employees.[79]

The Ohio governor also signed into law similar radical changes to the state's public employee bargaining but included safety and all other public employees. Through a public referendum, the new Ohio law was rejected in 2011 by 62 percent of the voters. Other states have introduced anti-union laws that attempt to limit the scope of bargaining, eliminate payroll deductions, prohibit arbitration over contract grievances, and increase pension contributions. Many of these proposed laws are still being debated, and others have been placed on hold by courts while appeals are pending.

Diversity in labor laws and bargaining practices among the states makes it difficult to generalize about collective bargaining and teachers' labor rights. State labor laws, state employment relations board rulings, and court decisions must be consulted to determine specific rights, because there is no federal labor law covering public school employees. Over two-thirds of the states have enacted bargaining laws, ranging from very comprehensive laws controlling most aspects of negotiations to laws granting the minimal right to meet and confer. Still other states, in the absence of legislation, rely on judicial rulings to define the basic rights of public employees in the labor relations arena. In this section, the legal structure in which bargaining occurs and public school teachers' employment rights under state labor laws are examined. Specific topics include bargaining subjects, dues and service fees, grievances, negotiation impasse, and strikes.[80]

Because of the variations in labor laws, as well as the lack of such laws in some states, substantial differences exist in bargaining rights and practices. A few states, such as New York, have a detailed, comprehensive collective bargaining statute that delineates specific bargaining rights. In contrast, negotiated contracts between teachers' organizations and school boards are prohibited in North Carolina. Under North Carolina law, all contracts between public employers and employee associations are invalid.[81]

---

[77]2011 Wis. Act 10.

[78]Wis. Educ. Ass'n Council v. Walker, 824 F. Supp. 2d 856, 876 (W.D. 2012); *see also* Madison Teachers Inc. v. Walker, No. 11CV3774 (Dane Cnty. Cir. Ct. Sept. 14, 2012) (holding that the Wisconsin bargaining law violated union members' speech and association rights under both the federal and state constitutions), *appeal granted*, No. 2012AP002067 (Wis. Ct. App. 2012); Joseph Slater, Am. Constitution Soc'y for Law & Policy *The Assault on Public Sector Collective Bargaining: Real Harms and Imaginary Benefits* (June 2011), https://www.acslaw. org/sites/default/files/Slater_Collective_Bargaining.pdf.

[79]Wis. Educ. Ass'n Council v. Walker, 705 F.3d 640 (7th Cir. 2013).

[80]As collective bargaining has matured in the public sector, state labor relations board decisions have become a substantial source of legal precedent for each state, with courts rendering fewer decisions in the labor arena. In fact, courts defer to the boards' rulings unless they are clearly contrary to law. While specific rulings of labor boards are not included in this chapter, educators are encouraged to examine that extensive body of law if a board governs negotiations in their state.

[81]N.C. GEN. STAT. § 95-98 (2012).

In contrast to North Carolina, other states without legislation have permitted negotiated agreements. The Kentucky Supreme Court ruled that a public employer may recognize an employee organization for the purpose of collective bargaining, even though state law is silent regarding public employee bargaining rights.[82] The decision does not impose a duty on local school boards to bargain, but merely allows a board the discretion to negotiate. This ruling is consistent with several other judicial decisions permitting negotiated contracts in the absence of specific legislation. The board's authority to enter into contracts for the operation and maintenance of the school system has been construed to include the ability to enter into negotiated agreements with employee organizations. Once a school board extends recognition to a bargaining agent and commences bargaining, the board's actions in the negotiation process are governed by established judicial principles.

Teachers' Statutory Bargaining Rights

In states with laws governing teachers' bargaining rights, school boards must negotiate with teachers in accordance with the statutorily prescribed process. Generally, public employee bargaining laws address employer and employee rights, bargaining units, scope of bargaining, impasse resolution, grievance procedures, unfair labor practices, and penalties for prohibited practices. Many states have established labor relations boards to monitor bargaining under their statutes. Although the specific functions of these boards vary widely, their general purpose is to resolve questions arising from the implementation of state law. Functions assigned to such boards include determination of membership in bargaining units, resolution of union recognition claims, investigation of unfair labor practices, and interpretation of the general intent of statutory bargaining clauses. Usually, judicial review cannot be pursued until administrative review before labor boards is exhausted. Thus, decisions of labor boards are an important source of labor law, since many of the issues addressed by boards are never appealed to courts. When the labor boards' decisions are challenged in court, substantial deference is given to their findings and determinations.[83]

Like the National Labor Relations Act (NLRA) in the private sector, state statutes require bargaining "in good faith." *Good faith bargaining* **has been interpreted as requiring parties to meet at reasonable times and attempt to reach mutual agreement without compulsion on either side to agree.** Many states have followed the federal law in stipulating that this "does not compel either party to agree to a proposal or to require the making of a concession."[84] Failure of the school board or teachers' organization to bargain in good faith can result in the imposition of penalties.

---

[82]Bd. of Trs. v. Pub. Emps. Council No. 51, 571 S.W.2d 616 (Ky. 1978); *see also* Independence-Nat'l Educ. Ass'n v. Independence Sch. Dist., 223 S.W.3d 131 (Mo. 2007), *overruling* City of Springfield v. Clouse, 206 S.W.2d 539, 542 (Mo. 1947) (holding that the state constitutional provision guaranteeing "employees" the right to organize and bargain collectively includes both public and private employees).

[83]*See, e.g.*, *In re* Kennedy, 27 A.3d 844 (N.H. 2011); Dodgeland Educ. Ass'n v. Wis. Emp't Relations Comm'n, 639 N.W. 2d 733 (Wis. 2002).

[84]29 U.S.C. § 158(d) (2012); *see also* Bd. of Educ. v. Sered, 850 N.E.2d 821 (Ill. App. Ct. 2006) (finding that a tentative oral agreement made by the board's representatives was valid; the board could not disregard or modify the terms of the agreement).

Statutes impose certain restrictions or obligations on both the school board and the employee organization. Violation of the law by either party can result in an unfair labor practice claim. Allegations of unfair labor practices are brought before the state public employee relations board for a hearing and judgment. Specific unfair labor practices, often modeled after those in the NLRA, are included in state statutes. The most common prohibited labor practice is that an employer or union cannot interfere with, restrain, or coerce public employees in exercising their rights under the labor law.[85] Among other prohibited *employer* practices are interference with union operations, discrimination against employees because of union membership, refusal to bargain collectively with the exclusive representative, and failure to bargain in good faith. *Unions* are prevented from causing an employer to discriminate against employees on the basis of union membership, refusing to bargain or failing to bargain in good faith, failing to represent all employees in the bargaining unit,[86] and engaging in unlawful activities, such as strikes or boycotts, identified in the bargaining law.

Upon completion of the negotiation process, the members of the bargaining unit and the school board ratify the written agreement (usually referred to as the *master contract*). These agreements often contain similar standard contract language and clauses, beginning with recognition of the exclusive bargaining representative and union security issues (i.e., fair share fees). Management rights and association rights also are detailed. Management clauses emphasize the board's control over the establishment of educational policies, and union clauses may include the right to use school facilities or communication systems. Other provisions relate to the scope of bargaining, which is defined by the state's labor law or common law. These items not only include salary and fringe benefits but also may address grievance procedures, employee evaluations, preparation time, length of workday, class size, procedures for employee discipline, transfers, layoff and recall procedures, assignment of duties, and processes for filling vacancies.

Scope of Negotiations

Should the teachers' organization have input into class size? Who will determine the length of the school day? How will extra-duty assignments be determined? Will reductions-in-force necessitated by declining enrollment be based on seniority or merit? These questions and others are raised in determining the scope of negotiations. *Scope* refers to the range of issues or subjects that are negotiable, and determining scope is one of the most difficult tasks in public-sector bargaining. Public employers argue that issues must be narrowly

---

[85]*See* Cal. Teachers Ass'n v. Pub. Emp't Relations Bd., 87 Cal. Rptr. 3d 530 (App. Ct. 2009) (holding that the act of organizing teachers through signing a letter was a protected act); Fort Frye Teachers Ass'n v. SERB, 809 N.E.2d 1130 (Ohio 2004) (ruling the nonrenewal of a teacher's contract for union activities constitutes an unfair labor practice).

[86]*See* United Teachers v. Sch. Dist. of Miami-Dade Cnty., 68 So. 3d 1003 (Fla. Dist. Ct. App. 2011) (finding that the bargained agreement denied nonunion teachers the right of representation at performance review proceedings; the union committed an unfair labor practice when it entered into the agreement); S. Sioux City Educ. Ass'n v. Dakota Cnty. Sch. Dist., 772 N.W.2d 564 (Neb. 2009) (ruling that school board committed a prohibited labor practice when it classified a certificated teacher as a long-term substitute rather than a probationary teacher, resulting in compensation less than bargained for in the contract).

defined to protect the government's policy-making role, whereas employee unions counter that bargaining subjects must be defined broadly to have meaningful negotiations.

Restrictions on scope of bargaining vary considerably among states. Consequently, to determine negotiable items in a particular state, the state's collective bargaining law, other statutes, and litigation interpreting these laws must be examined. The specification of negotiable items in labor laws may include broad guidelines or detailed enumeration of specific issues. As noted, many states have modeled their bargaining statutes after the NLRA, which stipulates that **representatives of the employer and employees must meet and confer "with respect to wages, hours, and other terms and conditions of employment."**[87] A few states deal directly with the scope of bargaining by identifying each item that must be negotiated. Some states specify prohibited subjects of bargaining. For example, Michigan's prohibited subjects include decisions related to the establishment of the starting date for the school year, composition of site-based decision-making bodies, interdistrict and intradistrict open enrollment opportunities, authorization of public school academies, and establishment and staffing of experimental programs.[88] Generally, statutory mandates cannot be preempted by collective bargaining agreements;[89] however, in a few states, the negotiated agreement prevails over conflicting laws, unless the laws are specifically exempted.[90] A Pennsylvania court held that a school board could not deny a female teacher's request to return to work early after a pregnancy under a policy in the negotiated agreement permitting the return.[91] The board had argued that the agreement violated public policy against sex discrimination because no provision was made for males to request an early return from leave.

Proposed subjects for negotiation can be classified as mandatory, permissive, or prohibited. *Mandatory* items must be negotiated.[92] Failure of the school board to meet and confer on such items is evidence of lack of good faith bargaining. *Permissive* items can be negotiated if both parties agree; however, there is no legal duty to consider the items. Furthermore, in most states, permissive items cannot be pursued to the point of negotiation impasse, and an employer cannot unilaterally change these items if no agreement is reached. *Prohibited* items are beyond the power of the board to negotiate; an illegal delegation of power results if the board agrees to negotiate these items. Since most statutory scope provisions are general in nature, courts or labor relations boards often have been asked to differentiate between negotiable and nonnegotiable items.

Defining managerial rights is a key element in establishing limitations on negotiable subjects at the bargaining table. **State laws specify that public employers cannot be**

---

[87]29 U.S.C. § 158(d) (2012).

[88]MICH. COMP. LAWS ANN. § 423.215(3)(4) (2012).

[89]Furthermore, collective bargaining agreements cannot deprive individuals of rights guaranteed by federal laws. *See, e.g.*, Abrahamson v. Bd. of Educ., 374 F.3d 66 (2d Cir. 2004).

[90]*See, e.g.*, Hickey v. N.Y.C. Dep't of Educ., 952 N.E.2d 993 (N.Y. 2011); Streetsboro Educ. Ass'n v. Streetsboro City Sch. Dist., 626 N.E.2d 110 (Ohio 1994).

[91]W. Allegheny Sch. Dist. v. W. Allegheny Educ. Ass'n, 997 A.2d 411 (Pa. Commw. Ct. 2010).

[92]Wages definitely fall within the mandatory category. A wage-related area that has received recent attention is the payment of "signing bonuses" to attract teachers for difficult-to-fill positions. Failure to bargain these payments may constitute an unfair labor practice. *See, e.g.*, Ekalaka Unified Bd. of Trs. v. Ekalaka Teachers' Ass'n, 149 P.3d 902 (Mont. 2006); Crete Educ. Ass'n v. Salie Cnty. Sch. Dist., 654 N.W.2d 166 (Neb. 2002).

required to negotiate governmental policy matters, and courts have held that it is impermissible for a school board to bargain away certain rights and responsibilities in the public policy area.[93] Generally, educational policy matters are defined through provisions in collective bargaining statutes, such as "management rights" and "scope of bargaining" clauses. Policy issues—such as class size, teacher evaluation criteria, and the award of tenure—are excluded as negotiable items in a few states; however, most states stipulate only that employers are not *required* to bargain such policy rights.

Public employee labor laws requiring the negotiation of "conditions of employment" can include far-reaching policy matters since most school board decisions either directly or indirectly affect the teacher in the classroom. The Maryland high court noted the difficulty in distinguishing between educational policy and matters relating to teachers' employment: "Virtually every managerial decision in some way relates to 'salaries, wages, hours, and other working conditions,' and is therefore arguably negotiable. At the same time, virtually every such decision also involves educational policy considerations and is therefore arguably nonnegotiable."[94] In many states, the interpretation of what is negotiable resides with the labor relations board. Often, these boards as well as courts employ a balancing test, beginning with an inquiry into whether a particular matter involves wages, hours, and terms and conditions of employment. If so, then the labor board or court must determine if the matter also is one of inherent managerial policy. If not, the matter is a mandatory subject of bargaining. However, if the issue also pertains to educational policy, the benefits of bargaining on the decision-making process must be balanced against the burden on the employer's authority. Accordingly, this process entails a fact-specific analysis.

Judicial decisions interpreting negotiability illustrate the range in bargainable matters. The Supreme Court of New Jersey narrowly interpreted *conditions of employment* to mean wages, benefits, and work schedules, thereby removing governmental policy items such as teacher transfers, course offerings, and evaluations.[95] Other courts, however, have construed the phrase in broader terms. For example, the Nevada Supreme Court ruled that items *significantly* related to wages, hours, and working conditions are negotiable.[96]

Courts agree that school boards cannot be *required* to negotiate inherent managerial rights pertaining to policy matters, but some states view these rights as *permissive* subjects of bargaining. That is, the board may agree to negotiate a particular "right" in the absence of statutory or judicial prohibitions. **If the board does negotiate a policy item, it is bound by the agreement in the same manner as if the issue were a mandatory item.**

---

[93]*See* City Univ. of N.Y. v. Prof'l Staff Cong., 837 N.Y.S.2d 121 (App. Div. 2007) (holding that the employer could not bargain away its right to inspect teacher personnel files; the agreement was against public policy to investigate discrimination complaints).

[94]Montgomery Cnty. Educ. Ass'n v. Bd. of Educ., 534 A.2d 980, 986 (Md. 1987).

[95]Ridgefield Park Educ. Ass'n v. Ridgefield Park Bd. of Educ., 393 A.2d 278 (N.J. 1978); *see also* Polk Cnty. Bd. of Educ. v. Polk Cnty. Educ. Ass'n, 139 S.W.3d 304 (Tenn. Ct. App. 2004) (ruling that a dress code policy constituted a "working condition," not a managerial prerogative).

[96]Clark Cnty. Sch. Dist. v. Local Gov't Employee-Management Relations Bd., 530 P.2d 114 (Nev. 1974); *see also* Governing Bd. v. Comm'n on Prof'l Conduct, 99 Cal. Rptr. 3d 903 (App. Ct. 2009) (finding that the negotiated agreement requiring all teachers to acquire English learner certification was "reasonably related" to hours, wages, and conditions of employment).

Union Security Provisions

To ensure their strength and viability, unions attempt to obtain various security provisions in the collective bargaining contract. The nature and extent of these provisions will depend on state laws and constitutional limitations.

In bargaining with employees, unions seek to gain provisions that require all employees either to join the association or to pay fees for its services. Since a union must represent all individuals in the bargaining unit, it is argued that such provisions are necessary to eliminate "free riders" (i.e., the individuals who receive the benefits of the union's work without paying the dues for membership).

Union security provisions take several forms. The *closed shop*, requiring an employer to hire only union members, does not exist in the public sector and is unlawful in the private sector. The *union shop* agreement requires an employee to join the union within a designated time period after employment to retain a position. Union shop agreements are prevalent in the private sector, but they are not authorized by most public-sector laws and are limited or proscribed in some states under "right-to-work" laws.[97] The security provisions most frequently found in the public sector are *agency shop* and *fair share* agreements—terms that often are used interchangeably. An agency shop provision requires an employee to pay union dues but does not mandate membership, whereas a fair share arrangement requires a nonmember simply to pay a service fee to cover the cost of bargaining activities.

Nonunion teachers have challenged mandatory fees as a violation of their First Amendment speech and association rights. The Supreme Court, however, upheld the payment of fair share fees by public employees in *Abood v. Detroit Board of Education*.[98] The Court rejected the nonunion members' First Amendment claims, noting the importance of ensuring labor peace and eliminating "free riders." Yet the Court concluded that **employees cannot be compelled to contribute to the support of ideological causes they oppose as a condition of maintaining employment as public school teachers.** In a recent case, Idaho's right-to-work law, which prohibits payroll deductions for political activities, was challenged as impermissible because it singled out political speech based on its content.[99] Disagreeing, the Supreme Court stated that the government must accommodate speech in certain contexts but certainly is not required to assist in subsidizing particular views.[100] The Court further commented: "Idaho does not suppress political speech but simply declines to promote it through public employer checkoffs for political activities."[101] Accordingly,

---

[97]In 2012, Michigan became the twenty-fourth state to sign a "right-to-work" law that specifically declares that an individual's employment cannot be conditioned on joining a union or paying fees to a union. A strong movement fueled by anti-union sentiment can be seen across states with right-to-work legislation being actively pursued in Missouri; Maine legislators continue to debate a right-to-work law, while New Hampshire soundly defeated a proposed law in February 2013.

[98]431 U.S. 209 (1977).

[99]Idaho Code §§ 44-2601–44-2605, § 44-2004 (2012). Political activities are defined as "electoral activities, independent expenditures, or expenditures made to any candidate, political party, political action committee, or political issues committee or in support of or against any ballot initiative." § 44-2602(1)(e).

[100]Ysursa v. Pocatello Educ. Ass'n, 555 U.S. 353 (2009).

[101]*Id.* at 361.

nonmember teachers cannot be forced to contribute to a union's political activities; fees must reflect only the costs of bargaining and contract administration.[102]

Although the Supreme Court has upheld fair share arrangements, they may not be permitted under some state laws. The Maine high court held that forced payment of dues was "tantamount to coercion toward membership."[103] The Maine statute ensures employees the right to join a union *voluntarily*, and the court interpreted this provision as including the right to *refrain* from joining. Similarly, the Vermont Supreme Court held that fees were prohibited under the Vermont Labor Relations for Teachers Act, which specified that teachers have the right to join or not to join, assist, or participate in a labor organization.[104]

Exclusive Privileges

The designated employee bargaining representative gains security through negotiating exclusive rights or privileges, such as dues checkoff, the use of the school mail systems, and access to school facilities. Although exclusive arrangements strengthen the majority union and may make it difficult for minority unions to survive, courts often support such arrangements as a means of promoting labor peace and ensuring efficient operation of the school system.

Dues Checkoff. The exclusive privilege most often included in collective bargaining contracts is dues checkoff, a provision that authorizes employers to deduct union dues and other fees when authorized by employees. Over half of the states with public employee bargaining laws specify dues checkoff as a mandatory subject for bargaining. The Supreme Court, however, has held that **employee unions have no constitutional right to payroll deductions.**[105] The Fourth Circuit ruled that state legislation permitting payroll deductions for charitable organizations but not labor unions was not an infringement of the First Amendment; the law did not deny the union members the right to associate, speak, publish, recruit members, or express their views.[106] Unless prohibited by state law, checkoff rights can be reserved for the exclusive bargaining unit and denied to rival unions.

---

[102]The Supreme Court ruled in 2007 that a state law requiring unions to obtain affirmative authorization from nonmembers prior to spending agency fees for election-related purposes is constitutional. The state gave the unions the right to collect the fees and could also place limitations on their use. Davenport v. Wash. Educ. Ass'n, 551 U.S. 177 (2007); *see also* Knox v. Serv. Emps. Int'l Union, 132 S. Ct. 2277 (2012) (finding that the union infringed on nonmembers' First Amendment rights by imposing an additional mandatory special fee for political purposes without informing the employees; such an assessment requires notice to the employees and affirmative consent from nonmembers).

[103]Churchill v. Sch. Adm'r Dist. No. 49 Teachers Ass'n, 380 A.2d 186, 192 (Me. 1977).

[104]Weissenstein v. Burlington Bd. of Sch. Comm'rs, 543 A.2d 691 (Vt. 1988). *But see* Nashua Teachers Union v. Nashua Sch. Dist., 707 A.2d 448 (N.H. 1998) (interpreting a state law that permits negotiation of "other terms and conditions of employment" as authorizing agency fees to promote labor peace).

[105]City of Charlotte v. Local 660, Int'l Ass'n of Firefighters, 426 U.S. 283 (1976).

[106]S.C. Educ. Ass'n v. Campbell, 883 F.2d 1251 (4th Cir. 1989).

State laws also may place other restrictions on unions' request for the use of the school district's payroll deduction system. The Michigan Education Association (MEA) entered into agreements with school districts across the state requiring the districts to administrator a payroll deduction plan for members to contribute to its political action committee (MEA-PAC). The deductions were challenged as a violation of the Michigan Campaign Finance Act, which prohibits public entities from using any public funds to make a contribution or expenditure for political purposes.[107] The Michigan Supreme Court declared that the payroll deductions to MEA-PAC were prohibited because they constituted a *contribution* as well as an *expenditure* in support of the MEA-PAC's partisan political activities related to elections and legislative and policy initiatives.

Use of School Mail Facilities.   Often unions negotiate *exclusive* access to the internal school mail system, which denies rival unions the right to use teachers' mailboxes. The Supreme Court clarified the constitutionality of exclusive use in an Indiana case where the negotiated agreement between the bargaining representative and an Indiana school board denied all rival unions access to the interschool mail system and teacher mailboxes.[108] One union challenged the agreement as a violation of the First and Fourteenth Amendments. The Supreme Court upheld the arrangement, reasoning that the First Amendment does not require "equivalent access to all parts of a school building in which some form of communicative activity occurs."[109] **The Court concluded that the school mail facility was not a public forum for communication, and thereby its use could be restricted to official school business.** The fact that several community groups (e.g., Boy Scouts, civic organizations) used the school mail system did not create a public forum. The Court noted that, even if such access by community groups created a limited public forum, access would be extended only to similar groups—not to labor organizations. The Court's emphasis on the availability of alternative channels of communication (e.g., bulletin boards and meeting facilities), however, indicates that total exclusion of rival unions would not be permitted.

Exclusive Recognition.   In most states, school boards negotiate only with the designated bargaining representative. Under this exclusive recognition, other unions and teacher groups can be denied the right to engage in official exchanges with an employer. The Supreme Court has held that nonmembers of a bargaining unit or members who disagree with the views of the representative have no constitutional right "to force the government to listen to their views."[110] The Court concluded that a Minnesota statute requiring employers to "meet and confer" only with the designated bargaining representative did not violate other employees' speech or associational rights as public employees or as citizens, because these sessions were not a public forum. According to the Court, "the Constitution does not

---

[107]Mich. Educ. Ass'n v. Sec'y of State, 801 N.W.2d 35 (Mich. 2011). *See* MICH. COMP. LAWS § 169.257(1) (2012).

[108]Perry Educ. Ass'n v. Perry Local Educators' Ass'n, 460 U.S. 37 (1983); *see also* San Leandro Teachers Ass'n v. Governing Bd., 209 P.3d 73 (Cal. 2009) (ruling that state law prohibits unions from using school mailboxes to distribute political endorsement information; the contested law does not violate the state and federal constitutions).

[109]*Perry Educ. Ass'n*, 460 U.S. at 44.

[110]Minn. State Bd. for Cmty. Colls. v. Knight, 465 U.S. 271, 283 (1984).

grant to members of the public generally a right to be heard by public bodies making decisions of policy."[111]

However, in a public forum, such as a school board meeting, **a nonunion teacher has a constitutional right to address the public employer, even concerning a subject of negotiation.** The Supreme Court concluded that a Wisconsin nonunion teacher had the right to express concerns to the school board.[112] In this case, negotiation between the board and union had reached a deadlock on the issue of an agency shop provision. A nonunion teacher, representing a minority group of teachers, addressed the board at a regular public meeting and requested postponement of a decision until further study of the proposal. The Court reasoned that the teacher was not attempting to negotiate, but merely was speaking on an important issue before the board—a right every U.S. citizen possesses.

Grievances

Disputes concerning employee rights under the terms of a collective bargaining agreement are resolved through the negotiated grievance procedures, which generally must be exhausted before pursuing review by state labor relations boards or courts. The exhaustion requirement ensures the integrity of the collective bargaining process, encouraging orderly and efficient dispute resolution at the local level. Grievance procedures usually provide for a neutral third party, generally an arbitrator, to conduct a hearing and render a decision. *Grievance* **arbitration, which addresses enforcement of contract rights, differs from** *interest* **arbitration, which may take place in resolving an impasse between parties in the bargaining process.**

Depending on state law and the negotiated contract, grievance arbitration decisions may be advisory or binding. Public employers, adhering to the doctrine of the sovereign power of government, have been reluctant to agree to procedures that might result in a loss of public authority. Allowing grievance procedures to include final decision making by a third party significantly lessens a school board's power, effectively equating the positions of the teachers' organization and the school board. Nevertheless, as bargaining has expanded, legislative bodies have favored binding arbitration to settle labor disputes. About half of the states have enacted laws permitting school boards to negotiate grievance procedures with binding arbitration, and several states require binding arbitration as the final step in the grievance procedure.[113] With the widespread acceptance of grievance arbitration, it has become one of the most contested areas in collective bargaining. Suits have challenged the arbitrator's authority to render decisions in specific disputes as well as the authority to provide certain remedies.[114]

---

[111]*Id.*

[112]City of Madison v. Wis. Emp't Relations Comm'n, 429 U.S. 167 (1976).

[113]Among the few states requiring binding grievance arbitration are Alaska, Florida, Illinois, Minnesota, and Pennsylvania. *See In re* Silverstein, 37 A.3d 382 (N.H. 2012) (finding that the state labor board had no authority to review a grievance under a bargaining contract that contained a final and binding grievance process within the district).

[114]*See, e.g.*, United Teachers of L.A. v. L.A. Unified Sch. Dist., No. S177403, 2012 Cal. LEXIS 6454 (Cal. June 28, 2012) (charter school petition); Kalispell Educ. Ass'n v. Bd. of Trs., 255 P.3d 199 (Mont. 2011) (teacher contract); *In re* Haessig and Oswego City Sch. Dist., 936 N.Y.S.2d 442 (App. Div. 2011) (teacher class loads).

Negotiation Impasse

An impasse occurs in bargaining when an agreement cannot be reached and neither party will compromise. When negotiations reach such a stalemate, several options are available for resolution: mediation, fact-finding, and arbitration. As discussed below, the most effective means for resolving negotiation impasse—the strike—is not legally available to the majority of public employees. Most comprehensive state statutes address impasse procedures, with provisions ranging from allowing impasse procedures to be negotiated to mandating detailed steps that must be followed.

Mediation is often the first step to reopening negotiations. A neutral third party assists both sides in working toward an agreement. The mediator serves as a facilitator rather than a decision maker, thus enabling the school board's representative and the teachers' association jointly to reach an agreement. Mediation may be optional or required by law; the mediator is selected by the negotiation teams or, upon request, appointed by a public employee relations board.

Failure to reach agreement through mediation frequently results in fact-finding (often called advisory arbitration). The process may be mandated by law or may be entered into by mutual agreement of both parties. Fact-finding involves a third party investigating the causes for the dispute, collecting facts and testimony to clarify the dispute, and formulating a judgment. Because of the advisory nature of the process, proposed solutions are not binding on either party. However, since fact-finding reports are made available to the public, they provide an impetus to settle a contract that is not present in mediation.

In a number of states, the final step in impasse procedures is fact-finding, which may leave both parties without a satisfactory solution. A few states permit a third alternative— binding interest arbitration. This process is similar to fact-finding except that the decision of the arbitrator, related to the terms of the negotiated agreement, is binding on both parties. States that permit binding arbitration often place restrictions on its use. For example, Ohio, Oregon, and Rhode Island permit binding arbitration on matters of mutual consent;[115] Maine allows binding arbitration on all items except salaries, pensions, and insurance.[116]

Although it is argued that there can be no true collective bargaining without the right to withhold services, which characterizes the bargaining process in the private sector, **state statutes or common law prohibit most public school teachers from striking.** In those states that grant public employees a limited right to strike, certain conditions, specified by statute, must be met prior to the initiation of a work stoppage.[117] Designated conditions vary but usually include (1) the exhaustion of statutory mediation and fact-finding steps, (2) expiration of the contract, (3) a required waiting period before commencing the strike, (4) written notice of the union's intent to strike, and (5) evidence that the strike will not constitute a danger to public health or safety. In contrast to the few states permitting strikes,

---

[115]Ohio Rev. Code § 4117(C) (2012); Or. Rev. Stat. § 243.712 (2)(e) (2012); R.I. Gen. Laws § 28-9.3-9 (2012).

[116]26 Me. Rev. Stat. § 979.D(4) (2012).

[117]A statutory limited right to strike exists for public employees in Alaska, Colorado, Hawaii, Illinois, Minnesota, Montana, Ohio, Oregon, Pennsylvania, and Vermont. Alaska's law has been interpreted as prohibiting teachers from striking even though most other public employees are permitted to strike. Anchorage Educ. Ass'n v. Anchorage Sch. Dist., 648 P.2d 993 (Alaska 1982).

most states with public employee collective bargaining statutes have specific "no-strike" provisions, and courts have generally denied the right to strike unless affirmatively granted by the state.

A strike is more than simply a work stoppage; states define the term broadly to include a range of concerted activities such as work slowdowns, massive absences for "sick" days, and refusal to perform certain duties. For example, the Massachusetts high court found that refusing to perform customary activities, such as grading papers and preparing lesson plans after the end of the school day, constituted a strike.[118] A Missouri appellate court upheld the right of the St. Louis school superintendent to request documentation from 1,190 teachers that a "sick" day was not related to a labor dispute surrounding the negotiation of a new contract.[119] Without documentation from the teachers, the school district could deny payment for the day.

State laws, in addition to prohibiting work stoppages, usually identify penalties for involvement in strikes. Such penalties can include withholding compensation for strike days, prohibiting salary increases for designated periods of time (e.g., one year), and dismissing participants in the strike. Penalties for illegal strikes also are imposed on unions. Sanctions may include fines, decertification of the union, and loss of certain privileges such as dues checkoff.

Despite statutory prohibitions on strikes, some teachers, as well as other public employees, participate in work stoppages. Public employers can seek a court injunction against teachers who threaten to strike or initiate such action. Most courts have granted injunctions, concluding, as did the Supreme Court of Alaska, that the "illegality of the strike is a sufficient harm to justify injunctive relief."[120] Failure of teachers and unions to comply with such a restraining order can result in contempt-of-court charges and resulting fines and/or imprisonment. For example, in South Bend, Indiana, refusal to comply with an injunction resulted in a contempt-of-court charge and fines totalling $200,000 against two unions.[121] Teachers illegally participating in a strike are subject to court-imposed penalties and, in most states, to statutory penalties. Refusal of teachers to return to the classroom can result in dismissal.

CONCLUSION

Individual state laws, school board regulations, and master contracts must be consulted to determine the specific terms and conditions of teachers' employment. Except for certain limitations imposed by constitutional provisions and federal civil rights laws, state statutes govern public educators' employment. The state prescribes general requirements for licensure, contracts, tenure, and employment. Local school boards are vested with the power to appoint teachers and to establish professional and academic employment standards above

---

[118]Lenox Educ. Ass'n v. Labor Relations Comm'n, 471 N.E.2d 81 (Mass. 1984).

[119]Franklin v. St. Louis Bd. of Educ., 904 S.W.2d 433 (Mo. Ct. App. 1995).

[120]Anchorage Educ. Ass'n v. Anchorage Sch. Dist., 648 P.2d 993, 998 (Alaska 1982).

[121]Nat'l Educ. Ass'n-S. Bend v. S. Bend Cmty. Sch. Corp., 655 N.E.2d 516 (Ind. Ct. App. 1995).

the state minimums. Also, a school board may assign or transfer a teacher to any school or grade at its discretion, so long as the assignment is within the teacher's licensure area and not limited by contract terms. Under state laws, school boards confer tenure, which ensures that dismissal is based on adequate cause and accompanied by procedural due process.

In some states, employment is further defined by negotiated collective bargaining agreements (often called master contracts) between school boards and teacher unions, which limit the discretionary power of school boards to make unilateral employment decisions. Specific bargaining rights are conferred through state statutes or judicial interpretations of state constitutions, thus creating wide divergence in teachers' bargaining rights across states. All teachers have a constitutionally protected right to form and join a union, but school boards are not required to bargain with employee organizations unless mandated to do so by state law. Negotiated agreements typically include the specification of salary and fringe benefits, and also typically address management and association rights, grievance procedures, employee evaluations, and procedural due process for employee discipline and reduction-in-force.

POINTS TO PONDER

1. After a two-year recruitment effort, a prominent, successful basketball coach moved across the state to accept a position to coach the boys' varsity basketball team and teach science in a well-known high school program. His failure to produce a championship basketball team led the school board to terminate his coaching contract four years later. Although he retained his teaching position, he challenged the board's decision, arguing that he was recruited primarily to coach basketball and that he had moved to the community, at great expense, for the coaching opportunity. What are the teacher-coach's legal rights?

2. You have been offered employment in a school district for next fall. With the offer of employment, the superintendent notes several requirements that must be met prior to final school board approval. In addition to the typical physical examination, the board requires that all new appointees consent to fingerprinting, a criminal records check, and a drug test. Do any of these requirements implicate protected privacy rights?

3. A high school principal refused to appoint a teacher, a former president of the teachers union, as chair of the history department. The teacher questioned the decision, claiming that the denial was based on her union activities. What are the teacher's protected rights?

4. Invoking the state Freedom of Information Act, a group calling itself Concerned Citizens for Improving Our Schools requested extensive financial data as well as personnel data from the local school district. Teachers objected to the release of personal data related to their sick leave records, teaching licenses, and annual evaluations. Does this request violate teachers' privacy rights? How do freedom of information laws affect these privacy rights?

5. After several weeks of noticing bruises on a ten-year-old boy, a teacher expressed her concern to the principal. The principal responded that she had no cause to worry, particularly since the boy's parents were prominent citizens in the community. What is the teacher's legal responsibility in this situation?

Report! Mandatory Reporting

CHAPTER TEN

TEACHERS' SUBSTANTIVE CONSTITUTIONAL RIGHTS

It is clear that teachers do not leave their constitutional rights at the schoolhouse gate. Yet limitations may be placed on the exercise of these rights because of the special context of the school environment. For teachers, it becomes difficult to navigate through what is protected and what can be restricted. This chapter presents an overview of the scope of teachers' constitutional rights as defined by the judiciary in connection with free expression, academic freedom, freedom of association, freedom of choice in appearance, and privacy rights. Some of the cases do not involve school situations, but the legal principles apply to all public employees.

FREEDOM OF EXPRESSION

Public employees' comments on matters of public concern are protected expression if they are made as a citizen and not pursuant to official job duties.

Until the mid-twentieth century, it was generally accepted that public school teachers could be dismissed or disciplined for expressing views considered objectionable by the school board. The private-sector practice of firing such employees was assumed to apply to public employment as well. Since the late 1960s, however, the Supreme Court has recognized that free expression rights are not forfeited by accepting public school employment, even though such rights must be weighed against the school district's interest in maintaining effective and efficient schools. This section reviews the evolution of legal principles and their application to specific school situations.

Legal Principles

Similar to student free speech cases, an initial determination must be made regarding whether the public employee's claim involves expression *at all*. An action constitutes expression for First Amendment purposes only if it attempts "to convey a particularized message" that will likely be understood by those receiving the message.[1] For example, a teacher's action in scheduling a student's therapy sessions and attending those sessions did not involve intent to convey any message deserving First Amendment protection.[2]

In the landmark 1968 decision, *Pickering v. Board of Education*, the Supreme Court recognized that teachers have a First Amendment right to air their views on matters of public concern.[3] Pickering wrote a letter to a local newspaper, criticizing the school board's fiscal policies, especially the allocation of funds between the education and athletic programs. The school board dismissed Pickering because of the letter, which included false statements allegedly damaging the reputations of school board members and district administrators, and the Illinois courts upheld his dismissal.

Reversing the state courts, the U.S. Supreme Court first identified expression pertaining to matters of public concern as constitutionally protected and reasoned that the funding and allocation issues raised by Pickering were clearly questions of public interest requiring free and open debate. **The Court then applied a balancing test, weighing the teacher's interest in expressing his views on public issues against the school board's interest in providing educational services.** The Court recognized that the school board would prevail if Pickering's exercise of protected expression jeopardized his classroom performance, relationships with his immediate supervisor or coworkers, or school operations. Concluding that Pickering's letter did not have a detrimental effect in any of these areas, the Court found no justification for limiting his contribution to public debate. Indeed, the Court noted that a teacher's role provides a special vantage point from which to formulate an informed opinion on the allocation of school district funds, thus making it essential for teachers to be able to speak about public issues without fear of reprisal, unless false statements are intentionally or recklessly made.[4]

In 1977, the Supreme Court in *Mt. Healthy City School District v. Doyle* established the principle that a public educator can be disciplined or dismissed if sufficient cause exists *independent* of the exercise of protected speech. In this case, a school board voted not to renew the contract of a nontenured teacher who had made a telephone call to a local radio station to comment on a proposed teacher grooming code. The teacher had been involved in several previous incidents, but in not renewing his contract, the board cited "lack of tact in handling professional matters" with reference only to the radio call and obscene gestures made to several female students.[5] The lower courts ruled in favor of the teacher, but the Supreme Court reversed and remanded the case. The Court held that on remand, the **burden of proof is on the employee to show that the speech was**

[handwritten in left margin: Pickering Test]

[handwritten in left margin: Mt. Healthy Standard ✗]

---

[1]Texas v. Johnson, 491 U.S. 397, 404 (1989). Conduct that does not possess sufficient communicative elements is not shielded by the First Amendment.

[2]*See* Montanye v. Wissahickon Sch. Dist., 218 F. App'x 126 (3d Cir. 2007).

[3]391 U.S. 563 (1968); *see also* Givhan v. W. Line Consol. Sch. Dist., 439 U.S. 410 (1979) (concluding that so long as the expression pertains to matters of public concern, rather than personal grievances, statements made in private or through a public medium are constitutionally protected; the forum where the expression occurs does not determine whether it is of public or private interest).

[4]*Pickering*, 391 U.S. at 572, 574.

[5]429 U.S. 274, 282 (1977).

constitutionally protected and was a substantial or motivating factor in the school board's adverse action. Once established, the burden then shifts to the school board to show by a preponderance of evidence that it would have reached the same decision in the absence of the teacher's exercise of protected speech. The Court reasoned that protected expression should not place a public employee in a better or worse position with regard to continued employment. On remand, the board established that there were sufficient grounds other than the radio station call to justify the teacher's nonrenewal.[6]

Connick principle (handwritten margin note)

In a significant 1983 decision, *Connick v. Myers*, the Supreme Court narrowed the circumstances under which public employees can prevail in free expression cases.[7] The case involved an assistant district attorney, dissatisfied with her proposed transfer, who circulated among coworkers a questionnaire concerning office operations and morale and was subsequently terminated. The Court ruled that the questionnaire related primarily to a personal employment grievance, which is not protected by the First Amendment, rather than to matters of public interest. Of particular importance was the Court's conclusion that **the *form* and *context* as well as the *content* of the expression should be considered in assessing whether it relates to public matters.**

Garcetti principle (handwritten margin note)

In 2006, the Supreme Court decided *Garcetti v. Ceballos*, adding another threshold question in assessing constitutional protection of public employees' expression and making it even more difficult for public employees to prevail on claims that their expression rights have been abridged (see Figure 10.1).[8] The Court established a bright-line rule that expression pursuant to official job responsibilities is not protected. **Thus, whether the employee is speaking as a private citizen or as an employee is the first consideration, because if speaking as an employee, there is no further constitutional assessment.**

In *Garcetti*, the Supreme Court ruled that the district attorney's office did not impair the free speech rights of Ceballos, an assistant district attorney, by allegedly denying him a promotion and retaliating against him in other ways for writing a memorandum indicating that the arresting deputy sheriff may have lied in the search warrant affidavit in a criminal case. The Supreme Court reasoned that Ceballos was speaking about a task he was paid to perform and concluded that "when public employees make statements pursuant to their official duties . . . the Constitution does not insulate their communications from employer discipline."[9] The majority reiterated that the forum where the comments were made was not the central consideration, but rather the controlling factor was whether the expression occurred as part of official responsibilities.[10]

---

[6]Doyle v. Mt. Healthy City Sch. Dist., 670 F.2d 59 (6th Cir. 1982).

[7]461 U.S. 138 (1983). *See also* Waters v. Churchill, 511 U.S. 661 (1994) (concluding that the government employer can reach its factual conclusions without being held to the evidentiary rules followed by courts; as long as the employer conducts an investigation and acts in good faith, it can discharge an employee for remarks *believed* to have been made); Rankin v. McPherson, 483 U.S. 378 (1987) (assessing the context, form, and content of a public employee's pejorative statement to a coworker following the assassination attempt on President Reagan and finding no basis for dismissal in the absence of interference with work relationships or performance).

[8]547 U.S. 410 (2006).

[9]*Id.* at 421.

[10]*Id.* at 419–24. But the Court specifically left open whether its analysis would apply to speech related to instruction. *Id.* at 425.

FIGURE 10.1   Analyzing Public Educators' Expression Rights

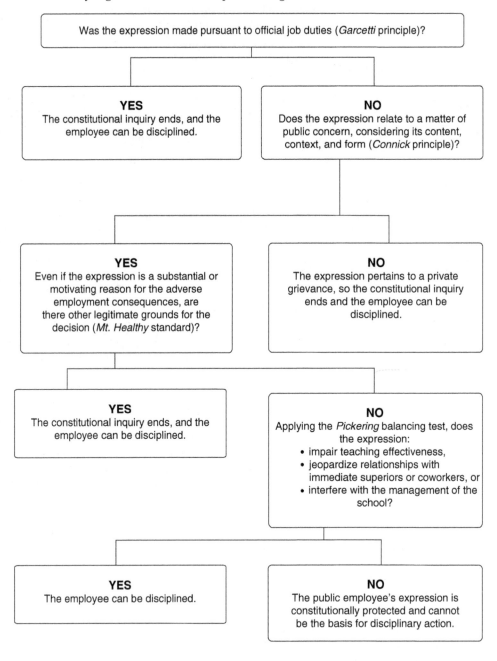

Application of the Legal Principles

In the majority of cases, public educators have challenged reprisals for their speech outside the classroom. Teachers' expression on the Internet has also been scrutinized by school districts. In addition, during the past couple of decades, educators' classroom expression has evoked litigation under the Free Speech Clause.

Expression Outside the Classroom.   During the 1970s and early 1980s, courts relied on the *Pickering* guidelines in striking down a variety of restrictions on teachers' rights to express views on matters of public interest. Since the early 1980s, however, courts have seemed increasingly inclined to view teachers' and other public employees' expression as relating to *private* employment disputes rather than to matters of public concern. Many courts relied on *Connick*[11] in broadly interpreting what falls under the category of unprotected private grievances. To illustrate, courts considered the following types of expression to be unprotected: discussing salaries during a lunch break;[12] filing a grievance about being assigned a job-sharing teaching position;[13] accusing the superintendent of inciting student disturbances;[14] sending sarcastic, critical memoranda to school officials;[15] protesting unfavorable performance evaluations;[16] criticizing harassment and oppression at the high school in a faculty newsletter;[17] commenting about class size and lack of discipline;[18] and complaining about the pace of an investigation into a school disciplinary matter.[19]

The *Garcetti* decision has added another initial consideration in deciding whether a public employee's expression will evoke the *Pickering* balancing test (see Figure 10.1). **If the expression is made pursuant to official job responsibilities, it is not protected, and it is thus unnecessary to establish that the expression pertains to a private grievance or has a negative impact on agency operations.** The content of the expression appeared to be the crucial consideration prior to the *Garcetti* ruling, but the role of the speaker now seems to trump the content. The broad protection once given to public educators' expression under *Pickering* currently is available only if the expression (1) does not occur pursuant to official duties, (2) relates to a public concern (considering its context and form as well as its content), and (3) is the motivating factor in the adverse employment action. *Pickering* has not been overturned, but far fewer circumstances trigger its balancing test.

In post-*Garcetti* decisions rejecting First Amendment claims, courts have tended to focus on whether the expression was made pursuant to job responsibilities. Whistleblowers

---

[11]461 U.S. 138 (1983).

[12]Koehn v. Indian Hills Cmty. Coll., 371 F.3d 394 (8th Cir. 2004); *see also* Bouma v. Trent, No. 10-0267, 2010 U.S. Dist. LEXIS 37565 (D. Ariz. Apr. 14, 2010) (finding that a complaint about a salary schedule was not a matter of public concern).

[13]Renfroe v. Kirkpatrick, 722 F.2d 714 (11th Cir. 1984).

[14]Stevenson v. Lower Marion Cnty. Sch. Dist. No. 3, 327 S.E.2d 656 (S.C. 1985).

[15]Hesse v. Bd. of Educ., 848 F.2d 748 (7th Cir. 1988).

[16]Day v. S. Park Indep. Sch. Dist., 768 F.2d 696 (5th Cir. 1985).

[17]Sanguigni v. Pittsburgh Bd. of Educ., 968 F.2d 393 (3d Cir. 1992).

[18]Cliff v. Bd. of Sch. Comm'rs of the City of Indianapolis, 42 F.3d 403 (7th Cir. 1995).

[19]Lucero v. Nettle Creek Sch. Corp., 566 F.3d 720 (7th Cir. 2009).

have not been as successful in securing legal redress for retaliation as they were prior to *Garcetti*. For example, the Fifth Circuit held that an athletic director who wrote a letter to the school's office manager about appropriations for athletic activities was speaking pursuant to his official duties and could not claim retaliation for being removed from the athletic director position and for his contract not being renewed.[20] The Eleventh Circuit similarly found that a teacher's questions about the fairness of cheerleading tryouts pertained to her duties as a cheerleading sponsor and were not protected expression relating to educational quality issues, as she claimed.[21] The Tenth Circuit also ruled that a superintendent's comments about the Head Start program and possible violations of federal law were not protected as they were made in the course of her job duties.[22] A Delaware federal district court held that a school psychologist's complaints about the school's noncompliance with the Individuals with Disabilities Education Act pertained to his job assignment and were not protected by the First Amendment.[23] A New York federal district court found that an office assistant's complaints to a supervisor about another school official who had encouraged her to misappropriate federal funds were made pursuant to her official job duties and thus were not protected by the First Amendment.[24]

Even where whistle-blowing is not at issue, public school personnel often have not prevailed in their free speech claims because courts have concluded that the expression at issue was pursuant to official job duties. To illustrate, the Eleventh Circuit rejected a terminated principal's claim that a Florida school board violated his First Amendment speech and association rights and his right to petition the government for redress of grievances.[25] He claimed that he was unconstitutionally terminated in retaliation for urging his teachers to support conversion of their school to a charter school. Noting that *Garcetti* shifted the threshold question from whether the employee is speaking on a matter of public concern to whether the employee is speaking as a private citizen, the Eleventh Circuit concluded that the principal was speaking in his professional role in seeking charter school status. Thus, his expression was not protected and could be the basis for dismissal. The court further found no evidence that the school board violated the principal's rights to association or to petition the government.

Likewise, the Sixth Circuit affirmed summary judgment in favor of the school district in a case involving a teacher who complained to her supervisors that her special education caseload violated the law. The court found that this complaint was not protected because the speech was made pursuant to her official job duties as a teacher.[26] The Second

---

[20]Williams v. Dallas Indep. Sch. Dist., 480 F.3d 689 (5th Cir. 2007).

[21]Gilder-Lucas v. Elmore Cnty. Bd. of Educ., 186 F. App'x 885 (11th Cir. 2006).

[22]Casey v. W. Las Vegas Indep. Sch. Dist., 473 F.3d 1323 (10th Cir. 2007) (holding, however, that her comments about the New Mexico Open Meetings Act were outside the scope of her job, so her claim of retaliation for those comments may be legally viable).

[23]Houlihan v. Sussex Tech. Sch. Dist., 461 F. Supp. 2d 252 (D. Del. 2006) (holding, however, that the school psychologist stated a valid cause of action for retaliation under the federal Rehabilitation Act, so the school district's motion to dismiss her claim under this law was denied).

[24]Williams v. Bd. of Educ., No. 07-cv-98c, 2012 U.S. Dist. LEXIS 36936 (W.D.N.Y. May 15, 2012).

[25]D'Angelo v. Sch. Bd., 497 F.3d 1203 (11th Cir. 2007).

[26]Fox v. Traverse City Area Pub. Schs., 605 F.3d 345 (6th Cir. 2010), *cert. denied*, 131 S. Ct. 643 (2010).

Circuit found that a teacher's complaint about an assistant principal forging her signature on a teaching evaluation form was not protected because the issue had no "practical significance to the general public."[27] In another Second Circuit case, a teacher's filing of a union grievance, after a school administrator failed to discipline a student who threw books at the teacher during class, was not protected speech because it was related to the teacher's "core duties" of "maintaining class discipline."[28]

Some employees, however, have succeeded in their expression claims in post-*Garcetti* cases. For example, the Sixth Circuit ruled in favor of a superintendent who claimed that he was not named Director of Schools when the superintendent position was abolished because he had expressed his view that associating with homosexuals is not immoral or improper, which the court considered a matter of public concern. The court reasoned that board members were not entitled to qualified immunity because the superintendent's expression rights were clearly established.[29] The Tenth Circuit ruled in favor of a speech-language pathologist who alleged First Amendment retaliation when adverse action was taken against her for advocating for students with disabilities in the school. The appellate court did not find that her advocacy was made pursuant to her official duties—her complaints went beyond her administrators and were made to the state board, which was not done pursuant to her official job duties.[30] The Tenth Circuit identified two factors to help determine if the employee is speaking as a private citizen as opposed to speaking pursuant to an official job duty: (1) the employee's job duties do not relate to the reporting of any wrongdoing, and (2) the employee went outside the chain of command. The court found that the speech pathologist's complaint satisfied both factors.

Even if protected speech is involved, courts have relied on *Mt. Healthy* to uphold terminations or transfers where other legitimate reasons justify the personnel actions. In an illustrative case, a principal who gave a speech at a public hearing expressing opposition to closing a school was demoted to a teaching position. He claimed retaliation for his protected expression, but a Kentucky federal court found no evidence that the speech was the motivating factor in the demotion.[31] The Seventh Circuit also rejected a teacher's challenge to disciplinary action for her critical comments pertaining to the need for additional textbooks at her school. The court ruled that the teacher failed to prove that her speech was a substantial or motivating factor in the disciplinary action, given the well-documented incidents of the teacher's misconduct or insubordination.[32] The Tenth Circuit similarly found that a director of bilingual education could not establish that speaking about the program's noncompliance with state guidelines and writing a letter to the editor of the local

---

[27]Nagle v. Marron, 663 F.3d 100, 107 (2d Cir. 2011) (holding, however, that the teacher's complaints about the abuse of students was speech that pertained to a matter of public concern and was protected).

[28]Weintraub v. Bd. of Educ., 593 F.3d 196, 198 (2d Cir. 2010), *cert. denied*, 131 S. Ct. 444 (2010).

[29]Scarbrough v. Morgan Cnty. Bd. of Educ., 470 F.3d 250 (6th Cir. 2006).

[30]Reinhardt v. Albuquerque Pub. Schs., 595 F.3d 1126 (10th Cir. 2010).

[31]Painter v. Campbell Cnty. Bd. of Educ., 417 F. Supp. 2d 854 (E.D. Ky. 2006).

[32]Smith v. Dunn, 368 F.3d 705 (7th Cir. 2004).

newspaper were the motivating factors in her termination and held instead that poor job performance justified the action.[33]

School authorities cannot rely on *Mt. Healthy* to justify termination or other disciplinary action if the school officials' stated reasons for personnel decisions are merely a pretext to restrict protected expression. For example, a federal district court denied a school district's motion for summary judgment because an administrator, who was allegedly fired for not complying with the district's school improvement plan, may have actually been fired in retaliation for complaining to the superintendent that many of the elementary school classrooms were racially segregated.[34]

Once determined that expression is protected, the employee then has the burden of demonstrating that it was a key factor in the dismissal or disciplinary decision. **Even if the employee can establish that expression on matters of public concern was the sole basis for the adverse action, the public employer still may prevail under the *Pickering* balancing test by showing that its interests in protecting the public agency outweigh the individual's free speech rights.**[35]

Courts also have upheld reasonable time, place, and manner regulations on educators' expression. Such restrictions must not be based on the content of the speech, and they must serve significant governmental interests and leave alternative communication channels open. Although prior restraints on educators' expression are legally vulnerable, reasonable time, place, and manner restrictions will be upheld if justified to prevent a disruption of the educational environment and if other avenues are available for employees to express their views.

Internet Speech

Educators' speech on social networking sites has been the subject of recent litigation. In some cases, courts have relied on *Garcetti* if the teacher wrote something on the Internet that was pursuant to his or her job responsibilities. For speech outside the scope of one's job duties, *Pickering* and *Connick* have also been used. For example, when a teacher made disparaging and unsubstantiated remarks about coworkers on his website, the West Virginia Supreme Court held that the teacher had no First Amendment right at stake because his statements both on and off the website would not be considered matters of public concern. The court further noted that the teacher's comments could have destroyed feelings of loyalty and confidence among his colleagues.[36]

The Ninth Circuit Court of Appeals also found that a curriculum specialist's postings on her personal blog, which included inappropriate comments about colleagues, were not

---

[33]Deschenie v. Bd. of Educ., 473 F.3d 1271 (10th Cir. 2007) (holding that the time between the expression and termination was too attenuated to show a causal connection).

[34]Howell v. Marion Sch. Dist. 1, No. 4:07:cv-1811, 2009 U.S. Dist. LEXIS 22723 (D.S.C. Mar. 19, 2009).

[35]*See* Fales v. Garst, 235 F.3d 1122 (8th Cir. 2001) (finding teachers' interests in speaking about incidents with special education students was outweighed by school district's interest in efficiently administering the middle school, given the upheaval caused by the expression).

[36]Alderman v. Pocahontas Cnty. Bd. of Educ., 675 S.E.2d 907 (W.Va. 2009).

protected speech. The court observed that although some of the comments on her blog may have related to a matter of public concern, the comments interfered with her relationships at school.[37] In another case, a teacher alleged that school officials violated his First Amendment rights when his contract was not renewed as a result of comments he had posted on his Myspace page. Holding in favor of the school district, the federal district court found no First Amendment violation because there was no connection between the teacher's postings and his dismissal. The court reasoned that even if there had been such a connection, the school district could have taken the same adverse actions because the teacher's speech was likely to disrupt school activities.[38]

Student teachers should also be cautious when using social networking sites. In a Pennsylvania case, a federal district court denied a student teacher injunctive relief in a case involving postings on her Myspace page. The student teacher was not awarded teacher certification after she received unsatisfactory ratings during student teaching as a result of her unprofessionalism involving her Myspace page that her students had viewed. The court determined that her postings related to only personal matters and did not touch upon matters of public concern.[39]

Problems with teachers posting inappropriate commentary on their Facebook pages has led some states to consider laws to regulate employees' Internet speech. Of course, such laws have created a backlash with employees arguing that the laws abridge First Amendment rights. Missouri had passed a law prohibiting teachers and students from being friends on Facebook, but the law was later repealed as a result of First Amendment concerns.[40]

Some controversies have focused on other forms of electronic communication. The Fourth Circuit held that public employees do not have a free speech right to use state computers for purposes not related to the agency's business and upheld restrictions on state employees using such equipment to access sexually explicit Internet materials.[41] Also, the Fifth Circuit reiterated that a state university's internal mail system is not a public forum and thus declined to interfere with an institution's use of e-mail spam guards and cancellation of adjuncts' e-mail accounts during semesters they are not teaching.[42] And the Seventh Circuit concluded that a part-time university employee could be required to remove a quotation she affixed to work-related e-mail messages because the employer considered a word in the quotation to be vulgar and inappropriate for workplace language.[43]

---

[37]Richerson v. Beckon, 337 F. App'x 637 (9th Cir. 2009).

[38]Spanierman v. Hughes, 576 F. Supp. 2d 292 (D. Conn. 2008).

[39]Snyder v. Millersville Univ., No. 07-1660, 2008 U.S. Dist. LEXIS 97943 (E.D. Pa. Dec. 3, 2008).

[40]David A. Lieb, *Missouri Repeals Law Restricting Teacher-Student Internet and Facebook Interaction*, HUFFINGTON POST (Oct. 21, 2011), http://www.huffingtonpost.com/2011/10/21/missouri-repeals-law-rest_n_1025761.html.

[41]Urofsky v. Gilmore, 216 F.3d 401 (4th Cir. 2000).

[42]Faculty Rights Coal. v. Shahrokhi, 204 F. App'x 416 (5th Cir. 2006); *see also* Educ. Minn. Lakeville v. Indep. Sch. Dist. No. 194, 341 F. Supp. 2d 1070 (D. Minn. 2004) (rejecting union's argument that the school district's policy prohibiting the use of internal communication channels to distribute literature endorsing political candidates violated the First Amendment).

[43]Pichelmann v. Madsen, 31 F. App'x 322 (7th Cir. 2002).

Classroom Expression

Traditionally, it has been assumed that restrictions can be placed on teachers' expressing their personal views to captive student audiences in their classrooms—a nonpublic forum. Since 1988, many courts have applied *Hazelwood v. Kuhlmeier* to assess the constitutionality of teachers' classroom expression of personal opinions,[44] holding that such expression could be curtailed for legitimate pedagogical reasons, an easy standard for school districts to satisfy. For example, the First Circuit held that a teacher's discussion of aborting fetuses with Down syndrome could be censored, noting that the school board may limit a teacher's classroom expression in the interest of promoting educational goals.[45] The Tenth Circuit relied on *Kuhlmeier* in upholding disciplinary action against a teacher who made comments during class about rumors that two students had engaged in sexual intercourse on the school tennis court during lunch hour, reasoning that the ninth-grade government class was not a public forum.[46] Also, a Missouri federal district court upheld termination of a teacher for making disparaging classroom comments about interracial relationships, finding no protected expression and noting that the teacher was aware of the district's anti-harassment policy.[47]

In several cases, public school teachers have not prevailed in their efforts to express their views via materials posted in their classrooms or on the adjacent hall walls. To illustrate, the Ninth Circuit agreed with the decision of school authorities to censor material a teacher had posted outside his classroom that denounced homosexuality and extolled traditional family values to offset the school district's materials recognizing Gay and Lesbian Awareness Month.[48] Reasoning that the teacher was speaking for the school, the court concluded that teachers are not entitled to express views in the classroom that are counter to the adopted curriculum. As discussed in Chapter 3, the Ninth Circuit held also that a math teacher had no First Amendment right to display religious banners in his classroom, observing that a public school teacher may not present his personal views of the role of God in class.[49]

The Sixth Circuit seemed to depart from the prevailing trend when it upheld a teacher's right to invite a guest speaker (actor Woody Harrelson) and present information to her fifth-grade class on the industrial and environmental benefits of hemp. Even though the teacher was speaking as an employee, the court concluded that the content of her speech

[44]484 U.S. 260 (1988).

[45]Ward v. Hickey, 996 F.2d 448 (1st Cir. 1993).

[46]Miles v. Denver Pub. Schs., 944 F.2d 773 (10th Cir. 1991)

[47]Loeffelman v. Bd. of Educ., 134 S.W.3d 637 (Mo. Ct. App. 2004).

[48]Downs v. L.A. Unified Sch. Dist., 228 F.3d 1003 (9th Cir. 2000); *see also* Newton v. Slye, 116 F. Supp. 2d 677 (W.D. Va. 2000) (finding no First Amendment right for a teacher to post outside his classroom door the American Library Association's pamphlet listing banned books, which the principal and superintendent felt potentially compromised the school's family life education program and other initiatives).

[49]Johnson v. Poway Unified Sch. Dist., 658 F.3d 954 (9th Cir. 2011), *cert. denied*, 132 S. Ct. 1807 (2012); text accompanying note 41, Chapter 3; *see also* Lee v. York Cnty. Sch. Div., 484 F.3d 687 (4th Cir. 2007) (finding a school district did not violate a teacher's rights when it ordered him to remove religious material from classroom bulletin board).

involved political and social concerns in the community.[50] Thus, the court found genuine issues of material fact regarding whether the school district's proffered grounds for terminating the teacher based on insubordination, conduct unbecoming a teacher, and other grounds were a pretext for the dismissal based on protected expression. The court recognized that the school district's interest in efficient and harmonious school operations did not outweigh the teacher's interests in speaking to her students about an issue of substantial concern in the state.

It is unclear how the *Garcetti* ruling will affect litigation pertaining to classroom expression. Indeed, the *Garcetti* majority emphasized that "we need not, and for that reason do not, decide whether the analysis we conduct today would apply in the same manner to a case involving speech related to scholarship or teaching."[51] Thus, some ambiguity remains regarding whether courts will continue to apply *Hazelwood* or will rely on *Garcetti* in assessing teachers' expression pursuant to their instructional duties.[52]

Some federal appellate courts have relied on *Garcetti* in this regard. The Seventh Circuit ruled that classroom expression clearly is part of public educators' official duties and can be censored to protect the captive student audience.[53] Accordingly, the court ruled that the teacher's expression of negative views about the war in Iraq during a current events session was not constitutionally protected. The court reasoned that *Garcetti* directly applied in this case because the teacher's current event lesson was an assigned classroom task.

Also, a few lower courts have addressed classroom expression issues. For example, a teacher in Michigan alleged that he was retaliated against after he wore a T-shirt to school that contained a printed message about the teachers' union not being under contract. The federal district court held that the T-shirt worn in his classes caused or had the potential to cause disharmony in the workplace. Although recognizing that the issue of labor negotiations touches on a matter of public concern, the court found the school district's interest in ensuring a professional workplace outweighed the teacher's rights in this instance. The court noted that under *Garcetti*, "government employers, like private employers, need a significant degree of control over their employees' words and actions; without it, there would be little chance for the efficient provision of public services."[54]

Litigation over teachers' classroom comments seems likely to continue. Whether courts apply *Garcetti* or *Hazelwood* may have little practical significance, because teachers' classroom expression has always been subject to restrictions to protect students from proselytization.

---

[50]Cockrel v. Shelby Cnty. Sch. Dist., 270 F.3d 1036 (6th Cir. 2001).

[51]Garcetti v. Ceballos, 547 U.S. 410, 425 (2006).

[52]*See, e.g.*, Sheldon v. Dhillon, No. C-08-03438, 2009 U.S. Dist. LEXIS 110275, at *14 (N.D. Cal. Nov. 25, 2009) (applying *Hazelwood*, the court noted that the Ninth Circuit has not yet determined if *Garcetti* applies to classroom speech). *But see* Evans-Marshall v. Bd. of Educ., 624 F.3d 332 (6th Cir. 2010) (finding that *Garcetti* does extend to a teacher's classroom speech), *cert. denied*, 131 S. Ct. 3068 (2011).

[53]Mayer v. Monroe Cnty. Cmty. Sch. Corp., 474 F.3d 477 (7th Cir. 2007).

[54]Montle v. Westwood Heights Sch. Dist., 437 F. Supp. 2d 652, 654 (E.D. Mich. 2006); *see also* Caruso v. Massapequa Union Free Sch. Dist., 478 F. Supp. 2d 377 (E.D.N.Y. 2007) (denying school district's motion for summary judgment because issues of fact existed about whether *Garcetti* applied in case involving a teacher who displayed only a picture of George Bush in her classroom during an election year).

FREEDOM OF ASSOCIATION

A public educator's participation in political activities outside the classroom cannot be the basis for adverse employment decisions unless the employee has policy-making responsibilities or such activities negatively affect job performance.

Although freedom of association is not specifically addressed in the First Amendment, the Supreme Court has recognized that associational rights are "implicit in the freedoms of speech, assembly, and petition."[55] The Court has consistently declared that infringements on the right to associate for expressive purposes can be justified only by a compelling government interest, unrelated to suppressing ideas, which cannot be achieved through less restrictive means.[56] Accordingly, public educators cannot be disciplined for forming or joining political, labor, religious, or social organizations.

Associational activities can be limited, however, if they disrupt school operations or interfere with teachers' professional duties. This section presents an overview of teachers' association rights in connection with political affiliations and activities. Public educators' rights to intimate association are discussed in the section on privacy rights, and labor union issues are addressed in Chapter 9.

Political Affiliations

Conditioning public employment on partisan political affiliation has been controversial. Historically, the patronage system governed public employment; when the controlling political party changed, non-civil-service employees belonging to the defeated party lost their jobs.[57] The Supreme Court held that the constant threat of replacing non-policy-making individuals, who cannot undermine the administration's policies, was considered detrimental to government effectiveness and efficiency. The Court subsequently ruled that promotions, transfers, recalls after layoffs, and hiring decisions based on political affiliation violates the constitutional rights of non-policy-making employees.[58]

Despite being insulated from partisan politics, in some instances, public educators have asserted that employment decisions have been based on their party affiliation. In such cases, the school employee has the burden of substantiating that protected political affiliation was the motivating factor in the board's employment decision.[59] If an employee satisfies this burden, then the board must demonstrate by a preponderance of evidence that it would have reached the same decision in the absence of the political association.

[55]Healy v. James, 408 U.S. 169, 181 (1972).

[56]*See, e.g.,* NAACP v. Button, 371 U.S. 415 (1963).

[57]*See* Elrod v. Burns, 427 U.S. 347 (1976).

[58]*See* Rutan v. Republican Party, 497 U.S. 62 (1990).

[59]*See* Piazza v. Aponte Roque, 909 F.2d 35 (1st Cir. 1990) (finding that nonrenewal of teachers' aides because of their political party affiliation impaired associational rights).

Political Activity

Teachers, like all citizens, are guaranteed the right to participate in the political process. First Amendment association as well as free speech rights have been invoked to protect public educators in expressing political views, campaigning for candidates, and running for office.

Campaigning and Other Activities. Public employees are constitutionally protected from retaliation for political participation at the local, state, and federal levels. For example, the Sixth Circuit held that the coordinator of gifted education, which was not a policy-making position, could not be reassigned for the exercise of constitutionally protected political expression and association in actively supporting an unsuccessful superintendent candidate.[60] The superintendent did not demonstrate that political loyalty was essential to the duties of this position. Of course, public employees in policy-making positions may be vulnerable to adverse employment consequences for their political activities that may preclude an effective relationship with the school board.[61]

Political activity that would cause divisiveness within the school district can be restricted. A federal district court upheld a regulation that prohibits political campaign buttons in school buildings because of legitimate pedagogical concerns related to entanglement of public education with partisan politics.[62] The court observed that the board's regulation of the campaign buttons was based on good faith professional judgment. **Teachers cannot take advantage of their position of authority with an impressionable captive audience to impose their political views.**[63] However, if campaign issues are related to the class topic, a teacher can present election issues and candidates in a nonpartisan manner.

Holding Public Office. Certain categories of public employees have been prevented from running for political office. In 1973, the Supreme Court upheld a federal law (the Hatch Act) that prevents *federal* employees from holding formal positions in political parties, playing substantial roles in partisan campaigns, and running for partisan office.[64] The Court recognized that legitimate reasons exist for restricting political activities of public employees, such as the need to ensure impartial and effective government, to remove employees from political pressure, and to prevent employee selection based on political factors. In a companion case, the Court upheld an Oklahoma law forbidding classified civil servants from running for paid political offices.[65] Lower courts similarly have endorsed

---

[60]Hager v. Pike Cnty. Bd. of Educ., 286 F.3d 366 (6th Cir. 2002). *But see* Beattie v. Madison Cnty. Sch. Dist., 254 F.3d 595 (5th Cir. 2001) (finding insufficient causal link between employee's termination and her support for the nonincumbent candidate for school superintendent).

[61]*See, e.g.*, Dabbs v. Amos, 70 F.3d 1261 (4th Cir. 1995) (unpublished); Kinsey v. Salado Indep. Sch. Dist., 950 F.2d 988 (5th Cir. 1992).

[62]Weingarten v. Bd. of Educ., 680 F. Supp. 2d 595 (S.D.N.Y. 2010); *see also* Turlock Joint Elementary Sch. Dist. v. Pub. Emp't Relations Bd., 5 Cal. Rptr. 3d 308 (Ct. App. 2003) (concluding that teachers could be prohibited from wearing union buttons while delivering instruction).

[63]*See* Mayer v. Monroe Cnty. Cmty. Sch. Corp., 474 F.3d 477 (7th Cir. 2007).

[64]U.S. Civil Serv. Comm'n v. Nat'l Ass'n of Letter Carriers, 413 U.S. 548 (1973); 5 U.S.C. § 7324 (2012).

[65]Broadrick v. Oklahoma, 413 U.S. 601 (1973).

certain restrictions on state and municipal employees running for elective office.[66] Conversely, the Court struck down a school board policy requiring any school employee who became a candidate for public office to take a leave of absence.[67]

Laws or policies prohibiting *all* public employees from running for *any* political office have been struck down as overly broad.[68] Several courts have held that public educators, unlike public employees who are directly involved in the operation of governmental agencies, have the right to run for and hold public office. The Utah Supreme Court, for example, ruled that public school teachers and administrators were not disqualified from serving in the state legislature.[69]

Although school boards must respect employees' associational rights, they are obligated to ensure that the political activities of public school personnel do not adversely affect the school. Disciplinary actions can be imposed if educators neglect instructional duties to campaign for issues or candidates, use the classroom as a political forum, or disrupt school operations because of their political activities. But school boards must be certain that constraints imposed on employees' freedom of association are not based on mere disagreement with the political orientation of the activities.

PERSONAL APPEARANCE

School officials can place constraints on educators' personal apperance if there is a rational basis for such restrictions.

Historically, school boards often imposed rigid grooming restrictions on teachers. In the 1970s, such attempts to regulate teachers' appearance generated considerable litigation, as did grooming standards for students. Controversies have subsided for the most part, but a few constraints on school employees' appearance continue to be challenged.[70] School boards have defended their efforts to regulate teacher appearance on the perceived need to provide appropriate role models, set a proper tone in the classroom, and enforce similar appearance and dress codes for students. Teachers have contested these requirements as abridgments of their constitutionally protected privacy, liberty, and free expression rights.

Most courts since the mid-1970s have supported school officials in imposing reasonable grooming and dress restrictions on teachers.[71] For example, the Second Circuit upheld a Connecticut school board's requirement that all male teachers wear ties as a

---

[66]*See, e.g.*, Fletcher v. Marino, 882 F.2d 605 (2d Cir. 1989); Cranston Teachers Alliance v. Miele, 495 A.2d 233 (R.I. 1985).

[67]*See* Dougherty Cnty. Bd. of Educ. v. White, 439 U.S. 32 (1978).

[68]*See, e.g.*, *Cranston Teachers Alliance*, 495 A.2d 233.

[69]Jenkins v. Bishop, 589 P.2d 770 (Utah 1978) (per curiam).

[70]*See* Polk Cnty. Bd. of Educ. v. Polk Cnty. Educ. Ass'n, 139 S.W.3d 304 (Tenn. Ct. App. 2004) (holding that the adoption of an employee dress code may be a management prerogative, but its enforcement must be bargained with the teachers' association).

[71]*See, e.g.*, Kelley v. Johnson, 425 U.S. 238 (1976) (upholding a hair grooming regulation for police officers).

rational means to promote respect for authority, traditional values, and classroom discipline.[72] Because of the uniquely influential role of teachers, the court noted that they may be subjected to restrictions in their professional lives that otherwise would not be acceptable. Applying similar reasoning, the First Circuit upheld a school board's dismissal of a teacher for wearing short skirts.[73]

Restrictions will not be upheld, however, if found to be arbitrary, discriminatory, or unrelated to a legitimate governmental concern. To illustrate, the Seventh Circuit overturned a school bus driver's suspension after he violated a regulation prohibiting school bus drivers from wearing mustaches.[74] Finding no valid purpose for the policy, the court noted that its irrationality was exemplified by the fact that the bus driver also was a full-time teacher but was not suspended from his teaching position.

■ ■ ■ ■ ■

CONSTITUTIONAL PRIVACY RIGHTS

Sanctions cannot be imposed solely because school officials disapprove of a teacher's private conduct, but restrictions can be placed on unconventional behavior that is detrimental to job performance or harmful to students.

Public employees have asserted the right to be free from unwarranted governmental intrusions into their personal activities.[75] The U.S. Constitution does not explicitly enumerate personal privacy rights, but the Supreme Court has recognized that certain *implied* fundamental rights warrant constitutional protection because of their close relationship to explicit constitutional guarantees. For example, protected privacy rights have been interpreted as encompassing personal choices in matters such as marriage, contraception, sexual relations, procreation, family relationships, and child rearing.[76] Employment decisions cannot be based on relinquishing such rights without a compelling justification. Litigation covered in this section focuses on constitutional privacy claims initiated under the Fourth Amendment (protection against unreasonable searches and seizures), the Ninth Amendment (personal privacy as an unenumerated right reserved to the people),

---

[72]E. Hartford Educ. Ass'n v. Bd. of Educ., 562 F.2d 838 (2d Cir. 1977).

[73]Tardif v. Quinn, 545 F.2d 761 (1st Cir. 1976).

[74]Pence v. Rosenquist, 573 F.2d 395 (7th Cir. 1978); *see also* Nichol v. Arin Intermediate Unit 28, 268 F. Supp. 2d 536 (W.D. Pa. 2003) (upholding an instructional assistant's right to wear a small cross and reasoning that the state's religious garb statute was overtly adverse to religion because it singled out and punished only religious, and not secular, symbolic expression).

[75]Most states have laws giving employees access to their personnel files and safeguarding the confidentiality of the records.

[76]*See* Lawrence v. Texas, 539 U.S. 558 (2003); Roe v. Wade, 410 U.S. 113 (1973); Loving v. Virginia, 388 U.S. 1 (1967); Griswold v. Connecticut, 381 U.S. 479 (1965); Skinner v. Oklahoma, 316 U.S. 535 (1942); Pierce v. Soc'y of Sisters, 268 U.S. 510 (1925).

and the Fourteenth Amendment (equal protection rights and protection against state action impairing personal liberties without due process of law).

In some instances, public employees have asserted that governmental action has impaired their privacy right to intimate association related to creating and maintaining a family. To assess such claims, courts must weigh the employee's rights against the government's interests in promoting efficient public services. For example, public educators cannot be deprived of their jobs because of the politics or other activities of their partners or spouses. Recognizing a classified employee's First Amendment right to associate with her husband who disagreed with policies of the school system, the Sixth Circuit found an inference that the superintendent's nonrenewal recommendation was impermissibly based on the employee's marital relationship.[77] However, public educators cannot assert an association or privacy right to disregard anti-nepotism policies that prohibit teachers from reporting to their spouses or working in the same building as their spouses.

The Fifth Circuit recognized that a teacher's interest in breast-feeding her child at school during noninstructional time was sufficiently close to fundamental rights regarding family relationships and child rearing to trigger constitutional protection.[78] The court acknowledged, however, that trial courts must determine whether school boards' interests in avoiding disruption of the educational process, ensuring that teachers perform their duties without distraction, and avoiding liability for potential injuries are sufficiently compelling reasons to justify restrictions imposed on teachers' fundamental privacy interests. Accordingly, courts in some cases have concluded that governmental interests in ensuring the welfare of students override teachers' privacy interests.[79]

Search and Seizure

Public educators, like all citizens, are shielded by the Fourth Amendment against unreasonable governmental invasions of their person and property. This amendment requires police officers and other state agents to secure a search warrant (based on probable cause that evidence of a crime will be found) before conducting personal searches. The Supreme Court has not addressed teachers' rights in connection with searches initiated by public school authorities, but it has upheld warrantless personal searches of students based on *reasonable suspicion* that contraband detrimental to the educational process is concealed.[80]

N.J. vs. TLO

[77]Adkins v. Bd. of Educ., 982 F.2d 952 (6th Cir. 1993).

[78]Dike v. Sch. Bd., 650 F.2d 783 (5th Cir. 1981).

[79]*See, e.g.,* Flaskamp v. Dearborn Pub. Schs., 385 F.3d 935 (6th Cir. 2004) (upholding suspension and denial of tenure to a teacher who had an intimate relationship with a former student; the school board could prohibit such activity within a year or two of graduation, given the importance of deterring student/teacher sexual relationships); Strong v. Bd. of Educ., 902 F.2d 208 (2d Cir. 1990) (ruling teacher's rights were not violated when the school board required her to submit medical records after an extended medical absence); Daury v. Smith, 842 F.2d 9 (1st Cir. 1988) (requiring principal to undergo psychiatric examination before returning to work because there was reason to believe that the welfare of students was at stake).

[80]New Jersey v. T.L.O., 469 U.S. 325 (1985). See text accompanying note 184–186, Chapter 8, for a discussion of the reasonable suspicion standard.

While technology has eased communication in the workplace, it has also presented privacy issues for public employees. In 2010, the Supreme Court held that a police department's search of an officer's employer-provided pager was reasonable under the Fourth Amendment. The police department searched the pager because the officer went over his allotted monthly text characters on the pager plan, and the employer was interested in learning whether the texting plan needed to be increased. During the search of the officer's pager, the police department found personal and sexually explicit text messages. The officer had signed a policy stating that pager users have no expectation of privacy.[81]

The judiciary has recognized that the reasonableness of a job-related search or seizure by a supervisor in public schools rests on whether educational interests outweigh the individual employee's expectation of privacy.[82] For example, a federal district court held that a teacher had a reasonable expectation of privacy with her password-protected e-mail account even though school officials had warned that e-mails may be discoverable.[83] The court reasoned that the district's acceptable use policy stated that teachers had a reasonable expectation of privacy, and it was not common practice to monitor the e-mail accounts of employees. It is important to note that when school districts have policies that clearly indicate employees' Internet activities may be monitored, expectation of privacy will be much lower.

In some cases employers have attempted to gain access to employees' Facebook pages. It is not surprising that requests by employers for job applicants' Facebook passwords have been criticized. In California, lawmakers are trying to make the practice of employers asking applicants for Facebook passwords illegal,[84] and Maryland has already made it illegal for employers and potential employers to do so.[85] The Fourth Amendment prohibits *arbitrary* invasions of teachers' personal effects by school officials, but in some situations, the school's interests are overriding.[86]

Public school employees' Fourth Amendment rights also have been asserted in connection with drug-screening programs. School boards can require employees to have physical examinations as a condition of employment, but mandatory screening for drugs has been challenged as impairing privacy rights. Teachers in a Tennessee school district secured an injunction prohibiting the school board from requiring all teachers to submit to

---

[81]City of Ontario v. Quon, 130 S. Ct. 2619 (2010); *see also* O'Connor v. Ortega, 480 U.S. 709 (1987) (finding that public employees have a reasonable expectation of privacy in their desks and files, but that a warrant was not required for work-related searches that are necessary to carry out the business of the public agency).

[82]*See, e.g.*, Gillard v. Schmidt, 579 F.2d 825 (3d Cir. 1978) (invalidating search of school counselor's desk by a school board member because the search was politically motivated and lacked sufficient work-related justification).

[83]Brown-Criscuolo v. Wolfe, 601 F. Supp. 2d 441 (D. Conn. 2009).

[84]Jessica Guynn, *Assembly Votes to Keep Facebook Passwords Private from Employers*, L.A. TIMES (May 10, 2012), http://articles.latimes.com/2012/may/10/business/la-fi-tn-assembly-votes-to-keep-facebook-passwords-private-from-employers-20120510.

[85]Joanna Stern, *Maryland Bill Bans Employers from Facebook Passwords*, ABC NEWS BLOGS (Apr. 11, 2012), http://abcnews.go.com/blogs/technology/2012/04/maryland-bill-bans-employers-from-facebook-passwords/.

[86]*See, e.g.*, Alinovi v. Worcester Sch. Comm., 777 F.2d 776 (1st Cir. 1985) (finding that a teacher had no expectation of privacy in withholding from the school administration a paper she had written for a graduate course—and shared with others—about a child with disabilities in her class).

random, suspicionless drug testing.[87] The court declared that the school district's policy as written and implemented was unconstitutional. Likewise, a North Carolina appellate court found a school board's policy requiring all employees to submit to random, suspicionless drug and alcohol testing violated the guarantee against unreasonable searches.[88] The court observed that there was no reason for the employees to have a reduced expectation of privacy because they worked in a public school and that there was no evidence of any drug problems among the school employees. A Georgia federal district court in an earlier case also struck down a statewide drug-testing law that would have required all new state employees and veteran employees transferring to another school district or state agency to submit to urinalysis screening.[89] The court reasoned that the general interest in maintaining a drug-free workplace was not a compelling governmental interest to justify testing *all* job applicants.

In contrast to *blanket* testing, support for *limited* drug testing of public employees can be found in two Supreme Court decisions outside the school domain that upheld mandatory drug testing of railroad employees involved in accidents[90] and customs employees who carry firearms or are involved in the interdiction of illegal drugs.[91] The Court found that the safety and security interests served by the programs outweighed employees' privacy concerns. The Fifth Circuit also let stand drug testing of school employees in safety-sensitive positions, including the school custodian, whose performance of maintenance duties affects almost 900 students.[92]

What constitutes safety-sensitive roles in the school context, however, remains unclear. Some courts now seem more inclined than they were in the past to interpret expansively the positions in this category. The Sixth Circuit upheld a school district's policy requiring suspicionless drug testing for all individuals who apply for, transfer to, or are promoted to safety-sensitive positions, including teachers who are entrusted with the care of children and are on the "frontline" of school security.[93] Furthermore, the court upheld drug testing of any individual for whom there was reasonable suspicion of drug possession

---

[87]Smith Cnty. Educ. Ass'n v. Smith Cnty. Bd. of Educ., 781 F. Supp. 2d 604 (M.D. Tenn. 2011) (distinguishing this case from the Sixth Circuit decision, Knox Cnty. Bd. of Educ., 158 F.3d 361 (6th Cir. 1998), that upheld a drug-testing policy specifically targeting only those teachers applying for teaching positions or those seeking promotion within the district) *see also* Am. Fed'n of Teachers-W. Va. v. Kanawha Cnty. Bd. of Educ., 592 F. Supp. 2d 883 (S.D. W. Va. 2009) (prohibiting school district from suspicionless drug testing of employees).

[88]Jones v. Graham Cnty. Bd. of Educ., 677 S.E.2d 171 (N.C. Ct. App. 2009).

[89]Ga. Ass'n of Educators v. Harris, 749 F. Supp. 1110 (N.D. Ga. 1990); *see also* Chandler v. Miller, 520 U.S. 305 (1997) (striking down a Georgia law requiring candidates for state office to pass a drug test; finding no special need based on public safety to override the individual's privacy interests).

[90]Skinner v. Ry. Labor Execs.' Ass'n, 489 U.S. 602 (1989). In this case, the Court also upheld alcohol testing of employees. *See* text accompanying note 196, Chapter 8.

[91]Nat'l Treasury Emps. Union v. Von Raab, 489 U.S. 656 (1989).

[92]Aubrey v. Sch. Bd., 148 F.3d 559 (5th Cir. 1998); *see also* English v. Talladega Cnty. Bd. of Educ., 938 F. Supp. 775 (N.D. Ala. 1996) (upholding random drug testing of school bus mechanics).

[93]*Knox Cnty. Educ. Ass'n*, 158 F.3d at 375.

or use, but it remanded the case for additional factual inquiry regarding the provision calling for alcohol testing of all employees.[94] A Kentucky federal district court subsequently upheld random, suspicionless drug testing of a school district's employees in safety-sensitive roles, including teachers, as justified to comply with the Drug-Free Workplace Act of 1988.[95] But the Fifth Circuit struck down policies in two Louisiana school districts that required employees injured in the course of employment to submit to urinalysis, finding an insufficient nexus between such injuries and drug use.[96]

Of course, employees, like students, can be subjected to alcohol and drug testing where there is reasonable suspicion that the individual is under the influence of those substances. For example, a Texas federal district court found that because two witnesses raised concerns about a teacher being under the influence of some substance, there was sufficient reason to justify drug testing the teacher.[97] Employees can be dismissed for refusing to submit to such a test,[98] but in some instances, such dismissals have been overturned when reasonable suspicion was not established to justify targeting particular individuals.[99] The law is still evolving regarding what constitutes individualized suspicion of drug use and the circumstances under which certain public employees can be subjected to urinalysis without such suspicion.

Out-of-School Conduct

The Supreme Court has acknowledged that a "teacher serves as a role model for . . . students, exerting a subtle but important influence over their perceptions and values."[100] Recognizing that teachers are held to a higher standard of conduct than general citizens, the judiciary has upheld dismissals for behavior that jeopardizes student welfare, even if it takes place during the summer break.[101]

In recent years, teachers frequently have challenged school officials' authority to place restrictions on their personal lifestyles or out-of-school conduct. Although the right to such personal freedom is not an enumerated constitutional guarantee, it is a right implied in the concept of personal liberty embodied in the Fourteenth Amendment. Constitutional protection afforded to teachers' privacy rights is determined not only by the *location* of the

---

[94] *Id.* at 386 (remanding this issue for the district court to determine whether the low level of alcohol impairment identified, .02, was reasonably related to the purpose of the testing program).

[95] Crager v. Bd. of Educ., 313 F. Supp. 2d 690 (E.D. Ky. 2004) (citing 41 U.S.C. § 702 (2012)). This law stipulates that federal grant and contract recipients cannot receive federal funds unless they implement policies to ensure that workplaces are free from the illegal use, possession, and distribution of controlled substances.

[96] United Teachers v. Orleans Parish Sch. Bd., 142 F.3d 853 (5th Cir. 1998).

[97] Catlett v. Duncanville Indep. Sch. Dist., No. 3:09-cv-1245-k, 2010 U.S. Dist. LEXIS 91931 (N.D. Tex. Sept. 2, 2010).

[98] *See, e.g.*, Hearn v. Bd. of Pub. Educ., 191 F.3d 1329 (11th Cir. 1999) (upholding termination of a teacher who refused to undergo urinalysis after a drug-detecting dog identified marijuana in her car).

[99] *See, e.g.*, Warren v. Bd. of Educ., 200 F. Supp. 2d 1053 (E.D. Mo. 2001) (finding genuine issues as to whether the teacher's behavior suggested drug use and whether she consented to the drug test).

[100] Ambach v. Norwick, 441 U.S. 68, 78–79 (1979).

[101] *See, e.g.*, Bd. of Educ. v. Wood, 717 S.W.2d 837 (Ky. 1986).

conduct but also by the *nature* of the activity. The judiciary has attempted to balance teachers' privacy rights against the school board's legitimate interests in safeguarding the welfare of students and the effective management of the school. Sanctions cannot be imposed solely because school officials disapprove of teachers' personal and private conduct, but restrictions can be placed on unconventional behavior that is detrimental to job performance or harmful to students. Educators can be terminated based on evidence that would not be sufficient to support criminal charges,[102] but they cannot be dismissed for unsubstantiated rumors.[103] Some courts have based termination decisions on whether teachers' out-of-school conduct had a negative impact on their teaching effectiveness.[104]

The precise contours of public educators' constitutional privacy rights have not been clearly delineated; constitutional claims involving pregnancies out of wedlock, unconventional living arrangements, homosexuality, and other alleged sexual improprieties usually have been decided on a case-by-case basis. Since many of these cases also are discussed in Chapter 12 in connection with dismissals based on charges of immorality, the following discussion is confined to an overview of the constitutional issues.

Recognizing that decisions pertaining to marriage and parenthood involve constitutionally protected privacy rights, courts have been reluctant to support dismissal actions based on teachers' unwed, pregnant status in the absence of evidence that the condition impairs fitness to teach.[105] Compelled leaves of absence for pregnant, unmarried employees similarly have been invalidated as violating constitutional privacy rights.[106]

Most courts have reasoned that public employees, including educators, have a protected privacy right to engage in consenting sexual relationships out of wedlock, and that such relationships cannot be the basis for dismissal unless teaching effectiveness is impaired.[107] Some courts, however, have upheld dismissals or other disciplinary actions based on public employees' lifestyles that involve adulterous or other unconventional

---

[102]*See, e.g.*, Montefusco v. Nassau Cnty., 39 F. Supp. 2d 231 (E.D.N.Y. 1999) (holding that although the criminal investigation surrounding the teacher's possession of candid pictures of teenagers taken at his home did not result in criminal charges, the school board could suspend the teacher with pay and remove extracurricular assignments).

[103]*See, e.g.*, Peaster Indep. Sch. Dist. v. Glodfelty, 63 S.W.3d 1 (Tex. App. 2001) (holding that widespread gossip triggered by unproven allegations of sexual misconduct could not be the basis for not renewing teachers' contracts).

[104]*See, e.g.*, Teacher Standards & Practices Comm'n v. Bergerson, 153 P.3d 84 (Or. 2007) (reinstating teacher who took large quantities of prescription drugs and ran her car into her estranged husband's truck, because there was no clear nexus between her misconduct and her professional duties); Land v. L'Anse Creuse Pub. Sch. Bd. of Educ., No. 288612, 2010 Mich. App. LEXIS 999 (Ct. App. May 27, 2010) (reinstating teacher who was terminated after pictures were posted on the Internet of her simulating the act of fellatio on a male mannequin at a bachelorette party, because her ability to teach effectively was not adversely impacted enough to justify the dismissal).

[105]*See, e.g.*, Andrews v. Drew Mun. Separate Sch. Dist., 507 F.2d 611, 614 (5th Cir. 1975) (equating birth of an illegitimate child with immoral conduct impairs equal protection and due process rights).

[106]*See* Ponton v. Newport News Sch. Bd., 632 F. Supp. 1056 (E.D. Va. 1986).

[107]*See, e.g.*, Littlejohn v. Rose, 768 F.2d 765 (6th Cir. 1985) (holding that a nonrenewal of a nontenured teacher's contract because of her involvement in a divorce abridged her constitutional privacy rights); *see also* Sherburne v. Sch. Bd., 455 So. 2d 1057 (Fla. Dist. Ct. App. 1984) (overturning school board's termination of an unmarried teacher for lacking good moral character because she spent the night with an unmarried man).

sexual relationships or activities that allegedly impaired job performance. To illustrate, the U.S. Supreme Court upheld the dismissal of a police officer for selling videotapes of himself stripping off a police uniform and masturbating.[108] The Court rejected the officer's assertion that his off-duty conduct was constitutionally protected expression unrelated to his employment. A New York federal court also upheld termination of a teacher for actively participating in a group supporting consensual sexual activity between men and boys, reasoning that his activities in this organization were likely to impair teaching effectiveness and disrupt the school.[109]

In a case involving privacy issues and the Internet, an English teacher in Georgia was forced to resign over two pictures posted on Facebook that showed her drinking while on vacation in Ireland. The teacher had activated privacy settings and had not communicated with her students via Facebook. School officials, however, learned about the pictures from a concerned parent. The teacher claimed that she was bullied into resigning and then sued the district when it refused to reinstate her. A state court judge ruled that she could not force school officials to give her a hearing because it was within the school district's legal rights to deny the request.[110] Had the teacher been dismissed as a result of the Facebook pictures instead of resigning—though her resignation was, in effect, a constructive discharge—it seems unlikely that the school district would have prevailed in this case.

Whether employment decisions can be based on a teacher's sexual orientation has been controversial, and the scope of constitutional protections afforded to lesbian, gay, bisexual, and transgendered (LGBT) educators continues to evolve. Among factors courts consider are the nature of the conduct (public or private), the notoriety it generates, and its impact on teaching effectiveness.[111]

In 2003, the Supreme Court delivered a significant decision, *Lawrence v. Texas*, in which it recognized a privacy right for consenting adults of the same sex to have sexual relations in the privacy of their homes by striking down a Texas law imposing criminal penalties for such conduct.[112] This ruling overturned a 1986 Supreme Court decision in which the Court upheld a Georgia law attaching criminal penalties to public *or private* consensual sodomy.[113] The Court in *Lawrence* emphasized that private, consensual sexual behavior in one's home is constitutionally protected and cannot be the basis for criminal action.

In addition to asserting protected privacy rights, some LGBT employees have claimed discrimination under the Equal Protection Clause of the Fourteenth Amendment. Discrimination in employment is discussed in detail in Chapter 11, so equal protection

---

[108]City of San Diego v. Roe, 543 U.S. 77 (2004) (finding no protected expression involved).

[109]Melzer v. Bd. of Educ., 196 F. Supp. 2d 229 (E.D.N.Y. 2002), *aff'd mem.*, 336 F. 3d 185 (2d Cir. 2003).

[110]Merritt Melancon, *Barrow Teacher Presses Forward with Facebook Lawsuit*, ATHENS BANNER-HERALD (Oct. 11, 2011), http://onlineathens.com/local-news/2011-10-11/barrow-teacher-denied-her-old-job-presses-forward-lawsuit.

[111]*See* Nat'l Gay Task Force v. Bd. of Educ., 729 F.2d 1270, 1274 (10th Cir. 1984), *aff'd by an equally divided court*, 470 U.S. 903 (1985).

[112]539 U.S. 558 (2003).

[113]Bowers v. Hardwick, 478 U.S. 186 (1986).

claims pertaining to LGBT educators are reviewed only briefly here. To substantiate an Equal Protection Clause violation, a teacher must prove that sexual orientation was the motivating factor in the adverse employment action and that there was no rational basis for the differential treatment.[114]

Dismissals of public educators based solely on sexual orientation, in the absence of criminal charges, have generated a range of judicial interpretations. During the 1970s and 1980s, a few courts permitted school districts to dismiss LGBT teachers or reassign them to nonteaching roles, even when there was no link to teaching effectiveness.[115] The Sixth Circuit upheld a school district in not renewing a guidance counselor's contract after she revealed her sexual orientation and that of two students to other school employees. Rejecting the claim that the nonrenewal impaired free speech rights, the court held that her statements regarding her sexual orientation were not matters of public concern.[116] Subsequently, the Tenth Circuit, even though recognizing that a principal's refusal to hire a teacher on the basis of perceived homosexual tendencies was arbitrary and capricious, nonetheless held that the law was not clearly established in this regard in 1988 and thus granted the principal immunity for his role in the personnel decision based on sexual orientation.[117]

Litigation since the 1990s requires school districts to provide evidence that one's sexual orientation has a negative impact on teaching effectiveness before disciplinary action can be imposed. To illustrate, a Utah federal court overturned the school district's removal of a girls' volleyball coach, finding no job-related reason for the coach's removal, which was based solely on the community's negative response to her sexual orientation. The court also noted that the school district could not instruct the coach to avoid mentioning her sexual orientation and ordered the school district to reinstate her and pay damages.[118] An Ohio federal district court similarly awarded a teacher reinstatement, back pay, and damages after finding that his contract was not renewed because of his sexual orientation rather than for his teaching deficiencies as the school board had asserted.[119]

A New Jersey teacher prevailed on his claim that he was harassed by teachers and students because he was gay, and that his resulting anxiety attacks forced him to take a

---

[114]*See* Romer v. Evans, 517 U.S. 620 (1996) (invalidating an amendment to the Colorado Constitution that prohibited all legislative, executive, or judicial action designed to protect gay individuals).

[115]*See, e.g.*, Burton v. Cascade Sch. Dist., 512 F.2d 850 (9th Cir. 1975); Acanfora v. Bd. of Educ., 491 F.2d 498 (4th Cir. 1974); Gaylord v. Tacoma Sch. Dist. No. 10, 559 P.2d 1340 (Wash. 1977). But some courts have required evidence of impaired teaching effectiveness to discharge teachers for private homosexuality. *See, e.g.*, Bd. of Educ. v. Jack M., 566 P.2d 602 (Cal. 1977); Morrison v. State Bd. of Educ., 461 P.2d 375 (Cal. 1969).

[116]Rowland v. Mad River Local Sch. Dist., 730 F.2d 444 (6th Cir. 1984) (rejecting also the Fourteenth Amendment equal protection claim because the counselor was not treated differently from other similarly situated employees facing nonrenewal of their contracts).

[117]Jantz v. Muci, 976 F.2d 623, 629 (10th Cir. 1992); *see also* Snyder v. Jefferson Cnty. Sch. Dist. R-1, 842 P.2d 624 (Colo. 1992) (upholding termination of a teacher who let his teaching certificate expire while on leave to have gender reassignment surgery).

[118]Weaver v. Nebo Sch. Dist., 29 F. Supp. 2d 1279 (D. Utah 1998).

[119]Glover v. Williamsburg Local Sch. Dist., 20 F. Supp. 2d 1160 (S.D. Ohio 1998).

leave of absence, after which his contract was not renewed.[120] A New York federal district court also held that a teacher had stated a valid claim, precluding summary judgment, that a school district violated her Fourteenth Amendment equal protection rights when it failed to discipline students who harassed the teacher because she was a lesbian and treated her differently from other similarly situated non-LGBT teachers.[121] However, the Seventh Circuit held that a school had not violated a teacher's equal protection rights in connection with parental and student harassment of the teacher based on sexual orientation, because school officials took some action to respond to the teacher's complaints of harassment and treated the allegations as they would treat harassment complaints filed by other teachers.[122]

The case law suggests that there has been a shift from condoning dismissals for merely being LGBT to requiring evidence that an individual's sexual orientation has an adverse impact on job performance. Teachers do not become poor role models simply because of their sexual orientation, and it would be difficult to produce a rational basis for terminating or treating LGBT teachers differently from other educators.

CONCLUSION

The United States Constitution places constraints on government, not private, action. Thus, public employees, but not usually those working in the private sector, can challenge employment decisions as violating their constitutional rights. If public employees can show that they have suffered adverse employment consequences because of the exercise of protected expression, association, or privacy rights, then the burden shifts to the employer to justify the restriction on protected rights as necessary to carry out the work of the government agency. In the school context, this means that the employee's action has impaired teaching effectiveness, relations with superiors, or school operations. The public employer also can prevail by showing that there are legitimate reasons for the personnel action aside from the exercise of protected expression or other constitutional rights. In short, under certain circumstances, restrictions on constitutional freedoms can be justified by overriding government interests.

POINTS TO PONDER

 1. A nontenured teacher has received mediocre evaluations for two years. The principal has provided him some instructional assistance but feels the teacher is not making sufficient progress. Thus, the principal recommends that the teacher's contract not be renewed. Before the school board acts on the recommendation, the teacher writes a letter to the newspaper criticizing the school board's adoption of a new math program for elementary

---

[120]Curcio v. Collingswood Bd. of Educ., No. 04-5100 (JBS), 2006 U.S. Dist. LEXIS 46648 (D.N.J. June 28, 2006); *see also* Murray v. Oceanside Unified Sch. Dist., 95 Cal. Rptr. 2d 28 (Ct. App. 2000) (ruling in favor of an award-winning biology teacher who used the California nondiscrimination law to challenge years of sexual orientation harassment by her colleagues).

[121]Lovell v. Comsewogue Sch. Dist., 214 F. Supp. 2d 319 (E.D.N.Y. 2002).

[122]Schroeder v. Hamilton Sch. Dist., 282 F.3d 946 (7th Cir. 2002).

grades. Is protected expression involved? Can the school board decide not to renew the teacher's contract?

2. A teacher complained to her principal that children with disabilities were being placed in the regular classroom for fiscal reasons, when the children needed more restrictive placements. Does such expression pertain to the teacher's job duties? Can the teacher be disciplined for the expression?

3. A school board is concerned about the mounting drug problem in the community and particularly in the public schools. To address the problem, the school has instituted a drug-education program and a drug-testing program for all students who participate in extracurricular activities. Now the board wants to adopt a requirement that all new teachers, as part of their preemployment medical exams, must submit to urinalysis screening for drug use. Are teachers in safety-sensitive roles? Can such a drug-screening program be justified without individualized suspicion?

4. A tenured gay middle school teacher has not mentioned his sexual orientation to his students. Yet he has been prominent in gay rights rallies and has been a guest on a radio talk show to advocate a law authorizing same-sex marriages. As a result, several parents have complained to the principal and asked that the teacher be dismissed. Can the teacher be removed from the classroom?

CHAPTER ELEVEN

DISCRIMINATION
IN EMPLOYMENT

All persons and groups are potential victims of discrimination in employment. People of color and women claim discrimination in traditionally segregated job categories, whereas Caucasians and males claim that affirmative action has denied them the right to compete on equal grounds. The young argue that the old already hold the good jobs and that entry is nearly impossible, and older employees contend that they often are let go when "downsizing" occurs. Religious minorities might not be allowed to dress the way they please or may be denied leave for religious observances, and religious majorities (particularly in private schools) have concerns about governmental intrusion into their homogeneous work environments. Likewise, persons with disabilities often complain that they are not given the opportunity to show what they can do, whereas employers may argue that the costs of accommodating those with disabilities can be significant and never ending. Given these diverse factors, it is not surprising that literally thousands of employment discrimination suits are filed each year.

LEGAL CONTEXT

Extending constitutional protections, numerous federal laws prohibit discrimination in public and private employment.

Most, but not all, forms of employment discrimination violate either federal or state law. Foremost among these legal protections are the Fourteenth Amendment to the United States Constitution and Title VII of the Civil Rights Act of 1964; both are discussed here, given their broad application. Other more narrowly tailored statutes are reviewed in the respective sections addressing discrimination based on race and national origin, sex, sexual orientation, religion, age, and disability (see Table 11.1).

TABLE 11.1   Selected Federal Laws Prohibiting Employment Discrimination

FEDERAL LAW	PUBLIC SCHOOLS	PRIVATE SCHOOLS	RECIPIENTS OF FEDERAL FINANCIAL ASSISTANCE	NUMBER OF EMPLOYEES NECESSARY FOR LAW TO APPLY	RACE	NATIONAL ORIGIN, ALIENAGE	SEX	AGE	RELIGION	DISABILITY
Fourteenth Amendment to the U.S. Constitution	X				X	X	X	X	X	X
42 U.S.C. § 1983	X				X	X	X	X	X	X
42 U.S.C. § 1981		X			X	X(i.e., ethnicity)				
Title VII of Civil Rights Act of 1964	X	X		15	X	X	X		X	
Equal Pay Act of 1963	X	X		20			X			
Section 504 of Rehabilitation Act of 1973			X							X
Americans with Disabilities Act	X	X		15						X
Age Discrimination in Employment Act	X	X		20				X		

Fourteenth Amendment

The Fourteenth Amendment to the United States Constitution mandates that no state shall deny any person within its jurisdiction equal protection of the laws. As noted in Chapter 6, the Equal Protection Clause of the Fourteenth Amendment requires the application of strict scrutiny in cases involving discrimination based on race, national origin, or alienage. Intermediate scrutiny is applied in cases in which sex discrimination is at issue. The lowest level of scrutiny, rational basis, is applied in sexual orientation and disability cases (see Figure 6.1, Chapter 6). The Equal Protection Clause has been interpreted as prohibiting intentional discrimination and applies to subdivisions of the state, including public school districts. Districts may be found guilty of facial discrimination (e.g., if the policy, on its face, is discriminatory, such as when an administrative position is reserved for a female applicant), or facially neutral discrimination (e.g., a school district's employment criteria results in hiring a disproportionately larger share of men than women from a qualified pool with equal numbers of men and women).

Title VII

Title VII is enforced by the Equal Employment Opportunity Commission (EEOC) and prohibits discriminating on the basis of race, color, religion, sex, or national origin and covers hiring, promotion, and compensation practices as well as fringe benefits and other terms and conditions of employment.[1] However, protection against discriminatory employment practices is not absolute for individuals within these classifications since both Congress and the courts have identified exceptions (e.g., employers might not accommodate a Jewish basketball coach's request to be excused from every Friday and Saturday night basketball game so that he may observe the Jewish Sabbath from sundown on Friday until sundown on Saturday if the accommodation creates an undue hardship on the school district). Also, in creating and amending Title VII over the years, Congress has expressly permitted employers to facially discriminate based on religion, sex, or national origin (but not on race or color) if they can show the existence of a bona fide occupational qualification (BFOQ) that is reasonably necessary to the normal operation of their particular enterprise (e.g., a parochial school could require that members of the teaching staff be of the same denomination).

Qualifying as an Employer. Title VII applies to employers with fifteen or more employees, each of whom works twenty or more weeks during the calendar year. Although this requirement is seemingly simple, its application has been complex. The Supreme Court resolved some of the issues in *Walters v. Metropolitan Educational Enterprises*,[2] in which it adopted the "payroll method" to assess when an employee is considered to be on the employer's payroll. All that is necessary under this approach is to determine when the employee began employment and when he or she left (if at all).[3]

---

[1] 42 U.S.C. § 2000e (2012).

[2] 519 U.S. 202 (1997).

[3] Although *Walters* is a Title VII retaliation case, the definition established by the Supreme Court has been applied to cases under the Americans with Disabilities Act (ADA), given the similarity of the two statutes. *See, e.g.*, Owens v. S. Dev. Council, 59 F. Supp. 2d 1210 (M.D. Ala. 1999).

Disparate Treatment and Impact.   When evaluating Title VII claims, courts have developed two legal theories: disparate treatment and disparate impact. *Disparate treatment* applies when an individual claims less favorable treatment as compared to other applicants or employees. *Disparate impact* is applicable when an employer's ostensibly neutral practice has a discriminatory impact on the class to which the claimant belongs. In proving disparate treatment, plaintiffs may use direct or circumstantial evidence to prove their employer's discriminatory intent.

Plaintiffs usually do not have direct evidence of discrimination (e.g., "you are fired for being too religious"[4]). Thus, they often rely on circumstantial evidence to substantiate that they received less favorable treatment and that such conduct, if otherwise unexplained, is "more likely than not based on the consideration of impermissible factors."[5] To support a circumstantial claim, the plaintiff must show that he or she:

- was a member of a protected class;
- applied for and was qualified for the job; and
- was denied the position, while the employer continued to seek applicants with the plaintiff's qualifications.

These criteria were articulated by the Supreme Court in 1973 in *McDonnell Douglas Corporation v. Green*[6] and, with some modification, are applied beyond claims of hiring discrimination to alleged disparate treatment in areas such as promotion, termination, and tenure.

If the claim is supported, the burden shifts to the employer to state a "legitimate nondiscriminatory" reason for its action that does not violate Title VII. Such a reason may be either objective (e.g., a higher-level academic degree), subjective (e.g., stronger interpersonal skills), or a combination. But given the ease of presenting a nondiscriminatory reason, employers in nearly every instance provide a response. After the employer provides a rebuttal, the employee then has the additional burden of proving by a preponderance of the evidence not only that the proffered reason was false, but also that it served as a pretext for prohibited intentional discrimination. In most instances of alleged discrimination, the plaintiff is unable to show that the employer's purported nondiscriminatory basis was pretextual.

In contrast to disparate treatment claims, to prove disparate impact, the plaintiff is not initially required to show discriminatory intent but must establish that an employer's facially neutral practice had a disproportionate impact on the plaintiff's protected class. This generally is accomplished through the use of statistics. Once this type of prima facie case is established, the employer then must show that the challenged policies or practices (or its employment practices in the aggregate) are job related and justified by a business necessity.

The Supreme Court has recognized, however, that mere awareness of a policy's adverse impact on a protected class does not constitute proof of unlawful motive; a discriminatory purpose "implies that the decisionmaker . . . selected or reaffirmed a particular

[4]Dixon v. Hallmark Cos., 627 F.3d 849, 853 (11th Cir. 2010).

[5]Furnco Constr. Corp. v. Waters, 438 U.S. 567, 577 (1978).

[6]411 U.S. 792, 802 (1973).

course of action at least in part 'because of,' not merely 'in spite of,' its adverse effects upon an identifiable group."[7] Nonetheless, foreseeably discriminatory consequences can be considered by courts in assessing intent, although more will be needed to substantiate unlawful motive. Furthermore, the employee may prevail if it is shown that the employer refused to adopt an alternative policy identified by the employee that realistically would have met the employer's business needs without resulting in disparate impact.

Retaliation.   By the time a complaint is filed with the EEOC or a state or federal court, the working relationship between the employer and the employee is strained, sometimes beyond repair. In response to filing, an employee may not be terminated, demoted, or harassed, but less extreme acts such as rudeness or "the cold shoulder" will not typically violate Title VII.[8] Where actionable behavior occurs, the employee may file a second claim alleging retaliation.[9] To support this type of case, the employee is required to show that he or she participated in statutorily protected activity (i.e., the filing of a complaint or suit), an adverse employment action was taken by the employer, and that a causal connection existed between the protected activity and the adverse action. If the employee can show that filing the complaint was the basis for the adverse employment decision, even if the original complaint of discrimination fails, the court will provide appropriate relief.[10]

Relief.   If it is proven that the employee was a victim of prohibited discrimination, courts have the authority to require a *make-whole remedy* where the person is placed in the same position he or she otherwise would have been, absent discriminatory activity. In meeting this objective, courts may:

- provide injunctive and declaratory relief;
- require that a person be reinstated, hired, tenured, or promoted;
- direct the payment of back pay, interest on back pay, or front pay;[11]
- assign retroactive seniority;
- provide attorneys' fees and court costs; and
- in cases in which intentional discrimination is proved, provide compensatory and punitive damages.

---

[7]Personnel Adm'r of Mass. v. Feeney, 442 U.S. 256, 279 (1979).

[8]David J. Walsh, Employment Law for Human Resource Practice (Mason, OH: Thomson Southwestern, 3d ed. 2010).

[9]*See* Thompson v. N. Am. Stainless, 131 S. Ct. 863 (2011) (finding that Title VII protected a worker who was fired in retaliation for a complaint made by his fiancé who was also an employee).

[10]*See* Jackson v. Birmingham Bd. of Educ., 544 U.S. 167 (2005) (holding that retaliation against a girls' basketball coach who had complained of discrimination could support a sex discrimination suit under Title IX, even though the coach's initial complaints of sex discrimination were unfounded).

[11]For example, if a teacher is denied a principalship because of race, the court may direct the district to hire the teacher for the next available position. And the court could require that the difference in salary be awarded to the teacher up to the time of promotion to a principalship. That portion of the salary paid in the future is termed "front pay," while the portion due for the period between the failure to hire and the court's ruling is termed "back pay."

RACE AND NATIONAL ORIGIN DISCRIMINATION

Without a proven history of prior discrimination, an employer may not use race as a factor in making employment decisions.

Race and national origin discrimination in employment continue in spite of nearly 140 years of protective statutes and constitutional amendments.[12] Lawsuits are filed under the Fourteenth Amendment, Title VII, and 42 U.S.C. § 1981. Section 1981 applies when either race or ethnicity discrimination is alleged in making, performing, modifying, and terminating contracts, as well as in the enjoyment of all benefits, privileges, terms, and conditions of the contractual relationship.

Hiring and Promotion Practices

Unless a school district is under a narrowly tailored court order to correct prior proven acts of race discrimination, it may not advantage or disadvantage an applicant or employee because of that individual's race. When unsuccessful candidates believe that race played a role in the decision-making process, they will generally allege disparate treatment, requiring the heightened proof of discriminatory intent. In attempting to support such a claim, many plaintiffs have difficulty overcoming employers' purported nondiscriminatory reasons for their decisions. For example, in a Fifth Circuit case, a substitute teacher alleged race discrimination and other claims under Title VII against a school district when she was not hired for three full-time history teaching positions. Instead of choosing the substitute teacher, the district hired one black male, one white female, and one white male for the three different positions. Finding in favor of the school district, the court held that the teacher failed to demonstrate pretext for discrimination or that her qualifications were not more impressive than those of the three candidates who were hired.[13] Because most qualifications for initial employment in educational settings (e.g., degree, licensure) are required to perform jobs satisfactorily and to meet state standards and accountability mandates, disparate impact claims are difficult to win.

At other times, plaintiffs are able to show that no legitimate bases supported the employer's decision and that the selection was based on impermissible factors.[14] A Fourth Circuit case focused on national origin discrimination; the teacher was of Russian descent and was not hired for a teaching position. Even though she had superior teaching credentials, the school district deviated from its hiring procedures and hired someone else. After

[12]*See* King v. Hardesty, 517 F.3d 1049 (8th Cir. 2008) (ruling that a statement made to an African American teacher about white teachers being able to teach African American students better than African American teachers was evidence that may be viewed as discriminatory).

[13]Godfrey v. Katy Indep. Sch. Dist., 395 F. App'x 88 (5th Cir. 2012); *see also* Brown v. Unified Sch. Dist. No. 501, 459 F. App'x 705 (10th Cir. 2012) (finding no showing of pretext in teacher's race discrimination claim when teacher was not rehired for three positions).

[14]*See, e.g.,* Stern v. Trs. of Columbia Univ., 131 F.3d 305 (2d Cir. 1997).

the teacher complained that the district had not followed hiring protocol by not interviewing the most qualified applicant, she was told that the district would not hire a Russian. Reversing the district court's dismissal of the complaint, the appellate court remanded the case because the applicant sufficiently stated a claim that she was the most qualified for the position.[15]

Testing. Among the more controversial objective measures used in hiring and promotion (e.g., academic degree level, a specified number of years' experience) is the use of standardized test scores. Tests may not be discriminatorily administered, nor may their results be discriminatorily used. Moreover, employers may not use different cutoff scores for different racial groups or adjust scores based on race.[16] The EEOC requires employers to conduct validity studies for tests used in making employment decisions if they result in adverse impact on a protected class. For tests with a disparate impact to be used, they must be reliable and valid, and they must qualify as a business necessity.[17] Also, tests may be administered to applicants for positions other than those for which the tests have been validated, but only if there are no significant differences in the skills, knowledge, and abilities required by the jobs.[18]

Notwithstanding the restrictions posed above, many employers (both small and large) feel that the use of tests is so important to the accomplishment of organizational goals that they are compelled to use them. For example, a state has the right to require its current and future teachers to demonstrate their general literacy as well as their content knowledge. In *United States v. South Carolina*, the Supreme Court affirmed a lower court's conclusion that South Carolina's use of the National Teachers Examination (NTE) for teacher certification and salary purposes satisfied the Equal Protection Clause.[19] The federal district court had held that the test was valid since it measured knowledge of course content in teacher preparation courses, and that it was not administered with intent to discriminate against minority applicants for teacher certification. The court also found sufficient evidence to establish a relationship between the use of the test scores in determining the placement of teachers on the salary scale and legitimate employment objectives, such as encouraging teachers to upgrade their skills. The option proposed by the plaintiffs (i.e., graduation from an approved teacher preparation program) was rejected by the court as incapable of ensuring minimally competent teachers because of the wide range in university admission requirements, academic standards, and grading practices.

It is likely that states, districts, and teacher-training institutions will continue to use tests as a requirement for admission to teacher education training programs; a prerequisite

---

[15]Dolgaleva v. Va. Beach City Pub. Sch., 364 F. App'x 820 (4th Cir. 2010).

[16]*See* Ricci v. DeStefano, 557 U.S. 557 (2009) (holding that city fire department's choice to ignore test results for promotions because no black firefighter scored high enough to be considered for promotion violated Title VII).

[17]Griggs v. Duke Power Co., 401 U.S. 424, 432 (1971). In *Griggs*, the Court held that a private company's use of both a high school diploma requirement and a test of general intelligence as prerequisites to initial employment and a condition of transfer violated Title VII; neither requirement was shown to be related to successful job performance, and both operated to disqualify minority applicants at a higher rate than those who were Caucasian.

[18]Albemarle Paper Co. v. Moody, 422 U.S. 405, 432 (1975).

[19]445 F. Supp. 1094 (D.S.C. 1977), *aff'd sub nom.* Nat'l Educ. Ass'n v. South Carolina, 434 U.S. 1026 (1978).

to licensure; and a basis for graduation, hiring, and promotion. To avoid discriminatory actions, test performance should not be the sole criterion for making personnel decisions.

Adverse Decisions

Employers cannot dismiss, decline to renew, or demote employees on the basis of race or national origin. In an illustrative case, a teacher established a Title VII claim for discrimination by submitting evidence that the principal made derogatory remarks about her Polish national origin, which could be linked to the teacher's contract not being renewed at the end of the year.[20] Reversing the district court's decision, the Seventh Circuit remanded the national origin claim because it was a question for the jury to decide regarding whether there was a connection between the principal's discriminatory statements and the nonrenewal of the teacher's contract.

In some cases, plaintiffs have difficulty showing that the conduct of their employers qualifies as adverse actions (e.g., change of school, grade level, teaching assignment). An Indian teacher, for example, failed to show that her dismissal was based on national origin discrimination.[21] The teacher taught third grade in the district and was reassigned to seventh grade as a result of budget cuts. She was later terminated because of her poor teaching evaluations. Her national origin discrimination claim failed when the Seventh Circuit ruled that being moved from third to seventh grade should not be considered an adverse employment action. Also, the principal's alleged statement that the teacher should try to find a job on "the North side where most of the Indians go" was not related to her discharge.[22]

Affirmative Action

Affirmative action within the context of employment has been defined as "steps taken to remedy the grossly disparate staffing and recruitment patterns that are the present consequences of past discrimination and to prevent the occurrence of employment discrimination in the future."[23] Correcting such imbalances requires the employer to engage in activities such as:

- expanding its training programs;
- becoming actively involved in recruitment;
- eliminating invalid selection criteria that result in disparate impact; and
- modifying collective bargaining agreements that impermissibly restrict the promotion and retention of minorities.

Courts will uphold most strategies that the Equal Employment Opportunities Commission (EEOC) identifies as affirmative action under both Title VII (for which the EEOC has

---

[20]Darchak v. Chi. Bd. of Educ., 580 F.3d 622 (7th Cir. 2009).

[21]Dass v. Chi. Bd. of Educ., 675 F.3d 1060 (7th Cir. 2012).

[22]*Id.* at 1071.

[23]U.S. Comm'n on Civil Rights, *Statement of Affirmative Action for Equal Employment Opportunities* (1973).

regulatory authority) and the Fourteenth Amendment (for which the EEOC does not have regulatory authority). However, courts will prohibit the use of affirmative action plans that provide a discriminatory "preference" rather than an "equal opportunity."

In 1989, the Supreme Court began to question a variety of public-sector practices that allowed racial preferences.[24] In the aggregate, these cases applied strict scrutiny to race-based affirmative action programs operated by federal, state, and local levels of government; discredited societal discrimination as a justification for such programs; required showing specific discriminatory action to impose a race-based remedy; and allowed only narrowly tailored plans that would further a compelling interest. Given these precedents, existing public-sector affirmative action plans that provide racial preferences without a proven history of discrimination or are based only on underrepresentation are likely to be found unconstitutional. To illustrate, the Eighth Circuit held that a white teacher presented sufficient evidence of unlawful discrimination and demonstrated that genuine issues of material fact remained about whether the school district's affirmative action policy was valid. The teacher claimed that she was not promoted to an assistant principal position because the district's affirmative action policy unlawfully required that at least one assistant principal at each school be a different race than the school's principal.[25]

In addition to affirmative action in hiring and promotion, efforts have been made to protect the diversity gained through court order and voluntary affirmative action by providing a preference in organization downsizing. When a reduction in school staff is necessary due to financial exigency, declining enrollment, or a change in education priorities, it generally is based, at least in part, on tenure and seniority within teaching areas. Accordingly, it is important for all employees to be in their rightful place on the seniority list.[26]

In 1986, the Supreme Court decided *Wygant v. Jackson Board of Education*, a case involving a voluntary affirmative action plan that included a layoff quota.[27] In this case, the Court struck down a school district's collective bargaining agreement that protected minority teachers from layoffs in order to preserve the percentage of minority personnel employed prior to the reduction in force (RIF). The Court reasoned that the quota system, which resulted in the release of some Caucasian teachers with greater seniority than some of the minority teachers who were retained, violated the Equal Protection Clause. Societal discrimination alone was not sufficient to justify the class preference. Recognizing that racial classifications in employment must be justified by a compelling governmental interest and that means must be narrowly tailored to accomplish that purpose, the Court concluded that the layoff provision did not satisfy either of these conditions. The Court further rejected the lower courts' reliance on the "role model" theory.[28]

---

[24]*See, e.g.*, Adarand Constructors v. Pena, 515 U.S. 200 (1995); Ne. Fla. Chapter of Associated Gen. Contractors of Am. v. City of Jacksonville, 508 U.S. 656 (1993); Martin v. Wilks, 490 U.S. 755 (1989).

[25]Humphries v. Pulaski Cnty. Special Sch. Dist., 580 F.3d 688 (8th Cir. 2009); *see also* Taxman v. Bd. of Educ., 91 F.3d 1547 (3d Cir. 1996) (concluding that an affirmative action plan preferring minority teachers over equally qualified nonminority teachers violated Title VII).

[26]*See, e.g.*, Franks v. Bowman Trans. Co., 424 U.S. 747 (1976).

[27]476 U.S. 267 (1986).

[28]*Id.* at 275–76.

- - - - - ▬▬▬▬▬▬▬▬▬▬▬▬▬▬▬▬▬▬▬▬▬▬▬▬▬▬▬▬▬

SEX DISCRIMINATION

Sex generally may not be used as a basis in determining whom to hire, what salary to provide, or any other term or condition of employment.

Prior to 1963, there were no federal statutes prohibiting discrimination based on sex. Women were commonly denied employment when qualified male applicants were in the pool, were offered less money for the same or similar job, or were expected to do work that would not have been asked of a man. Today, most forms of sex discrimination are prohibited, including those associated with hiring, promotion, and virtually all terms and conditions of employment. The Fourteenth Amendment, Title VII of the Civil Rights Act of 1964, and other federal and state laws have played significant roles in allowing victims of sex discrimination to attempt to vindicate their rights in court.

Hiring and Promotion Practices

Sex discrimination is facial when an employer openly seeks a person of a particular sex (e.g., the posting of a position for a female guidance counselor). It becomes illegal discrimination when being male or female is unrelated to meeting job requirements (e.g., hiring only males as basketball coaches).[29] At other times, employment practices are facially neutral (e.g., requiring head coaching experience in football in order to qualify as athletic director), but nevertheless result in nearly the same level of exclusion as when the discrimination is facial. If this occurs, an action will be upheld only if found to qualify as a business necessity, and other less discriminatory options do not meet the needs of the organization.

If applicants or employees have been treated unfairly solely because of their sex, a plaintiff typically files a Title VII suit alleging disparate treatment. The standards for a sex-based prima facie case are similar to those used for race. Also, assuming that a claim is supported, the employer then must identify a basis other than sex for its decision, such as showing that the successful applicant was equally or better qualified or that the plaintiff was unqualified.[30] Where a nondiscriminatory basis has been identified, applicants still may obtain relief if the reasons are shown to be pretextual.[31] For example, rejected applicants could likely prevail where employers base their decisions on stereotypic attitudes about the capabilities of the applicant's sex; job advertisements include phrases, "prefer male" or "prefer female"; or job descriptions are specifically drafted to exclude qualified applicants of a particular sex.

---

[29]*See, e.g.*, Fuhr v. Sch. Dist. of City of Hazel Park, 364 F.3d 753 (6th Cir. 2004) (upholding jury award because school board failed to appoint female to coach boys' basketball team, and evidence suggested the decision not to appoint her was motivated by sex).

[30]*See, e.g.*, Straughter v. Vicksburg Warren Sch. Dist., 152 F. App'x 407 (5th Cir. 2005).

[31]*See, e.g.*, Goodwin v. Bd. of Trs. Univ. of Ill., 442 F.3d 611 (7th Cir. 2006).

One of the most significant cases involving sex-based discrimination in promotion was a 1981 Supreme Court decision, *Texas Department of Community Affairs v. Burdine*.[32] In this case, a female accounting clerk was denied promotion and later was terminated along with two other employees, although two males were retained. In response to the female's prima facie case, the public employer claimed that the three terminated employees did not work well together and that the male who was promoted to the position sought by the female employee was subjectively better qualified, although he had been her subordinate prior to the promotion. In rendering its decision, the Court emphasized that Title VII does not require the hiring or promotion of equally qualified women or the restructuring of employment practices to maximize the number of underrepresented employees. Instead, the employer has the discretion to choose among *equally qualified* candidates so long as the decision is not based on unlawful criteria. In this case, the female employee failed to show pretext, resulting in a decision for the employer.

Not all sex-based distinctions are prohibited, as Title VII explicitly allows for a bona fide occupational qualification (BFOQ) exception. For a BFOQ to be upheld, it needs to be narrowly defined and applied only when necessary to achieve the employer's objectives. There have been few school-based BFOQ cases, since the vast majority of jobs in education can be performed by either males or females. The only readily identifiable BFOQ in education would be the hiring of a female to supervise the girls' locker room and the hiring of a male to supervise the boys' locker room.

Compensation Practices

Claims of sex-based compensation discrimination involving comparative entry salaries, raises, supplemental or overtime opportunities, or other perquisites and benefits are not uncommon within business and industry and even occur at times in higher education. The U.S. Supreme Court in *Ledbetter v. Goodyear Tire and Rubber Co.* held that the statute of limitations for alleging an equal pay lawsuit begins when the employer makes the initial discriminatory wage decision.[33] As a result of the public outcry related to this decision concerning the statute of limitations, Congress passed the Lilly Ledbetter Fair Pay Act of 2009, which addresses the time for filing a claim under Title VII for sex discrimination in employment.[34] These amendments to the Civil Rights Act of 1964 changed the 180-day statute of limitations for filing an equal pay lawsuit. Under the amended law, notice of pay discrimination resets with the issuance of each new discriminatory paycheck. This Act allows plaintiffs who allege compensation discrimination a much longer window to file their claims. Although the Act would apply to the public school context, most PK–12 salary decisions are based on objective criteria such as seniority and degree level. Teachers, staff, and administrators have challenged the use of facially neutral salary adjustments, such as "head of household" or "principal wage earner" allowances. These practices have been invalidated if not shown to be job related.[35]

---

[32]450 U.S. 248 (1981).

[33]550 U.S. 618 (2007).

[34]42 U.S.C. § 2000e-5(e) (2012).

[35]*See, e.g.*, EEOC v. Fremont Christian Sch., 781 F.2d 1362 (9th Cir. 1986).

The Fourteenth Amendment, Title VII, and the Equal Pay Act (EPA) of 1963 may be used where plaintiffs claim that their salaries are based in whole or in part on their sex. The EPA applies only when the dispute involves sex-based wage discrimination claims of unequal pay for equal work.[36] As a result, the Act does not apply when race-based or age-based salary differences are challenged or when the work is unequal.[37] The plaintiff need not prove that the employer intended to discriminate, as with Title VII disputes; proof that the compensation is different and not based on factors other than sex will suffice. Furthermore, the law prohibits the lowering of the salaries for the higher paid group and therefore requires the salaries for the lower paid group to be raised. It is important to note that relief under the EPA is not barred by Eleventh Amendment immunity.[38] In one case, a principal argued that the district discriminated against her by paying male principals more in violation of the EPA. The female principal argued that five male principals at other similarly situated high schools had higher salaries, bonuses, and other financial incentives. Holding in favor of the district, the federal district court ruled that the female principal failed to produce any evidence that the male principals had comparable job duties.[39]

Because the EPA is limited to controversies dealing with equal work, its application is restricted to those circumstances where there are male and female employees performing substantially the same work but for different pay. Accordingly, if there are no male secretaries for a salary comparison, there can be no EPA violation, regardless of how abysmal the salaries of female secretaries may be.

Termination, Nonrenewal, and Denial of Tenure

In Title VII disparate treatment cases based on sex discrimination, the employee is required to prove that the employer elected to terminate or not renew the employee's contract due to sex rather than job performance, inappropriate conduct, interpersonal relationships, financial exigency, or other just cause. As in most cases where proof of intent is required, employees alleging sex discrimination often have difficulty supporting their claims, even if true. Occasionally, however, corroborating evidence will be inadvertently provided by officials responsible for making personnel decisions.

In a Tenth Circuit case, a female former principal was "bumped" by an associate superintendent who assumed her position as well as his own. The district initially proposed that the RIF was necessary due to financial exigency but later claimed that the female principal had continuing difficulty with her faculty, which allegedly was the basis for her contract not being renewed. The appeals court found the evidence to be contradictory, including the superintendent's annual evaluation of the principal in which she received

---

[36]29 U.S.C. § 206(d) (2012).

[37]*See, e.g.*, Vasquez v. El Paso Cnty. Cmty. Coll., 177 F. App'x 422 (5th Cir. 2006). In the 1980s, the comparable worth doctrine had been used as an attempt to remedy pay inequity that resulted from a history of sex-segregation in employment. For example, if working in child care (historically a profession dominated by females) is as important and difficult as working as a butcher (historically a profession dominated by males), then child-care workers and butchers should receive similar pay. Although courts have been skeptical of this doctrine, its merits continue to be debated.

[38]See Chapter 12, note 106, for an explanation of Eleventh Amendment immunity.

[39]Musgrove v. District of Columbia, 775 F. Supp. 2d 158 (D.D.C. 2011), *aff'd*, 458 F. App'x 1 (D.C. Cir. 2012).

high marks for establishing and maintaining staff cooperation and creating an environment conducive to learning. Given such discrepancies, the appeals court reversed the lower court's grant of summary judgment for the school district.[40]

Where facial discrimination does not exist, most plaintiffs will attempt to show that persons of the opposite sex were treated differently (e.g., required to meet different standards, assessed differently in meeting the same standards). With this approach, however, it often is difficult to identify a comparable party or to challenge subjective judgments regarding performance or potential.

Sexual Harassment

Sexual harassment generally refers to repeated and unwelcome sexual advances, sexually suggestive comments, or sexually demeaning gestures or acts. Both men and women have been victims of sexual harassment from persons of the opposite or same sex.[41] The harasser may be a supervisor, an agent of the employer, a coworker, a nonemployee, or even a student. Critical to a successful claim is proof that the harassment is indeed based on sex. There are two types of harassment cognizable under Title VII:[42] quid pro quo and hostile work environment. Each is reviewed briefly here.

Quid Pro Quo.   Quid pro quo literally means "this for that" or, in this context, giving something for something. To establish a prima facie case of quid pro quo harassment against an employer, the employee must show that:

- he or she was subjected to unwelcome sexual harassment in the form of sexual advances or requests for sexual favors;
- the harassment was based on the person's sex; and
- submission to the unwelcome advances was an express or implied condition for either favorable actions or avoidance of adverse actions by the employer.

Although only a preponderance of evidence is required in such cases, acquiring the necessary 51 percent can be difficult, particularly given that the violator is unlikely to provide corroborating testimony. If the employee succeeds, however, the law imposes strict liability on the employer because of the harasser's authority to alter the terms and conditions of employment.

Hostile Work Environment.   To prevail under this theory, the plaintiff must show that the environment in fact was hostile. The harassment needs to be severe or pervasive,

[40]Cole v. Ruidoso Mun. Sch., 43 F.3d 1373 (10th Cir. 1994). *But see* Atkinson v. LaFayette Coll., 460 F.3d 447 (3d Cir. 2006) (determining that the university administration provided sufficient documentation showing that the plaintiff had alienated others in her leadership role and that her ineffective interpersonal skills created poor relations and low morale within her unit).

[41]*See, e.g.*, Oncale v. Sundowner Offshore Servs., 523 U.S. 75 (1998).

[42]In addition to filing a Title VII claim, plaintiffs may file charges under state employment law or state tort law. Tort claims may include intentional infliction of emotional distress, assault and battery, invasion of privacy, and defamation. See Chapter 2 for a discussion of tort law.

unreasonably interfere with an individual's work performance (actual physical or psychological injury is not required),[43] **and be either threatening or humiliating.** A single offensive utterance generally will be insufficient.[44] If the victims are able to substantiate their claims, the employer may be vicariously liable for the acts of its supervisors who have immediate authority over an alleged victim.[45] However, the employer may raise an affirmative defense to liability if the employee suffered no tangible employment loss. Such a defense requires that the employer exercise reasonable care to prevent or promptly correct harassing behavior *and* that the employee failed to take advantage of preventive and corrective opportunities provided by the employer. Accordingly, to guard against liability, school districts should:

- prepare and disseminate sexual harassment policies;
- provide appropriate in-service training;
- establish appropriate grievance procedures, including at least two avenues for reporting in case one avenue is blocked by the harasser or supportive colleague;
- take claims seriously and investigate promptly;
- take corrective action in a timely manner; and
- maintain thorough records of all claims and activities.

Furthermore, investigators should have no stake in the outcome of the proceedings, and both male and female investigators should be available.

Employer liability in hostile environment claims is more difficult to establish than in quid pro quo claims, but it may be easier to substantiate in light of *Burlington Industries v. Ellerth*[46] and *Faragher v. City of Boca Raton*.[47] In these cases, the Supreme Court proclaimed that an employer is subject to vicarious liability for the acts of its supervisors with immediate authority over an alleged victim. However, the employer may raise an affirmative defense to liability if the employee suffered no tangible employment loss. Such a defense requires that the employer be able to show that it exercised reasonable care to prevent or promptly correct harassing behavior *and* that the employee failed to take advantage of the preventive and corrective opportunities provided by the employer.[48] While most of this discussion has focused on employers harassing employees, there have been some cases where teachers have alleged under Title VII that they were harassed by students.[49]

---

[43]Meritor Savs. Bank v. Vinson, 477 U.S. 57 (1986).

[44]Harris v. Forklift Sys., 510 U.S. 17 (1993).

[45]Faragher v. City of Boca Raton, 524 U.S. 775 (1998).

[46]524 U.S. 742 (1998).

[47]524 U.S. 775 (1998).

[48]*See* Pa. State Police v. Suders, 542 U.S. 129 (2004) (holding that although the employee did not avail herself of her employer's anti-harassment procedures, a question of triable fact remained regarding the adequacy of those procedures). The employer is expected to ensure that the reasons for any tangible loss, such as dismissal, are legitimate; thus, an affirmative defense cannot be asserted in those cases.

[49]*See* Lucero v. Nettle Creek Sch. Corp., 566 F.3d 720 (7th Cir. 2009) (rejecting teacher's claim that she had been harassed by students because students had been disciplined by school officials); Mongelli v. Clay Consol. Sch. Dist., 491 F. Supp. 2d 467 (D. Del. 2007) (finding harassment of teacher by special education student was actionable under Title VII).

Pregnancy Discrimination

Under the Pregnancy Discrimination Act (PDA),[50] an amendment to Title VII enacted in 1978, employers may not discriminate based on pregnancy, childbirth, or related medical conditions.[51] As such, pregnancy may not be used as a basis for refusing to hire an otherwise qualified applicant; denying disability, medical, or other benefits; or terminating or nonrenewal of employment. To succeed, the employee must show that the employer knew she was pregnant prior to the adverse action and that the pregnancy, rather than some other factor, was the basis of an adverse decision.[52]

If an employer requires a doctor's statement for other conditions, it also may require one for pregnancy prior to granting leave or paying benefits.[53] And, if employees are unable to perform their jobs due to pregnancy, the employer is required to treat them the same as any other temporarily disabled person.[54] Possible forms of accommodation may include modified tasks, alternate assignments, or disability leave (with or without pay). If a pregnant employee takes a leave of absence, her position must be held open the same length of time that it would be if she were sick or disabled. Moreover, maternity leave cannot be considered an interruption in employment for the purposes of accumulating credit toward tenure or seniority if employees retain seniority rights when on leave for other disabilities.[55]

Mandatory pregnancy leave policies requiring teachers to take a leave of absence prior to the birth of their children and specifying a return date also violate the Due Process Clause by creating an *irrebuttable presumption* that all pregnant teachers are physically incompetent as of a specified date.[56] School boards, however, may establish maternity leave policies that are justified by a business necessity, such as the requirement that the employee notify the administration of her intended departure and return dates, assuming this is required for other forms of extended personal leave. The business necessity of such a policy is to allow for planning and staffing in the employee's absence.

Retirement Benefits

Women live longer than men, which traditionally resulted in differential treatment of women with respect to retirement benefits. Specifically, employers either required women

---

[50]42 U.S.C. § 2000e(k) (2012).

[51]The PDA was passed in response to two Supreme Court decisions in which the denial of benefits for pregnancy-related conditions was found not to violate either Title VII or the Fourteenth Amendment. *See* Gen. Elec. Co. v. Gilbert, 429 U.S. 125 (1976); Geduldig v. Aiello, 417 U.S. 484 (1974).

[52]*See, e.g.*, Silverman v. Bd. of Educ. of City of Chi., 637 F.3d 729 (7th Cir. 2011) (holding that a principal's decision not to renew a teacher's contract was not pregnancy discrimination because the principal's decision was based on the need to eliminate a teaching position).

[53]EEOC v. Elgin Teachers Ass'n, 27 F.3d 292, 295 (N.D. Ill. 1994) (validating the association's maternity leave procedures, which conditioned the teacher's pay on a showing of "actual inability to work" during the six-week period).

[54]29 C.F.R. pt. 1604 app. (2012).

[55]Nashville Gas Co. v. Satty, 434 U.S. 136 (1977).

[56]Cleveland Bd. of Educ. v. LaFleur, 414 U.S. 632 (1974).

to make a higher contribution or awarded them lower annual benefits upon retirement. But in 1978, the Supreme Court rejected the use of sex-segregated actuarial tables in retirement benefits programs. The Court invalidated a retirement program requiring women to make a higher contribution to receive equal benefits on retirement, noting that sex was the only factor considered in predicting life expectancy.[57] This case established that women cannot receive lower benefits for equal contributions either.

SEXUAL ORIENTATION DISCRIMINATION

An employee's sexual orientation should not be the basis for negative employment decisions.

When public employees are discriminated against because of sexual orientation in hiring, promotion, termination, or any other term or condition of employment, they may file suit under the Fourteenth Amendment. Both public-sector and private-sector employees also may base related complaints on state statutes and local ordinances, where they exist. Although Title VII does not specifically prohibit discrimination based on sexual orientation, the EEOC ruled recently that Title VII protections extend to transgendered employees.[58]

Access to Benefits and Other Rights

Some states, locales, and employers—through their constitutions, statutes, ordinances, policies, or common law—have elected to permit same-sex partners to receive benefits. But unless restricted by state law or local ordinance, school districts may limit the availability of family benefits to legal spouses and dependents. Likewise, in states that recognize only heterosexual marriages, benefits such as retirement, death, health care, eye care, and dental are not generally available to same-sex partners or the children of same-sex partners unless the children have been legally adopted by the employee.[59] This position was fortified in 1996 by the passage of the Defense of Marriage Act (DOMA).[60] That statute gives states the option of refusing to extend marriage benefits to same-sex partners who were legally married in another state, territory, or country, but this statute has been under scrutiny. In 2011, the Obama Administration stated it would no longer defend the constitutionality of the DOMA in court.[61] Also, in 2012, the First Circuit and Second Circuit declared part of

[57]City of L.A. Dep't of Water & Power v. Manhart, 435 U.S. 702 (1978).

[58]Macy v. Holder, Appeal No. 0120120821 (EEOC Apr. 20, 2012) The EEOC observed that "intentional discrimination against a transgender individual because that person is transgender is, by definition, discrimination 'based on . . . sex,' and such discrimination therefore violates Title VII."

[59]Rutgers Council of AAUP Chapters v. Rutgers, 689 A.2d 828 (N.J. Super. Ct. App. Div. 1997).

[60]28 U.S.C. § 1738C (2012).

[61]See Press Release, Dep't of Justice, *Statement of the Attorney General on Litigation Involving the Defense of Marriage Act* (Feb. 23, 2011), http://www.justice.gov/opa/pr/2011/February/11-ag-222.html.

DOMA to be unconstitutional because it discriminates against married same-sex couples by denying them the same benefits afforded to heterosexual couples.[62] The Supreme Court will address many of these unsettled issues in 2013.

Adverse Employment Decisions

Terminating or not renewing employment of a public employee solely due to sexual orientation is unlikely to meet even rational basis scrutiny under the Equal Protection Clause.[63] School personnel might also rely on Title VII if school officials retaliated against them.[64] A private-sector employee must seek protection under either state law or local ordinance and must show that sexual orientation was in fact the basis of the adverse action to substantiate a valid discrimination claim. Such state and local provisions may not violate federal constitutional rights in their application, however.[65]

DISCRIMINATION BASED ON RELIGION

An employee's religion may not be used as a basis for negative employment decisions; however, it also may not be used by the employee to acquire benefits for opportunities that are rightfully determined by seniority or negotiated agreement.

The United States is now more culturally and religiously diverse than at any time in its history. When discrimination based on religion occurs, or an employer fails to provide reasonable accommodations, First and Fourteenth Amendment claims have been filed, as well as claims under Title VII.[66] At times, employees have claimed religious discrimination when they have been transferred, demoted, not renewed, terminated, or denied tenure. As with other claims of employment discrimination, the burden is on the employee to prove that the adverse action was motivated by an impermissible reason—specifically, the employee's

---

[62]*See* Massachusetts v. U.S. Dep't of Health & Human Servs., 682 F.3d 1 (1st Cir. 2012); Windsor v. United States, 699 F.3d 169 (2d Cir. 2012), *cert. granted*, 133 S. Ct. 786 (Dec. 7, 2012); *see* text accompanying note 47, Chapter 9.

[63]*See, e.g.*, Weaver v. Nebo Sch. Dist., 29 F. Supp. 2d 1279 (D. Utah 1998) (finding no job-related basis for the coach's removal, which was based solely on the community's negative response to her sexual orientation).

[64]*See* Birkholz v. City of N.Y., No. 10-cv-479, 2012 U.S. Dist. LEXIS 22445 (E.D.N.Y. Feb. 22, 2012).

[65]*See, e.g.*, Boy Scouts of Am. v. Dale, 530 U.S. 640 (2000) (ruling that a state law requiring the Boy Scouts to admit gay assistant scout masters violated the organization's expressive associational rights).

[66]If an employee claims an Equal Protection Clause violation due to religious-based facial discrimination by the government, either strict scrutiny or rational basis scrutiny could apply, depending on the form of the discrimination. When the government infringes upon the employee's First Amendment right to exercise religious beliefs (a fundamental right), strict scrutiny is applied. On the other hand, if the employee is a victim of discrimination based on religion, rational basis scrutiny is applied. Intent must be proved in cases involving facially neutral discrimination.

religious beliefs, practices, or affiliation. Employees experience difficulty in winning such cases because employers typically can identify one or more legitimate bases for the adverse action (e.g., lack of commitment,[67] excessive absenteeism[68]).

The first issue in such cases is whether the discrimination is based on sincerely held religious beliefs. A person's religion does not have to be organized, recognized, or well known. Curiously, even opposition to abortion, the draft, and nuclear power have qualified as "religious" beliefs,[69] although a belief in veganism has not.[70] Nonetheless, employers generally should accept an employee's representation of a sincerely held belief, at least for accommodation purposes.[71] Where the employee suffers an adverse employment outcome due to religion, the employer then must show either that an accommodation was offered but not taken, or that no reasonable accommodation existed that would not result in hardship for the employer.

Hiring and Promotion Practices

Private religious organizations are exempt from First and Fourteenth Amendment claims and in large part from the religious restrictions imposed by Title VII.[72] As a result, they are not generally prohibited from establishing religion as a *bona fide occupational qualification* (BFOQ) (e.g., when a Methodist theological seminary requires that its instructors be Methodists) or from making employment decisions that are consistent with the tenets of their particular faith.

In contrast, **religion will never qualify as a BFOQ in public education, and public employers may not inquire as to an applicant's religious beliefs, use the interview process as an opportunity to indoctrinate, or require prospective employees to profess a belief in a particular faith or in God.**[73] A person's religious affiliation or practice, if any, should not be considered in making an employment decision.

Accommodation

Recommended forms of religious accommodation include activities such as accepting voluntary substitutions and assignment exchanges, using a flexible schedule, and modifying

---

[67]*See, e.g.*, Lee v. Wise Cnty. Sch. Bd., No. 97-1471, 1998 U.S. App. LEXIS 367 (4th Cir. Jan. 12, 1998).

[68]*See, e.g.*, Rosenbaum v. Bd. of Trs. of Montgomery Cmty. Coll., No. 98-1773, 1999 U.S. App. LEXIS 4744 (4th Cir. Mar. 19, 1999).

[69]*See, e.g.*, Wilson v. U.S. W. Commc'ns, 58 F.3d 1337 (8th Cir. 1995).

[70]Friedman v. S. Cal. Permanente Med. Group, 125 Cal. Rptr. 2d 663 (Ct. App. 2002).

[71]*But see* Bushhouse v. Local Union 2209, 164 F. Supp. 2d 1066 (N.D. Ind. 2001) (concluding that there was no Title VII violation when a union sought to verify the religious beliefs of an employee who did not want to pay dues based on those beliefs).

[72]42 U.S.C. § 2000e-1(a) (2012); *see also* Hosanna-Tabor Evangelical Lutheran Church v. EEOC, 132 S. Ct. 694 (2012) (recognizing a ministerial exception to Title VII, which barred teacher's lawsuit involving an Americans with Disabilities Act claim against her parochial school; the decision allows religious institutions to discriminate against employees considered ministers and applies to other employment discrimination laws in addition to the ADA).

[73]Torcaso v. Watkins, 367 U.S. 488 (1961).

job assignments. If requested accommodations would compromise the constitutional, statutory, or contractual rights of others (e.g., interfere with a bona fide seniority system) or result in undue hardship, Title VII does not require the employer to make the accommodation.[74] **Undue hardship results when extensive changes are required in business practices or when the costs of religious accommodations are more than minimal.** Some of the more often litigated controversies regarding religious accommodation in public education involve dress codes, personal leave, and job assignments.

Attire Restrictions. As a general rule, public school district restrictions on the wearing of religious apparel, even if also purportedly cultural, will be upheld where young and impressionable students would perceive the garment as religious. In an illustrative case, the Third Circuit held that a district's refusal to accommodate a Muslim substitute teacher who sought to wear religious attire in the public school classroom did not violate Title VII.[75] The district's action was pursuant to a state statute that regarded the wearing of religious clothing as a significant threat to the maintenance of a religiously neutral public school system. A similar decision was reached by a federal court in Mississippi when it upheld the termination of a teacher's aide who refused to comply with the school's dress code proscribing religious attire.[76]

Personal Leave. Although most public school calendars allow time off for Christmas and Easter to coincide with semester and spring breaks, holy days of religions other than Christianity are not so routinely accommodated. But when a school district serves a significant number of students or employs a large number of teachers or staff of another religion, it is not uncommon for schools to be closed on several of the more significant days of worship for that religion as well. The "secular purpose" of such an act is the need to operate the school efficiently.

Modest requests for religious absences are typically accommodated, but others may result in hardship both for the district as well as for students.[77] The Supreme Court has held that an employer could satisfy Title VII by offering a reasonable accommodation, which may or may not be the one the employee preferred. Where leave has been provided, some employees have been satisfied when allowed to have the day off without adverse impact; others have requested that leave be accompanied with full or partial pay. In *Ansonia Board of Education v. Philbrook*, a teacher asserted that the negotiated agreement violated Title VII by permitting employees to use only three days of paid leave for religious purposes,

---

[74]Harrell v. Donahue, 638 F.3d 975 (8th Cir. 2011) (determining that it would be an undue hardship and a violation of the collective bargaining agreement to accommodate a postal employee who is a Seventh Day Adventist by not scheduling him to work on Saturdays).

[75]United States v. Bd. of Educ., 911 F.2d 882 (3d Cir. 1990). *But see* Brown v. F.L. Roberts & Co., 896 N.E.2d 1279 (Mass. 2008) (overturning summary judgment for the employer and holding that a Rastafarian service technician may have had a legitimate religious discrimination claim under state law after the employer required him to have short hair and to shave).

[76]McGlothin v. Jackson Mun. Separate Sch. Dist., 829 F. Supp. 853 (S.D. Miss. 1992).

[77]*See* Trans World Airlines v. Hardison, 432 U.S. 63 (1977) (finding no Title VII violation involving an employee who, for religious reasons, could not work on Saturdays; the employer was not required to bear more than minimal costs in making religious accommodations).

whereas three additional days of paid personal business leave could be used for specified secular activities.[78] The teacher proposed either permitting the use of the paid personal business leave days for religious observances or allowing employees to receive full pay and cover the costs of substitute teachers for each additional day missed for religious reasons. The Supreme Court, in upholding the agreement, held that the employer was not required to show that each of the plaintiff's proposed alternatives would result in undue hardship, and noted that the employer could satisfy Title VII by offering a reasonable accommodation, which may or may not be the one the employee preferred.

It is important to note that religious leave need not be paid unless compensation is provided for other forms of leave. In a Tenth Circuit case, the court rejected a teacher's claim that the school district's leave policy violated Title VII and burdened his free exercise of religion because he occasionally had to take unpaid leave to observe Jewish holidays.[79] The policy allowed teachers two days of paid leave that could be used for religious purposes. The court concluded that the availability of unpaid leave for additional religious observances constituted a reasonable accommodation under Title VII and did not place a substantial burden on free exercise rights. In another case, a Muslim teacher sued the school district for religious discrimination when she was denied an unpaid three-week leave of absence so she could make a pilgrimage to Mecca, Saudi Arabia. The once-in-a-lifetime pilgrimage, or Hajj, is considered one of the most important religious requirements for the Muslim faith. The U.S. Department of Justice reached a settlement with the school district, which accommodated the teacher with unpaid leave.[80]

■ ■ ■ ■ ■

AGE DISCRIMINATION

Under the Age Discrimination in Employment Act, persons age forty and over may claim age discrimination when the criteria used to make the adverse decision are only correlated with age (e.g., seniority, vesting in retirement).

Unlike other characteristics that generate charges of discrimination, age is unique in that everyone is subject to the aging process and eventually will fall within the age-protected category. Age discrimination employment claims may be filed under the Equal Protection Clause (any age),[81] the Age Discrimination in Employment Act (ADEA) (over age

---

[78]479 U.S. 60 (1986).

[79]Pinsker v. Joint Dist. No. 28J, 735 F.2d 388 (10th Cir. 1984).

[80]Manya A. Brachear, *Settlement Reached in Muslim's Suit Over Denial of Time Off for Hajj*, Chi. Trib. (Oct. 19, 2011), http://articles.chicagotribune.com/2011-10-19/news/ct-met-hajj-time-off-20111019_1_safoorah-khan-hajj-pilgrimage.

[81]Facially discriminatory procedures and practices that classify individuals on the basis of age can satisfy the Equal Protection Clause if they are rationally related to a legitimate governmental objective, whereas facially neutral criteria may be successfully challenged only with proof of discriminatory intent.

forty),[82] and state statutes. The Equal Employment Opportunities Commission is responsible for the enforcement of the ADEA.

The purpose of the ADEA is to promote the employment of older persons based on their ability, to prohibit arbitrary age discrimination in employment, and to find ways of addressing problems arising from the impact of age on employment. The ADEA specifically stipulates that "it shall be unlawful for an employer . . . to fail or refuse to hire or to discharge any individual or otherwise discriminate . . . with respect to his compensation, terms, conditions, or privileges of employment, because of such individual's age."[83] However, if the employment decision is based on any reasonable factor other than age, even though correlated with or associated with age, there is no violation of the ADEA. This standard requires less than is mandated under Title VII (i.e., intent in disparate treatment cases; proof that the practice, policy, or requirement was job related and justified by a business necessity in disparate impact cases). Moreover, if a reasonable factor is identified, the employer avoids liability even if other factors with less discriminatory impact are available and not used. Also, for a violation to be substantiated, age must play a role in the decision-making process *and* have a determinative influence on the outcome.[84]

Future application of the ADEA in public school cases may be limited at times, however, because the Supreme Court in *Kimel v. Florida Board of Regents* held that Eleventh Amendment immunity may be claimed as a defense where money damages to be paid out of the state treasury are sought in federal court.[85] Accordingly, immunity may be claimed when state laws consider school districts to be "arms of the state" rather than political subdivisions. But even when the Eleventh Amendment is used as a defense, plaintiffs can sue under comparable state statutes to vindicate their rights.

Hiring and Promotion Practices

As indicated, under the ADEA, except in those circumstances where age qualifies as a bona fide occupational qualification, selection among applicants for hiring or promotion may be based on any factor other than age. Although a BFOQ defense in an educational setting is unlikely in cases involving staff, teachers, or administrators, claims could conceivably be made for school bus drivers and pilots. Where a BFOQ is applied, the employer carries the burden of persuasion to demonstrate that there is reasonable cause to believe that all, or substantially all, applicants beyond a certain age would be unable to perform a job safely and efficiently. With Title VII cases, most employers who are alleged to have engaged in age discrimination simply respond that a better qualified applicant was hired, irrespective of age. In the effort to show pretext, an employee need not discredit each and every proffered reason for the rejection, but must cast substantial doubt on many, if not most, of the

[82]29 U.S.C. § 621 (2012).

[83]29 U.S.C. § 623(a)(1) (2012).

[84]*See, e.g.*, Hazen Paper Co. v. Biggins, 507 U.S. 604, 617 (1993).

[85]528 U.S. 62 (2000).

purported bases so that a fact finder then could rationally disbelieve the remaining reasons given the employer's loss of credibility.

In an illustrative Second Circuit case, a less experienced, unqualified, younger teacher was selected over the plaintiff.[86] The school district purported that the selected applicant performed better during the interview and was chosen largely on that basis. In ruling that pretext had been shown, the court noted that the successful candidate did not possess the specified degree and had submitted an incomplete file; that the employer had made misleading statements and destroyed relevant evidence; and that the plaintiff possessed superior credentials, except perhaps as to the interview. The fact that the previously selected applicant also was over the age of forty was irrelevant; what mattered was that she was substantially younger (i.e., age forty-two) than the plaintiff (age sixty-four).[87]

Termination, Nonrenewal, or Reduction- in-Force

The termination of at-will employees[88] is comparatively simple, as are the removal of non-tenured teachers and the elimination of unnecessary teaching and administrative positions, assuming strict adherence to approved policy. In contrast, to terminate tenured employees, as well as those working within a long-term contract, a "for cause" hearing will be required to permit the school district to show why the removal of the employee is necessary.[89] Although many factors may be considered in making such decisions (e.g., morality, efficiency), the employee's age may not be used, unless age qualifies as a BFOQ.

Retirement

Given that the mandatory retirement of school employees has been eliminated, districts have attempted to entice older employees to retire through attractive retirement benefits packages. **Under the ADEA, employers can follow the terms of a bona fide retirement plan so long as the plan is not a subterfuge to evade the purposes of the Act.**[90] Also, employers may not reduce annual benefits or cease the accrual of benefits after employees attain a certain age as an inducement for them to retire.[91]

In a 1993 Supreme Court decision, *Hazen Paper Co. v. Biggins*, the plaintiff was fired at age sixty-two, only a few weeks before completing ten years of service and being vested in his pension plan.[92] Two issues before the Supreme Court were whether the

---

[86]Byrnie v. Town of Cromwell, Bd. of Educ., 243 F.3d 93 (2d Cir. 2001).

[87]*See also* Brennan v. Metro. Opera Ass'n, 192 F.3d 310 (2d Cir. 1999) (noting that the fact that the replacement is substantially younger than the plaintiff is a more valuable indicator of age discrimination than whether the replacement was over age forty).

[88]At-will employees have no contract or job expectation and may leave or be terminated at any time. In many states, charter school employees are "at-will," even though they are considered public school employees.

[89]*See also* text accompanying notes 23–40, Chapter 12.

[90]*See, e.g.*, United Air Lines v. McMann, 434 U.S. 192 (1977).

[91]29 U.S.C. § 623(i)(1) (2012).

[92]507 U.S. 604 (1993).

employer's interference with the vesting of pension benefits violated the ADEA *and* whether the standard for liquidated damages[93] applied to informal age-based decisions by employers in addition to those that were based on formal policies that facially discriminate based on age. In a unanimous opinion, the Court vacated and remanded the lower court decision for a determination of whether the jury had sufficient evidence to find an ADEA violation.

Although it is difficult to prevail in an age-discrimination claim, expect the number of cases to remain high as the "baby boomers" become sexagenarians and septuagenarians over the next decade. Some will be denied employment, promotion, or vesting, whereas others may be disappointed in their retirement packages. Plaintiffs will allege age discrimination, but in most instances, those claims will be successfully rebutted by employers.

DISABILITY DISCRIMINATION

Federal disability law protects only those individuals who can show that they qualify as disabled and are otherwise qualified for the job.

Prior to 1973, federal claims regarding disability discrimination in employment were filed under the Equal Protection Clause.[94] The Fourteenth Amendment is now less often used due to the applicability of two federal statutes: **the Rehabilitation Act of 1973 (particularly § 504**[95]**), which applies to recipients of federal financial assistance, and Title I of the Americans with Disabilities Act of 1990 (ADA),**[96] **which applies to most employers with fifteen or more employees.** These statutes require nondiscrimination against employees with disabilities involving any term, condition, or privilege of employment. Section 504 complaints are submitted to the Office for Civil Rights within the Department of Education.[97] In comparison, the Equal Employment Opportunity Commission, the Department of Justice, and private litigants have enforcement rights under the ADA.

---

[93]For a discussion of liquidated damages, see *Trans World Airlines v. Thurston*, 469 U.S. 111, 126 (1985).

[94]The Fourteenth Amendment requires the application of rational basis scrutiny in cases where disability discrimination is facial and proof of intent where the alleged discrimination is facially neutral.

[95]29 U.S.C. § 794 (2012). The Supreme Court has held that a state employer is immune from paying damages in an ADA case. *See* Bd. of Trs. of Univ. of Ala. v. Garrett, 531 U.S. 356 (2001).

[96]42 U.S.C. § 12101 (2012).

[97]Complaint forms must be filed in a timely manner and signed by the employee. *See* Fry v. Muscogee Cnty. Sch. Dist., 150 F. App'x 980 (11th Cir. 2005) (concluding that an employee with morbid obesity failed to sign and thereby verify her ADA complaint—her attorney had signed it for her, but later failed to acquire her signature or properly amend the claim).

Qualifying as Disabled

When cases are filed, courts often are asked to resolve questions regarding whether the plaintiff is in fact disabled and, if so, what accommodations are required. A person qualifies as disabled under § 504 and the ADA if he or she:

- has a physical or mental impairment that substantially limits one or more major life activities;
- has a record of impairment;[98] or
- is regarded as having an impairment.[99]

However, more is required than simple knowledge of a condition that is physically or mentally limiting for the employee to establish that the employer regarded the employee as having an impairment. To illustrate, the Eighth Circuit granted the school district's motion for summary judgment because a teacher with multiple sclerosis did not demonstrate that she had an impairment that substantially limited a major life activity, had a record of impairment, or was regarded as having an impairment. The court reasoned that the school district's knowledge of the teacher's physical impairments did not establish that school officials regarded her as disabled, nor did the accommodations that were provided establish such.[100]

Although federal regulations define physical or mental impairment broadly,[101] persons who currently are involved in the use of illegal drugs,[102] are unable to perform the duties of the job due to alcohol use, have a contagious disease,[103] or otherwise represent a direct threat to the safety or health of themselves or others do not qualify as disabled. If the individual is disqualified because of health issues, the decision must be based on current medical evidence, and not on stereotypes or fears. Likewise, persons claiming discrimination due to pedophilia, exhibitionism, voyeurism, sexual behavior disorders, compulsive gambling, kleptomania, pyromania, and psychoactive substance use disorders resulting from current illegal drug use are not protected by either the ADA or § 504.

Qualifying as disabled requires a two-step process: identifying a physical or mental impairment and **determining whether the impairment substantially limits a major life activity.** The EEOC identifies several major life activities (i.e., walking, seeing,

---

[98]For example, when a person is discriminatorily treated because of having a history of hospitalization due to tuberculosis, alcoholism, or drug addiction, the person would qualify for protection as he is viewed as having a record of impairment.

[99]To illustrate, when a person is discriminatorily treated because of being HIV positive, but does not have AIDS or any type of current physical impairment limiting a major life activity, the person would qualify for protection as he is regarded as having an impairment.

[100]Nyprov v. Indep. Sch. Dist., 616 F.3d 728 (8th Cir. 2010).

[101]34 C.F.R. § 104.3(j)(2)(i) (2012).

[102]*See, e.g.*, McKissick v. Cnty. of N.Y., No. 1:09-cv-1840, 2011 U.S. Dist. LEXIS 123158 (M.D. Pa. Oct. 25, 2011) (noting that drug addiction can constitute a physical or mental impairment under the ADA, but the term "qualified individual with a disability" does not include individuals currently using illegal drugs).

[103]*But see* P.R. v. Metro. Sch. Dist. of Wash. Twp., No. 1:08-cv-1562, 2010 U.S. Dist. LEXIS 116223 (S.D. Ind. Nov. 1, 2010) (finding HIV infection is a physical impairment that substantially limits a major life activity).

hearing, speaking, breathing, learning, and working) in its guidelines for the ADA[104] and others in related manuals (i.e., caring for oneself, sitting, standing, lifting, concentrating, thinking, and interacting with others),[105] while the Supreme Court has expanded the list also to include both reproduction and performing manual tasks.[106] It is important to note that in 2008, the ADA was amended to clarify that mitigating measures should not be considered when determining whether someone has a disability under the ADA. In other words, even individuals who are able to control their disabilities with medication would still be considered disabled.[107]

Performance is substantially limited when an employee is unable to perform, or is significantly restricted in performing, a major life activity that can be accomplished by the average person in the general population. The nature, severity, duration, and long-term impact of the impairment are considered when determining whether a condition is substantially limiting.[108] Also, an impairment that is substantially limiting for one person may not be for another. To qualify, it must prevent or restrict an individual from performing tasks that are of central importance to most people's daily lives. If the life activity claimed is working, impairments are not substantially limiting unless they restrict the ability to perform a broad range of jobs and not just a single or specialized job.[109] In such cases, courts will consider the geographic area to which the plaintiff has reasonable access and the nature of the job from which the individual was disqualified, as well as other jobs that require similar training, knowledge, ability, or skill.[110] When contagious disease is involved, the employer should consider how the disease is transmitted, how long the employee is infectious, the potential harm to others, and the probability of transmission.

Otherwise Qualified

If a person qualifies as disabled, it then must be determined whether he or she is "otherwise qualified." **To be an otherwise qualified individual with a disability, the applicant or employee must be able to perform the essential functions of the job in spite of the disability, although reasonable accommodation at times may be necessary.** Generally, employers should not impose a blanket exclusion of persons with particular disabilities, but rather should provide individual review of each person. Only in rare instances will a particular disability disqualify an applicant (e.g., where federal or state law establishes health or ability requirements for particular types of employment).

---

[104]29 C.F.R. §1630.2(i) (2012).

[105]EEOC, *Technical Assistance Manual on the Employment Provisions (Title I) of the Americans with Disabilities Act* II-3 (Jan. 1992), http://archive.org/details/technicalassista00unse; EEOC, *Enforcement Guidance on the Americans with Disabilities Act and Psychiatric Disabilities*, No. 915.002, 6-7 (Mar. 25, 1997), http://www.eeoc.gov/policy/docs/psych.html.

[106]Bragdon v. Abbott, 524 U.S. 624 (1998) (reproduction); Toyota Motor Mfg. v. Williams, 534 U.S. 184 (2002) (manual tasks).

[107]Americans with Disabilities Amendments Act of 2008, 42 U.S.C. § 12101 (2012).

[108]29 C.F.R. § 1630.2(j)(1), (2) (2012).

[109]*See, e.g.*, Samuels v. Kansas City Mo. Sch. Dist., 437 F.3d 797 (8th Cir. 2006).

[110]29 C.F.R. § 1630.2(j)(2)(3) (2012).

In identifying the essential functions of the job, courts will give consideration to what the employer perceives to be essential. So long as each identified requirement for employment is either training related (for initial employment) or job related, the employer should not have difficulty in substantiating its claim of business necessity. For example, being on time to work and being at work on a regular daily basis can qualify as a business necessity for most positions in education as well as elsewhere. Employees often have claimed that their respective disabilities were the basis for their lateness or nonarrival. Although this may have been true, courts generally have not found such employees to be otherwise qualified.[111]

In *School Board of Nassau County, Florida v. Arline*, a teacher had three relapses of tuberculosis over a two-year period for which leave was given, and she was terminated prior to returning to work following the third leave.[112] The Supreme Court held that the teacher qualified as disabled under § 504 due to her record of physical impairment and hospitalization, but remanded the case for the district court to determine whether risks of infection to others precluded her from being otherwise qualified and whether her condition could be reasonably accommodated without an undue burden on the district. Following remand, the teacher was found to be otherwise qualified since she posed little risk of infecting others, and was ordered reinstated with back pay.

Reasonable Accommodation

Persons with disabilities must be able to perform all of the essential functions of the position, either with or without accommodation. Employers are responsible for providing reasonable accommodations, such as making necessary facilities accessible and usable, restructuring work schedules, acquiring or modifying equipment, and providing readers or interpreters.[113] Also, when not restricted by bargaining rights or other entitlements, transfer within the organization may qualify as a reasonable accommodation.[114] However, federal law does not require the employer to bump a current employee to allow a person with a disability to fill the position, to fill a vacant position it did not intend to fill, to violate seniority rights, to refrain from disciplining an employee for misconduct, to eliminate essential functions of the job, or to create a new unnecessary position. Moreover, an employer need not transfer the employee to a better position, or select a less-qualified or unqualified applicant solely because of disability.[115] Such forms of accommodation may be theoretically possible but would result in undue hardship to the employer and discriminate against other employees.

---

[111]*But see* Sch. Bd. of Nassau Cnty. v. Arline, 480 U.S. 273 (1987) (finding that a teacher who had three relapses of tuberculosis qualified as disabled under § 504 due to her record of physical impairment; on remand, she was found to be otherwise qualified).

[112]480 U.S. 273 (1987), *on remand*, 692 F. Supp. 1286 (M.D. Fla. 1988).

[113]*See* Lowe v. Indep. Sch. Dist. No. 1, 363 F. App'x 548 (10th Cir. 2010) (holding that school district failed to identify an appropriate accommodation for a teacher with a post-polio condition who resigned after being reassigned to a small and crowded classroom); Ekstrand v. Sch. Dist. of Somerset, 583 F.3d 972 (7th Cir. 2009) (finding that a jury could determine that the school district was required under the ADA to provide a classroom with natural light for a teacher who suffered from seasonal affective disorder), *aff'd*, 683 F.3d 826 (7th Cir. 2012).

[114]*See, e.g.*, Smith v. Midland Brake, 180 F.3d 1154 (10th Cir. 1999) (en banc).

[115]*See, e.g.*, Lors v. Dean, 595 F.3d 831 (8th Cir. 2010) (finding that the ADA is not an affirmative action statute).

Courts determine whether undue hardship results after a review of the size of the program and its budget, the number of employees, the type of facilities and operation, and the nature and cost of accommodation. Because there is no fixed formula for calculations, courts have differed markedly in identifying what they consider reasonable.

Termination and Nonrenewal

There are more individuals with disabilities in the workplace today than ever before, with many achieving leadership positions. Not all persons with disabilities have fared well, however, as some have not been selected for initial employment, granted tenure, promoted, or paid fairly, or have been arbitrarily discharged or forced to resign or retire.[116] At times, such adverse decisions were due to inadequate qualifications or skills, better-qualified applicants, poor job performance, posing a risk, or criminal wrongdoing.[117]

To support a disparate treatment adverse action claim, employees must show that they:

- have a disability that substantially limits a major life activity compared with the average person in the population;
- were the target of an action that qualified as adverse; and
- were denied employment or retention in employment due to disability.[118]

Claims of employment discrimination based on disabilities are more likely to focus on the ADA rather than § 504, given its broader application. School officials continue to search for effective, cost-efficient accommodations in their good faith efforts to comply with federal and state disability laws.

CONCLUSION

Federal law requires that employment decisions be based on qualifications, performance, merit, seniority, and the like, rather than factors such as race, national origin, sex, religion, age, or disability. Statutes vary considerably, however, about what they require. Moreover, federal regulations are extensive, complex, and at times confounding. As a result, courts differ in applying the law.

When preparing a policy related to personnel, it will be important to consider (1) whether it facially discriminates only in legal and appropriate ways and (2) whether it adversely affects a protected class, even though the policy may be facially neutral. Treating all persons the same may not accommodate individual needs and may inadvertently result in subtle forms of discrimination. In the alternative, treating persons differently may

---

[116]*See, e.g.*, Cigan v. Chippewa Falls Sch. Dist., 388 F.3d 331 (7th Cir. 2004).

[117]*See, e.g.*, Haulbrook v. Michelin N. Am., 252 F.3d 696 (4th Cir. 2001) (unable to perform job duties); Borgialli v. Thunder Basin Coal Co., 235 F.3d 1284 (10th Cir. 2000) (not qualified for position).

[118]*See, e.g.*, Macy v. Hopkins Cnty. Sch. Bd. of Educ., 484 F.3d 357 (6th Cir. 2007).

advantage some over others. Given the different types of discrimination that can be present in the workplace and the complexities of the law, there is no simple solution.

POINTS TO PONDER

1. A math and science teacher at an elite (selective admissions) public magnet school had a knowledge base measured in the 99th percentile of all persons taking a standardized math test. He was hired because of his knowledge of math and his ability to teach (as evidenced by the exceptional evaluations he received at his former school in China, his native country). Unfortunately, little effort was made to determine his English-language speaking skills, although his written English proficiency scores were satisfactory. After two semesters of unsuccessful teaching, his contract was not renewed. He was not tenured and did not have the guarantee of employment beyond the one-year contract that had just expired. He then sued the school under Title VII and the Fourteenth Amendment, alleging national origin discrimination. School officials claimed that he was not renewed because of his horrible teaching evaluations (based overwhelmingly on poor verbal communication skills) and not because of national origin. Two other Chinese teachers remained on staff. Is the nonrenewed teacher likely to win this suit? Why or why not?

2. All candidates for promotion are required to take a standardized test. Only persons scoring in the top 10 percent make the first cut and are allowed to proceed to the interview portion of the promotion process. You did poorly on the test, as did several others within your racial group. In fact, only 2 percent of those within your racial classification were in the top 10 percent, notwithstanding the fact that your race represents 25 percent of those in the pool of candidates who had the seniority to be considered for promotion. Performance on the test has been shown to be predictive of success on the job. You sued under Title VII, claiming disparate impact. Will you be successful in this suit? Why or why not?

3. A physically disabled school maintenance worker was terminated because of poor job performance. As a form of accommodation, he had requested either additional time (with additional compensation) to perform the job or an assistant to do a portion of the work for him—he can perform two-thirds of the daily work assignment within an eight-hour day. Following his termination, he filed suit under § 504 of the Rehabilitation Act of 1973. The school district, which receives federal funds, claimed that he was not otherwise qualified to meet the essential functions of the job. How will this legal challenge be decided? Why?

4. A well-qualified male applicant for a first grade teaching position was not hired, admittedly because of his sex. There were no other applicants for the position. The male principal made it clear that only females historically had been first grade teachers and that they, by their nature, were better suited for such positions. Moreover, he encouraged the male to apply for a middle school position, for which he also was licensed, and virtually guaranteed the applicant that he would be selected. Following his initial rejection, the male applicant filed suit against the district under Title VII. Is he likely to win this case? Why or why not?

CHAPTER TWELVE

TERMINATION OF EMPLOYMENT

State laws delineate the authority of school boards in terminating school personnel. Generally, these laws specify the causes for which a teacher may be terminated and the procedures that must be followed. The school board's right to determine the fitness of teachers is well established; in fact, courts have declared that school boards have a duty as well as a right to make such determinations. This chapter provides an overview of due process in connection with nonrenewal and dismissal, specific procedural requirements, judicial interpretations of state laws regarding causes for dismissal and an overview of remedies available to teachers for violation of their protected rights.

PROCEDURAL DUE PROCESS IN GENERAL

A teacher is entitled to procedural due process if termination of employment impairs a property or liberty interest.

Basic due process rights are embodied in the Fourteenth Amendment, which guarantees that no state shall "deprive any person of life, liberty, or property without due process of law."[1] Due process safeguards apply not only in judicial proceedings but also to acts of governmental agencies such as school boards. As discussed in Chapter 1, constitutional due process entails *substantive* protections against arbitrary governmental action and *procedural* protections when the government threatens an individual's life, liberty, or property interests. Most teacher termination cases have focused on procedural due process requirements.

The individual and governmental interests at stake and applicable state laws influence the nature of procedural due process required. **Courts have established that a teacher's interest in public employment may entail significant "property" and "liberty" rights necessitating due process prior to employment termination.** A *property interest* is a legitimate claim of entitlement to continued employment that is created

---

[1]As noted in Chapter 1, the Fourteenth Amendment restricts state, in contrast to private, action.

by state law.[2] The granting of tenure conveys such a right to a teacher. Also, a contract establishes a property right to employment within its stated terms. A property interest in continued employment, however, does not mean that an individual cannot be terminated; it simply means that an employer must follow the requirements of due process and substantiate cause.

The judiciary has recognized that Fourteenth Amendment *liberty rights* encompass fundamental constitutional guarantees, such as freedom of speech. Procedural due process is always required when a termination implicates such fundamental liberties. A liberty interest also is involved when termination creates a stigma or damages an individual's reputation in a manner that forecloses future employment opportunities. If protected liberty or property interests are implicated, the Fourteenth Amendment entitles the teacher at least to notice of the reasons for the school board's action and an opportunity for a hearing. Employment terminations are classified as either dismissals or nonrenewals. The distinction between the two has significant implications for teachers' procedural rights.

Dismissal

Dismissal refers to the termination for cause of any tenured teacher or of a probationary teacher within the contract period. Both tenure statutes and employment contracts establish a property interest entitling teachers to full procedural protection. Beyond the basic constitutional requirements of appropriate notice and an opportunity to be heard, state laws and school board policies often contain detailed procedures that must be followed. Failure to provide these additional procedures, however, results in a violation of state law, rather than constitutional law. Statutory procedures vary as to specificity, with some states enumerating detailed steps and others identifying only broad parameters. In addition to complying with state law, a school district must abide by its own procedures, even if they exceed state law. For example, if school board policy provides for a preliminary notice of teaching inadequacies and an opportunity to correct remediable deficiencies prior to dismissal, the board must follow these steps.

A critical element in dismissal actions is a showing of justifiable cause for termination of employment. If causes are identified in state law, a school board must base dismissal on those grounds. Failure to relate the charges to statutory grounds can invalidate the termination decision. Because statutes typically list broad causes—such as incompetency, insubordination, immorality, unprofessional conduct, and neglect of duty—notice of discharge must indicate specific conduct substantiating the legal charges. Procedural safeguards ensure not only that a teacher is informed of the specific reasons and grounds for dismissal but also that the school board bases its decision on evidence substantiating those grounds. Detailed aspects of procedural due process requirements and dismissal for cause are addressed in subsequent sections of this chapter.

Nonrenewal

Unless specified in state law, procedural protections are not accorded the probationary teacher when the employment contract is not renewed. At the end of the contract period,

---

[2]*See* Bd. of Regents v. Roth, 408 U.S. 564 (1972).

employment can be terminated for any or no reason, so long as the reason is not constitutionally impermissible (e.g., denial of protected speech).[3] The most common statutory requirement is notification of nonrenewal on or before a specified date prior to the expiration of the contract. When a statute designates a deadline for nonrenewal, a school board must notify a teacher on or before the established date. The timeliness of nonrenewal notices is strictly construed. The fact that the school board has set in motion notification (e.g., mailed the notice) generally does not satisfy the statutory requirement; the teacher's actual receipt of the notice is critical. A teacher, however, cannot avoid or deliberately thwart delivery of notice and then claim insufficiency of notice.[4] Failure of school officials to observe the notice deadline may result in a teacher's reinstatement for an additional year or even the granting of tenure in some jurisdictions.

In the nonrenewal of teachers' contracts, some states require a written statement of reasons and may even provide an opportunity for a hearing at the teacher's request. Unlike evidentiary hearings for dismissal of a teacher, the school board is not required to show cause for nonrenewal; a teacher is simply provided the reasons underlying the nonrenewal and an opportunity to address the school board. When a school board is required to provide reasons, broad general statements such as "the school district's interest would be best served," "the district can find a better teacher," or "the term contract has expired" will not suffice; the teacher must be given specific information about deficiencies, such as lack of classroom control or ineffective classroom instruction. Although statements must inform the teacher of specific deficiencies, school officials must be careful to avoid communicating stigmatizing reasons that would require a name-clearing hearing. Additionally, when state law establishes specific requirements and procedures for nonrenewal, failure to abide by these provisions may invalidate a school board's decision. A school board must not only follow state law but must also comply substantially with its own nonrenewal procedures.

Although state laws may not provide the probationary teacher with specific procedural protections, a teacher's interest in continued public employment may be constitutionally protected if a liberty or property right guaranteed by the Fourteenth Amendment has been abridged. Infringement of these interests entitles a probationary teacher to due process rights similar to the rights of tenured teachers.

Establishing Protected Property and Liberty Interests

The United States Supreme Court addressed the scope of protected interests encompassed by the Fourteenth Amendment in 1972 in two significant decisions: *Board of Regents v. Roth*[5] and *Perry v. Sindermann*.[6] These decisions addressed whether the infringement of

---

[3]*See, e.g.*, Grossman v. S. Shore Pub. Sch. Dist., 507 F.3d 1097 (7th Cir. 2007); Back v. Hastings, 365 F.3d 107 (2d Cir. 2004); Flaskamp v. Dearborn Pub. Schs., 385 F.3d 935 (6th Cir. 2004); see also Chapter 10 for a discussion of teachers' constitutional rights.

[4]*See* Sullivan v. Centinela Valley Union High Sch. Dist., 122 Cal. Rptr. 3d 871 (Ct. App. 2011) (finding a notice adequate when a teacher avoided timely notification by not attending work and leaving his home for the day).

[5]408 U.S. 564 (1972).

[6]408 U.S. 593 (1972).

a liberty or property interest entitles a probationary teacher to due process rights similar to the rights of tenured teachers. The cases involved faculty members at the postsecondary level, but the rulings are equally applicable to public elementary and secondary school teachers.

In *Roth*, the question before the Court was whether a nontenured teacher had a constitutional right to a statement of reasons and a hearing prior to nonreappointment. Roth had been hired on a one-year contract, and the university elected not to rehire him for a second year. Because Roth did not have tenure, there was no entitlement under Wisconsin law to an explanation of charges or a hearing. Roth challenged the nonrenewal, alleging that failure to provide notice of reasons and an opportunity for a hearing impaired his due process rights.

The Supreme Court held that nonrenewal does not require procedural protection unless impairment of a protected liberty or property interest can be shown. To establish infringement of a liberty interest, the Court held that the teacher must show that the employer's action (1) resulted in damage to his or her reputation and standing in the community or (2) imposed a stigma that foreclosed other employment opportunities. The evidence presented by Roth indicated that there was no such damage to his reputation or future employment. Accordingly, the Court concluded: "It stretches the concept too far to suggest that a person is deprived of 'liberty' when he simply is not rehired in one job but remains as free as before to seek another."[7] In rejecting Roth's claim that he had a protected property interest to continued employment, the Court held that **in order to establish a valid property right, an individual must have more than an "abstract need or desire" for a position; there must be a "legitimate claim of entitlement" grounded in state laws or employment contracts.**[8]

On the same day it rendered the *Roth* decision, the Supreme Court in the *Sindermann* case explained the circumstances that might create a legitimate expectation of reemployment for a nontenured teacher.[9] Sindermann was a nontenured faculty member in his fourth year of teaching when he was notified, without a statement of reasons or an opportunity for a hearing, that his contract would not be renewed. He challenged the lack of procedural due process, alleging that nonrenewal deprived him of a property interest protected by the Fourteenth Amendment and violated his First Amendment right to freedom of speech.

In advancing a protected property right, Sindermann claimed that the college, which lacked a formal tenure system, had created an informal, or de facto, tenure system through various practices and policies. Specifically, Sindermann cited a provision in the faculty guide stating: "The College wishes the faculty member to feel that he has permanent tenure so long as his teaching services are satisfactory."[10] The Supreme Court found that Sindermann's claim, unlike Roth's, might have been based on a legitimate expectation of reemployment promulgated by the college. According to the Court, the lack of a formal tenure

---

[7]*Roth*, 408 U.S. at 575.

[8]*Id.* at 577; *see also* Lautermilch v. Findlay City Schs., 314 F.3d 271 (6th Cir. 2002) (finding that a substitute teacher without a contract did not have a protected property interest in continued employment).

[9]408 U.S. 593 (1972).

[10]*Id.* at 600.

system did not foreclose the possibility of an institution fostering entitlement to a position through its personnel policies.

In assessing Sindermann's free speech claim, **the Supreme Court confirmed that a teacher's lack of tenure does not void a claim that nonrenewal was based on the exercise of constitutionally protected conduct.** Procedural due process must be afforded when a substantive constitutional right is violated.

The *Roth* and *Sindermann* cases are the legal precedents for assessing the procedural rights of nontenured teachers. To summarize, the Supreme Court held that a nontenured teacher does not have a constitutionally protected property right to employment requiring procedural due process before denial of reappointment. Certain actions of the school board, however, may create conditions entitling a nontenured teacher to notice and a hearing similar to the tenured teacher. Such actions would include:

- nonrenewal decisions damaging an individual's reputation and integrity;
- nonrenewal decisions foreclosing other employment opportunities;
- policies and practices creating a valid claim to reemployment; and
- nonrenewal decisions violating fundamental constitutional guarantees (e.g., freedom of expression, equal protection of the laws).

Because the Supreme Court has held that impairment of a teacher's property or liberty interests triggers procedural protections, the question arises as to what constitutes a violation of these interests. Courts have purposely avoided precisely defining the concepts of liberty and property, preferring to allow experience and time to shape their meanings. Since 1972, the Supreme Court and federal appellate courts have rendered many decisions that provide guidance in understanding these concepts.

Property Interest. In general, a nontenured employee does not have a property claim to reappointment unless state or local governmental action has clearly established such a right. Protected property interests are not created by mere longevity in employment. Issuing an employee a series of annual contracts does not constitute a valid claim to continued employment in the absence of a guarantee in state law, local policy, or an employment contract.[11] Similarly, a statute or collective bargaining agreement providing a teacher, upon request, a hearing and statement of reasons for nonrenewal does not confer a property interest in employment requiring legally sufficient cause for termination. Such a provision simply gives the teacher an opportunity to present reasons that the contract should be renewed.

Protected property interests are not created by mere longevity in employment. Both the Fourth and Tenth Circuits found that issuing an employee a series of annual contracts did not constitute a valid claim to continued employment in the absence of a guarantee in

---

[11]*See* Halfhill v. Ne. Sch. Corp., 472 F.3d 496 (7th Cir. 2006) (concluding that a nontenured teacher could not assert a property interest in continued employment based on a principal's positive midyear evaluation that indicated the teacher's contract would be renewed; the teacher demonstrated a lack of professionalism in handling several incidents with students after the evaluation).

state law, local policy, or an employment contract.[12] Also, a statute or collective bargaining agreement providing a teacher, upon request, a hearing and statement of reasons for nonrenewal does not confer a property interest in employment requiring legally sufficient cause for termination. The provision simply gives the teacher an opportunity to present reasons the contract should be renewed.

Liberty Interest.   As noted previously, liberty interests encompass fundamental constitutional guarantees such as freedom of expression and privacy rights. If governmental action in the nonrenewal of employment threatens the exercise of these fundamental liberties, procedural due process must be afforded.[13] Most nonrenewals, however, do not overtly implicate fundamental rights, and thus the burden is on the aggrieved employee to prove that the proffered reason is pretextual to mask impermissible grounds.

A liberty interest also may be implicated if the nonrenewal of employment damages an individual's reputation. The Supreme Court established in *Roth* that damage to a teacher's reputation and future employability could infringe Fourteenth Amendment liberty rights. In subsequent decisions, the Court identified prerequisite conditions for establishing that a constitutionally impermissible stigma has been imposed. According to the Court, **procedural protections must be afforded only if stigma or damaging statements are related to loss of employment, publicly disclosed, alleged to be false, and virtually foreclose opportunities for future employment.**[14]

Under this *stigma-plus test*, governmental action damaging a teacher's reputation, standing alone, is insufficient to invoke the Fourteenth Amendment's procedural safeguards.[15] While many employment actions may stigmatize and affect a teacher's reputation, they do not constitute a deprivation of liberty in the absence of loss of employment.[16] As the Ninth Circuit noted, "nearly any reason assigned for dismissal is likely to be to some extent a negative reflection on an individual's ability, temperament, or character," but circumstances giving rise to a liberty interest are narrow.[17] Charges must be serious implications against character, such as immorality and dishonesty, to create a stigma of constitutional magnitude that virtually forecloses other employment.

---

[12]Martin v. Unified Sch. Dist. No. 434, 728 F.2d 453 (10th Cir. 1984); Robertson v. Rogers, 679 F.2d 1090 (4th Cir. 1982); *see also* Ray v. Nash, 438 F. App'x 332 (5th Cir. 2011) (holding that a teacher's expectancy of reemployment because she had been successful in her teaching did not create a protected property interest).

[13]Violations of teachers' fundamental constitutional rights are discussed in Chapter 10; this section focuses on the violations of liberty rights where a teacher's reputation is damaged in the process of nonrenewal.

[14]Codd v. Velger, 429 U.S. 624 (1977); *see, e.g.*, O'Connor v. Pierson, 426 F.3d 187 (2d Cir. 2005); Bordelon v. Chi. Sch. Reform Bd. of Trs., 233 F.3d 524 (7th Cir. 2000).

[15]State constitutions, however, may provide greater protection of due process rights encompassing damage to reputation alone.

[16]*See, e.g.*, Brown v. Simmons, 478 F.3d 922 (8th Cir. 2007); Ulichny v. Merton Cmty. Sch. Dist., 249 F.3d 686 (7th Cir. 2001). *But see* Winegar v. Des Moines Indep. Cmty. Sch. Dist., 20 F.3d 895 (8th Cir. 1994) (holding that a teacher's disciplinary transfer to another school because of the physical abuse of a student involved a significant liberty interest necessitating an opportunity to be heard).

[17]Gray v. Union Cnty. Intermediate Educ. Dist., 520 F.2d 803, 806 (9th Cir. 1975).

According to the Fifth Circuit, a charge must give rise to "a 'badge of infamy,' public scorn, or the like."[18]

Among accusations that courts have found to necessitate a hearing are a serious drinking problem, emotional instability, mental illness, dishonesty, immoral conduct, child molestation, and extensive professional inadequacies.[19] Reasons held to pose no threat to a liberty interest include job-related comments such as personality differences and difficulty in working with others, hostility toward authority, incompetence, aggressive behavior, ineffective leadership, and poor performance.[20] **Charges relating to job performance may have an impact on future employment but do not create a stigma of constitutional magnitude.**

Liberty interests are not implicated unless damaging reasons are publicly communicated in the process of denying employment.[21] The primary purpose of a hearing is to enable individuals to clear their names. Without public knowledge of the reasons for nonreappointment, such a hearing is not required. Furthermore, a protected liberty interest generally is affected only if the *school board* (rather than an individual, media, or another source) *publicizes* the stigmatizing reasons. Accordingly, statements that are disclosed in a public meeting requested by the teacher or made by the teacher to the media or others do not require a name-clearing hearing. Likewise, rumors or hearsay remarks surfacing as a result of nonrenewal do not impair liberty interests.

PROCEDURAL REQUIREMENTS IN DISCHARGE PROCEEDINGS

When a liberty or property interest is implicated, the Fourteenth Amendment requires that a teacher be notified of charges and provided with an opportunity for a hearing that usually includes representation by counsel, examination and cross-examination of witnesses, and a record of the proceedings.

Since termination of a tenured teacher or a nontenured teacher during the contract period requires procedural due process, the central question becomes, what process is due? Courts have noted that no fixed set of procedures apply under all circumstances. Rather, due process entails a balancing of the individual and governmental interests affected in

---

[18]Ball v. Bd. of Trs., 584 F.2d 684, 685 (5th Cir. 1978).

[19]Knox v. N.Y.C. Dep't of Educ., 924 N.Y.S.2d 389 (App. Div. 2011); Donato v. Plainview-Old Bethpage Cent. Sch. Dist., 96 F.3d 623 (2d Cir. 1996); Vanelli v. Reynolds Sch. Dist. No. 7, 667 F.2d 773 (9th Cir. 1982) ; Carroll v. Robinson, 874 P.2d 1010 (Ariz.Ct. App. 1994).

[20]Gilder-Lucas v. Elmore Cnty. Bd. of Educ., 186 F. App'x 885 (11th Cir. 2006); Lybrook v. Members of Farmington Mun. Schs. Bd., 232 F.3d 1334 (10th Cir. 2000); Hayes v. Phoenix-Talent Sch. Dist. No. 4, 893 F.2d 235 (9th Cir. 1990).

[21]*See, e.g.*, Vega v. Miller, 273 F.3d 460 (2d Cir. 2001); Vandine v. Greece Cent. Sch. Dist., 905 N.Y.S.2d 428 (App. Div. 2010); *see also* Segal v. City of New York, 459 F.3d 207 (2d Cir. 2006) (holding that placement of damaging statements in a teacher's personnel file can meet the public disclosure aspect of a stigma-plus claim; future employers may have access to the file).

FIGURE 12.1   Procedural Due Process Elements in Teacher Termination Proceedings

- Notification of charges
- Opportunity for a hearing
- Adequate time to prepare a rebuttal to the charges
- Access to evidence and names of witnesses
- Hearing before an impartial tribunal
- Representation by legal counsel
- Opportunity to present evidence and witnesses
- Opportunity to cross-examine adverse witnesses
- Decision based on evidence and findings of the hearing
- Transcript or record of the hearing
- Opportunity to appeal an adverse decision

each situation. Minimally, the Fourteenth Amendment requires that dismissal proceedings be based on established rules or standards. Actual procedures will depend on state law, school board regulations, and collective bargaining agreements, but they cannot drop below constitutional minimums. For example, a statute requiring tenured teachers to pay half the cost of a hearing that the school board must provide was found to impair federal rights.[22]

In assessing the adequacy of procedural safeguards, the judiciary looks for the provision of certain basic elements to meet constitutional guarantees.[23] Courts generally have held that **a teacher facing a severe loss such as termination must be afforded full procedural due process** (see Figure 12.1 for elements).[24] Beyond the constitutional considerations, courts also strictly enforce any additional procedural protections conferred by state laws and local policies. Examples of such requirements might be providing detailed performance evaluations prior to termination, notifying teachers of weaknesses, and allowing an opportunity for improvement before dismissal. Although failure to comply with these stipulations may invalidate the school board's action under state law, federal due process rights per se are not violated if minimal constitutional procedures are provided. Except in limited circumstances, individuals are required to exhaust administrative procedures, or the grievance procedures specified in the collective bargaining agreement, prior to seeking judicial review. Pursuing an administrative hearing promotes resolution of a controversy at the agency level.

Various elements of due process proceedings may be contested as inadequate. Questions arise regarding issues such as the sufficiency of notice, impartiality of the board members, and placement of the burden of proof. The aspects of procedural due process that courts frequently scrutinize in assessing the fundamental fairness of school board actions are examined next.

---

[22]Rankin v. Indep. Sch. Dist. No. I-3, 876 F.2d 838 (10th Cir. 1989).

[23]At the same time, courts will not find a deprivation of procedural due process rights if educators do not avail themselves of the offered safeguards. *See, e.g.*, Segal v. N.Y. City, 459 F.3d 207 (2d Cir. 2006); Christensen v. Kingston Sch. Comm., 360 F. Supp. 2d 212 (D. Mass. 2005).

[24]This chapter focuses on procedural protections required in teacher terminations. It should be noted, however, that other school board decisions (e.g., transfers, demotions, or mandatory leaves) may impose similar constraints on decision making.

Notice of Charges

In general, **a constitutionally adequate notice is timely, informs the teacher of specific charges, and allows the teacher sufficient time to prepare a response.** Beyond the constitutional guarantees, state laws and regulations as well as school board policies usually impose very specific requirements relating to form, timeliness, and content of notice.[25] In legal challenges, the adequacy of a notice is assessed in terms of whether it meets constitutional and other requirements. Failure to comply substantially with mandated requisites will void school board action.

The form or substance of notice is usually stipulated in state statutes. In determining appropriateness of notice, courts generally have held that substantial compliance with form requirements (as opposed to strict compliance required for notice deadlines) is sufficient. Under this standard, the decisive factor is whether the notice adequately informs the teacher of the pending action. For example, if a statute requires notification by certified mail and the notice is mailed by registered mail or is personally delivered, it substantially complies with the state requirement. However, oral notification will not suffice if the law requires written notification. If the form of the notice is not specified by statute, any timely notice that informs a teacher is adequate.

For a notice to comply with constitutional due process guarantees, reasonable efforts must be made for the teacher to receive the notice. In a New York case, the board of education mailed the notice of intent to terminate a teacher's employment by certified and regular mail to an outdated address.[26] The regular mail copy was not returned, but the certified copy was returned as unclaimed. Consequently, the teacher argued he did not receive the notice and could not request a hearing. The court held that the notice did not meet statutory requirements because the board of education was aware that the notice was returned as unclaimed and did not make additional efforts, such as hand delivery of the notice to the teacher in his classroom.

Although form and timeliness are important concerns in issuing a notice, the primary consideration is the statement of reasons for an action. **With termination of a teacher's contract, school boards must bring specific charges against the teacher,** including not only the factual basis for the charges but also the names of accusers. State laws may impose further specifications, such as North Dakota's requirement that reasons for termination in the notice must be based on issues raised in prior written evaluations.[27] If the state law identifies grounds for dismissal, charges also must be based on the statutory causes. But a teacher cannot be forced to defend against vague and indefinite charges that simply restate the statutory categories, such as incompetency or neglect of duty. Notice must include specific accusations to enable the teacher to prepare a proper defense. The Arkansas Supreme Court interpreted its state Teacher Fair Dismissal Act as requiring sufficient notice "such

---

[25]*See* Sajko v. Jefferson Cnty. Bd. of Educ., 314 S.W.3d 290 (Ky. 2010) (interpreting state law that requires a teacher challenging a dismissal to notify school officials within ten days of the receipt of termination notice to mean *actual receipt—not postmarked within ten days*).

[26]Norgrove v. Bd. of Educ., N.Y.C., 881 N.Y.S.2d 802 (Sup. Ct. 2009).

[27]Hoffner v. Bismarck Pub. Sch. Dist., 589 N.W.2d 195 (N.D. 1999).

that *a reasonable teacher* could defend against the reasons given."[28] Furthermore, only charges identified in the notice can form the basis for dismissal.

Hearing

In addition to notice, **some type of hearing is required *before* an employer makes the initial termination decision;** post-termination hearings do not satisfy federal constitutional due process requirements.[29] Courts have not prescribed in detail the procedures to be followed in administrative hearings. Basically, the fundamental constitutional requirement is fair play—that is, an opportunity to be heard at a meaningful time and in a meaningful manner. Beyond this general requirement, the specific aspects of a hearing are influenced by the circumstances of the case, with the potential for grievous losses necessitating more extensive safeguards. According to the Missouri Supreme Court, a hearing generally should include a meaningful opportunity to be heard, to state one's position, to present witnesses, and to cross-examine witnesses; the accused also has the right to counsel and access to written reports in advance of the hearing.[30] Implicit in these rudimentary requirements are the assumptions that the hearing will be conducted by an impartial decision maker and will result in a decision based on the evidence presented. This section examines issues that may arise in adversarial hearings before the school board.

Adequate Notification of Hearing. As noted, due process rights afford an individual the opportunity to be heard at a meaningful time. This implies sufficient time between notice of the hearing and the scheduled meeting. Unless state law designates a time period, the school board can establish a reasonable date for the hearing, taking into consideration the specific facts and circumstances. In a termination action, the school board would be expected to provide ample time for the teacher to prepare a defense; however, the teacher bears the burden of requesting additional time if the length of notice is insufficient to prepare an adequate response.

Waiver of Hearing. Although a hearing is an essential element of due process, a teacher can waive this right by failing to request a hearing, refusing to attend, or walking out of the hearing.[31] Voluntary resignation of a position also waives an individual's entitlement to a hearing. In some states, a hearing before the school board may be waived if an employee

---

[28]Russell v. Watson Chapel Sch. Dist., 313 S.W.3d 1 (Ark. 2009).

[29]Cleveland Bd. of Educ. v. Loudermill, 470 U.S. 532 (1985); *see also* Curtis v. Montgomery Cnty. Pub. Schs., 242 F. App'x 109 (4th Cir. 2007) (concluding that the predismissal process provided to a teacher, including notice that he was being investigated regarding serious allegations and placed on suspension, satisfied pre-termination rights).

[30]Valter v. Orchard Farm Sch. Dist., 541 S.W.2d 550 (Mo. 1976); *see also* McClure v. Indep. Sch. Dist. No. 16, 228 F.3d 1205 (10th Cir. 2000) (holding that a teacher was deprived of due process rights when she was not allowed to cross-examine witnesses who provided testimony by affidavit at her termination hearing).

[31]*See, e.g.*, Jefferson v. Sch. Bd., 452 F. App'x 356 (4th Cir. 2011); Miller v. Clark Cnty. Sch. Dist., 378 F. App'x 623 (9th Cir. 2010); Schimenti v. Sch. Bd., 73 So. 3d 831 (Fla. Dist. Ct. App. 2011); Smith v. Caddo Parish Sch. Bd., 69 So. 3d 543 (La. Ct. App. 2011).

elects an alternative hearing procedure, such as a grievance mechanism or an impartial referee. For example, the Third Circuit held that an employee's choice of *either* a hearing before the school board *or* arbitration under the collective bargaining agreement met the constitutional requirements of due process; the school board was not required to provide the individual a hearing in addition to the arbitration proceeding.[32]

Impartial Hearing. A central question raised regarding hearings is the school board's impartiality as a hearing body. This issue arises because school boards often perform multiple functions in a hearing; they may investigate the allegations against a teacher, initiate the proceedings, and render the final judgment. Teachers have contended that such expansive involvement violates their right to an unbiased decision maker. Rejecting the idea that combining the adjudicative and investigative functions violates due process rights, courts generally have determined that prior knowledge of the facts does not disqualify school board members.[33] In addition, the fact that the board makes the initial decision to terminate employment does not render its subsequent review impermissibly biased. Neither is a hearing prejudiced by a limited, preliminary inquiry to determine if there is a basis for terminating a teacher. Since hearings are costly and time consuming, such a preliminary investigation may save time as well as potential embarrassment.

In *Hortonville Joint School District No. 1 v. Hortonville Education Association*, the United States Supreme Court firmly established that **the school board is a proper review body to conduct dismissal hearings.**[34] The Court held that a school board's involvement in collective negotiations did not disqualify it as an impartial hearing board in the subsequent dismissal of striking teachers. The Court noted that "a showing that the Board was 'involved' in the events preceding this decision, in light of the important interest in leaving with the board the power given by the state legislature, is not enough to overcome the presumption of honesty and integrity in policymakers with decision-making power."[35]

Although the school board is the proper hearing body, bias on the part of the board or its members is constitutionally unacceptable. A teacher challenging the impartiality of the board has the burden of proving actual, not merely potential, bias. This requires the teacher to show more than board members' predecision involvement or prior knowledge of the issues.[36] A high probability of bias, however, can be shown if a board member has a personal interest in the outcome of the hearing or has suffered personal abuse or criticism from a teacher.

Evidence. Under teacher tenure laws, the burden of proof is on the school board to show cause for dismissal. The standard of proof generally applied to administrative bodies is to

---

[32]Pederson v. S. Williamsport Area Sch. Dist., 677 F.2d 312 (3d Cir. 1982).

[33]*See, e.g.*, Withrow v. Larkin, 421 U.S. 35 (1975).

[34]426 U.S. 482 (1976).

[35]*Id.* at 496–97; *see also* James v. Indep. Sch. Dist. No. I-050, 448 F. App'x 792 (10th Cir. 2011) (ruling that board members' previous criticisms of administrators' performance did not render them biased when they eliminated positions due to urgent financial conditions).

[36]*See, e.g.*, Say v. Umatilla Sch. Dist. 6, 364 F. App'x 385 (9th Cir. 2010); Beischel v. Stone Bank Sch. Dist., 362 F.3d 430 (7th Cir. 2004).

produce a *preponderance of evidence*. Administrative hearings are not held to the more stringent standards applied in criminal proceedings (i.e., clear and convincing evidence beyond a reasonable doubt). Proof by a preponderance of evidence simply indicates that the majority of the evidence supports the board's decision or, as the New York high court stated, is "such relevant proof as a reasonable mind may accept as adequate to support a conclusion."[37] If the board fails to meet this burden of proof, the judiciary will not uphold the termination decision. For example, the Nebraska Supreme Court, in overturning a school board's dismissal decision, concluded that dissatisfaction of parents and school board members was not sufficient evidence to substantiate incompetency charges against a teacher who had received above-average performance evaluations during her entire term of employment.[38]

Only relevant, well-documented evidence presented at the hearing can be the basis for the board's decision. Unlike formal judicial proceedings, hearsay evidence may be admissible in administrative hearings.[39] Courts have held that such evidence provides the background necessary for understanding the situation. Comments and complaints of parents have been considered relevant, but hearsay statements of students generally have been given little weight.[40]

DISMISSAL FOR CAUSE

Causes for dismissal vary widely among the states, but usually include such grounds as incompetency, immorality, insubordination, unprofessional conduct, neglect of duty, and other good and just cause.

Tenure laws are designed to assure competent teachers continued employment so long as their performance is satisfactory. **With the protection of tenure, a teacher can be dismissed only for cause and only in accordance with the procedures specified by law.** Tenure rights accrue under state laws and therefore must be interpreted in light of each state's provisions.

When grounds for dismissal of a permanent teacher are identified by statute, a school board cannot base dismissal on reasons other than those specified. To cover unexpected matters, statutes often include a catchall phrase such as "other good and just cause." Causes

[37]Altsheler v. Bd. of Educ., 464 N.E.2d 979, 979–80 (N.Y. 1984).

[38]Schulz v. Bd. of Educ., 315 N.W.2d 633 (Neb. 1982); *see also* Weston v. Indep. Sch. Dist. No. 35, 170 P.3d 539 (Okla. 2007) (ordering the school district to reinstate a teacher because officials did not prove by a preponderance of evidence that dismissal was warranted).

[39]*See, e.g.,* Colon v. N.Y.C. Dep't of Educ., 941 N.Y.S.2d 628 (App. Div. 2012); Drummond v. Todd Cnty. Bd. of Educ., 349 S.W.3d 316 (Ky. Ct. App. 2011); *see also* Waisanen v. Clatskanie Sch. Dist. #6J, 215 P.3d 882 (Or. Ct. App. 2009) (holding that student's polygraph exam results were admissible, particularly since student was subject to cross-examination).

[40]*See, e.g.,* Daily v. Bd. of Educ., 588 N.W.2d 813 (Neb. 1999); *see also* Gongora v. N.Y.C. Dep't of Educ., 930 N.Y.S.2d 757, 773 (Sup. Ct. 2010) (holding that a student's hearsay evidence of "uncertain reliability" was not a consideration in determining a preponderance of evidence; the student did not appear at the hearing, so credibility of statements could not be assessed).

included in statutes vary considerably among states and range from an extensive listing of individual grounds to a simple statement that dismissal must be based on cause. The most frequently cited causes are incompetency, immorality, and insubordination.

Since grounds for dismissal are determined by statute, it is difficult to provide generalizations that apply to all teachers. The causes are broad in scope and application; in fact, individual causes often have been attacked for impermissible vagueness. It is not unusual to find dismissal cases with similar factual situations based on different grounds. In addition, several grounds often are introduced and supported in a single termination case. Illustrative case law is examined here in relation to the more frequently cited grounds for dismissal.

Incompetency

Incompetency is legally defined as the "lack of ability, legal qualifications, or fitness to discharge the required duty."[41] Although incompetency has been challenged as unconstitutionally vague, courts have found the word sufficiently precise to give fair warning of prohibited conduct. These cases often involve issues relating to teaching methods, grading procedures, classroom management, and professional relationships.

Dismissals for incompetency are generally based on several factors or a pattern of behavior rather than isolated incidents. Indicators of incompetency might include poor rapport with students, inappropriate use of class time, irrational grading of students, lack of student progress, and deficiencies in judgment and attitude. Termination for incompetency usually requires school officials systematically to document a teacher's performance. Providing opportunities and support for a teacher to achieve expected performance standards can be an important component in substantiating that a teacher had adequate notice of deficiencies.

Immorality

Immorality, one of the most frequently cited causes for dismissal, is typically not defined in state laws. The judiciary has tended to interpret immorality broadly as unacceptable conduct that affects a teacher's fitness to teach. **The teacher is viewed as an exemplar whose conduct is influential in shaping the lives of young students, so educators are held to a higher level of discretion than required for the general public.**

Sexually related conduct per se between a teacher and student has consistently been held to constitute immoral conduct justifying termination of employment. The Supreme Court of Colorado stated that when a teacher engages in sexually provocative or exploitative conduct with students, "a strong presumption of unfitness arises against the teacher."[42] Similarly, a Washington appellate court found that a male teacher's sexual relationship with a minor student justified dismissal.[43] The court declined to hold that an adverse effect

---

[41]BLACK'S LAW DICTIONARY (9th ed. 2009).

[42]Weissman v. Bd. of Educ., 547 P.2d 1267, 1273 (Colo. 1976).

[43]Denton v. S. Kitsap Sch. Dist. No. 402, 516 P.2d 1080 (Wash. Ct. App. 1973); *see also* Gongora v. N.Y.C. Dep't of Educ., 951 N.Y.S.2d 137 (App. Div. 2012) (finding that calling a student's home, asking the student out on a date, and urging the student not to report the call constituted sexual misconduct justifying the termination of a teacher).

on fitness to teach must be shown. Rather, the court concluded that when a teacher and a minor student are involved, the board might reasonably decide that such conduct is harmful to the school district. In upholding the termination of a teacher involved in a sexual relationship with a minor, the Supreme Court of Delaware declared that such sexual contact directly relates to a teacher's fitness to teach and affects the community.[44]

In addition to sexual improprieties with students, which clearly are grounds for dismissal, other conduct that sets a bad example for students may be considered immoral under the "role model" standard. **Courts, however, generally have required school officials to show that misconduct or a particular lifestyle has an adverse impact on fitness to teach.** They have recognized that allowing dismissal merely based on a showing of immoral behavior without consideration of the nexus between the conduct and fitness to teach would be an unwarranted intrusion on a teacher's right to privacy.

A California appellate court examined whether a teacher's immoral conduct rendered him unfit to teach.[45] In this case, the teacher, also a dean of students in a middle school, posted a sexually explicit ad with pornographic images of himself on Craigslist in the "men seeking men" category. An anonymous report to the local police led to the police notifying local school officials and the subsequent termination of the teacher. Although the teacher argued that no connection existed between his behavior and his teaching effectiveness, the appellate court disagreed, noting that at least one parent and several school officials had seen the ad. In upholding the termination, the court noted: "There are certain professions which impose upon persons attracted to them, responsibilities and limitations on freedom of action which do not exist in regard to other callings."[46] The court also noted that judges, police officers, and teachers are in this category.[47]

Teachers' sexual orientation has been an issue in several controversial dismissal cases. Although these cases often have raised constitutional issues related to privacy and freedom of expression, courts also have confronted the question of whether sexual orientation per se is evidence of unfitness to teach or whether it must be shown that this lifestyle impairs teaching effectiveness.[48] Courts have rendered diverse opinions regarding lesbian, gay, bisexual, and transgender (LGBT) educators. According to the Supreme Court of California, immoral or unprofessional conduct or moral turpitude must be related to

---

[44]Lehto v. Bd. of Educ., 962 A.2d 222 (Del. 2008); *see also* State v. Edwards, No. 106,435, slip op. at 3 (Kan. App. Ct. Nov. 2, 2012) (upholding the constitutionality of a statute that makes a sexual relationship between a teacher and a student a crime; with the disparity in power between a teacher and student, the court concluded that "the right of privacy does not encompass the right of a high school teacher to have sex with students enrolled in the same school system").

[45]San Diego Unified Sch. Dist. v. Comm'n on Prof'l Competence, 124 Cal. Rptr. 3d 320 (Ct. App. 2011).

[46]*Id.* at 327.

[47]The California court cited a U.S. Supreme Court decision holding that a police officer could be terminated for selling sexually explicit videos of himself on eBay, establishing that termination for public distribution or posting of such material does not violate constitutional rights of public employees. *See* City of San Diego v. Roe, 543 U.S. 77 (2004).

[48]See the section entitled "Sexual Orientation Discrimination" in Chapter 11, for a discussion of claims of discrimination based on sexual orientation and the section in Chapter 10 entitled "Constitutional Privacy Rights" for a discussion of constitutionally protected privacy rights.

unfitness to teach to justify termination.[49] Yet the Supreme Court of Washington upheld the dismissal of a teacher based simply on the knowledge of his homosexuality.[50] The court feared that public controversy could interfere with the teacher's classroom effectiveness.

In recent years, however, courts have been reluctant to support the dismissal of an LGBT educator simply because the school board does not approve of a particular private lifestyle. For example, an Ohio federal court concluded that the nonrenewal of a teacher because of his homosexuality did not bear a rational relationship to a legitimate government purpose, thereby violating the Equal Protection Clause.[51]

Whereas many teacher terminations for immorality involve sexual conduct, immorality is broader in meaning and scope. As one court noted, it covers conduct that "is hostile to the welfare of the school community."[52] Such hostile conduct has included, among other things, dishonest acts, criminal conduct, and drug-related conduct. Specific actions substantiating charges of immorality have included misrepresenting absences from school as illness,[53] being involved in the sale of illegal drugs,[54] pleading guilty to grand larceny,[55] altering student transcripts,[56] reporting to school under the influence of marijuana,[57] and pressuring a young incarcerated woman to give up her eleven-month-old child for adoption.[58]

Although immorality is an abstract concept that can encompass broad-ranging behavior, it is understood to refer to actions that violate moral standards and render a teacher unfit to teach. Courts consistently hold that to justify termination for immorality, school officials must link the challenged conduct to impairment of the teacher's effectiveness in the classroom.

Insubordination

Insubordination is generally defined as the willful disregard of or refusal to obey school regulations and official orders. Teachers can be dismissed for violation of administrative regulations and policies even though classroom performance is satisfactory; school officials are not required to establish a relationship between the insubordinate conduct and fitness to teach.

With the plethora of regulations enacted by school districts, wide diversity is found in the types of behavior adjudicated as insubordination. Dismissals based on insubordination have been upheld in cases involving refusal to abide by specific school directives,

---

[49]Morrison v. State Bd. of Educ., 461 P.2d 375 (Cal. 1969).

[50]Gaylord v. Tacoma Sch. Dist. No. 10, 559 P.2d 1340 (Wash. 1977).

[51]Glover v. Williamsburg Local Sch. Dist., 20 F. Supp. 2d 1160 (S.D. Ohio 1998).

[52]Jarvella v. Willoughby-Eastlake City Sch. Dist., 233 N.E.2d 143, 145 (Ohio 1967).

[53]Riverview Sch. Dist. v. Riverview Educ. Ass'n, 639 A.2d 974 (Pa. Commw. Ct. 1994).

[54]Woo v. Putnam Cnty. Bd. of Educ., 504 S.E.2d 644 (W. Va. 1998).

[55]Green v. N.Y. City Dep't of Educ., 793 N.Y.S.2d 405 (App. Div. 2005); *see also* Patterson v. City of N.Y., 946 N.Y.S.2d 472 (App. Div. 2012) (finding misconduct justifying dismissal when a teacher provided an Albany address to avoid paying New York City income taxes).

[56]Hill v. Indep. Sch. Dist. No. 25, 57 P.3d 882 (Okla. Civ. App. 2002).

[57]Younge v. Bd. of Educ., 788 N.E.2d 1153 (Ill. App. Ct. 2003).

[58]Homa v. Carthage R-IX Sch. Dist., 345 S.W.3d 266 (Mo. Ct. App. 2011).

unwillingness to cooperate with superiors, unauthorized absences, and numerous other actions. Since conduct is measured against the existence of a rule or policy, a school board may more readily document insubordination than most other legal causes for dismissal.

Many state laws and court decisions require that acts be "willful and persistent" to be considered insubordinate. A Florida teacher's continued refusal to provide lesson plans during school absences resulted in termination for insubordination. A Florida appellate court, affirming the dismissal, noted insubordination under state law as "constant or continuing intentional refusal to obey a direct order, reasonable in nature, and given by and with proper authority."[59] A California appellate court upheld the termination of a tenured teacher for repeatedly refusing to pursue certification to teach English language learners (ELLs) as required for all teachers.[60] The court ruled that it was within the school board's authority to impose this additional requirement.

Teachers cannot ignore reasonable directives and policies of administrators or school boards. If the school board has prohibited corporal punishment or prescribed procedures for its administration, teachers must strictly adhere to board requirements. In upholding the termination of a Colorado teacher, the state supreme court ruled that tapping a student on the head with a three-foot pointer supported termination when the teacher had been warned and disciplined previously for using physical force in violation of school district policy.[61] The Eleventh Circuit found that insubordination was established when a teacher refused to undergo a urinalysis drug test within two hours of the discovery of marijuana in her car in the school parking lot as required by school board policy.[62] The Eighth Circuit upheld the dismissal of a teacher for violating a school board policy that prohibited students' use of profanity in the classroom; students had used profanity in various creative writing assignments such as plays and poems.[63] The key determinant generally is whether the teacher has persisted in disobeying a *reasonable* school policy or directive.

Unprofessional Conduct

Some states identify either unprofessional conduct or conduct unbecoming a teacher as cause for dismissal. A teacher's activities both inside and outside of school can be used to substantiate this charge when it interferes with teaching effectiveness. Dismissals for

[59]Dolega v. Sch. Bd., 840 So. 2d 445, 446 (Fla. Dist. Ct. App. 2003); *see also* Miller v. Clark Cnty. Sch. Dist., 378 F. App'x 623 (9th Cir. 2010) (holding that evidence showing prior warnings, admonitions, and suspensions established grounds to dismiss a teacher for insubordination); Chattooga Cnty. Bd. of Educ. v. Searels, 691 S.E.2d 629 (Ga. Ct. App. 2010) (finding termination justified when a teacher continued to make inappropriate statements about students after repeated warnings from her principal).

[60]Governing Bd. v. Comm'n on Prof'l Conduct, 99 Cal. Rptr. 3d 903, 913 (Ct. App. 2009); *see also* Overton v. Bd. of Educ., 900 N.Y.S.2d 338, 339 (App. Div. 2010) (ruling that both misconduct and insubordination were established by the teacher's "pattern of poor work performance and disruptive behavior").

[61]Bd. of Educ. v. Flaming, 938 P.2d 151 (Colo. 1997). *But see In re* Principe v. N.Y.C. Dep't of Educ., 941 N.Y.S.2d 574 (App. Div. 2012) (finding the termination of a middle school dean of students for violating the policy against corporal punishment excessive when he physically restrained students in two separate incidents; the action was found not to be premeditated and was taken in his role as disciplinarian), *review denied*, 976 N.E.2d 238 (N.Y. 2012).

[62]Hearn v. Bd. of Pub. Educ., 191 F.3d 1329 (11th Cir. 1999).

[63]Lacks v. Ferguson Reorganized Sch. Dist. R-2, 147 F.3d 718 (8th Cir. 1998).

unprofessional conduct, neglect of duty, and unfitness to teach often are based on quite similar facts. Facts that establish unprofessional conduct in one state may be deemed neglect of duty in another state. Most courts have defined *unprofessional conduct* as actions directly related to the fitness of educators to perform in their professional capacity.[64] The working definition adopted by the Supreme Court of Nebraska specified unprofessional conduct as breaching the rules or ethical code of a profession or "unbecoming a member in good standing of a profession." Under this definition, the court reasoned that a teacher had engaged in unprofessional conduct when he "smacked" a student on the head hard enough to make the student cry, thereby violating the state prohibition against corporal punishment.[65]

Courts have upheld dismissal for unprofessional conduct based on several grounds, such as taking photos of a female student nude above the waist,[66] engaging in sexual harassment of female students,[67] wrapping a student in an electrical cord and verbally humiliating him in front of other students,[68] losing complete control of the classroom,[69] engaging in inappropriate touching of students,[70] and showing a sexually explicit film to a classroom of adolescents without previewing it.[71] As with dismissals based on incompetency, **courts often require prior warning that the behavior may result in dismissal.**

Neglect of Duty

Neglect of duty arises when an educator fails to carry out assigned duties. This may involve an intentional omission or may result from ineffectual performance. In a Colorado case, neglect of duty was found when a teacher failed to discipline students consistent with school policy.[72] Similarly, the Louisiana high court ruled that a teacher repeatedly sending unescorted students to the principal's office in violation of school policy substantiated willful neglect of duty.[73] The Oregon appellate court concluded that a teacher's failure to maintain a professional working relationship with students, parents, staff, and other teachers constituted neglect of duty.[74]

---

[64]*See, e.g.*, Fed. Way Sch. Dist. v. Vinson, 261 P.3d 145 (Wash. 2011).

[65]Daily v. Bd. of Educ., 588 N.W.2d 813, 824 (Neb. 1999). Following a hearing to consider termination of employment, the school board instead gave the teacher a thirty-day suspension.

[66]Dixon v. Clem, 492 F.3d 665 (6th Cir. 2007).

[67]Conward v. Cambridge Sch. Comm., 171 F.3d 12 (1st Cir. 1999).

[68]Johanson v. Bd. of Educ., 589 N.W.2d 815 (Neb. 1999).

[69]Walker v. Highlands Cnty. Sch. Bd., 752 So. 2d 127 (Fla. Dist. Ct. App. 2000).

[70]*In re* Watt, 925 N.Y.S.2d 681 (App. Div. 2011).

[71]Fowler v. Bd. of Educ., 819 F.2d 657 (6th Cir. 1987).

[72]Bd. of Educ. v. Flaming, 938 P.2d 151 (Colo. 1997); *see also* Flickinger v. Lebanon Sch. Dist., 898 A.2d 62 (Pa. Commw. Ct. 2006) (concluding that the principal's failure to respond immediately to a report of a gun in the middle school established willful neglect of duty; school procedures specified that such a crisis situation must be handled without delay).

[73]Wise v. Bossier Parish Sch. Bd., 851 So. 2d 1090 (La. 2003).

[74]Bellairs v. Beaverton Sch. Dist., 136 P.3d 93 (Or. Ct. App. 2006).

The United States Supreme Court upheld the dismissal of an Oklahoma teacher for "willful neglect of duty" in failing to comply with the school board's continuing education requirement.[75] For a period of time, lack of compliance was dealt with through denial of salary increases. Upon enactment of a state law requiring salary increases for all teachers, the board notified teachers that noncompliance with the requirement would result in termination. Affirming the board's action, the Supreme Court found the sanction of dismissal to be rationally related to the board's objective of improving its teaching force through continuing education requirements.

The Nebraska high court, however, held that a superintendent's failure to file a funding form did not constitute neglect of duty to support the termination of his contract.[76] Similarly, a Louisiana appellate court held that a teacher's showing of an R-rated film did not warrant dismissal for neglect of duty and incompetence.[77] The Louisiana Supreme Court concluded that a teacher bringing a loaded gun to school in his car did not substantiate willful neglect of duty to support termination.[78] The court commented that his action was certainly a mistake and possibly endangered students, but it did not involve a failure to follow orders or an identifiable school policy that required dismissal under state law.

Teachers can be discharged for neglect of duty when their performance does not meet expected professional standards in the school system. Often charges relate to a failure to perform but also can be brought for ineffective performance. Again, as with other efforts to terminate employment, documentation must substantiate that performance is unacceptable.

Other Good and Just Cause

Not unexpectedly, "other good and just cause" as grounds for dismissal has frequently been challenged as vague and overbroad. Courts have been faced with the task of determining whether the phrase's meaning is limited to the specific grounds enumerated in the statute or whether it is a separate, expanded cause. An Indiana appellate court interpreted it as permitting termination for reasons other than those specified in the tenure law if evidence indicated that the board's decision was based on "good cause."[79] As such, dismissal of a teacher convicted of a misdemeanor was upheld even though the teacher had no prior indication that such conduct was sufficient cause. A Connecticut court found good cause to be any ground put forward in good faith that is not "arbitrary, irrational, unreasonable, or irrelevant to the board's task of building up and maintaining an efficient

---

[75]Harrah Indep. Sch. Dist. v. Martin, 440 U.S. 194 (1979).

[76]Boss v. Fillmore Sch. Dist. No. 19, 559 N.W.2d 448 (Neb. 1997). *But see* Smith v. Bullock Cnty. Bd. of Educ., 906 So. 2d 938 (Ala. Civ. App. 2004) (ruling that a principal's failure to establish procedures to prevent the theft of about $25,000 of athletic funds was neglect of duty).

[77]Jones v. Rapides Parish Sch. Bd., 634 So. 2d 1197 (La. Ct. App. 1993).

[78]Howard v. W. Baton Rouge Parish Sch. Bd., 793 So. 2d 153 (La. 2001). *But see* Sias v. Iberia Parish Sch. Bd., 74 So. 3d 800 (La. Ct. App. 2011) (ruling that school board had sufficient evidence to substantiate willful neglect of duties when a principal was arrested for possession of various drugs, weapons, and counterfeit money in his house).

[79]Gary Teachers Union, Local No. 4, AFT v. Sch. City of Gary, 332 N.E.2d 256, 263 (Ind. Ct. App. 1975); *see also* Hierlmeier v. N. Judson-San Pierre Bd., 730 N.E.2d 821 (Ind. Ct. App. 2000) (ruling that sexual harassment of female students and other inappropriate conduct toward students substantiated good and just cause for termination).

school system."[80] Terminating a teacher for altering students' responses on state mandatory proficiency tests was held to be relevant to that task.

The Supreme Court of Iowa applied a statute permitting teachers to be terminated during the contract year for "just cause" to support the termination of a teacher for shoplifting.[81] Although the teacher claimed that her compulsion to shoplift was related to a mental illness, the court found substantial evidence to terminate the teacher's employment, weighing the teacher's position as a role model, the character of the illness, and the school board's needs. In a subsequent case, the Iowa high court ruled "just cause" existed to terminate a teacher who had knowledge of her son and his high school friends drinking at a campsite on her property. She failed to monitor their activities, and four students who left to buy more beer died in a car crash. The court agreed with the school board that the teacher's effectiveness as a role model was significantly diminished.[82]

Reduction-in-Force

In addition to dismissal for causes related to teacher performance and fitness, legislation generally permits the release of teachers for reasons related to declining enrollment, financial exigency, and school district consolidation. Whereas most state statutes provide for such terminations, some states have adopted legislation that specifies the basis for selection of released teachers, procedures to be followed, and provisions for reinstatement. These terminations, characterized as reductions-in-force (RIF), also may be governed by board policies and negotiated bargaining agreements.

Unlike other termination cases, the employee challenging a RIF decision shoulders the burden of proof. There is a presumption that the board has acted in good faith with permissible motives. Legal controversies in this area usually involve questions related to the necessity for the reductions, board compliance with mandated procedures, and possible subterfuge for impermissible termination (such as denial of constitutional rights, subversion of tenure rights, or discrimination).

If statutory or contractual restrictions exist for teacher layoffs, there must be substantial compliance with the provisions. One of the provisions most frequently included is a method for selecting teachers for release. **In general, reductions are based on seniority, and a tenured teacher, rather than a nontenured teacher, must be retained if both are qualified to fill the same position.** State statutes usually require that both licensure and seniority be considered; a teacher lacking a license in the area would not be permitted to teach, while a teacher with proper credentials but less seniority would be dismissed. Along with seniority, merit-rating systems may be included in the determination of reductions. School districts in Pennsylvania use a combination of ratings and seniority; ratings are the primary determinant unless there is no substantial difference in ratings, and then seniority becomes the basis for the layoff.[83] Both the Montana and Nebraska high courts concluded

---

[80]Hanes v. Bd. of Educ., 783 A.2d 1, 6 (Conn. App. Ct. 2001).

[81]Bd. of Dirs. v. Davies, 489 N.W.2d 19 (Iowa 1992).

[82]Walthart v. Bd. of Dirs., 694 N.W.2d 740 (Iowa 2005).

[83]24 PA. STAT. ANN. § 11-1124 (2012).

that school boards have broad discretion in deciding what factors to use in their RIF policies and how to weight those factors.[84] Guidelines or criteria established by state or local education agencies, however, must be applied in a uniform and nondiscriminatory manner. For example, under New Mexico law, the school board must determine that no other positions exist for teachers targeted for release.[85]

The Fourteenth Amendment requires procedural protections in dismissals for cause, but courts have not clearly defined the due process requirements for RIFs. The Eighth Circuit noted that tenured teachers possess a property interest in continued employment and thereby must be provided notice and an opportunity to be heard.[86] Specific procedural protections for employees vary according to interpretations of state law, bargaining agreements, and board policy. The court emphasized that the law protected the released teacher, who, subject to qualifications, was entitled to the next vacancy. Similarly, a Pennsylvania commonwealth court held that a hearing must be provided to assure the teacher (1) that termination was for reasons specified by law and (2) that the board followed the correct statutory procedures in selecting the teacher for discharge.[87]

State law or other policies may give employment preference to teachers who are released because of a reduction-in-force. Typically, under such requirements, a school board cannot hire a nonemployee until each qualified teacher on the preferred recall list is reemployed.[88] Although statutes often require that teachers be appointed to the first vacancy for which they are licensed and qualified, courts have held that reappointment is still at the board's discretion. In addition, a board is generally not obligated to realign or rearrange teaching assignments to create a position for a released teacher.

REMEDIES FOR VIOLATIONS OF PROTECTED RIGHTS

Wrongfully terminated employees may be entitled to compensatory and punitive damages, reinstatement with back pay, and attorneys' fees for the violation of their constitutional rights.

When it can be established that school districts or officials have violated an employee's rights that are protected by federal or state law, several remedies are available to the

---

[84]Scobey Sch. Dist. v. Radakovich, 135 P.3d 778 (Mont. 2006); Nickel v. Saline Cnty. Sch. Dist. No. 163, 559 N.W.2d 480 (Neb. 1997).

[85]Aguilera v. Bd. of Educ., 132 P.3d 587 (N.M. 2006).

[86]Boner v. Eminence R-1 Sch. Dist., 55 F.3d 1339 (8th Cir. 1995).

[87]Fatscher v. Bd. of Sch. Dirs., 367 A.2d 1130 (Pa. Commw. Ct. 1977).

[88]*See* Davis v. Chester Upland Sch. Dist., 786 A.2d 186 (Pa. 2001) (ruling that teachers who challenged the school district's failure to recall them must exhaust collective bargaining grievance procedures before filing for judicial review). *But see* Chi. Teachers Union v. Bd. of Educ., 476 F. App'x 83 (7th Cir. 2012) (vacating an injunction after the Supreme Court of Illinois, at 963 N.E.2d 918 (Ill. 2012), ruled that teachers had no recall rights under the state law; thus, such rights would exist only if specified in the negotiated agreement).

aggrieved individual. In some situations, the employee may seek a court injunction ordering the unlawful action to cease. This remedy might be sought if a school board has unconstitutionally imposed restraints on teachers' expression. Where terminations, transfers, or other adverse employment consequences have been unconstitutionally imposed, courts will order school districts to return the affected employees to their original status with back pay.

Educators also can bring damages suits for actions that violate their federally protected rights under 42 U.S.C. § 1983, which imposes personal liability on any person who acts under color of law to deprive another individual of rights secured by the U.S. Constitution. This law, originally enacted in 1871 to prevent discrimination against African American citizens, has been broadly interpreted as conferring liability on school personnel and school districts, not only for racial discrimination but also for actions that may result in the impairment of other federally protected rights.[89]

Suits seeking damages under § 1983 for violations of federal rights can be initiated in federal or state courts, and exhaustion of state administrative remedies is not required before initiating a federal suit. When a federal law authorizes an exclusive nondamages remedy, however, a § 1983 suit is precluded.[90] This section focuses on the liability of school officials and school districts for the violation of protected rights and on the types of damages available to aggrieved employees.

Liability of School Officials

In § 1983 claims, **public school employees acting under color of state law can be held personally liable for actions abridging students' or teachers' federal rights.** The Supreme Court, however, has recognized that government officials cannot be held liable under § 1983 for the actions of their subordinates, thus rejecting the doctrine of respondeat superior, even when school officials have general supervisory authority over the activities of the wrongdoers. In order to be found liable, the officials must have personally participated in or had personal knowledge of the unlawful acts or promulgated official policy under which the acts were taken.[91] Furthermore, the Supreme Court in 1998 ruled that public officials are absolutely immune from suit under § 1983 for their legislative activities.[92] These actions involve discretionary policy-making decisions and enactment of regulations, often with budgetary implications. Subsequently, courts have clarified that employment

---

[89]Maine v. Thiboutot, 448 U.S. 1 (1980).

[90]*See, e.g.,* Gonzaga Univ. v. Doe, 536 U.S. 496 (2002); Blessing v. Freestone, 520 U.S. 329 (1997). The Supreme Court, however, has ruled that damages can be sought under § 1983 for Fourteenth Amendment equal protection violations if a federal statute lacks an expressed private remedy. Specifically, the Court held that Title IX of the Education Amendments of 1972 (20 U.S.C.S. § 1681) does not preclude individuals from also pursuing a § 1983 damages claim for unconstitutional sex discrimination under the Equal Protection Clause. Fitzgerald v. Barnstable Sch. Comm., 555 U.S. 246 (2009).

[91]*See* Ashcroft v. Iqbal, 556 U.S. 662 (2009); Am. Mfrs. Mut. Ins. Co. v. Sullivan, 526 U.S. 40 (1999); Rizzo v. Goode, 423 U.S. 362 (1976).

[92]Bogan v. Scott-Harris, 523 U.S. 44 (1998).

decisions related to individual employees (such as hiring, dismissal, or demotion) are administrative, not legislative, in nature.[93]

The Supreme Court has recognized that in some circumstances, school officials can claim qualified immunity to avoid personal liability. In *Harlow v. Fitzgerald*, the Court ruled: "Government officials performing discretionary functions generally are shielded from liability for civil damages insofar as their conduct does not violate clearly established statutory or constitutional rights of which a reasonable person would have known."[94] In 2002, the Supreme Court emphasized that the overriding issue regarding qualified immunity was whether the law at the time an individual acted gave "clear and fair warning" that rights were established.[95] The "clear and fair warning" standard, however, has resulted in a range of interpretations by lower courts. The Supreme Court provided further clarification of this standard when it examined the reasonableness of school officials' strip search of a thirteen-year-old student. The Court in *Safford Unified School District #1 v. Redding*[96] held the actions violated the basic legal framework established in *New Jersey v. T.L.O.*[97] However, the Court ruled that school officials were entitled to qualified immunity based on lower courts' "divergent conclusions regarding how the *T.L.O.* standard applied to school searches."[98] The Court did caution that divergent views among other courts regarding a right "does not automatically render the law unclear" if the Supreme Court has been clear.[99]

School officials have been denied qualified immunity when they have disregarded well-established legal principles in areas such as due process, protected expression, and privacy.[100] Public officials are not expected to predict the future course of constitutional law, but they are expected to adhere to principles of law that were *clearly established* at the time of the violation.

---

[93]*See, e.g.*, Canary v. Osborn, 211 F.3d 324 (6th Cir. 2000); Harhay v. Town of Ellington Bd. of Educ., 323 F.3d 206 (2d Cir. 2003).

[94]457 U.S. 800, 818 (1982); *see also* Filarsky v. Delia, 132 S. Ct. 1657 (2012) (unanimously ruling that a private individual employed by the government to perform a job can claim qualified immunity from suit under 42 U.S.C. § 1983).

[95]Hope v. Pelzer, 536 U.S. 730 (2002); *see also* Ashcroft v. al-Kidd, 131 S. Ct. 2074, 2085 (2011) (holding that qualified immunity gives officials "breathing room to make reasonable but mistaken judgments about open legal questions"; if properly applied, "it protects 'all but the plainly incompetent or those who knowingly violate the law'" (quoting Malley v. Briggs, 475 U.S. 335, 341 (1986)).

[96]557 U.S. 364 (2009); *see* text accompanying notes 93–96, Chapter 8.

[97]469 U.S. 325 (1985); *see* text accompanying notes 62–66, Chapter 8.

[98]*Safford*, 557 U.S. at 378.

[99]*Id.* Reconsidering an earlier high court decision that mandated lower courts initially to assess whether the facts of a case establish a constitutional violation prior to determining immunity, the Supreme Court more recently granted lower courts discretion to consider whether immunity exists prior to considering the alleged constitutional violation. Pearson v. Callahan, 555 U.S. 223 (2009).

[100]*See, e.g.*, Evans-Marshall v. Bd. of Educ., 428 F.3d 223 (6th Cir. 2005); Baird v. Bd. of Educ., 389 F.3d 685 (7th Cir. 2004).

Liability of School Districts

In 1978, the Supreme Court ruled that local governments are considered "persons" under § 1983.[101] In essence, **school districts can be assessed damages when action taken pursuant to official policy violates federally protected rights.** To prevail against a school district, an individual must present evidence that the district acted with deliberate indifference in establishing and maintaining a policy, practice, or custom that directly deprived an individual of his or her constitutionally protected rights.

The governmental unit (like the individual official), however, cannot be held liable under the respondeat superior doctrine for the wrongful acts committed solely by its employees. Liability under § 1983 against the agency can be imposed only when execution of official policy by an individual with final authority impairs a federally protected right.[102] The Supreme Court has held that a single egregious act by a low-level employee does not imply an official policy of inadequate training and supervision,[103] but an agency can be liable if "deliberate indifference" in ensuring adequately trained employees is established.[104]

The Supreme Court has ruled that school districts and other governmental subdivisions cannot claim qualified immunity based on good faith actions of their officials. The Court acknowledged that under certain circumstances, sovereign immunity can shield municipal corporations from state tort suits, but concluded that § 1983 abrogated governmental immunity in situations involving the impairment of federally protected rights.[105]

To avoid liability for constitutional violations, school districts have introduced claims of Eleventh Amendment immunity. The Eleventh Amendment, explicitly prohibiting citizens of one state from bringing suit against another state without its consent, has been interpreted also as precluding federal lawsuits against a state by its own citizens.[106] A state can waive this immunity by specifically consenting to be sued, and Congress can abrogate state immunity through legislation enacted to enforce the Fourteenth Amendment. Such congressional intent, however, must be explicit in the federal legislation.[107]

School districts have asserted Eleventh Amendment protection based on the fact that they perform a state function. Admittedly, education is a state function, but it does

---

[101]Monell v. Dep't of Soc. Servs., 436 U.S. 658 (1978).

[102]*See, e.g.,* Collins v. City of Harker Heights, 503 U.S. 115 (1992); Langford v. City of Atl. City, 235 F.3d 845 (3d Cir. 2000); Seamons v. Snow, 206 F.3d 1021 (10th Cir. 2000).

[103]Okla. City v. Tuttle, 471 U.S. 808 (1985).

[104]City of Canton, Ohio v. Harris, 489 U.S. 378 (1989).

[105]Owen v. City of Independence, Mo., 445 U.S. 622 (1980). See text accompanying note 37, Chapter 2, for a discussion of governmental immunity under tort law.

[106]*See* Hans v. Louisiana, 134 U.S. 1 (1890); *see also* Will v. Mich. Dep't of State Police, 491 U.S. 58 (1989) (holding that § 1983 does not permit a suit against a state; Congress did not intend the word "person" to include states).

[107]For example, the Supreme Court held that the Family Educational Rights and Privacy Act of 1974 does not explicitly confer individually enforceable rights. Gonzaga Univ. v. Doe, 536 U.S. 273 (2002). Also, in ruling that an individual cannot sue a state for money damages in federal court under the Americans with Disabilities Act of 1990, the Supreme Court reasoned that Congress did not act within its constitutional authority when it abrogated Eleventh Amendment immunity under that law. Bd. of Trs. v. Garrett, 531 U.S. 356 (2001).

not necessarily follow that school districts gain Eleventh Amendment immunity against claims of constitutional abridgments. For the Eleventh Amendment to be invoked in a suit against a school district, the state must be the "real party in interest." In many states, the Eleventh Amendment question with respect to school district immunity was resolved in the *Mt. Healthy* case.[108] The Supreme Court concluded that the issue in this case hinged on whether, under Ohio law, a school district is considered an arm of the state as opposed to a municipality or other political subdivision. Considering the taxing power and autonomy of school district operations, the Supreme Court found school districts to be more like counties or cities than extensions of the state. As a result, Eleventh Amendment immunity does not apply.

Remedies

Judicial remedies for the violation of protected rights depend on employment status, federal and state statutory provisions, and the discretion of courts. Federal and state laws often identify damages that may be recovered or place limitations on types of awards. Unless these provisions restrict specific remedies, courts have broad discretionary power to formulate equitable settlements.

Damages. When a school official or school district is found liable for violating an individual's protected rights, damages are assessed to compensate the claimant for the injury. **Actual injury, however, must be shown for the aggrieved party to recover damages; without evidence of monetary or mental injury, the plaintiff is entitled only to nominal damages (not to exceed one dollar), even though an impairment of protected rights is established.**[109] Significant monetary damages, however, may be awarded for a wrongful termination if a teacher is able to demonstrate substantial losses. At the same time, individuals must make an effort to mitigate damages by seeking appropriate employment.

In some instances, aggrieved individuals have sought punitive as well as compensatory damages. The judiciary has ruled that school officials can be liable for punitive damages (to punish the wrongdoer) if a jury concludes that the individual's conduct is willful or in reckless and callous disregard of federally protected rights.[110] Punitive and compensatory

---

[108]Mt. Healthy City Sch. Dist. v. Doyle, 429 U.S. 274 (1977); *see* Adams v. Recovery Sch. Dist., 463 F. App'x 297 (5th Cir. 2012); Woods v. Rondout Valley Cent. Sch. Dist. Bd. of Educ., 466 F.3d 232 (2d Cir. 2006). *But see* Belanger v. Madera Unified Sch. Dist., 963 F.2d 248 (9th Cir. 1992) (holding that California school boards are indivisible agencies of the state and thus entitled to Eleventh Amendment immunity).

[109]*See* Farrar v. Hobby, 506 U.S. 103 (1992) (concluding that an award of nominal damages is mandatory when a procedural due process violation is established but no actual injury is shown); Carey v. Piphus, 435 U.S. 247 (1978) (holding that pupils who were denied procedural due process in a disciplinary proceeding would be entitled only to nominal damages unless it was established that lack of proper procedures resulted in actual injury to the students).

[110]*See* Smith v. Wade, 461 U.S. 30 (1983). In 1991, the Supreme Court refused to place a limit on the amount of punitive damages that properly instructed juries may award in common law suits, but it did note that extremely high awards might be viewed as unacceptable under the Due Process Clause of the Fourteenth Amendment. Pac. Mut. Life Ins. Co. v. Haslip, 499 U.S. 1 (1991).

damages were assessed against a principal and superintendent who, without authority, discharged a teacher in retaliation for the exercise of protected speech.[111]

In 1981, the Supreme Court ruled that **§ 1983 does not authorize the award of punitive damages against a municipality.**[112] Recognizing that compensation for injuries is an obligation of a municipality, the Court held that *punitive* damages were appropriate only for the *individual* wrongdoers and not for the municipality itself. The Court also noted that punitive damages constitute punishment against individuals to deter similar conduct in the future, but they are not intended to punish innocent taxpayers. This ruling does not bar claims for punitive damages for violations of federal rights in school cases, but such claims must be brought against individuals rather than against the school district itself.

Reinstatement. Whether a court orders reinstatement as a remedy for school board action depends on the protected interests involved and the discretion of the court, unless an explicit provision for reinstatement is specified in state law. When a tenured teacher is unjustly dismissed, the property interest gives rise to an expectation of reemployment; reinstatement in such instances is usually the appropriate remedy. A nontenured teacher, wrongfully dismissed during the contract period, however, is normally entitled only to damages, not reinstatement unless the termination involves the violation of a constitutionally protected right.

A valid property or liberty claim entitles a teacher to procedural due process, but the teacher can still be dismissed for cause after proper procedures have been followed. Courts will order reinstatement when a teacher is terminated without proper procedures and can establish that the action is not justified. If it is proven that the actual reason for the nonrenewal of a teacher's contract is retaliation for the exercise of constitutional rights (e.g., protected speech), reinstatement would be warranted, although substantiation of such a claim is difficult.

The failure to comply with statutory requirements in nonrenewals and dismissals may result in reinstatement. When statutory dates are specified for notice of nonrenewal, failure to comply strictly with the deadline provides grounds for reinstatement of the teacher. Courts may interpret this as continued employment for an additional year or reinstatement with tenure if nonrenewal occurs at the end of the probationary period. In contrast to the remedy for lack of proper notice, the remedy for failure to provide an appropriate hearing is generally a remand for a hearing, not reinstatement.[113]

Attorneys' Fees. Attorneys' fees are not automatically granted to the teacher who prevails in a lawsuit, but are dependent on statutory authorization. At the federal level, the Civil Rights Attorneys' Fees Award Act gives federal courts discretion to award fees in

---

[111]Fishman v. Clancy, 763 F.2d 485 (1st Cir. 1985); *see also* Ciccarelli v. Sch. Dep't, 877 N.E.2d 609 (Mass. App. Ct. 2007) (upholding a $50,000 punitive damages award to a provisional teacher who was not rehired after her name appeared on a witness list for another teacher who had filed a sex discrimination complaint).

[112]City of Newport v. Fact Concerts, 453 U.S. 247 (1981).

[113]*See* Snowden v. Adams, 814 F. Supp. 2d 854 (C.D. Ill. 2011) (noting that an inadequate name-clearing hearing may entitle an individual to compensatory damages when remand for another hearing would be too late to remedy the damage to reputation).

civil rights suits.[114] In congressional debate concerning attorneys' fees, it was stated: "Private citizens must be given not only the right to go to court but also the legal resources. If the citizen does not have the resources, his day in court is denied him."[115]

To receive attorneys' fees, the teacher must be the prevailing party; that is, damages or some form of equitable relief must be granted to the teacher. The Supreme Court has held that a prevailing party is one who is successful in achieving some benefit on any significant issue in the case, but not necessarily the primary issue. The Court ruled that at a minimum, "the plaintiff must be able to point to a resolution of the dispute which changes the legal relationship between itself and the defendant."[116] If a plaintiff achieves only partial success, the fees requested may be reduced.

It has been established that the plaintiff who prevails in a civil rights suit may, at the court's discretion, be entitled to attorneys' fees, but the same standard is not applied to defendants. The Supreme Court has held that such fees cannot be imposed on a plaintiff unless the claim was "frivolous, unreasonable, or groundless."[117] Although awards of damages to prevailing defendants have not been common, in some situations, awards have been made to deter groundless lawsuits.

CONCLUSION

Through state laws and the U.S. Constitution, extensive safeguards protect educators' employment security. Most states have adopted tenure laws that precisely delineate teachers' employment rights in termination and disciplinary proceedings. Furthermore, in the absence of specific state guarantees, the Fourteenth Amendment ensures that teachers will be afforded procedural due process when property or liberty interests are implicated. At a minimum, the employee is entitled to notice of the charges and an opportunity to be heard. Legal decisions interpreting both state and federal rights in dismissal actions have established broad guidelines about when due process is required, the types of procedures that must be provided, and the legitimate causes required to substantiate dismissal action.

Causes for dismissal vary widely among the states but usually include such grounds as incompetency, neglect of duty, immorality, insubordination, unprofessional conduct, and other good and just cause. These causes relate not only to classroom performance but also to other conduct that may have a negative impact on a teacher's effectiveness in the school system. If educators' constitutional rights are impaired in connection with termination actions, school officials and school districts can be held liable for damages. An individual, however, can recover only nominal damages for such impairment unless monetary, emotional, or mental injury can be proven.

[114]42 U.S.C. § 1988 (2012).

[115]122 Cong. Rec. 33,313 (1976).

[116]Tex. State Teachers Ass'n v. Garland Indep. Sch. Dist., 489 U.S. 782, 792 (1989).

[117]Christiansburg Garment Co. v. EEOC, 434 U.S. 412, 422 (1978); *see* Jefferson v. Jefferson Cnty. Pub. Sch. Sys., 360 F.3d 583 (6th Cir. 2004); Potlatch Educ. Ass'n v. Potlatch Sch. Dist., 226 P.3d 1277 (Idaho 2010).

POINTS TO PONDER

1. An elementary school teacher was not renewed for failure to meet the school district's teaching expectations as she completed her third year of employment. A mentor teacher had worked closely to assist the teacher in pedagogical and classroom management issues, but little progress had been made. Her sixth-grade students consistently scored lower than other students in the school district, and parents frequently complained to the principal about her teaching. Upon receipt of the nonrenewal notice, the teacher asked for a hearing, claiming that the school board's decision had severely damaged her reputation and affected her ability to obtain another position. Is she entitled to a hearing? Does the school board's action violate her protected liberty interests?

2. A school board sent a tenured teacher a notice of its intent to terminate him for insubordination after he repeatedly refused to develop a personal growth plan as required by school district policy. Even though he had not complied with the policy, the principal had given the teacher good teaching evaluations each year. Can the school board terminate his employment? What are the teacher's rights if the school board pursues termination?

3. A tenured veteran teacher received a notice from the school board of its intent to terminate her employment for lack of teaching effectiveness. The brief letter cited the statutory language permitting teacher termination for cause and indicated that a hearing would be held in ten days. Does this constitute adequate notice?

4. After two convictions for driving while intoxicated, a tenured middle school teacher was dismissed on grounds of immorality. The teacher argued that the convictions did not relate to his teaching effectiveness, the students had been unaware of the incidents until his termination, and he was in a treatment program for his drinking problem. Do you think his termination will be upheld? Support your answer.

5. A male teacher was arrested and charged with propositioning a male undercover police officer. Subsequently, the charges were dropped, but the school board, with no statement of reasons, did not renew the teacher's contract at the end of the school year. Although state law and local policies do not provide for a hearing in nonrenewals, the teacher requested an opportunity to appear before the school board. Is he entitled to such a hearing? Why or why not?

CHAPTER THIRTEEN

SUMMARY OF LEGAL GENERALIZATIONS

In the preceding chapters, principles of law have been presented as they relate to specific aspects of teachers' and students' rights and responsibilities. Constitutional and statutory provisions, in conjunction with judicial decisions, have been analyzed in an effort to portray the current status of the law. Many diverse topics have been explored, some with clearly established legal precedents and others about which the law is still evolving.

The most difficult situations confronting school personnel are those without specific legislative or judicial guidance. In such circumstances, educators must make judgments based on their professional training and general knowledge of the law as it applies to education. The following broad generalizations, synthesized from the preceding chapters, are presented to assist educators in making such determinations.

GENERALIZATIONS

The Legal Control of Public Education Resides with the State as One of Its Sovereign Powers.   In attempting to comply with the law, school personnel must keep in mind the scope of the state's authority to regulate educational activities. Courts consistently have held that state legislatures possess plenary power in establishing and operating public schools; this power is restricted only by federal and state constitutions and civil rights laws. Where the federal judiciary has interpreted the United States Constitution as prohibiting a given practice in public education, such as racial discrimination, the state or its agents cannot enact laws or policies that conflict with the constitutional mandate. In contrast, if the Federal Constitution and civil rights laws have been interpreted as permitting a certain activity, such as corporal punishment in public schools, states retain discretion in either restricting or expanding the practice. Under such circumstances, standards vary across states, and legislation becomes more important in specifying the scope of protected rights. For example, the U.S. Supreme Court has rejected the claim that probationary teachers have an inherent federal right to due process prior to contract nonrenewal, but state legislatures have the authority to create such a right under state law. Similarly, the Supreme Court has found no Fourth Amendment violation in blanket or random drug testing of public school students who participate in extracurricular activities; however, state law may place restrictions on school authorities in conducting such searches. Also, the Supreme Court has found no Establishment Clause violation in the participation of sectarian schools in state-supported voucher programs to fund education, but these programs might run afoul of state constitutional provisions prohibiting the use of public funds for religious purposes.

Unless constitutional rights are at stake, courts defer to the will of legislative bodies in determining educational matters. State legislatures have the authority to create and redesign school districts; to collect and distribute educational funds; and to determine teacher qualifications, curricular offerings, and minimum student performance standards. With the pervasive control vested in the states, a thorough understanding of the operation of a specific educational system can be acquired only by examining an individual state's statutes, administrative regulations, and judicial decisions interpreting these provisions.

Certain prerequisites to public school employment are defined through statutes and state board of education regulations. For example, all states stipulate that public school teachers must possess a valid teaching license based on satisfying specified requirements. State laws also delineate the permanency of the employment relationship, dismissal procedures for tenured and nontenured teachers, and the extent to which teachers can engage in collective bargaining.

State laws similarly govern conditions of school attendance. Every state has enacted a compulsory attendance statute to ensure an educated citizenry. These laws are applicable to all children, with only a few legally recognized exceptions. In addition to mandating school attendance, states also have the authority to prescribe courses of study and instructional materials. Courts will not invalidate these decisions unless constitutional rights are abridged.

Courts also apply comparable reasoning in upholding the state's power to establish academic standards and graduation requirements. To determine whether students and school districts are progressing consistently with state standards and federal expectations, students are being subjected to more testing than ever before. Assessments determine the level and type of instruction provided; whether the child should be promoted from grade to grade or is eligible for graduation; and if the local school district has achieved required outcomes. Increasingly, states and local districts are enacting policies that base the evaluation of school personnel in part on student performance on standardized tests.

It is a widely held perception that local school boards control public education in this nation, but local boards hold only those discretionary powers conferred by state law. Depending on the state, a local board's discretionary authority may be quite broad, narrowly defined by statutory guidelines, or somewhere in between. School board regulations enacted pursuant to statutory authority are legally binding on employees and students. For example, school boards can place conditions on employment beyond state minimums, if not prohibited by law (e.g., continuing education requirements, residency requirements).

In some states, policy-making authority in certain domains (e.g., curriculum, personnel) has been delegated to school-based councils, and the relationship between local boards and school-based councils is still being defined. Courts will not overturn decisions made by school boards or site-based councils unless they are clearly arbitrary, discriminatory, or beyond their scope of authority.

School board and/or council discretion, however, may be limited by negotiated contracts with teachers' associations. Negotiated agreements may affect the terms and conditions of employment in areas such as teacher evaluation, work calendar, teaching loads, extra-duty assignments, and grievance procedures. It is imperative for educators to become familiar with all of these sources of legal rights and responsibilities.

All School Policies and Practices That Impinge on Protected Personal Freedoms Must Be Substantiated as Necessary to Advance the School's Educational Mission.   The state and its agents have broad authority to regulate public schools, but policies that impair federal constitutional rights must be justified by an overriding public interest. Although courts do not enact laws like legislative bodies, they do significantly influence educational policies and practices by interpreting constitutional and statutory provisions. Both school attendance and public employment traditionally were considered privileges bestowed at the will of the state, but the Supreme Court has recognized that teachers and students do not shed their constitutional rights at the schoolhouse door. The state controls education, but this power must be exercised in conformance with the U.S. Constitution.

It is important to keep in mind that the Bill of Rights places restrictions on governmental, not private, action that interferes with personal freedoms. To illustrate, the public schools may have to tolerate private student expression under certain circumstances, but expression representing the school can be censored for educational reasons. Similarly, the Establishment Clause prohibits public school employees from directing or condoning devotional activities in public education, whereas student-initiated religious groups in secondary schools must be treated like other student groups in terms of school access during noninstructional time. Furthermore, community religious groups, even those involved in religious instruction targeting elementary school children, must be treated like other community groups during nonschool hours.

In balancing public and individual interests, courts weigh the importance of the protected personal right against the governmental need to restrict its exercise. For example, courts have reasoned that there is no overriding public interest to justify compelling students to salute the American flag if such an observance conflicts with religious or philosophical beliefs. In contrast, public educators can be required to be U.S. citizens because public school teaching is so intimately connected to the operation of the state to justify such a condition on public school employment. Also, mandatory vaccination against communicable diseases has been upheld as a prerequisite to school attendance, even if opposition to immunization is based on religious grounds. Courts have reasoned that the overriding public interest in safeguarding the health of all students justifies such a requirement.

Restrictions can be placed on students' activities if necessary to advance legitimate school objectives. The judiciary has recognized that students' constitutional rights must be assessed in light of the special circumstances of the school. Consequently, school authorities can bar attire that is disruptive. They also can impose dress codes, and even uniforms, if shown to advance legitimate educational objectives, such as reducing disciplinary problems and gang influences, and the requirement is not intended to stifle expression. School authorities, although considered state officials, can conduct warrantless searches of students based on reasonable suspicion that they are concealing contraband that poses a threat to the school environment. Similarly, vulgar speech or expression promoting illegal activity that might be protected by the First Amendment for adults can be curtailed among public school students to further the school's legitimate interest in maintaining standards of decency. As noted, student expression that gives the appearance of representing the school also can be censored to ensure its consistency with educational objectives. And even personal student expression of ideological views, including electronic expression initiated off school grounds, can be restricted if linked to a disruption of the educational process.

Similarly, constraints can be placed on school employees if justified by valid school objectives. Prerequisites to employment, such as examinations and residency requirements, can be imposed if necessary to advance legitimate governmental interests. Furthermore, restrictions on teachers' rights to govern their appearance and their out-of-school conduct can be justified when appearance or lifestyle impinges on their effectiveness in the classroom. Although teachers enjoy a First Amendment right to express views on matters of public concern, expression pursuant to job responsibilities is not protected by the First Amendment. Even if educators are speaking as citizens and not employees, expression relating to private employment grievances, rather than public concerns, can be the basis for disciplinary action. And teachers' expression on public issues can be curtailed if it impedes the management of the school, work relationships, or teaching effectiveness. Also, educators' expression on school-owned computers, pagers, and other equipment can be monitored for educational reasons.

Every regulation that impairs individual rights must be based on valid educational considerations and be necessary to carry out the school's mission. Such regulations also should be clearly stated and well publicized so that all individuals understand the basis for the rules and the penalties for infractions.

School Policies and Practices Must Not Disadvantage Selected Individuals or Groups. The inherent personal right to remain free from governmental discrimination has been emphasized throughout this book. Strict judicial scrutiny has been applied in evaluating state action that creates a suspect classification, such as race. In school desegregation cases, courts have charged school officials with an affirmative duty to take the necessary steps to overcome the lingering effects of past discrimination. Similarly, intentional racial discrimination associated with testing methods, suspension procedures, employee hiring, and promotion practices has been disallowed. Whether voluntary race-based school or program assignments that further the goal of diversity will be upheld in de facto segregated school districts will depend on the ability of school officials to devise narrowly tailored means to achieve their desired objective.

In contrast, neutral policies, uniformly applied, are not necessarily unconstitutional, even though they may have a disparate impact on minorities. For example, prerequisites to employment, such as tests that disqualify a disproportionate number of minority applicants, have been upheld so long as their use is justified by legitimate employment objectives and not accompanied by discriminatory intent. Also, the placement of a disproportionate number of minority students in lower instructional tracks is permissible if such assignments are based on legitimate educational criteria that are applied in the best interests of students.

Likewise, school segregation that results from natural causes rather than intentional state action does not implicate constitutional rights.

In addition to racial classifications, other bases for distinguishing among employees and students have been invalidated if they disadvantage individuals. Federal civil rights laws, in conjunction with state statutes, have reinforced constitutional protections afforded to various segments of society that traditionally have suffered discrimination. Indeed, the judiciary has recognized that legislative bodies are empowered to go beyond constitutional minimums in protecting citizens from discriminatory practices. Accordingly, laws have been enacted that place specific responsibilities on employers to ensure that employees are not disadvantaged on the basis of gender, age, religion, national origin, or disability. If an inference of discrimination is established, employers must produce legitimate nondiscriminatory reasons to justify their actions. School officials can be held liable for damages if it is substantiated that benefits have been withheld from certain individuals because of their inherent characteristics.

Federal and state mandates also stipulate that students cannot be denied school attendance or otherwise disadvantaged based on characteristics such as race, sex, disability, national origin, marriage, or pregnancy. Also, disciplinary procedures that disproportionately disadvantage identified groups of students are vulnerable to legal challenge. Educators should ensure that all school policies are applied in a nondiscriminatory manner.

Courts will scrutinize grouping practices to ensure that they do not impede students' rights to equal educational opportunities. Nondiscrimination, however, does not require identical treatment. Students can be classified according to their unique needs, but any differential treatment must be justified in terms of providing more appropriate services. Indeed, judicial rulings and federal and state laws have placed an obligation on school districts to provide appropriate programs and services to meet the needs of children with disabilities and to eliminate the language barriers of those with English-language deficiencies.

Due Process Is a Basic Tenet of the United States System of Justice—the Foundation of Fundamental Fairness.   The notion of due process, embodied in the Fifth and Fourteenth Amendments, has been an underlying theme throughout the discussion of teachers' and students' rights. The judiciary has recognized that due process guarantees protect individuals against arbitrary governmental action impairing life, liberty, or property interests and ensure that procedural safeguards accompany any governmental interference in these interests.

In the absence of greater statutory specificity, courts have held that the U.S. Constitution requires, at a minimum, notice of the charges and a hearing before an impartial decision maker when personnel actions impair public educators' property or liberty rights. A property claim to due process can be established by tenure status, contractual agreement, or school board action that creates a valid expectation of reemployment. A liberty claim to due process can be asserted if the employer's action implicates constitutionally protected rights or damages the teacher's reputation by imposing such a stigma that the opportunity to obtain other employment is foreclosed.

Many state legislatures have specified procedures beyond constitutional minimums that must be followed before a tenured teacher is dismissed. The provision of due process does not imply that a teacher will not be dismissed or that sanctions will not be imposed.

But it does mean that the teacher must be given the opportunity to refute the charges and that the decision must be made fairly and be supported by evidence.

Students, as well as teachers, have due process rights. Students have a state-created property right to attend school that cannot be denied without procedural requisites. The nature of the proceedings depends on the deprivation involved, with more serious impairments necessitating more formal proceedings. If punishments are arbitrary or excessive, students' substantive due process rights may be implicated. Children with disabilities have due process rights in placement decisions as well as in disciplinary matters. Since school authorities are never faulted for providing too much due process, at least minimum procedural safeguards are advisable when making any nonroutine change in a student's status.

Inherent in the notion of due process is the assumption that all individuals have a right to a hearing if state action impinges on personal freedoms. Such a hearing need not be elaborate in every situation; an informal conversation can suffice under some circumstances, such as for brief student suspensions from school. Moreover, an informal hearing can serve to clarify issues and facilitate agreement, thus eliminating the need for more formal proceedings. The crucial element is for all affected parties to have an opportunity to air their views and present evidence that might alter the decision.

Educators Are Expected to Follow the Law, to Act Reasonably, and to Anticipate Potentially Adverse Consequences of Their Actions. Public school personnel are presumed to be knowledgeable of federal and state constitutional and statutory provisions as well as school board policies affecting their roles. The Supreme Court has emphasized that ignorance of the law is no defense for violating clearly established legal principles. For example, ignorance of the Supreme Court's interpretation of Establishment Clause restrictions would not shield educators from liability for conducting devotional activities in public schools.

Educators hold themselves out as having certain knowledge and skills by the nature of their special training and licenses. Accordingly, they are expected to exercise sound professional judgment in the performance of their duties. To illustrate, in administering student punishments, teachers are expected to consider the student's age, mental condition, and past behavior as well as the specific circumstances surrounding the rule infraction. Failure to exercise reasonable judgment can result in dismissal or possibly financial liability for impairing students' rights.

Teachers also are expected to make reasonable decisions pertaining to the academic program. Materials and methodology should be appropriate for the students' age and educational objectives. If students are grouped for instructional purposes, teachers are expected to base such decisions on legitimate educational considerations.

In addition, educators are held accountable for reasonable actions in supervising students, providing appropriate instructions, maintaining equipment in proper repair, and warning students of any known dangers. Teachers must exercise a standard of care commensurate with their duty to protect students from unreasonable risks of harm. Personal liability can be assessed for negligence if a school employee should have foreseen that an event could result in injury to a student.

Educators also are expected to exercise sound judgment in personal activities that affect their professional roles. Teachers do not relinquish their privacy rights as a condition of public employment, but private lifestyles that impair teaching effectiveness or disrupt the school can be the basis for adverse personnel action. As role models for students, teachers and other school personnel are held to a higher level of discretion in their private lives than is expected of the general public.

CONCLUSION

One objective of this book has been to alleviate educators' fears that the scales of justice have been tipped against them. It is hoped that this objective has been achieved. In most instances, courts and legislatures have not imposed on school personnel any requirements that fair-minded educators would not impose on themselves. Courts have consistently upheld reasonable policies and practices based on legitimate educational objectives. If anything, legislative and judicial mandates have clarified and supported the authority as well as the duty of school personnel to make and enforce regulations that are necessary to maintain an effective and efficient educational environment.

The federal judiciary in the late 1960s and early 1970s expanded constitutional protection of individual liberties against governmental interference. Since the 1980s, however, federal courts have exhibited more restraint and reinforced the authority of state and local education agencies to make decisions necessary to advance the school's educational mission, even if such decisions impinge on protected personal freedoms. Courts do continue to invalidate school practices and policies if they are arbitrary, unrelated to educational objectives, or impair protected individual rights without an overriding justification.

Because reform is usually easier to implement when designed from within than when externally imposed, educators should become more assertive in identifying and altering those practices that have the potential to generate legal intervention. Internet censorship; peer sexual harassment; social media policies for personnel; and bullying, hazing, and other intimidating behaviors are a few issues now requiring educators' attention. Furthermore, school personnel should stay abreast of legal developments, since new laws are enacted each year, and courts are continually interpreting constitutional and statutory provisions.

In addition to understanding basic legal rights and responsibilities, educators are expected to transmit this knowledge to students. Students also need to understand their constitutional and statutory rights, the balancing of interests that takes place in legislative and judicial forums, and the rationale for legal enactments, including school regulations. Only with increased awareness of fundamental legal principles can all individuals involved in the educational process develop a greater respect for the law and for the responsibilities that accompany legal rights.

absolute privilege protection from liability for communication made in the performance of public service or the administration of justice.

additur the trial court's power to assess damages or increase the amount of an inadequate jury award, which can be a condition of denying a motion for a new trial.

amicus brief brief provided by nonparties to inform or perhaps persuade the court (also termed "*amicus curiae*" briefs or "friend-of-the-court" briefs).

appeal a petition to a higher court to alter the decision of a lower court.

appellant an individual who appeals a court decision because s/he lost in the lower court. The appellant may be called the petitioner in some jurisdictions.

appellate court a tribunal having jurisdiction to review decisions on appeal from lower courts.

appellee an individual who won in the lower court but now must defend that decision because the lower court case has been appealed. The appellee may be called the respondent in some jurisdictions.

arbitration (binding) a process whereby an impartial third party, chosen by both parties in a dispute, makes a final determination regarding a contested issue.

assault the placing of another in fear of bodily harm.

battery the unlawful touching of another with intent to harm.

certiorari a writ of review whereby an action is removed from a lower court to an appellate court for additional proceedings.

civil action a judicial proceeding to redress an infringement of individual civil rights, in contrast to a criminal action, which is brought by the state to redress public wrongs.

civil right a personal right that accompanies citizenship and is protected by the Constitution (e.g., freedom of speech, freedom from discrimination).

class-action suit a judicial proceeding brought on behalf of a number of persons similarly situated.

common law a body of rules and principles derived from usage or from judicial decisions enforcing such usage.

compensatory damages monetary award to compensate an individual for injury sustained (e.g., financial losses, emotional pain, inconvenience) and restore the injured party to the position held prior to the injury (also termed "money damages").

concurring opinion a statement by a judge or judges, separate from the majority opinion, that endorses the result of the majority decision but offers its own reasons for reaching that decision.

consent decree an agreement, sanctioned by a court, that is binding on the consenting parties.

consideration something of value given or promised for the purpose of forming a contract.

contract an agreement between two or more competent parties that creates, alters, or dissolves a legal relationship.

criminal action a judicial proceeding brought by the state against a person charged with a public offense.

damages an award made to an individual because of a legal wrong.

declaratory relief a judicial declaration of the rights of the plaintiff without an assessment of damages against the defendant.

de facto segregation separation of the races that exists but does not result from action of the state or its agents.

de jure segregation separation of the races by law or by action of the state or its agents.

de minimis something that is insignificant, not worthy of judicial review.

de novo a new review.

defamation false and intentional communication that injures a person's character or reputation; slander is spoken and libel is written communication.

defendant the party against whom a court action is brought.

dictum a statement made by a judge in delivering an opinion that does not relate directly to the issue being decided and does not embody the sentiment of the court.

directed verdict the verdict provided when a plaintiff fails to support a prima facie case for jury consideration or when the defendant fails to present a necessary defense.

discretionary power authority that involves the exercise of judgment.

dissenting opinion a statement by a judge or judges who disagree with the decision of the majority of the justices in a case.

en banc the full bench; refers to a session where the court's full membership participates in the decision rather than the usual quorum of the court.

fact-finding a process whereby a third party investigates an impasse in the negotiation process to determine the facts, identify the issues, and make a recommendation for settlement.

fraudulent conveyance a transfer of property intended to defraud or hinder a creditor or to put such property beyond the creditor's reach.

friend-of-the-court briefs briefs provided by nonparties to inform or perhaps persuade the court (also termed *"amicus curiae"* briefs).

governmental function activity performed in discharging official duties of a federal, state, or municipal agency.

governmental immunity the common law doctrine that governmental agencies cannot be held liable for the negligent acts of their officers, agents, or employees.

impasse a deadlock in the negotiation process in which parties are unable to resolve an issue without assistance of a third party.

injunction a writ issued by a court prohibiting a defendant from acting in a prescribed manner.

in loco parentis in place of parent; charged with rights and duties of a parent.

liquidated damages contractual amounts representing a reasonable estimation of the damages owed to one of the parties for a breach of the agreement by the other.

mediation the process by which a neutral third party serving as an intermediary attempts to persuade disagreeing parties to settle their dispute.

ministerial duty an act that does not involve discretion and must be carried out in a manner specified by legal authority.

negligence the failure to exercise the degree of care that a reasonably prudent person would exercise under similar conditions; conduct that falls below the standard established by law for the protection of others against unreasonable risk of harm.

per curiam a court's brief disposition of a case that is not accompanied by a written opinion.

plaintiff the party initiating a judicial action.

plenary power full, complete, absolute power.

precedent a judicial decision serving as authority for subsequent cases involving similar questions of law.

preponderance of evidence a standard that requires more evidence to support than refute a claim; it also is termed the 51 percent rule.

prima facie on its face presumed to be true unless disproven by contrary evidence.

probable cause reasonable grounds, supported by sufficient evidence, to warrant a cautious person to believe that the individual is guilty of the offense charged.

procedural due process the fundamental right to notice of charges and an opportunity to rebut the charges before a fair tribunal if life, liberty, or property rights are at stake.

proprietary function an activity (often for profit) performed by a state or municipal agency that could as easily be performed by a private corporation.

punitive damages a monetary punishment where the defendant is found to have acted with either malice or reckless indifference.

qualified immunity an affirmative defense that shields public officials performing discretionary functions from civil damages if their conduct does not violate clearly established statutory or constitutional rights.

qualified privilege protection from liability for communication made in good faith, for proper reasons, and to appropriate parties.

reasonable suspicion specific and articulable facts, which, taken together with rational inferences from the facts, justify a warrantless search.

remand to send a case back to the original court for additional proceedings.

remittitur the trial court's power to reduce a jury's excessive award of damages, which may be a condition of denying a motion for a new trial.

respondeat superior a legal doctrine whereby the master is responsible for acts of the servant; a governmental unit is liable for acts of its employees.

save harmless clause an agreement whereby one party agrees to indemnify and hold harmless another party for suits that may be brought against that party.

stare decisis the doctrine of abiding by decided cases; adhering to precedent.

statute   an act by the legislative branch of government expressing its will and constituting the law within the jurisdiction.

substantive due process   requirements embodied in the Fifth and Fourteenth Amendments that legislation must be fair and reasonable in content as well as application; protection against arbitrary, capricious, or unreasonable governmental action.

summary judgment   disposition of a controversy without a trial when there is no genuine dispute over factual issues.

tenure   a statutory right that confers permanent employment on teachers, protecting them from dismissal except for adequate cause.

tort   a civil wrong, independent of contract, for which a remedy in damages is sought.

ultra vires   beyond the scope of authority to act on the subject.

vacate   to set aside; to render a judgment void.

verdict   a decision of a jury on questions submitted for trial.

SELECTED SUPREME COURT CASES

INDEX